Civilizing the West

Civilizing the West

 The University of Alberta Press

*The Galts
and the
development of
western Canada*

A. A. den Otter

First published by
The University of Alberta Press
Edmonton, Alberta, Canada

First paperback edition published 1986.

ISBN 0-88864-111-7

Canadian Cataloguing in Publication Data

   Otter, A.A. den (Andy Albert), 1941–
      Civilizing the West

      ISBN 0-88864-111-7
      1. Galt, A.T. (Alexander Tilloch), Sir, 1817-1893.
      2. Galt family. 3. Canada, Western—History.* I. Title.
      FC471.G3087   971.04′9′0924   C81-091228-7
      F1032.G34087

Printed by Hignell Printing Limited, Winnipeg, Manitoba, Canada

Voor
Pa en Moe
die in dit land
een nieuwe toekomst zochten

Contents

Preface

A mere five years after George Stephenson opened the world's first railway in England, enthusiasts began to propose schemes for a railway to span British North America from coast to coast. These visionaries, to be sure, based their plans only on superficial reading rather than on sound geographic and economic studies. Yet, because Stephenson's invention promised an efficient means of transportation into the western interior of the British possessions, it kindled in many minds an interest in the fertile soil resource of the territories. Throughout the following decades, plans for transcontinental railways, as a preliminary step to colonization, were periodically revived and reshelved. Also, businessmen from the Canadas increasingly supported such schemes as an answer to their provinces' need for agricultural and commercial expansion. In the late 1850s, after two government inquiries and two scientific expeditions pronounced that much of the plains was suitable for agricultural settlement, the calls for western development and railways grew more strident.

The growing popularity of the Northwest coincided with a remarkable convergence of several strands in European and American thought. By the mid-nineteenth century, the old belief that man was master over nature had culminated in the view that this mastery implied domination and exploitation. The consequent loss of respect for nature coincided with the completion of the steam phase of the industrial revolution, the period that created the tools, such as the steamship and the railway, which made possible the conquest of a vast territory like the western plains. Moreover, the industrial revolution, the factory system, and the wholesale adoption of the capitalist ethic spawned a new class of businessmen and entrepreneurs who had the managerial skill and determination to tame the forces of nature. Indeed, the marriage of business and technology sparked a tremendous optimism and a fervent faith in historical progress.

In Canada, this boisterous self-confidence translated into a strong desire to get on with the job of opening the West to settlement and commerce. "The non-occupation of the North West Territory is a blot upon our character for enterprise," wrote the editor of the Toronto *Globe*, "We settle down quietly within the petty limits of a province while a great empire is offered to our ambition."[1] This challenge found a ready response elsewhere in British North America. Even Joseph Howe, the prominent Nova Scotia opponent to the union of the British American provinces, claimed that the undeveloped state of the northwestern territories, when contrasted to the progressive American West, was "a standing reproach to the British Government and a blot upon our civilization."[2]

Howe's reference to "civilization" was common among the promoters of the Northwest. By this word, they meant primarily the complex social and cultural institutions of Great Britain and Canada—the manners and mores, the schools, the representative institutions, and above all, the churches. This cultural imperialism was most explicit in the persistent efforts to civilize the Indian. But civilization was more than that. It also encompassed the whole economic paraphernalia of railways, banks, mines, and particularly modern agriculture. Howe and *The Globe* lamented that it was a "blot upon our civilization" that the enormous expanse of grass and parklands of the Northwest was idle and unproductive. The land had to be civilized; it had to be integrated into the economy of the new technological society. The principle of efficiency, the goal of progress, and the drive for expansion had to be applied to the western plains. In other words, they equated western expansion with the very spread of civilization itself.

One prominent Canadian who saw the exploitation of the Northwest as a civilizing mission was Sir Alexander Galt, a financier and father of confederation. For Galt, civilizing the empty western lands was an undertaking well worth any investment in time and money. In 1879, on the eve of his departure to London to take up his new post as high commissioner for Canada, he spoke glowingly of the "laborious task of opening up [the Northwest] and bringing [it] under civilization."[3] Implicit in his statement was the belief that a civilized economy was the basis, even the rationale, for cultural and political expansion. The schools, the churches, and even the farms were adjuncts of the railways, the coal-mines, and the warehouses. The construction of this basic economic framework would be expensive, of course, and he was the first to admit that "it would require an enormous outlay to bring [the West] under cultivation and civilization." Yet, the rewards promised to be proportionally great, both for the private businessman and for the nation. In fact, he believed that his prime function as high commissioner was to persuade the British that civilizing the West was an enterprise which would bring enormous benefits to the whole empire. It was an imperial business and consequently the burden must be borne also by the imperial government.

The first part of this study examines Alexander Galt's concept of the West and the role he felt it should play in the economic growth of a confederated Canada and a more closely integrated British empire. Part 2 describes the process whereby Galt, as a businessman, employed the relatively new techniques of mines and railways to implement in southern Alberta a miniature version of his larger vision. The final part of the book relates how Sir Alexander's eldest son, Elliott Galt, constructed an irrigation system to complete the transformation of the supposedly empty grasslands of this region into cultivated fields and meadows, thus realizing in a small way his father's vision of a truly civilized world.

The Galts, then, viewed civilization through an economic prism. Their story—particularly why they expanded their modest coal-mining enterprise into a million-dollar railway, irrigation, and colonization company—is a striking commentary about the over-emphasis on economic development which dominated Canada in the nineteenth century. The drive to encourage businessmen to make the enormous investments needed to exploit the prairies' resources became the most important component in the government's policies, and blinded administrators, as well as businessmen, to broader, long-range considerations. The operation of a coal-mine, for example, meant importing a labour force, which in turn required a town. The livelihood of the miners and the survival of the town depended upon the collieries' production, which in its turn was intimately connected with the western economy. The drive to civilize the West affected all those who wanted to make their homes in the new land; it also came to permeate the very fabric and design of the new society. This study then also examines the establishment and early years of the mining town of Lethbridge, and the work of the miners and their relations with the company as notable examples of the impact of the techniques of a civilized society upon a new frontier.

Acknowledgements

This study of the Galts could not have been done without the generous financial assistance of several institutions. The author is grateful to the Canada Council, the J. S. Ewart Memorial Fund, and the Vice-President of Memorial University of Newfoundland's Research Fund for providing the moneys needed to visit some of the far-flung archives of Canada and Great Britain. Memorial University of Newfoundland also granted me a sabbatical leave, matched by a Canada Council Leave fellowship, so that I could spend one year in Ottawa to complete the research and write the final draft of the book. I am also indebted to Dr. Leslie Harris, the former Vice-President of Memorial University of Newfoundland, for making funds available to prepare the index. Finally, this book has been published with the help of a grant from the Social Science Federation of Canada, using funds provided by the Social Sciences and Humanities Research Council of Canada.

It is impossible to thank all the archivists who in one way or another helped me to uncover the basic information without which I could not have written the Galt story. Nevertheless, Sheilagh S. Jameson and Georgeen Klassen of the Glenbow-Alberta Institute and James Parker of the University of Alberta Archives (and their staff) merit special mention for making my hurried visits to their archives always productive and always pleasant. John Gerla, Lethbridge's city clerk, went far beyond the call of duty to find long-lost, dusty documents and to make avail-

able the mayor's air-conditioned office when outside temperatures soared over 100°F. The clergy at St. Augustine and Knox
churches, likewise, were most co-operative. I am also indebted to
the staff of the Hudson's Bay Company Archives at the Public
Archives of Manitoba, the W. H. Smith Company archives and the
Public Record Office in London, the Provincial Archives of Alberta
in Edmonton, and the Sir Alexander Galt Museum in Lethbridge.
The archivists at the Public Archives of Canada, despite their
large numbers and busy schedules, are always personal and help-
ful. Canadian historians are well served by their archivists.

I have also accumulated a large debt to those friends and
colleagues who directly or indirectly shared their ideas, offered
suggestions, or made corrections. David Breen, J. M. S. Careless,
Joe Cherwinski, Lewis H. Thomas, and William Wonders provided
valuable commentaries on an early draft of the manuscript. Rod
Macleod saved me much time with detailed short cuts to the
RCMP papers. Lethbridge historian Alex Johnston answered all
my queries promptly and gave me a memorable historical tour of
Lethbridge and environs. William Baker, Doug Hay, Harry Kiefte,
and Ted Regehr ferreted out many annoying errors in grammar
and historical fact. Hugh Tuck deserves special mention for actually having read, with his usual painstaking care and attention, the
entire manuscript at least once and several sections twice. Susan
Snook, Eileen Dalton, and Diane Fry managed somehow to translate my illegible handwriting into readable typescript, cheerfully
made the many revisions, and unscrambled the footnotes. Kather-
ine K. Wensel of the University of Alberta Press carefully polished
the manuscript and competently guided it to its completion.
Despite all this assistance, the final product remains my own and
I accept full responsibility for advice rejected and corrections not
made.

The most invaluable help came from my wife, Dini. While she
did some of the typing in the very early stages of the work, her
major contribution has been in providing the moral support only a
loving wife can give and in making available the extra time needed
to write a book. Not only did she assume many of the tasks of a
busy household, but she cheerfully endured forced vacations in
our fragile tent-trailer, which we usually parked in crowded urban
campgrounds located near the various archives.

Maps and tables

Abbreviations

AR&CCo	Alberta Railway and Coal Company
AR&ICo	Alberta Railway and Irrigation Company
CPR	Canadian Pacific Railway
GAI	Glenbow-Alberta Institute
HBCA, PAM	Hudson's Bay Company Archives, Public Archives of Manitoba
NWC&NCo	North Western Coal and Navigation Company
NWMP	North West Mounted Police
PAC	Public Archives of Canada
PRO	Public Record Office
RNWMP	Royal North West Mounted Police
UMWA	United Mine Workers of America

Part 1

The need to expand

Such a country cannot now remain unpeopled. It offers temptations to the emigrant nowhere excelled. It invites alike the mechanic and the farmer. Its rivers and rolling prairies and accessible mountain passes, secure to it advantages which must belong to a highway to the Pacific.... What can impede its development?

Nor'-Wester (Red River), 28 December 1859

1

The break
in the cycle

For countless ages the southwestern corner of the Canadian prairies had camouflaged its dynamic diversity. Most visitors saw only an endless sea of waving, yellow grass, interrupted occasionally by a grey sage-brush or other dry-soil plant, a vast landscape, its monotony accentuated occasionally by the gleaming white shore of an alkali slough, a low gravel hill, or an odd sand dune where the wind willed it. A closer examination, however, would have revealed a more complex character. The dry prairie of the extreme south was surrounded by a wide arc of more fertile soil, taller grasses, and greater rainfall. To the west stood the glistening white peaks of the Rockies, their majesty enhanced by the dark green Porcupine Hills and the light blue sky, while to the south the Milk River Ridge trimmed the shimmering horizon. Several large rivers, Waterton, St. Mary, and Belly, converged into the Oldman, whose rushing spring runoff had through the centuries gouged a huge valley into the soft prairie soil, three hundred feet deep and a mile across from rounded edge to rounded edge. The Oldman, snaking its way eastward, joined the South Saskatchewan, which ultimately delivered its waters to the icy Hudson Bay. At the same time, just a few miles from the source of the St. Mary, the Milk River commenced its meandering course through the grassy plains to meet the Missouri, which in turn emptied into the warm waters of the Gulf of Mexico. The river valleys were not the only scars in the gently rolling countryside.

Numerous glacial spillways, known as coulees, had cut deeply into the surface of the land. In sharp contrast to the windy, treeless plains, these sheltered coulees and river valleys supported a wide variety of plants, bushes, and trees.

Ecologically this was a region of perpetual contrasts. Most years the hot, searing winds, robbed of their moisture by the towering Rockies, drove temperatures up into the high nineties, causing an aridity only rarely but spectacularly relieved by heavy and brief rainstorms often accompanied by violent thunder and lightning. Before the parched plants could fully quench their thirst, the dry winds usually returned to soak up the surface moisture. During these prolonged dry spells, small plants withered and were replaced by a hardier short grass, but the rainfall—too infrequent to permit the growth of trees—was never scanty enough to create a sandy desert. At other times a number of wet years, often marked by flooding, restored the taller grasses and larger plants, creating an appearance of lushness. Thus the ground-cover changed repeatedly and altered the landscape, a delicate ecological cycle little understood by early observers.[1]

Based on reports from Indian residents, a few explorers who actually visited the southwestern portion of the territories commented on its dryness. Henry Kelsey and Anthony Henday, for example, described at second hand the arid country in the south, and others, like Alexander Mackenzie and David Thompson, compared the bleak southern expanse with the seemingly more hospitable northern region. Thus was created the general opinion that the western interior contained a dry prairie, a belief reinforced by two expeditions in the late 1850s. One, a Canadian party led by H. Y. Hind, visited southern Manitoba and parts of Saskatchewan and in its report differentiated between fertile and desert-like areas. The other, a British group under the leadership of Captain John Palliser, travelled through the southern territories to the Rockies and popularized Hind's terms, "fertile belt" and "central desert." This qualitative distinction, linked with Palliser's name, and soon associated with good and bad lands, made a lasting impression upon the public mind.[2] Although some individuals like Lorin Blodgett, an American climatologist, maintained that the Northwest was suitable for agriculture because the average temperature was warmer and the annual precipitation was greater than previously believed, the notion of aridity persisted.[3]

While regional rainfall was inadequate for nineteenth-century agricultural methods, there was an abundance of water. The western foothills were scored by countless streams fed by melted water from the Rocky Mountains. Every spring this runoff transformed the playful currents into raging torrents that surged into the rivers and rushed toward the sea. Although the creeks virtually dried up in the summer and the rivers became shallow and lazy, water remained plentiful, a valuable resource unrecognized until late in the nineteenth century. Moisture was also provided by the immense quantities of snow which fell each winter and were melted periodically by the warm Chinook winds. These hard winds came whistling through the mountain passes, drove down onto the prairies where the heated, compressed air drove out the cold, and a forty-degree rise in temperature was possible. Thus the Chinook, by baring winter forage, made survival possible for grazing animals during the long, harsh winters on the windswept, unsheltered plains.[4]

The popular perception of a dry, lifeless plain also failed to realize that the many streams and nutritious grasses generously supported vast numbers of wildlife. Enormous herds of bison ranged at will and at times formed an uninterrupted shaggy carpet of brown hides or an endless line of plodding beasts. Side by side with the ponderous buffalo, the graceful pronghorn grazed on the broad-leaved plants scorned by the larger animals. The grizzly, wolf, and fox hunted freely and found abundant prey. Slithering through the grass, many snakes gorged themselves upon numerous toads, gophers, and mice. The muskrat and beaver made their homes in the several lakes, while on the shores the porcupine rustled and the ground-squirrels played their games. The skies were filled with falcons, hawks, eagles, larks, ducks, blackbirds, whooping cranes, and trumpeter swans. The land was rich and, to those adapted to it, food was plentiful.

The native American Indian fitted well into this ecological system because he lived in harmony with the slowly pulsating rhythm of prairie life. For hundreds of years the Blackfoot, Piegan, and Sarcee freely followed the grazing buffalo and antelope across the northern plains. Since the red man did not recognize the great fertility of the prairie soil nor the enormous potential energy of the rich black coal cropping out of the river banks, he hardly disturbed his environment. Although he killed more than he needed, his small numbers and limited hunting techniques scarcely affected the vast bison herds. Thus, while man, animal, and even such natural phenomena as rain, wind, and fire, constantly altered the landscape, its essential grassland features hardly changed in thousands of years.[5]

The first major disruption of this fragile scene occurred in the 1850s with the invasion of the white men from the south. Most of the newcomers were blind to the beauty of the land and indifferent to the delicate balance of life; they viewed both the animals and the Indians as items of easy profit and exploitation. Greedy robe hunters and wolfers, operating out of Fort Benton, Montana, wantonly butchered the buffalo and pronghorn for the hides, the bones, or only the tongues. Aided by their counterparts in American territory, the killers decimated wildlife and within twenty years virtually destroyed the buffalo, pronghorn, and deer. Avaricious merchants, hiding in strong forts with fitting names like Robber's Roost, Stand-Off, and Whisky Gap, cheated and debauched naive Indian hunters by selling them poisonous, adulterated alcohol. Of all these posts, Fort Whoop-Up was the worst. Built at the junction of the St. Mary and Oldman rivers, near present-day Lethbridge, the solid, squared-log structure, guarded by one bristling cannon, protected plunderers from their whisky-maddened victims.[6] The degradation of the Indians and the general lawlessness of the whisky trade caused much concern in the East, and in 1874 the Canadian government sent the North West Mounted Police to the region to blot out the smuggling. The police accomplished the task within months. But, tragically, a quarter-century of rot-gut had crushed the red man's spirit, and his dignity was further stripped by starvation as the buffalo disappeared. Thus the once proud nomad of the plains was reduced to a servile refugee, totally dependent upon the good will of the Canadian government.

After the whisky trade was effectively curbed, the NWMP could turn to their second task, the removal of the Indians to reservations in order to make room for the anticipated influx of white settlers. The programme, embodied in a number of treaties of which the seventh, signed in 1877, covered the southwestern natives, was administered by Edgar Dewdney, the Indian commissioner, and his able assistant, Elliott Galt, the son of a well-known Montreal financier and politician. Their task and that of the police was made so much easier because disease, alcohol, and starvation had done the essential work and had made the Indians docile subjects.[7] By 1880 government officials claimed that the Canadian Northwest was generally peaceful and ready for settlement.

In the ten years since it had taken control over the territories in 1870, the government had introduced a rudimentary system of management of which the Mounted Police was its most efficient agent. This administrative superstructure, haphazardly superimposed upon prairie life, was designed to facilitate the rapid exploitation of some of the region's valuable resources. Although the government had acted to stop the cancerous whisky trade, it too was primarily interested in the wealth of the land. It differed from the smugglers, however, in that its purpose was not destructive; it viewed the Northwest as an essential component in the new transcontinental economy, as a vital prerequisite for national prosperity. To nineteenth-century government officials, resources had value only when developed. That the countless bison no longer covered the prairies, that the nomadic Indian no longer roamed the plains, was of little concern. Scarcely did they realize that without the wildlife, without the natives, the grasslands had truly become a wilderness. Blinded by a view of progress that had no place for the red man or the buffalo, they could not appreciate what had existed before. Instead they believed that the way had been opened for a much better utilization of the fertile soil. Thus Canadian politicians actively encouraged businessmen to exploit these natural resources for the benefit of Canada: many entrepreneurs readily accepted the opportunity and worked tirelessly and even devoutly in pursuit of this economic objective.

One individual who exemplified this outlook was Sir Alexander Galt, entrepreneur and father of confederation. In 1882 the sixty-five-year-old promotor willingly endured the considerable discomfort of a wagon trip across the desolate prairies to investigate these investment opportunities at first hand. In passing he noted the dearth of wildlife. "We saw no game," he wrote his wife, "except a few antelope."[8] Despite the threatened extinction of this species, the businessman lamented his failure to shoot one. The reaction was typical: Galt was not interested in the preservation of wildlife nor in the conservation of the grasslands for their own intrinsic worth. As a believer in man's mastery over nature, he considered resources to be valuable only when utilized. The wilderness had to be made productive. He envisioned a beehive of human activity: cowboys herding cattle on the range, farmers cultivating the soil, loggers cutting timber in the foothills, and miners excavating coal. Galt's vision expressed both personal and Canadian aspirations. And Galt, an industrious promoter and developer, transformed part of this dream into reality. Within three years of his visit he had built a sawmill in the Porcupine Hills, a colliery and town on the banks of the Oldman, and a hundred miles of railway to transport the coal. Within the next five years he added two more shafts to the coal-mine and sixty miles of railway. By the turn of the century his son Elliott brought irrigation to thousands of acres of fertile lands. In just fifteen years these bustling promoters, with the generous support of the federal government, had transformed the desolate treeless plains into prosperous irrigated farmlands dotted with tree-lined towns. In that time technological man had brought about greater changes than centuries of winds, rains, fires, animals, or native people.

2

The practical visionary

Early in July 1858 the Canadian Legislative Assembly was locked in a rancorous debate on constitutional reform. The political equality of French- and English-speaking Canadians had created deep sectional rifts which virtually paralyzed the government. For several days speaker after speaker passionately advanced various answers to the union's dilemma but each proposal was rejected with equal ardour. On the afternoon of 5 July 1858 Alexander Tilloch Galt, the young and wealthy member for Sherbrooke, Quebec, rose to offer a fresh solution to what he thought was basically a racial and religious problem. Applying his usual broad perspective in search of a cure for Canada's ills, Galt urged his fellow legislators to break out of their restrictive parochial wranglings and consider a comprehensive scheme for the federation of all the British North American colonies. Such a union would permit the two racial groups to control their cultural affairs at a local level while freeing the national government to manage broad economic matters.

Although the concept of a federal union of British North America was not new, Galt's approach was novel in that he made the annexation of Rupert's Land an integral feature of his plan. This immense region was increasingly coming into public view. In 1857 Lorin Blodgett's *Climatology of the United States* claimed that the vastness of the interior plains moderated temperatures, meaning that the Canadian portion was warmer and wetter than previously believed, making the land suitable for agriculture. In addition the gold-rush into the interior of British Columbia and the advance of American traders into the Red River area drew the attention of Upper Canadians to the Northwest. To a province plagued by chronic unemployment and a nagging shortage of land, the open expanse of the territories beckoned as a splendid opportunity for expansion. The government waffled on the issue because it feared French opposition, yet was afraid of losing the region by default to the Americans. Thus in 1857, when a British parliamentary committee held an inquiry into the Hudson's Bay Company's license over the territories, Canada made only a half-hearted, legalistic presentation. Later in the summer the colonial government yielded to the insistent demands of opposition leader George Brown, who as editor of the Toronto *Globe* was a leading advocate of western expansion, for a scientific assessment of the plains by S.J. Dawson and H. Y. Hind. Since the imperial government had also appointed an exploration party, led by John Palliser, to evaluate the Northwest, it meant that in 1857 two scientific expeditions were in the region gauging its suitability for agriculture.

The acquisition of the Northwest appealed to Alexander Galt's expansionist imagination and business acumen. Clearly recognizing that the rich natural resources of the territories promised limitless opportunities for new investments and economic growth, he urged his fellow legislators to stop thinking of this immense region as merely "a bagatelle to be disposed of like a township on the Ottawa."[1] Did they not know that the Northwest "comprised a region ten times as large as the settled part of Canada—1,000 miles long by 700 broad, and capable of sustaining thirty millions of souls?" Did they not realize that "such a thing had never yet occurred to any one people, as to have the offer of half a continent to be handed over to the control of the Legislature?" The wealth of the Northwest could transform the small provinces into a powerful nation but, so he warned them, they must act quickly to open the doors "for the young men of Canada to go into that country, otherwise the Americans would certainly go there first." In an emotional, almost angry conclusion, Galt pleaded with his colleagues to stop squabbling over trivialities. "Half a continent is ours if we do not keep on quarrelling about petty matters and lose sight of what interests us most," he shouted. If Canadians wanted to prosper, they must adopt a "firm national policy," a comprehensive programme which would transform several insignificant provinces into one mighty nation spanning the continent.

Galt's proposition was a natural sequel in a highly successful career dedicated to economic expansion. His entire experience was linked in one way or another with resource development and colonization schemes. His father, John Galt, a tall and restless Scottish businessman, political agent, textbook writer, and novelist, had assembled a group of prominent British businessmen who founded the Canada Company, which sought to develop a large tract of land near Lake Huron.[2] John Galt moved to Canada in 1826 as the project's manager, and with great enthusiasm began to implement his grandiose settlement plans. His large expenditures on public improvements, assisted passage for immigrants, and advertising caused great alarm among the cautious board members in London, and when Galt also became involved in a quarrel with the colony's political establishment they refused to rehire him. In 1828 he returned to London, and to his extreme chagrin found himself in debtors' prison. With all his flamboyant pretensions to being a high-level promoter, John Galt had failed to manage his personal finances effectively and had fallen into debt. He was freed several months later and doggedly worked to restore his financial position by writing novels, virtually on order. In 1831 he was appointed honorary secretary of the British American Land Company, but chronic illness curtailed his activities and instead it was his son, Alexander, who became important in the colonization company's success.

Alexander Galt, the youngest of the three sons of John and Elizabeth Galt, was born in London on 6 September 1817.[3] Although his father was often away on business trips, Alexander was deeply influenced by John Galt. In 1828 the family came to Canada where Elizabeth joined her husband in Guelph and the boys attended school in Lower Canada. John Galt's failure in Canada and his imprisonment for debt made a lasting impression on Alexander, who retained a deep fear of bankruptcy throughout his life. He also shared his father's overbearing egotism and grating temper which flared quickly when it encountered opposition in a manner which could be abrasive rather than conciliatory. But the youngest son also inherited from his father an optimistic self-confidence firmly supported by stubborn perseverance. Like his father, Alexander thrived on weighty discussions with influential people. His incisive mind quickly grasped complex details, exposed fuzzy thinking and, by placing the problems in broad perspective, emerged with clear and novel solutions. He was a romantic imbued with grandiose ideas, but like his father he was also very practical and efficient, always determined to force his visions to fulfilment. Innovation and expansion were his trademarks, two attributes he clearly demonstrated soon after arriving in Canada in 1835 as a junior clerk with the British American Land Company.

At the time A. T. Galt joined this British-based colonization company, it was experiencing serious financial difficulties. The scheme had been launched in 1824 by a group of Montreal merchants who, with the backing of prominent London financiers, had purchased nearly eight hundred thousand acres of land around Sherbrooke in the Eastern Townships of Lower Canada. Both colonial and imperial officials had balked at approving a venture obviously speculative in nature, but in 1833 they reluctantly gave way under the persistent pressure from influential London and Montreal financiers.[4] Montrealers Peter McGill, a wealthy banker, and George Moffatt, a rich merchant and member of the Legislative Assembly, were appointed Canadian commissioners, while Samuel Brooks, of the City Bank of Sherbrooke and also a member of the provincial assembly, was named secretary. Because of the corporation's close connections with the commercial and political elite of Montreal, the British American Land Company was greatly disliked by French-Canadian reformers who argued that corporate involvement in the sale of crown lands could only serve to increase prices. The critics of the company also charged that the large land payments the company made to the provincial government increased the independence of an administration already insensitive to popular opinion. In addition, they accused the English establishment of alienating from the overcrowded French-Canadian seigneurial system a large segment of undeveloped and fertile land. Thus embroiled in the political turmoil of the time, the company did not attract many settlers to its lands. The problem was aggravated by the high cost of public improvements and the losses caused by dishonest land agents. Only a few years of operations had demonstrated that this land development scheme would not be the fast and easy way to wealth imagined by its promoters.[5]

Some reforms were obviously needed, and in 1840 the company turned to Alexander Galt, who had distinguished himself with his quick grasp of business principles and clear insight into intricate financial details. They asked him to devise a method of collecting the many overdue debts. He surprised them by not recommending a means of foreclosures but suggesting instead larger and easier credit as well as payments made in labour or produce. The directors were impressed by the young man's assertive authority and accepted his proposals. Later, in 1842, when their financial problems became especially critical, they invited him to London to make further recommendations. This time Galt urged comprehensive reforms including: vigorous recruiting of prospective settlers in England, the United States, and French Canada; inducements to manufacturers; and greater powers to the local commissioners. The board took nearly a year to approve Galt's bold suggestions and then appointed him secretary with powers to execute his proposals. Under Galt's enthusiastic direction, the fortunes of the company changed so much for the better that in 1844 the directors promoted him to commissioner with a free hand and sufficient time to incorporate reforms. His striking ability to define problems clearly and seek their solution in expansion had brought him full control over a very large land settlement scheme when he was not yet twenty-seven years of age.

Under Galt's guidance the changes in the company's fortunes were nothing less than spectacular. During his twelve years as commissioner, land sales rose from fifteen hundred to twelve thousand acres per year and the company's assets began to outweigh its liabilities.[6] Although economic conditions were in his favour and Canada experienced an unprecedented surge of immigration, Galt's uncanny ability to recognize opportunities and to exploit them in an imaginative, expansionist manner was a crucial factor in the firm's success. When British colonists proved reluctant to settle in a French province, he turned to French Canadians and attracted them with easy credit terms. He was not afraid to spend considerable sums of money to make the lands more attractive to colonists; he built roads, mills, and stores, and he established several small industries in Sherbrooke. While most of his actions were based on common sense and contemporary business principles, he had also taken some novel and several enterprising steps to improve the company's investments.

The reforms initiated by Alexander Galt were not confined to more effective management of the company's properties, but he leaped beyond them to encompass the entire Great Lakes region in his ideas. In 1845 when John A. Poor, a lawyer from Bangor, Maine, proposed the construction of a railway from Montreal to Portland, Maine, Galt immediately recognized that the projected railway could be made to bisect the British American holdings and provide essential transportation to markets and supplies. A railway could also stimulate land sales, which in turn would increase property values. While the immediate benefits to the company were obvious, he also realized that the economic growth of Montreal depended upon a year-round access to the Atlantic. In a clearly argued, published letter, brimming with authoritative statistics, he reasoned that because transportation costs from the Great Lakes to Montreal were less than to New York or Boston, a railway connection to Portland would enable the merchants of Montreal to expand beyond the confines of Canada and compete with the American ports for the rich and growing markets south of the Great Lakes. He challenged his readers to consider "that the same causes which render New York or Boston the seaports for Canada West, equally entitle Montreal or Quebec to compete with them for the trade of the vast territory of the United States, around or near the Great Lakes."[7] This region, which already had a population "of five million, and [was] increasing with unexampled rapidity," would dwarf the existing provincial market and bring untold wealth to British and Canadian investors. Galt's panoramic vision had placed the economic welfare of Montreal, the Eastern Townships, and particularly the British American Land Company within the broad context of North American trading patterns. This grand dream, only the first of many, illustrates the working of Galt's expansionist imagination, his ability to synchronize several known ideas into an unique, comprehensive concept.

Galt, who was no impractical visionary, took a leading role in implementing the railway scheme. He persuaded several of his Montreal friends to form the St. Lawrence and Atlantic Railway Company to build a line from Montreal to Vermont to meet with the Atlantic and St. Lawrence coming from Portland. Although the list of incorporators was an impressive cross-section of wealthy Montrealers, the group was too timid to finance such a long-term, unprecedented venture completely by themselves, and so they dispatched Galt to London in the summer of 1845 to seek financial support among his business associates. Fortune smiled but briefly. Reaching London at the height of a railway-building mania, Galt quickly gathered sufficient backing only to lose it within the year when the boom collapsed. Most of the Montrealers wanted to withdraw as well, but Galt, unabashed, persuaded a few directors to sign a commitment to begin construction in the spring of 1846. This audacious move, only narrowly approved by the entire board, was followed by a highly successful campaign among the citizens of Montreal for support and culminated in an equally successful bid for government aid. Although provincial governments had assisted the construction of canals in the past, they proved reluctant to contribute to the advancement of the new transportation technology. Without government backing, the St. Lawrence and Atlantic project could not attract sufficient capital and its construction had to be postponed.

By 1849, however, the economic and political climate in the Canadas had changed drastically. Beginning in 1846, with the repeal of the Corn Laws, Britain adopted a free trade policy. The declared obsolescence of the mercantilistic system destroyed Canada's preferential position in the British grain market and exposed Montreal to the ruinous competition of New York and Boston. To meet the crisis, Montreal had to reduce its transportation costs and seek an ice-free outlet to the Atlantic. The need for a year-round port became painfully apparent in the winter of 1848. Shortly after the annual freeze-up, grain prices dropped sharply in Britain and the value of wheat stockpiled in Montreal fell accordingly. Irate businessmen calculated that the losses incurred could have paid for the Canadian portion of the proposed railway to the Atlantic, and they prodded the government to subsidize the venture. In the summer of 1849 the provincial assembly, which included several directors of the St. Lawrence and Atlantic, passed the Guarantee Act which secured a six percent interest per year on the bonds of any railway at least seventy-five miles long and half completed. The government's action encouraged the City of Montreal, the Sulpician Seminary, and the British American Land

Company to make significant investments in the railway.

Britain's free trade policy, as well as the full implementation of responsible government for the Canadas, also forced Montrealers to re-examine their commercial policies. They felt betrayed by the imperial government and believed that the unity of the empire had been broken. In reaction, they began to discuss union with the United States and in the fall of 1849 issued the Annexation Manifesto. This remarkable document, signed also by Alexander Galt, protested Britain's abandonment of her colony and stated that, consequently, Canada's future in trade and wealth lay within a continental framework. Although the change of loyalties was dramatic, it was easily made. These businessmen were more committed to the mercantilistic position of their city than to any empire of culture or sentiment. The manifesto also revealed that Montrealers were ready to sacrifice the fledgling economic nationalism of the Canadas in favour of a continental policy. Economic efficiency, so they argued, demanded that obsolete policies be dismantled in favour of new means; business principles required Montreal's extension into the financial and transportation system of the United States.[8]

Although Montreal's business establishment had embraced a continental policy and adopted the new technology of railways, the financial difficulties of the St. Lawrence and Atlantic were not yet solved. Serious mismanagement of company funds had created a staggering debt. Once again crisis spelled opportunity for Galt. The desperate directors asked him to take complete charge of the project and late in 1849 elected him president. Galt faced a formidable situation, a predicament so critical that at one time a banker refused to lend him a paltry few hundred pounds. Day after day, he and fellow director John Young, a promoter and politician, worked tirelessly for the railway and finally, by various expedients, completed enough of the road to qualify for the government guarantee.[9]

The completion of the railway, administrative reform, and policy changes were the most tangible factors in Galt's revitalization of the British America Land Company. More difficult to measure but none the less real was his political influence. Company affairs often brought him into contact with government leaders and ultimately steered him into a new direction. Early in

1849 he accepted the nomination for Sherbrooke County, a seat left vacant by the death of Samuel Brooks. When his employers objected strongly to this move, Galt wrote them a strong letter which bluntly stated that he could more easily influence the assembly as a member than as a lobbyist. Clearly annoyed, he pointed out that the future of the British American Land Company depended upon the government's ability to stimulate the Canadian economy. As long as people were leaving Canada for the more prosperous United States, no amount of wise management could increase land sales. "I will frankly admit to the court," he fumed, "that if instructed to confine myself to the sale of land and collection of debt, I cannot adequately give value for my salary, and that it is only by striving to remove the weighty evils that press on the country that the Company itself can prosper."[10] Once again Galt the practical visionary placed the private concerns of his employers squarely within the public problems of the provincial economy. "I consider the interests of the Company and the country to be identical," he added, and as a politician he faithfully followed his own prescription. Although he claimed to be an independent, he voted against the Rebellion Losses Bill and signed the Annexation Manifesto. Both moves were logical reactions for the commissioner of the British American Land Company and the president of the St. Lawrence and Atlantic Railway.

Politics and railways drew Galt out of his total preoccupation with company affairs; they widened his horizons, made him more aware of his own potential, and brought him in ever closer contact with the commercial establishment of Montreal. The connection became a social one in 1848 when he married Elliott Torrance, the daughter of John Torrance, an influential banking and shipping magnate as well as a director of the St. Lawrence and Atlantic. Elliott Galt died in May 1850 shortly after the birth of their first son, Elliott; a year later Alexander Galt married her younger sister Amy Gordon, with whom he was to share a lifetime of close and loving companionship.

Galt worked comfortably in the Tory world of conservative politics and progressive economics. These were exciting years for him because Canada was entering a restless age in which enterprising men boldly embraced the latest technological and scientific doctrines to induce rapid development and create a new civilization. These men were truly entrepreneurs because they almost instinctively sensed the worth of new ideas; they were receptive to untried processes as long as they promised greater efficiency, greater profits. To them, the novel technologies of railways, steamboats, telegraphs, mines, and even business itself opened up exciting new vistas sure to lead them into a promised land. To their surprise, no one limited their ambitions, no one restricted their growth. Progress became a dream shared by everyone. In Canada, for example, critics may have denounced the profiteering of particular businessmen and politicians, but they still held the broad assumption that the highest good for all was to move forward into a world of growth. Enchanted by the heady prospects of unlimited expansion, investors cheerfully assumed enormous risks and walked on the precipice of ruin. They accepted almost as a matter of fact the hazards on their search for still greater fields to conquer and their desire to do things better than ever before. Once the men of business, spurred on by public applause, grasped the full potential of technology, economic development mushroomed and society became wedded to change.[11]

Galt enjoyed this dynamic society and he readily accepted its new watchwords of efficiency and profitability. He recognized the usefulness of the railway as a tool for economic development. He supported the Portland railway as the most efficient technique for moving goods from Montreal to the Atlantic. In this way he was a bold visionary; yet, he was also shrewdly practical. The railway was also a means to enhance the property values of his employers, the British American Land Company. And when the road was finished, Galt had learned some valuable lessons. He had discovered that the formula for personal success was stunningly simple: form a company, retain a controlling interest in the stock, float public bonds secured by an accommodating government, award fat construction contracts to insiders, and reap the profits in the end. Thus the experience gained in service of the St. Lawrence and Atlantic launched a short but highly successful career in railroading.

The timing was crucial. In the early 1850s Canada embraced the new technology of railways as a means to inevitable prosperity. The province rushed headlong into an incredibly wild railway-building boom which revolutionized her transportation industry. Throughout the decade, railways dominated public discussions, stimulated private enterprise, and determined government policy. As the public demanded that rails be laid anywhere at any cost, the affairs of businessmen and politicians became intimately intertwined and nearly indistinguishable. Galt, too, took full advantage of the optimistic, reckless spirit of the day: the excitement matched his own buoyant, aggressive temperament and he, more than anyone else in the colony, was fully prepared for the moment.

Early in the 1850s Galt established several close personal business alliances which greatly advanced his railway career. The first was a partnership with Casimir Gzowski, the son of a Polish nobleman, participant in the Polish insurrection of 1830 and refugee to the United States. Despite his complete ignorance of the English language upon arrival, Gzowski managed to become a lawyer and later an engineer. He moved to Canada to take a position with the public works department but at Galt's urging resigned to become the chief engineer for the St. Lawrence and Atlantic.[12] By building quickly and cheaply, Gzowski had managed to qualify the railway for government guarantees. He and Galt next acquired a charter to construct a railway from Kingston, Ontario, to Montreal, linking the Great Lakes to Portland, Maine, by way of the St. Lawrence and Atlantic. A little later, Luther Holton and David L. Macpherson, two giants in the Canadian transportation industry, joined Galt's team. Although Holton and Macpherson were fierce competitors in St. Lawrence shipping, they merged their talents with those of Galt and Gzowski into an extremely efficient construction firm, Gzowski and Company, using Galt as negotiator, Holton as financier, Macpherson as administrator, and Gzowski as builder. The first charter obtained by this quartet was the Toronto and Guelph Railway. Construction of the road, begun in 1852, was in accordance with high British standards, yet costs were relatively low because Gzowski utilized new labor-saving devices for cutting, grading, and track-laying. By being involved in these schemes and associated with these powerful promoters, the thirty-five-year-old Galt became one of the major figures in Canadian railway construction.

In 1852 the British construction firm of Peto, Brassey, Betts, and Jackson, with railway contracts all over the world, teamed up with the prestigious banking concerns of Glyn, Mills, and Company and the Baring Brothers to persuade the Canadian government to subsidize the construction of a trunk railway from Montreal to Hamilton. The spirit of the era was ripe for this enormous project and Francis Hincks, the inspector general of Canada, willingly concluded an agreement with the construction and banking giants to guarantee the bonds of the proposed Grand Trunk Railway. But no sooner had the negotiators signed the contract than they discovered a deadly flaw, namely Galt and Gzowski's Kingston-Montreal charter. Their line, if linked to the St. Lawrence and Atlantic system, would drain all traffic from the Grand Trunk, which had no access to the Atlantic. To survive this lethal hemorrhage of traffic the new company had to come to terms with Galt; therefore in 1853 John Ross, solicitor general of Canada, A.M. Ross, chief engineer of the Grand Trunk, Samuel Peto, George Carr Glyn, and Thomas Baring sat down with Galt, and in four months of intense negotiations they hammered out a complex agreement. Galt drove a hard bargain. For the right to incorporate the Montreal-Kingston charter into the Grand Trunk system, Galt demanded that the new company take over the Toronto-Guelph Railway and extend the route to Sarnia, the entire section to be built at a very handsome profit by Gzowski and Company. Galt also insisted that the railway company purchase the assets of the St. Lawrence and Atlantic and lease the equipment of the Atlantic and St. Lawrence. The Grand Trunk representatives paid an exorbitant price for the Atlantic connection because the Canadian section was poorly built and the American part sometimes impassable; the cost of upgrading the road became a very heavy burden for the young company.[13]

The failure of the Grand Trunk to become a profitable venture was in no small measure due to the activities of Canadian entrepreneurs, like Alexander Galt, who were aided in this by their British cohorts. Businessmen on both sides of the ocean recognized that the application of the new transportation technology, the railway, meant huge profits. As community after community in Canada demanded rail service at any price, businessmen as well as politicians scrambled in unscrupulous haste for easy profits and ignited one of the greatest railway booms in Canadian history. A parliamentary inquiry, chaired by George

Brown, uncovered an incredible tangle of confusion, waste, and corruption, especially among some prominent politicians. No official investigation was required, however, to reveal that this duplicity critically undermined the solvency of the Grand Trunk and weakened the economic stability of Canada.

Alexander Galt, a product of this milieu, competed with other Canadian businessmen and politicians for the fabulous spoils. He saw no conflict between personal profits and the prosperity of Canada. Flagrant dishonesty was not in harmony with his spiritual convictions. While he was not a great churchman, he was deeply religious. He faithfully taught his children about God and the Christian values of honour, uprightness, and generosity. Before embarking on any voyage he always assembled his family to pray for God's blessing on the venture;[14] the private correspondence with his wife indicates that he always sought divine guidance in crucial decisions. But the moral sensitivity and the warm compassionate understanding taught by his faith did not reach into the secular business world where the sharp dealer was admired, maximum profit was the prime criterion, and poor management was immoral. Using these standards he could cripple the Grand Trunk with exorbitant terms, a ploy which made him very rich. Yet, he also instinctively understood the need for railways to grow in order to survive. Thus he was pleased that his clever bargaining had forced the British backers to expand the project from a mere local line to what was at that time the longest railway in the world; he had forced the Grand Trunk investors to implement the scheme that he had advocated for many years, an efficient means of transportation which would permit the merchants of Montreal to compete with their American counterparts for the expanding market of the United States. Galt had intermingled his private aims with the public good, but this time in a personally more profitable and ethically more ambiguous fashion than in his earlier land dealings.

The completion of the Grand Trunk negotiations marked another transition in Galt's career. He virtually disassociated himself from the railway except for occasional consultations requested by its president, John Jones Ross. In 1855 he broke all his ties with the British American Land Company. Three years later he resigned from the Gzowski firm, shifting his attention to insurance and real estate. He served on the Montreal board of the Standard Life Assurance Company and was involved in bringing to Canada the European Life and Guarantee Company of London. He also purchased wharf properties in Portland and, in partnership with Luther Holton, bought a number of houses in Montreal and Toronto.

With his financial position secure, Galt wanted to devote most of his time to political affairs. He was re-elected in 1853, this time from Sherbrooke town. Politically beholden to no one, he could follow an independent course: by the mid-1850s he called himself a Liberal but flirted with the Rouges; he sat on the opposition benches but supported the government when expedient. As an able debater and influential speaker, his political stature grew quickly and he became a politician of note, speaking out often on the issues of the day, particularly those concerned with finance. He was unable to shed his Grand Trunk past, however, and as he became more and more recognized as the spokesman for the Montreal business establishment, his opponents were many and increasingly vocal. They needled him about his wealth and his financial connections. These barbs annoyed him and he always retorted angrily that he had acted only in the best interest of the country.[15] This professed altruism may have been questioned in his past activities but it was becoming more real in the new Galt. Although his perspective remained that of the nineteenth-century entrepreneur, Galt's driving quest for personal profit was muted. His political career became, in fact, a liability to his financial affairs. The rewards he expected were no longer to be direct monetary gain but honour, political power, and the chance to initiate more efficient techniques for expanding the nation's business.

Reform in public policy certainly was necessary by the late 1850s. Among the most pressing problems were the cultural quarrels between French- and English-speaking Canadians, which virtually caused a deadlock in the government and threatened to stifle economic growth. To Galt's business mind, Canadian affairs were being conducted in an inefficient and unproductive manner, and on 5 July 1858 he intervened in the bitter constitutional debate to propose a radical renovation of the union's constitution and the expansion of her influence to the rich Northwest.

On 8 July 1858 Galt introduced three ingeniously interrelated motions that were designed to accomplish his aims in three consecutive stages. The first resolution requested a commission to report on the feasibility of dividing the Province of Canada into two parts, with each region controlling its local affairs but unified by a general government dealing with national interests. Once Canadians had established this federal framework and thereby solved their religious and racial problems, Galt's second resolution proposed that the Northwest should be annexed and governed by the federal administration until its population warranted provincial status. The third step proposed by Galt was the further expansion of Canadian territory to include the Pacific coast and the Maritime provinces.[16] The three resolutions were an imaginative solution to Canada's political dilemma as well as a creative outline for the merger of the isolated regional economies.

While the resolutions sparked some heated debate, they did not result in immediate political action. In fact the plans were momentarily lost in the melee of the last week of July when the Macdonald-Cartier administration suddenly resigned to be replaced by the Brown-Dorion alliance. Due to a legal technicality the new ministry fell within forty-eight hours of assuming office and Governor-General Head, who appeared to be very impressed with A. T. Galt's federation proposal, invited him to form the next government. Galt, who had no real political following except among the St. Lawrence commercial establishment, wisely refused, but he did consent to serve as inspector-general in the administration of his close friend, George Etienne Cartier.

Galt's appointment, which was in effect the finance ministry, was sharply criticized by the Toronto *Globe*. "No one will deny [Galt] greater skill and resources than his predecessor, but as to honesty, economy, or desire to bring the finances of the country to a proper condition, we believe he is even worse than Mr. Cayley." Still smarting from the humiliation suffered by its editor, the paper elaborated on its denunciation:

Mr. Galt is a more dangerous man than Mr. Cayley. He will be far more dexterous in the treatment of figures—far more clever in humbugging the House; but as to economy, he is incapable of it. He has not the courage of a mouse; nor has he the sense of right, the desire for the public good, necessary

to induce him to apply the pruning knife to the expenses of
the country. He is a jobber at heart; the benefit of the people
is his last thought in considering a public question.[17]

If Canada's economy needed a parsimonious minister of finance,
The Globe's comments on Galt's lack of frugality were valid because
he was a man of expansion, never of retrenchment.

As a condition for accepting office, Galt insisted that the new
government actively pursue the objective of federal union. Accordingly Prime Minister Cartier announced that he and Galt
would travel to London to seek imperial sanction for the plan. The
French-Canadian prime minister had accepted Galt's scheme because federalism promised local and therefore French control over
cultural affairs. Cartier, however, was more than a defender of
French-Canadian rights, for he was also the chief solicitor for the
Grand Trunk Railway and greatly admired this venture as a
symbol of economic advancement. To his mind a union of the
British American colonies would provide a broad credit base to
shore up the financially troubled corporation. That the railway
was an important function of the mission to London was evident
in that the third delegate, John Jones Ross, was the president of the
Canadian executive council as well as president of the Grand
Trunk. Ross was an ardent expansionist who agreed with Cartier
that the economic salvation of his company depended upon a
strengthening of colonial credit, but he also believed it depended
upon the expansion of the line westward to the Pacific coast.[18]
Galt, too, was interested in a Pacific railway. Only four years
earlier in company with friends like Poor, Augustin Morin, Young,
and others, he had petitioned the Canadian legislature on behalf of
the Northern Pacific Railroad Company for a charter to build a
railway westward from Montreal by way of the Ottawa valley,
into Michigan between Lakes Superior and Huron, and proceed
across American territory to the Pacific coast. The project, premature for Canadian ambitions, was rejected, but the idea of a
transcontinental railway was never far from Galt's mind.[19] Thus
in October 1858, three Canadians travelled to London to seek
imperial approval for a political union of British North America, to
negotiate the withdrawal of the Hudson's Bay Company from the
Northwest, and to request financial assistance for an intercolonial

railway from Quebec City to Halifax and for the tottering Grand Trunk Railway.[20]

While in London, Galt composed and wrote two memorials explaining the federation scheme. His statements emphasized the need for a strongly centralized federal government with overriding power in such economic areas as commerce, finance, and transportation. In the provisions for the annexation of the Northwest, for example, the documents clearly stipulated a measure of local government as an inducement to settlers but they also implied that the rich resources of the territories were to be administered for the benefit of the nation. Galt, the entrepreneur turned politician, wanted a general government with sufficient power to properly manage and develop the wealth of British North America. At the same time, he placed cultural and social affairs in the hands of the provincial legislatures.[21] In this way he not only suggested the creation of a transcontinental state but he also drafted the rough outlines of its structure.

The colonials were given a flattering reception, including an audience with the Queen and numerous social invitations, but a decision on unification and financial assistance was assiduously avoided. Finally, by the end of the year, the imperial government decided that the federal scheme was but a Canadian solution to a purely Canadian problem, and that without Maritime consent further action was impossible. Britain also refused to assist the colony's ambitious transcontinental railway programmes and declined to make a pronouncement on the Hudson's Bay Company's position in the Northwest. Galt viewed these rejections as a personal defeat and, in a passionate rebuttal, warned that the failure to unite the North American colonies would inevitably lead to their absorption into the United States.[22] His plea was to no avail. The federal scheme was obviously premature, and both the imperial and colonial governments decided to shelve it for an indefinite time.

The Clear Grit opposition, however, kept the issue very much alive. A year earlier, at the Reform Convention of 1857, the party had made federal union of the Canadas and western annexation the two important planks in their platform. Throughout the next decade its newspaper, the Toronto *Globe*, published a relentless stream of editorials and articles denouncing Hudson's Bay

Company control over the Northwest, extolling the riches of the region, and pleading for its union with Canada. Although the paper's editor, George Brown, dismissed Galt's 1858 confederation proposal as premature, opportunistic, and a front for Grand Trunk ambitions, the essence of his economic goals differed little from those of the finance minister. The two men disagreed strongly on the alliance of government and business in economic development, but both Brown and Galt called for rapid economic growth to be attained through western expansion. In November 1859 George Brown gave a speech which could have been written by Galt:

> I do hope that there is not one Canadian ... who does not look forward with great hope to that day when these northern colonies shall stand out among the nations of this world as one great confederation. What true Canadian can witness the tide of immigration now commencing to flow into the vast territories of the North-West without longing to have a share in the first settlement of that great fertile country? Who does not feel that to us rightfully belong the right and duty of carrying the blessings of civilization throughout those boundless regions, and of making our country the highway of traffic to the Pacific?[23]

Although the scheme "to carry the blessings of civilization" to the Northwest was officially rejected, as finance minister Galt did implement an important aspect of the plan. When he assumed office, Canada's financial situation was extremely critical. A serious depression had cut deeply into government revenues, almost entirely based on tariffs, at a time when enormous railway debts were driving the country to bankruptcy. Thanks in part to his financial expertise and his long and friendly relations with leading London financiers, especially Thomas Baring and George Carr Glyn, Galt managed to retain the confidence of British investors in the provincial economy. Of greater consequence, in 1859 Galt significantly raised the import duties on manufactured goods. A year earlier in his federation speech he had called for an increase in tariffs to give "vitality" to certain "languishing" branches of Canadian manufacturing. Thus in one move, the new minister of finance effectively increased government revenues and provided a protective barrier for Canada's infant industries. To smooth the ruffled feathers of British industrialists, Galt wrote a forceful pamphlet, *Canada 1849-1859*, a lively and lucid account of Canada's economic progress and an incisive defense of the tariff. Galt pointed out that Canada, having attained responsible government, must also exercise the right to control her economic affairs. He justified Canada's expensive canal and railway programmes as essential measures to enable her to compete with New York and Boston for a good portion of North American trade. "The public of England can now judge," he challenged his readers, "how far the expenditures of Canada have been reckless and unwise, or whether it has not been incurred for objects in which the prosperity of the country was wholly bound up, and which fully justified the sacrifices which have been made to attain them."[24] Forgetting that excessive speculation and corruption had grossly inflated railway construction costs, Galt justified the tariff on the grounds that it was necessary to pay for the enormous public debt generated by the expensive railway programme, so essential to facilitate the trade which, in turn, would prevent the fusion of Canada's economy into that of the United States. Reversing his American annexationist stand of 1849, by 1858 Galt had come to fear a closer integration with the powerful American economy whose large and wealthy corporations could easily overpower Canadian firms. Galt's tariff also significantly shifted Canada's traditional emphasis on agriculture to a new concern with industrialization.[25] Thus he laid a tentative basis for his "firm national policy," in which a protective tariff would foster an independent northern economy based on the factories of central Canada, sustained by the resources and markets of the Northwest and Maritimes, and bound together by railways.

Meanwhile, events were rapidly pushing Canada toward a radical renovation of her political structures. Increased sectional strife, the threat of American invasion, and deepening economic difficulties were only some of the factors leading British North American politicians to reconsider the feasibility of a federal union. This was to bring Galt the greatest achievement of his life. In his forties, thickset, balding slightly, wearing a wisp of a beard, he played a crucial role in the negotiations leading to confederation. In 1864 he served on George Brown's select committee of the assembly inquiring into the feasibility of colonial union. A few weeks later, he and John A. Macdonald visited Brown to arrange the remarkable coalition government which opened the way to federal union. At the Charlottetown and Quebec conferences Galt explained the complicated financial details of confederation. These were his greatest moments as he confidently explained his invention, the largest and most intricate corporate reorganization of his career, the formation of a transcontinental nation. His speeches, loaded with sweeping generalizations and spiced with rhetorical flourishes, were authoritatively annotated with specific statistics. With fluid eloquence the practical visionary unfolded the comprehensive scheme of an expansive nation bound together by railways carrying an unhindered flow of products from east and west. He helped to pacify the restive Maritimers with an ingenious system of subsidies, division of revenues, and the absorption of provincial debts by the federal government. In the end his infectious enthusiasm, which had inspired so many others to support his financial schemes, disarmed the suspicious Atlantic representatives, and he won their reluctant approval.[26] Once again Galt's keen sensitivity to the aspirations of his generation had made him a leader in a popular movement.

During the debates on confederation in Canada's legislative assembly, Galt was called upon to defend the economic implications of the union.[27] While other speakers covered the political, national, and defensive advantages, Galt, in one of the greatest speeches of his career, painted a vivid picture of a new mercantilistic economy with commerce and manufacturing centred on the St. Lawrence and its resource supply and markets lying on the periphery. "Possessing as we do, in the far western part of Canada, perhaps the most fertile wheat-growing tracts on this continent—in central and eastern Canada facilities for manufacturing such as cannot anywhere be surpassed,—and in the eastern or Maritime Provinces an abundance of that most useful of all minerals, coal, as well as the most magnificent and valuable fisheries in the world—,"[28] Canada could become as prosperous as the United States. The amalgamation of regional resources would create a diversified and, therefore, stable economy. To Galt's practical business mind it was sad that the British American colonies, instead of building coherent, unrestricted trade patterns among themselves, had chosen to strengthen their economic ties with the United States. The time had arrived to reverse this trend and to break down the barriers to intercolonial trade, opening markets to the different industries of each region. "In this manner we may hope to supply Newfoundland and the great fishing districts of the Gulf, with the agricultural products of Western Canada; we may hope to obtain from Nova Scotia our supply of coal; and the manufacturing industries of Lower Canada may hope to find more extensive outlets in supplying many of those articles which are now purchased in foreign markets." In other words, an integrated economy was Galt's answer to the repeal of the Reciprocity Treaty. Of course, as Galt pointed out, resource development required large investments, and he urged his listeners not to be afraid to make large expenditures, especially in the West. Confederation would enable Canada to marshall all her resources to develop the Northwest. "The reason why we have not been able to assume possession of that territory and open it up to the industry of the youth of this country who, in consequence of the want of some such field for the employment of their energies, have been obligated to go off to the States in thousands, especially to those states possessing the boundless resources of the great North-West," he reasoned, "is because these sources of Canada ... have been inadequate for the development of this great district." One of the first acts of the new, enlarged government must be the "opening up and developing [of] that vast region, and of making it a source of strength instead of a burden to us." In a crescendo of challenges, Galt warned his colleagues against allowing the small details of the plan to obscure its magnificent whole, or permitting a niggardly attention to expenditures to cause the loss of the incredibly rich resources which would make Canada a wealthy nation. His speech concluded, he sat down amid wild cheering.

Early in 1865 Galt and Cartier travelled to London and were joined a few weeks later by Macdonald and Brown to present the new arrangements to the imperial government. The energetic Galt soon tired of the dilatory, polite negotiations and seemingly endless social gatherings. He felt uneasy in the indolent world of aristocrats; while flattered by the honour, he disliked the slow pace of life:

We are decidedly in the "haute monde" at present, but I
confess I would rather mix with my own class. It shows,
however, that politics form the only short cut from the
middle to the upper ranks. No amount of wealth would secure
the attention we receive, and the attentions are given not to
us but to our offices, and in compliment to our people. . . . Still
it is pleasant to be the recipient of marks of attention.[29]

Galt returned to Canada to face a nasty clash with George
Brown concerning the threatened abrogation of the Reciprocity
Treaty by the Americans. The two men were never comfortable
together—largely because they were so much alike and shared
similar interests. Both were proud, at times even vain; both had
stubborn independent minds; they were temperamental and very
sensitive to criticism. They were at odds because Galt was the
more creative and politically more successful of the two. Like Galt,
Brown was a prosperous businessman, prominent in the commercial life of the province, and equally interested in economic
development especially in the Northwest; yet, he had never been
able to surpass Galt's pre-eminence as the financial wizard of
confederation. As a liberal, the editor of *The Globe* had always been
a cutting critic of the Tory entrepreneur-politician's actions, especially his close involvement with the Grand Trunk and the
Montreal business establishment. Thus when Galt wanted to go
to Washington to persuade the United States to continue or
perhaps modify the terms of the reciprocity agreement, Brown
objected strenuously. He did not trust Galt with this sensitive
mission to the United States because he believed Galt was too
liable to rash decisions. His concern was not unfounded and, when
Galt did reach unauthorized understandings with the Americans
in December of 1865, Brown resigned from the cabinet because he
felt that the Maritimes had not been consulted on this very
important matter, a slight which could jeopardize the confederation agreement.[30]

Less than a year later Galt himself resigned. He had publicly
pledged to seek specific minority rights for English-speaking
Protestants in Quebec. Such guarantees became politically unfeasible when the Roman Catholics of Canada West demanded

similar provisions for their province, a demand repugnant to English-speaking Upper Canadians. Galt fully understood the political implications and agreed that the concessions could not be made, yet he felt bound to resign symbolically from the cabinet.

Although Galt had resigned his post, his fiscal talents were still required and he was asked to serve on the last delegation which met in London to work out the final details of confederation. The request was a recognition of the prominent part he had played in the federation movement. His expansive 1858 design, embodied in the memorials presented to the imperial government, was accepted virtually without amendment. When first proposed the plan was too grandiose and premature for the time, but within a decade various circumstances and other equally strong personalities had pushed the great scheme to its logical conclusion. The essential features of the proposal were not invented by him for he had borrowed freely such useful concepts as federalism, annexation of the Northwest, union with the Maritimes, and transcontinental railways; however, the integrated coherence of the new nation's structure was his innovation. He applied his entrepreneurial techniques to the realm of politics and worked for a merger of several isolated economic and political entities into one efficient, enlarged nation. Others, like John A. Macdonald, George Etienne Cartier, Charles Tupper, Leonard Tilley, and George Brown, had all performed equally well to carry out their special tasks. They had worked together as a close-knit team of which Macdonald, the smooth conciliator, had assumed leadership. Only he had been able to reconcile the manifold interests, to convince these diverse characters of the inherent logic of Galt's plan. Unfortunately the British government destroyed the unity of the effort by awarding Macdonald the Knight Commander of the Bath while bestowing some of the others the lesser Companion of the Bath. At first Galt accepted the differentiation, but when Cartier refused to accept acknowledgement of a lesser role, he too declined the honour. Cartier's "refusal will necessarily involve mine," Galt explained to his wife, "as I cannot accept that which he declines without either declaring that I think he is wrong, which I do not, or that his services have been more important than my own, a position of inferiority that I cannot voluntarily assume."[31] The incident was regrettable because it marred the ultimate friendship among the three and artificially ranked the contributions of the fathers of confederation.

With the completion of the union in 1867, Galt lost interest in politics. His personal financial position had deteriorated gravely; he needed to devote more time to his private concerns. Only under strong pressure from friends did he accept a post as Canada's first minister of finance, but he did not stay long. In October 1867 the Commercial Bank, of which he was a director, faced bankruptcy and as finance minister Galt recommended that the government aid the struggling bank in order to prevent serious repercussions in the nation's banking circles. When the cabinet refused, the Commercial closed its doors, triggering a bank panic which had to be stopped by government intervention. Galt, who suffered considerable financial loss, accused the government of lack of confidence in his advice and on 3 November 1867 resigned.[32] Macdonald accepted the resignation reluctantly and on several occasions tried to woo him back, but to no avail. Having reached a plateau in his political career and facing personal financial difficulties,[33] Galt wanted to be rid of the drudgery of a position he had held for over seven years.

Relieved of his heavy political responsibilities, Galt had more time to devote to his private affairs, most of which had fared badly while he was in office. His investments in a copper mine in the Eastern Townships, some warehouses in Portland, and his real estate holdings in Montreal had not lived up to expectations. To recoup these losses he hoped to secure new opportunities, particularly in western Canada. Such openings were plentiful. He received a fascinating offer from Lord Northcote of the Hudson's Bay Company who asked Galt to draft a new company policy now that the Northwest was joined to Canada. Acknowledging Galt's entrepreneurial skill and his expertise on land settlement, Northcote wrote, "We have no officer capable of taking a really comprehensive view of the question, which closely affects the interests not only of our company but of Canada likewise."[34] The challenge tempted Galt but he refused probably because he wished to work on a project of his own.

Galt's quest for investment opportunities centred on railway construction in western Canada. The era was reminiscent of the frenetic Grand Trunk building boom; once again the prospect of a gigantic railway project liberally endowed by an eager government exploded into a heady turbulence in which aggressive entrepreneurs welded alliances, plotted their schemes, and grimly fought each other for the government's favour. Galt, who had always been a promoter, especially of the Northwest, became deeply involved in the struggle for the Pacific contract. Shortly after his resignation from the cabinet he received a nostalgic invitation to re-establish the old Gzowski-Macpherson relationship. "With you as leader keeping sharp lookout for good things and doing 'general tactics,' and Mac. on the nigh side labouring among the political altesse, and your humble servant to do the grubbing and digging, Holton's principle of division of labour will work well," Gzowski wrote him, "All joking aside, the only big thing left on this Confederated continent in the shape of railway enterprises can, I am sure, if properly managed, be made to fall into our hands."[35] In 1870 the proposition was made more concrete and Galt was asked to join David Macpherson in his claim for the government's Pacific contract. Although tempted, he declined. Why he refused his friends is not entirely clear except that at the time he was deeply involved in his own western railway scheme.

Although the details of Galt's plans are lost in the murky complexities of the battle for the Pacific contract, it is clear that he was allied with the Grand Trunk campaign. Both its president, Edward Watkin, and its managing director, C. J. Brydges, were strong advocates of western annexation and Grand Trunk expansion south of the Great Lakes and westward across Rupert's Land to the west coast. Galt had a close relationship with these men, a personal friendship which went back a number of years. As early as 1861 he had joined Watkin in the British North American Association, a powerful lobby for colonial development which also included such prominent individuals as Tilley, Joseph Howe, Baring, and several officials from the Hudson's Bay Company.[36] Some years later in 1867, while on government business in London, Galt met with the Grand Trunk president. "I had a long talk with Watkin and we agreed to act together in several important matters," he confided to Amy. "The Grand Trunk and I are to have a league, offensive and defensive."[37] No definite plans were worked out involving the Grand Trunk in a Pacific railway, but in

Portrait of Sir Alexander Tilloch Galt taken four years
after confederation when he was fifty-two years old.
(Public Archives of Canada)

July 1869 C. J. Brydges came forward with a definite proposal. He wrote Galt:

> While in Toronto, I saw Ross and [F. W.] Cumberland, and we have talked over a North-West scheme which we want to discuss with you.... The idea has not gone beyond us three, and further participants must be settled when we meet you. The notion is to get a charter next session for a Company to build a railway through the Territory, getting a bonus of £5,000 a mile and a large land grant, to enlist the Hudson's Bay people in it, to take advantage of the political necessity in England just now of saving the NW from the Yankees, etc. etc. I think the scheme a feasible and profitable one, and it can do us no harm at any rate to talk it over quietly.[38]

This proposition was the most attractive to Galt and it seemed the most likely to succeed. Both he and Brydges were good friends of John A. Macdonald, having shared rooms with him for some years in Ottawa. In addition to this special access to the prime minister, as the leading agent of the Grand Trunk in Canada as well as a commissioner of the Intercolonial, Brydges represented the strongest and in many ways the most practical strategy for a transcontinental railway. Like Galt and Macdonald, he strongly believed that the road had to be entirely controlled by Canadians. In part his bid for the contract was a diversionary tactic designed to forestall a Canadian-American alliance that could cripple the Grand Trunk,[39] but he also believed that Canadian ownership was necessary to gain British financial support. "I do not myself think that any good could result from joining [the Americans]...," he explained to Macdonald, "To be of any use for the purpose of raising money in England the whole composition of the scheme must be essentially British."[40] Of course, as he had implied in his letter to Galt, nationalist sentiment could be utilized as a weapon to gain government support. In January 1870, Brydges warned Macdonald of a plot by the Northern Pacific Railroad to establish a monopoly in the Northwest by extending branch lines into the territories; in reply the prime minister urged him to propose a definite plan and promised him government assistance in the form of a large land grant of alternate sections.[41] The railway man countered by suggesting a cash subsidy of about five to seven thousand dollars per mile and by firmly rejecting an all-Canadian route. "I have no belief myself in any line of railway running to Fort Garry for a long time to come through British territory," Brydges wrote a friend later, "I am quite clear that railways from Fort Garry around the north shore of Lake Superior and Lake Nipissing could not be built except at a frightful cost, when built could not be worked successfully in winter, and if it could be worked would have no traffic to carry upon it."[42] The alternative to the Canadian route was given concrete form in 1871 when Alexander Galt, George Stephen of the Bank of Montreal, and Donald Smith of the Hudson's Bay Company applied for charters to build railways from Pembina on the American border to Fort Garry and from that point eastward to the head of Lake Superior.[43] The intent of the charters may have been to duplicate Galt's highly successfuly 1853 Grand Trunk gambit, that is, an attempt to hold to ransom any rival projects with a crippling bypass through the United States. It may also have been a way of utilizing Lake Superior in the summer and an American railway in the winter as a link between the Grand Trunk and the proposed Pacific railway. In either case, Brydges stood for a group of businessmen who believed in Canadian financial control over the transcontinental but refused to assume the risk of an all-Canadian route.

Although the backers of the scheme were among the most powerful men in British and Canadian finance, railways, and politics, they could not win Sir John A. Macdonald's approval. The prime minister was deeply committed to an all-Canadian railway; therefore he refused to subsidize the project and rejected Galt's branch line charters in Manitoba. The group concluded that without government assistance they could never float another issue of railway bonds on a market depressed by the financial difficulties of the Northern Pacific.[44] Thus they withdrew from contention and Galt missed being a part of the road to the Pacific.

At the same time that Galt was promoting an American bypass for the trans-Canada railway he took a seemingly paradoxical, even quixotical, stand on the danger of American annexation. As early as the mid-1860s he had sensed that many British politicians and businessmen believed that Canada would eventu-

ally leave the empire and he grew apprehensive about the ease
with which imperial officials approved confederation. "You must
say nothing of it to anyone," he confided to Amy in 1865, "but I
have the conviction we shall effect nothing satisfactory to our
people. It is very grievous to see half a continent slipping away
from the grasp of England with scarcely an effort to hold it."[45]
Galt, who believed that the "connection between Canada &
England is now one of sentiment," felt that if these feelings were
permitted to deteroriate even further Canada would eventually
drift into the arms of the United States, a move which threatened
Canada's economic independence and thus was undesirable to
Canada's business community. On the eve of confederation, his
fears were even stronger and he penned a pessimistic letter to his
wife:

> I am more than ever disappointed at the tone of feeling here
> as to the Colonies. I cannot shut my eyes to the fact that they
> want to get rid of us. They have a servile fear of the United
> States and would rather give us up than defend us, or incur
> the risk of war with that country. Day by day I am more
> oppressed with the sense of responsibility of maintaining a
> connection undesired here and which exposes us to such peril
> at home. I pray to God to show me the right path. But I doubt
> much whether Confederation will save us from Annexation.[46]

The only alternative to the crumbling imperial ties and subsequent American annexation, according to Galt, was a vibrant
Canadian nationalism. During the session of 1870 he vigorously
opposed the Conservative administration on their lacklustre performance regarding Canadian economic nationalism. In a parliamentary speech he attacked their failure to understand the full
significance of confederation. "The intention of ... [confederation]
he believed, was to secure by the union of all the scattered British
North American Colonies, a united country of sufficient power,
population, and wealth, to be able to maintain itself alone. That
policy was to a certain extent carried out by the British North
America Act and his complaint against the Government was that
they had not made use of the prestige which Confederation gave
them; that they had not been successful in their efforts to con-

solidate Confederation."[47] In other words, Galt actively urged Canadians to pursue the establishment of a strong transcontinental economy, and to be more assertive in their dealings with the United States and Great Britain. He was too loyal to Britain and too sensitive to reality to advocate Canadian independence.[48] Total separation was in his opinion a needless shattering of the empire and would only lead to eventual economic and political absorption into the United States. A strong nationalistic self-respect, however, would result in a proudly independent nation, spiritually but securely attached to the British empire. Once again Galt freely mixed public and private motives; the cold calculations of the Montreal financier and railway promoter were roughly integrated into a warm attachment to his adopted country and his motherland.

Galt's strong statements brought him into conflict with his friend, Sir John A. Macdonald. He had never been a loyal party man and his political vacillations were always disconcerting to the prime minister. Macdonald voiced this frustration in response to C. J. Brydges who, while working on the Pacific railway proposal, wanted Galt as leader. Although he grudgingly admitted that Galt's "suggestiveness and versatility of resource would be of great value," Macdonald added, "But he is as unstable as water, and no one can depend upon continuous exertion in one direction with him for 48 hours. If he is the guiding mind, there will be great uncertainty, great delays, and I fear, a want of success."[49] Macdonald's biting comments reflected his growing impatience with Galt's erratic political behaviour. He could not understand the analytical business mind which accepted new ideas so easily yet calculated profits and risks so carefully. Surely Galt's espousal of greater Canadian independence while planning a Canadian transcontinental railway by way of the United States must have bewildered, even irritated, Sir John. From Galt's viewpoint, however, an all-Canadian route was wildly irresponsible. "I consider the proposition perfectly monstrous that for the sake of the sparse population on the Pacific Coast, the prosperity of the four million people east of Lake Superior should be arrested and their political independence jeopardized,"[50] he wrote a friend. His business instinct told him that the Canadian route was premature, that Canada could not afford a project which would drive taxes so high that they would discourage potential immigrants to the Northwest. For once Galt's visionary boldness left him. He allowed his pragmatic assessment of profitability to obscure the fact that a Pacific railway connected into the American network might endanger his own strident calls for increased national awareness as an antidote to American annexation. Unlike the prime minister, who saw full, physical control over transportation as an absolute prerequisite to political nationhood, Galt the railway promoter did not necessarily equate closer economic ties with political independence.

In March 1870, Galt further aggravated the dispute with a speech in the House of Commons calling for Canadian commercial treaty-making powers. For Galt the proposal was a logical extension of the 1859 tariff and the principle of confederation, but to Macdonald it was "nonsense" because it divorced economic considerations from the integrated fabric of imperialism. Galt, the entrepreneur turned politician, over-emphasized the economic sphere of social activity while Macdonald, the party leader, stressed the delicate political balance of the new dominion. Politically, Galt's position was untenable and he had become an embarrassment to the Conservatives. To Macdonald's relief, however, Galt openly severed his relations with the party. "Galt came out, I am glad to say, formally in opposition, and relieved me of the difficulty connected with him," Macdonald confided to a friend, "But he is now finally dead as a Canadian politician...and I shall take precious good care to keep him where he is."[51] The clash, caused by conflicting perceptions of Canada's nationhood, resulted in their political separation.

The breach in their friendship flared into open conflict shortly after the general election of 1872. Galt had refused to run in that election and was in London on business when the Liberals exposed the sordid details of massive contributions to the Conservative campaign by Sir Hugh Allan, the winner of the Pacific contract. Galt adopted a stringent moralistic tone and refused to aid the distressed Macdonald. Later he broke publicly with Macdonald, and in an open letter to Senator Ferrier,[52] he acknowledged the country's debt to Macdonald's statesmanship but stated that he could not condone the indiscretions of the Conservative leader. He harshly condemned Macdonald, writing, "I regard his election as leader of the opposition a grave mistake" which would lead to wholesale desertions of Conservatives to the Liberal party. Galt's letter also condemned the Conservative's Pacific railway policy. Still believing it foolish to risk bankruptcy for an all-Canadian railway, Galt stated that British Columbia had to be told: "the engagement was improvident and its fulfilment impossible." In Galt's view, if she could not accept these conditions she should leave the union. Given the tone of the argument, it was little wonder that Alexander Mackenzie, the new prime minister, invited Galt to renegotiate the agreement with British Columbia. Galt did not accept the assignment for personal reasons.

Galt's harsh condemnation of Macdonald and his policies was not merely a sanctimonious rebuke from the too-clever entrepreneur of the Grand Trunk era who had freely mixed politics and profits, nor was it just a sullen reproach from the disappointed railway promoter who had lost in the scramble for the contract. It was also a bitter denunciation from an inveterate businessman who disliked bribery because it transgressed his moral code and served as an example of unfair competition which violated the rules of the game. Galt appreciated Macdonald's practical outlook and deep devotion to his duty, but he could not condone outright corruption to attain the ends of the party nor the subjugation of principle for the sake of political expediency. Galt's business ethics, basically the inexorable creed of survival of the fittest, allowed him to be a relentless bargainer, exacting the utmost from a deal, unforgiving of a weaker opponent; yet his pious Christianity forbade him to be a dishonest dealer, deriving profits through graft. This was their basic difference in perspective: the shrewd, harsh, but honest business ethic against the cunning, complaisant, and pliable political morality.

The Ferrier letter hurt Macdonald deeply and temporarily shattered his friendship with Galt. It remained so until October 1876 when Galt made overtures for a reconciliation. He probably regained his admiration for the elderly Macdonald, who once again inspired people with a vision of a strong, unified nation, invigorated by massive immigration, sustained by the resources of western Canada, and bound together by the steel of the transcontinental. Although the two men renewed their friendship, the scars of the conflict remained. Macdonald continued to be suspicious of Galt's openness to new ideas and his eagerness to adopt new concepts. In

Macdonald's opinion, these were marks of instability, characteristics unsuitable for party politics. In Macdonald's eyes, Galt was
simply not a reliable party man.

This basic difference in perspective caused several more quarrels to erupt between them. One of these, while minor, clearly
illustrates their fundamental difference in thought. In 1876 Galt
published a pamphlet entitled *Civil Liberties in Lower Canada*, in which
he expressed his alarm about the activities of Roman Catholic
Bishop Bourget of Montreal. Galt, who firmly believed in the clear
separation of church and state, felt that the bishop was too actively
involved in politics. He warned that the civil liberties of English-
speaking Protestants as well as those of the French Roman Catholics in Quebec were in jeopardy. The public reaction to the tract
came largely from Catholic church officials and was quite hostile;
therefore, Galt wrote a second booklet, *Church and State*, which
refuted his critics and listed specific instances of ecclesiastical
interference in secular affairs. He tried to enlist Macdonald's
support, but that wily politician wanted no part in any anti-clerical
campaign which could upset the delicate structure of the Conservative party. The prime minister must have wondered at Galt's
incursion into the church and state battle. Surely it was a curious
departure from the promoter's usual pragmatic, business-like
ways? Yet Galt was a pious Calvinist whose religion was a precious
possession; he always lived in a close relationship with God and
always sought guidance in prayer. At the same time he cherished
liberty and always made stirring references to freedom in most of
his writings and speeches. Furthermore, as a member of a minority
group in Quebec, he felt threatened and as a man of resolute action
he decided to take a definite and strong stand. In all his activities
Galt was never equivocal.

Macdonald, the cautious politician who never acted until
absolutely necessary, could not understand Galt's obsession with
long range, broad issues which might never come before parliament. Nor could he bear the political maverick who chafed under
party restraints, his fickle temper, and the narrow emphasis upon
economic considerations. Yet, Macdonald admired Galt's resourceful mind, his familiarity with the London business world and his
understanding of the requirements for economic development and
nation building. He recognized that western expansion required

massive foreign investments and knowledge; thus, when the Con-servatives returned to power in 1878, the new prime minister turned quite naturally to this talented Canadian entrepreneur.

By the end of the 1870s, Galt had established himself as a prominent modern businessman and public figure. His career had shown the remarkable flexibility of those who eschew normal practices whenever these traditions bar the way to new ideas. His role in the confederation movement is a testimony to his imagina-tive yet pragmatic mind. He was among the first who recognized the utility of the railway as a tool for territorial expansion, but he was also among the few who realized that, conversely, western annexation was necessary for the survival of the railway. Further-more, he envisioned this interdependence of technology and re-source development as the basis of a new, national, and industrial state. The vision was bold, but he helped to make it a reality. Freely borrowing those ideas and concepts he found useful, Galt worked out the initial proposal for an integrated political and economic structure as the foundation of a modern northern state. He also counted the costs and risks very carefully and, it was (for example) the fear of potential losses which prevented him from accepting an all-Canadian route for the transcontinental railway. In this way too, Galt revealed that he had completely accommodated himself to the dawning age of technology: efficiency and profitability were his measure, expansion and change his creed.

This nineteenth-century technician of finance used his insight and experience to reap a personal fortune; his own ventures certainly stood to benefit from confederation and western coloniz-ation. His sense of what was profitable and efficient, however, was not confined to his own concerns or those of his colleagues. Galt's interests extended beyond his companies to embrace those of his adopted country. He had a vision of a colonized Northwest, occupied by industrious settlers busily reconstructing the land, as the basis for a dynamic Canadian nation. In his estimation, the resources of the Northwest, its coal, its rivers, and its soil, were valueless unless mobilized into a productive and remunerative process. He believed that the seemingly static wilderness had to be transformed into a dynamic civilization, a hospitable setting for the surplus population of an overcrowded Britain. For twenty years he had preached the need to civilize the western territories whose fabulous wealth could make Canada a prosperous and mighty nation. When Prime Minister Macdonald needed a salesman to promote the Northwest abroad, he chose a successful businessman. He asked Sir Alexander Galt to bring the dream into practical reality.

3

Salesman of
western Canada

In October 1878 the Canadian electorate returned Sir John A. Macdonald's Conservatives to office and entrusted them with the task of strengthening the weak framework of an independent Canadian economy. Although confederation successfully bound the far-flung provinces together politically, its economic purpose was in danger of collapse. The powerful lure of affluent and technological American society persistently drew trade southward, preventing a strong economic cohesion among Canada's diverse regions and threatening to reduce Canada to the limited role of supplier of raw materials for a prosperous and growing neighbour. To counteract these compelling forces of continental integration, and to keep Canada on its path to industrialization, the Conservatives planned to construct a high tariff wall between the two countries. Safely tucked behind such a barrier Canadian industries certainly would flourish, selling their products to the Maritimers as well as to the envisioned multitude of settlers on the western plains. The newly acquired Northwest became the most important ingredient in the government's formula. As Charles Tupper put it, "Under the National Policy...we must look forward not only to building up thriving centres of industry and enterprises all over this portion of the country, but to obtaining a market for those industries after they have been established; and I say where is there a greater market than the magnificent granary of the North-West?"[1] A settled West could not only raise grains

from its fertile soil to exchange for central Canadian manufactured goods, but its lands could be sold to pay for the transcontinental railway, the vital transportation chain needed to facilitate
the exchange of goods among Canadians. In this way, the national
policies so clearly expressed in the Conservative platform gave
concrete shape to one of the fundamental concepts underlying
confederation, the creation of a separate northern economy.

To accomplish these objectives, Prime Minister Macdonald
gathered about himself his old compatriots. Obviously, the team
that had initiated confederation was going to carry that project to
its logical conclusion. Macdonald took for himself the ministry of
the interior, a portfolio created in 1873 to manage Canada's
westward expansion and promote western settlement. He assigned the key ministries of finance and of railways and canals to
veterans Leonard Tilley and Charles Tupper. These powerful
politicians were to erect the tariff barricade and supervise the
construction of the Pacific railway.

To Sir Alexander Galt went the task of defining Canada's
relations with foreign nations, particularly with Great Britain, still
Canada's major trading partner and source of capital. By the end of
the 1870s Macdonald had come to accept the broad outlines of
Galt's nationalistic views. The prime minister had rejected his
arguments earlier because they had clashed with the mainstream
of Canadian thought; his sensitive political instincts refused to
espouse any concept not yet demanded by the voters. The depression of the mid-1870s, however, had forced the Conservatives to
adopt certain national policies which, in their call for industrialization and a western wheat economy, implied a vigorous expansion of foreign trade. The programme, which attested to Macdonald's intense faith in the Canadian nationality, was also in
perfect harmony with Galt's 1859 tariff, his long campaign for
federal union, and his call for independent treaty-making powers
for Canada. Both men had always shared a strong fundamental
belief in the ability of Canada, with its abundant natural resources,
to mature economically apart from the United States. Moreover,
like Galt, Macdonald knew that the empire was no longer held
together by diplomatic bonds but by the financial commitments
made by many influential British investors. Since the disruption of
political ties would no longer shatter the empire, Macdonald also

accepted Galt's position that Canada must aggressively pursue her own commercial policy and no longer timidly accept British foreign agreements detrimental to Canada's interests.[2]

The need for greater diplomatic representation became very evident in 1878. Hoping to counteract the crippling depression by increasing trade with Latin America, late in that year the government asked Galt if he would undertake a mission to Madrid to negotiate an agreement with the Spanish colonies of Cuba and Puerto Rico. En route, Galt was instructed to settle a tariff dispute with France. Both assignments, however, had to be discharged under the strict supervision of the imperial and colonial offices as well as the consuls in both capitals. When Galt finally unsnarled the red tape, he learned only that neither Spain nor France were able to make immediate decisions. So the disillusioned amateur diplomat returned to Canada in the spring of 1879 to report that his many meetings had not borne fruit but might in the distant future. This frustrating experience hardened Galt's conviction that Canada's foreign affairs had to be freed from British interference. He resented his subordinate role in the negotiations as the "humble hodman" gathering materials but possessing no power to make decisions. More than ever before, he urged Macdonald to secure some form of diplomatic voice for the Canadian nation.[3]

In this way the idea of a permanent representative abroad became an integral part of Canada's economic development policy. In the summer of 1879, when Macdonald, Tilley, Tupper, and Galt met with British officials in London, the Canadians sought imperial approval for the establishment of a permanent Canadian representative in London. Macdonald and his team were in England primarily to seek imperial support for the proposed railway to the Pacific. At the same time the colonists had to justify their recently imposed protective tariff. To appease the disgruntled British officials, Macdonald proposed a preferential tariff system for the empire, in other words, a reincarnation of the Corn Laws with favoured treatment for Canadian products. Although the device was cleverly designed to create an assured market for western grain, it was largely bombastic and totally unacceptable to the doctrinaire free traders. The request for financial assistance for the western railway was also denied. The only benefit gleaned was a reluctant recognition of a new office, the high commissioner of Canada in London, a concession which would not cost the imperial government any money.

The Pacific railway negotiations aroused Galt's entrepreneurial instincts, and he wanted to become involved in its construction. He urged Macdonald to fire Sandford Fleming, the government's engineer, for working too slowly and too expensively. Galt charged that Fleming was "incapable of grasping the idea of what the country wants and what its resources enable it to do and I must say with frankness that I trust you will pardon that his continuence on the direction of the Pacific Railway will defeat all our plans for the development of that country."[4] Galt implied that if anyone knew what the country needed and what the resources of the Northwest could do for Canada, he did. He suggested that, with his friends Brydges and Gzowski, he study the transcontinental project and afterwards supervise the railway's construction and land sales.

Macdonald, who still did not trust Galt's railway ambitions, took little note of his gratuitous advice and instead named him Canada's first high commissioner. Galt was the logical choice because he, with the prime minister, had drafted the structure of the new office. He also was the most experienced diplomat in Canada and had close friends in the London business world. Most important from Macdonald's point of view, Galt clearly recognized the needs of Canada's economy. Galt, like Macdonald, was an expansionist who fully understood that without massive emigration from the British Isles, the potential market for central Canadian goods would vanish, the tracks of the costly Pacific railway would rust, and the dreams of a national economy would disintegrate. While Macdonald could sketch the broad outlines of the national policies, he needed Galt's technically sharp mind to fill in the details by creating and executing a bold yet carefully prepared scheme to attract immigrants to the Canadian rather than the American prairies. Galt's entire career, both public and private, had been devoted to expansionary schemes: the British American Land Company and the Atlantic and Grand Trunk railways were projects intended to spark economic growth; the 1859 tariff was a plan designed to stimulate the colonial economy; and in his mind, confederation had been a scheme largely intended to expand

Canadian influence across the continent. Now Galt's place was obviously in London. Since Canada had neither the financial nor human resources to utilize the tremendous potential of the Northwest, his task was to capture the imaginations of British financiers and government officials. He had to make them aware of the boundless opportunities in the West and encourage them to invest in large-scale emigration and resource exploitation enterprises. Although he would have preferred to remain in Canada and work on western rail and land developments, once named to the new post he enthusiastically devoted himself to the responsibility of implementing one part of the western development plan he had advocated for over twenty years.

Once committed to the new task, Galt took up its challenge so eagerly that he left for London even before the Parliament of Canada had approved the new position and its first occupant. At a farewell dinner held in Montreal at the end of March 1880, Galt forcefully but carefully explained in detail his conception of the comprehensive nature of the new post. Noting that his first duty was the management of Canada's financial affairs, Galt was quick to point out that the "subject of immigration...is perhaps the most important that we have or are likely to have for many years to consider."[5] Playing on the strains of imperialism emerging at the time, Galt declared that "the laborious task of opening up and bringing under civilization" the immense Canadian prairies was an "imperial responsibility—a task to which Canada with its limited resources could only pledge its co-operation." He readily admitted that the colonization of the Northwest was "a most direct means of restoring to the commerce of Montreal that pre-eminence which we desire it should have," and that it "opens up to Canada a future which enables us to look forward to the attainment at a very early day of that national power and strength which we looked for when we entered Confederation." But he also urged his audience to remember that the United Kingdom had as large a stake as Canada had in this programme. The expansive plains beckoned the overcrowded population of the British Isles. Western Canada's fertile soils promised to relieve Britain's dependency upon foreign countries for food. Reiterating Canada's official position, Galt declared that "this half of the continent was not obtained directly by ourselves but we took it over at the instance of the Imperial Government, which knew at that time that it would require enormous outlay to bring it into cultivation and civilization." The most urgent task of the high commissioner, therefore, was to convince Great Britain that she must help to meet the staggering expense of railway construction, law enforcement, and civil administration in the Northwest. Ancillary to this mission was the need to establish diplomatic relations with other countries in order to meet Canada's special requirements. Galt hastened to explain, however, that Canada would not act as an independent nation but as a dominion working within the broad framework of British policy and utilizing her superb diplomatic corps. Galt argued that the imperial connection, although now only one of sentiment, was still very important. In fact he planned to work for the creation of an imperial customs union, a *Zollverein*, which could make the empire a completely self-sufficient economic unit. Once again his penchant for expansion placed the specific problem of western Canadian development into the sweeping panorama of a new imperialism.

Galt's official instructions differed little from his speech, an indication of his influence in their formulation.[6] Since the imperial government was unlikely to accept the *Zollverein* idea, the document cautioned the high commissioner to give the subject only his "best attention," merely test the idea, and keep the cabinet informed of public opinion on the issue. The memorandum, however, strongly reiterated Galt's stress on western expansion. "The most important subject which can engage the attention of the High Commissioner in England is the development of the North West Territory,"[7] the paper affirmed. It further echoed Galt's argument that the transfer of the Hudson's Bay lands had "imposed upon the present population of Canada burdens and responsibilities far exceeding any possible interest (great though that may be) which they could themselves directly have in it." In other words, the Canadian government was determined to continue its old policy. Although strongly desiring western extension and its great benefits, the government of Canada continued to shrink from shouldering the high cost of the project.

Despite his eagerness, Galt's first year in office was disappointing. The failure was due in some measure to his own attitude. The cost of moving and supporting his large family of eight daughters and one son, the high rent of a large, prestigious house near Hyde Park, as well as the expensive entertainments expected of a diplomat, were not adequately covered by his salary of ten thousand dollars.[8] The deficient compensation made it difficult for the parsimonious Galt to muster the buoyant enthusiasm so necessary for a salesman of western Canada. His spirits were dampened even more when the general elections held just prior to his arrival in London replaced his Tory friends with Gladstone's Liberals. The situation demanded discreet action on the part of Galt; instead he openly expressed his conservative politics and joined the Tory Carlton Club.

Galt encountered another protocol problem which not only hurt his feelings but also hampered his effectiveness. Imperial officials refused to award diplomatic status to the high commissioner, and throughout his entire stay in London, Galt doggedly fought this studied neglect partly to satisfy his pride, partly to enhance the stature of Canada, but mainly to increase his diplomatic influence. In a world where the slightest nuance in title could either open or close doors, the relatively low position of the Canadian representative curtailed his diplomatic activities. For example, Galt conducted only sporadic talks with Spanish and French representatives, partly because he did not want to make commitments before securing a preferential trade agreement with Britain, but mainly because the United Kingdom herself was negotiating with these countries and claimed prior rights over the Dominion. This diplomatic inferiority angered the sensitive Galt and the intentional slight became a frequent subject of irate letters to Macdonald.

Of smaller consequence but nevertheless annoying for the temperamental Galt was the question of his marital status. English law still did not recognize the validity of marriage with a deceased wife's sister. Therefore, when Sir Alexander wanted Amy to be at his side during his presentation to the queen, court officials declared that this was impossible. In retaliation, Galt impetuously threatened to resign, but personal intervention by the Prince of Wales and the fact that the marriage was solemnized in the United States where such unions were legal resulted in a reversal of the edict. Galt and his wife were jointly presented to Queen Victoria and diplomatic embarrassment was avoided.

Galt's touchy personality was not the only block marring his effectiveness. He soon discovered that colonial officials anticipated all his moves because Canada's governor-general routinely forwarded them copies of all his correspondence. He had carefully planned his course of action: his first step was to gain an imperial commitment to assist emigration as "the thin end of the wedge" which could lead to the second step, aid to the Pacific railway, and ultimately to the grand conclusion, support for a *Zollverein*.[9] With imperial officials privy to this plan, the high commissioner did not enjoy the luxury of such tactical manoeuvres.

Galt's worries were merely trivialities to Prime Minister Macdonald, who looked for immediate results. "The emigration matter is of more importance to Canada just now than any other aspect," he reminded Galt, "and it is therefore desirable that you should take direct charge of the question as a whole."[10] Macdonald allowed the high commissioner a free hand in the reorganization of the ineffective emigration office in London, a task which Galt carried out quickly and thoroughly. He placed the office on a "business-like" basis by rearranging the localities of subagencies and centralizing the entire recruitment procedures. He publicized the attractions of the Northwest through new pamphlets, public speeches, and newspaper articles.[11] He supported the work of philanthropic organizations and negotiated with steamship companies for lower rates and the use of their advertising facilities. In sum, Galt worked diligently to present to the British public the opportunities offered by the Canadian prairies.

Yet much of the effort was in vain. While Galt's reforms certainly streamlined Canada's publicity campaign, he could not overcome the competition from more attractive countries like the United States, New Zealand, and Australia. What was needed, according to Galt, was a massive removal of entire families from impoverished regions in the British Isles to western Canada, a gigantic project workable only if subsidized by the Canadian and imperial governments. Yet, he could make no headway with Colonial Secretary Lord Kimberley on the issue. "Most unsatisfactory interview with Colonial Minister respecting emigration," Galt cabled Macdonald shortly after his first meeting with Kimberley, "He holds out no expectation of assistance."[12] Galt, ever impatient with diplomatic niceties, urged Macdonald to let him take the issue right to the British cabinet; the politically more astute Macdonald, wary of the colonial secretary's brusque nature, firmly rejected such a precipitous move. Galt, on his part, interpreted the cool reception by Kimberley as a final answer, and that added to all other irritations caused him to submit his resignation only months after taking office.[13] Ironically, Galt, ever so sensitive concerning his own prerogatives, failed to appreciate those of others, a serious flaw which made him a poor diplomat.

Macdonald simply refused to accept the resignation and in July 1880 he travelled to London primarily to negotiate the contract for the Pacific railway but also to help Galt prepare the plans for large-scale western settlement. The first objective was completed in October 1880 when an agreement was signed with the Canadian Pacific Railway, headed by George Stephen, a Montreal banker. Since the project aroused little interest among British investors, most of its funding would have to come from Canada. To aid in this enormous undertaking, the Canadian government granted the Canadian Pacific Railway very generous land and cash subsidies, a policy which virtually committed the government to a partnership with the company. This link clearly demonstrated the deep commitment that Macdonald's administration had made to western settlement.

Understandably then, increasing the flow of emigrants to Canada was Macdonald's other objective in London. In co-operation with Galt and Stephen he drafted a scheme whereby the CPR in concert with the Canadian and imperial governments would carry out a wholesale transplant of Irish to Canada. When the general idea received favourable response, Galt was instructed to fill in the details. The final version of the plan, submitted to the Canadian cabinet and the colonial office in November 1880, called for use of the Homestead Act to provide two reserved sections of land near the CPR main line for each Irish family. Departing from the ordinary, the plan further proposed that the government build a house and plow and plant part of one section prior to the settlers' arrival. Transportation and improvement costs, estimated at seventy-five to eighty pounds per family, would be advanced by the imperial government to be repaid by the settler at low interest rates. Lastly Galt suggested that the proceeds from the pre-emption sales could finance future emigrants.[14] While

Galt received some cautious support in London for the concept, he believed that at least two years were needed to implement the policy.[15]

Theoretically the proposal had considerable merit; it promised to help Canada settle the Northwest at minimal cost and at the same time alleviate much suffering in over-populated Ireland. The most enthusiastic supporter of the scheme was George Stephen, whose company stood to gain much if the plan worked. In December 1880 he travelled to London to help Galt sell the project to British politicians. When he returned to Canada in April 1881, he was still certain of eventual success. He had encountered strong vocal support, and in his eyes the problem was primarily bureaucratic sluggishness. "It takes time to create anything in this slow moving country," he wrote Macdonald, but at the same time expressed confidence that Gladstone would ultimately support an assisted emigration scheme.[16]

Stephen's high hopes for an early and favourable response to the Irish emigration plan were unfounded. One of his colleagues, Sir John Rose, a former Canadian minister of finance and until recently an agent for Canada in London, confided to Macdonald that he was "much disappointed at the lukewarmness of the Government here in reference to Emigration. The subject requires to be worked up and public opinion brought to bear on them."[17] Rose correctly sensed that imperial politicians had serious reservations about the proposition. Although Gladstone was searching for a solution to the problem, his administration was reluctant to subsidize Irish emigration for fear that the Irish might interpret this as a plot to depopulate and weaken their country. British officials also disliked the close association of the CPR with the project. As one of them noted, "Still the whole scheme partakes of the nature of a commercial speculation nor would it be desirable to set such a precedent."[18] The principle of large-scale subsidized emigration was still unacceptable to any nation and therefore much basic work was needed before the British public would accept, and their government assist, massive emigration to the Canadian West.

In May 1881 Sir John A. Macdonald once again sailed to England, ostensibly for health reasons but also to push the Irish emigration programme, designed as Stephen put it, "to rope in" the British government.[19] Macdonald interviewed not only Gladstone, Kimberley, and the Marquis of Lansdowne but also several Irish landholders and even the Roman Catholic leader, Cardinal Manning. He argued that a mass movement of Irish to Canada would benefit both countries, but was met with little sympathy. Gladstone agreed only to include a provision in the Irish Land Act of 1881 granting some aid to Irish emigrants, but to any country of their choice. Since the imperial government refused to specify the country to which subsidies would apply, the concession was of little benefit to Canada. Macdonald was disappointed but with the approach of the summer season little more could be done until the fall.[20] The first attempt to gain assisted emigration had failed.

Alexander Galt had never been enthusiastic about the Irish emigration scheme. He privately advised Macdonald that Gladstone would not provide a "copper of public funds" to any Irish colonization plan.[21] Still very much the businessman, Galt preferred a completely different approach. He believed that private enterprise, motivated by the drive for profits, was the best means of stimulating emigration. Consequently he wanted to restore the system that had worked so well for him in the 1840s—the private land company. Among the first persons he visited in London were Alexander Gillespie, the former chairman of the Canada Company, and Thomas Brassey, one of the builders of the Grand Trunk. Galt suggested to both men that they should form colonization companies to take up under the homestead regulations several million-acre blocks of western lands. Like the CPR, these firms might earn a substantial part of their land as a subsidy for building colonization railways to their holdings. As a sop to the government, Galt recommended that each corporation should make available to indigent families a number of eighty-acre plots. When both British financiers appeared receptive to the idea, Galt was ecstatic. He impulsively advised the Canadian government to buy all the Hudson's Bay Company's lands for five hundred thousand pounds in order to make a handsome profit on sales to land companies.[22]

The concept of colonization companies was strongly opposed by George Stephen. Quite naturally the president of the CPR was suspicious of any railway-settlement scheme that threatened to compete with his own railway. Nevertheless he accurately assessed Galt's motives in proposing the land companies. He wrote Macdonald that he believed the high commissioner was "very anxious to strike something that will have the effect of opening the N.W. and at the same time do something for its investors and promoters."[23] Stephen had a point. Galt's entire career was mute testimony to the charge that his ideas were never far removed from personal profits. Interestingly enough, however, Stephen, who was as much a profit-seeking businessman as Galt, opposed the plan because the land companies would certainly become speculators. "Far better ... to refuse such operations," he advised Macdonald. "It is settling not selling that we must aim at." He recommended that the land companies should pay at least five dollars per acre for the land and be required to settle speedily. Of course, Stephen's position was clouded by the fact that massive land sales at a high price would automatically escalate the value of his CPR land grant. In fact, his attitude toward colonization was really no different than that of Galt; the only difference was that he wanted the CPR to be the prime benefactor of western settlement.

Government officials dismissed Stephen's objections and in general approved the notion of colonization companies. In their eyes the western lands were virtually unlimited but valuable only when developed. J. S. Dennis, Canada's surveyor-general, applauded the Brassey and Gillespie projects because they would open up some of the richest land and timber areas in the territories.[24] Although Prime Minister Macdonald vetoed Galt's concept of selling solid blocks of land to colonization companies and awarding them free grants of land for constructing railways, his creed of rapid progress at minimal cost to the government heartily approved the basic principle of development by private enterprise.[25] On 23 December 1881 cabinet bowed to strong popular pressure and issued a number of regulations which permitted the sale of odd-numbered sections of land to any business concern that satisfied the government of its good will, capabilities, and sincere interests.[26] It was an important amendment in policy, a modification which once again demonstrated that the government was willing to loosen its regulations in order to encourage the rapid exploitation of western Canadian resources, and "at the same time do something for its investors and promoters."

The new regulations proved to be extremely popular and many Canadian businessmen, including politicians from both parties, eagerly rushed to avail themselves of the opportunity. Because Galt had played a significant role in this policy change, government officials considered him an expert in emigration and colonization matters, and often sought his advice.[27] To Galt his new status seemed to be the only achievement of his career as high commissioner. The negotiations with Spain and France were faltering; the Irish emigration scheme had failed. Gillespie had still made no definite commitments to any colonization scheme, while Brassey lamely explained that all his financial resources were tied up in American projects.[28] It was all very discouraging for Galt. As far as he was concerned the year in London had been a total waste of time. In his constant stream of letters to Macdonald he fretted about the bad weather, his failing health, and the frustrating apathy among imperial officials. Above all he complained about the high cost of living in London; he grumbled that he could no longer afford to spend more on the high commissionership than it paid because he was suffering reverses in his unattended business concerns.[29] The Canadian government's refusal to incur more expenses on diplomacy and Macdonald's flippant suggestion that Galt reduce expenditures "and let the dignity of the office as far as hospitalities etc. are concerned go to the devil,"[30] only served to embitter Galt further. He impressed upon the prime minister that effective action depended upon personal contacts, chatting with influential men at their clubs, at dinners, or in their homes. Since he could no longer afford to entertain guests, he was refusing invitations from prominent officials and consequently was no longer in touch with the policy makers. "You can get a hundred men quite as good as I am to sit in my office and write letters," he grumbled, "but if you ever expect real service from me, it could only be in the personal influences I could exercise in the circles referred to."[31] It all added up to a strong desire to return to private life and Galt resubmitted his resignation. He even asked George Stephen for a position with the CPR.[32] Macdonald, who still had confidence in Galt's entrepreneurial skills, urged him to remain in London and promised him a summer trip to western Canada to look after his personal coal-mining and colonization venture there. While Galt did not withdraw the resignation, he accepted

the western jaunt and reluctantly agreed to return to London in
the fall to resume the negotiations. To save money, his family
would remain in Montreal.

The western Canadian tour momentarily recharged Galt's
enthusiasm. The prospects for his personal western business
venture looked promising and the future of the Northwest appeared bright. The summer's journey and the previous year's
work as high commissioner, however, had revealed to him a harsh
truth: before the West could be settled in any extensive manner,
enormous sums of money would be necessary not only to subsidize emigration but to finance the technology necessary to tame
the environment. While Canadians could provide some of the
required capital themselves, to build such necessities as railways
and coal-mines, the bulk of the funds would have to be sought
outside the country. Canadian businessmen needed the support of
their British colleagues and the imperial government in their
mission to exploit the bountiful resources of the plains. Even
though the wealth of the prairies was enormous and promised
handsome returns on investments, the task of luring money to the
Northwest had proved to be extremely difficult so far, mainly
because in England there was a lack of knowledge about and
confidence in western Canada. Clearly, every foreign investment
dollar would require prolonged and often discouraging negotiations. Invigorated by the trip to the Northwest, Sir Alexander
once again undertook the task of promoting the great possibilities
of western Canada.

On the surface, the potential for success was greater than the
year before. A land boom in Manitoba, closely associated with
railway construction, lured thousands of settlers to the province
and dramatically increased its population. The land mania proved
that the CPR could draw immigrants because rail transportation
made settlement on the plains feasible. But not enough colonists
were coming and the far-flung prairies still needed thousands of
farmers, labourers, and businessmen. Galt's mission was to attract
them.

Sir Alexander was still convinced that the answer to the
settlement problem was the creation of favourable conditions for
large settlement companies. Periodically, he revealed to Macdonald grand schemes using the British American Land Company

as a model, and requested the relaxation of the land regulations to permit the purchase of large solid tracts of land.[33] The prime minister, well aware of the poor record of large settlement companies, routinely dismissed such concessions and therefore no large British-owned colonization companies were established in the Northwest. One of Galt's successful projects, however, was the settlement of about fifteen hundred Jews near Moosomin, Saskatchewan. The high commissioner convinced the Rothschilds to subsidize a colony in the West for persecuted Russian Jews then living in London. Although Galt was not keen on a large influx of Jews into Canada, he swallowed his prejudice because these were mainly prosperous farmers and skilled workers who would certainly go to the United States instead.[34] Apart from this sizeable group, Galt dealt largely with individual settlers who merely continued to dribble onto the prairies.

By February 1882 Galt was again so discouraged by his lack of progress that he renewed his resignation. He informed Macdonald that there was little hope for the assisted Irish emigration scheme because of the deteriorating relationship between Ireland and the imperial government. He also grumbled about the continuing British reluctance to award him proper diplomatic status, which so greatly curtailed his effectiveness. He advised Macdonald that there was little to hold him in London; the emigration matters were so minor that they could be handled by a clerk, and the French and Spanish negotiations could easily await his successor. What bothered Galt the most, however, was the high cost of serving his country. In the confidential and "personal request to go home," addressed to Macdonald, Galt confided that his business affairs were suffering again and needed his undivided attention. "I want to go to the North West country this summer and my land interests in Montreal demand that I should be there in April," he wrote Macdonald and lamented, "All my own matters seem to go to the bad when I am away which is a good reason for going back."[35] Galt also attributed his chronic illness to the London climate. All in all, the high commissionership had given Galt no pleasure, but only worry and anxiety. "I have been now in office for two years," he concluded, "and I cannot truly say that I have had a happy time." He longed to return to Canada and immerse himself in a familiar business world, to tend his personal affairs, especially his coal-mining and colonization prospects.

Macdonald, who still believed in Galt's negotiating abilities, took great pains to refute all the high commissioner's arguments. In a long letter he cleverly argued that the usefulness of the commissionership was just beginning and that if he resigned, the credit for a number of significant achievements initiated by him would be awarded to his successor. Macdonald further flattered Galt by saying that an experienced Canadian diplomat was needed to interpret the faltering treaty talks of England with Spain and France and to look after Canada's interests. The upcoming international fisheries conference in London also needed a skilled negotiator. According to Macdonald, only Galt could fill the need. Furthermore, the prime minister pointed out, the Jewish emigration scheme was an important development because the Rothschilds had always refused to invest in Canada before. "I should prefer *you* to write another epistle to the Hebrews, rather than a newcomer,"[36] he added. In conclusion he informed Galt that Archbishop Lynch of Toronto was being sent to Britain to stir up interest among the Roman Catholic hierarchy for the lagging Irish emigration scheme. Surely Lynch's visit would bring results and possibly a million Irishmen would come to Canada. "Obtain [Irish emigration], and you are King of the Northwest," he promised Galt. Therefore, by appealing to his vanity, the wily Macdonald charmed Galt into remaining at his post; he also granted him leave to visit Montreal and the Northwest to tend to his personal affairs.

Before Galt could leave for Canada he had to prepare the way for Archbishop Lynch's visit to England. Prime Minister Macdonald hoped that Lynch could persuade the Roman Catholic hierarchy to sway the Irish public in favour of large-scale emigration. In an interview with Cardinal Manning, the head of the Roman church in England, Galt had learned that the cardinal feared the repercussions of a massive drain of people from Ireland but knew that such a movement was inevitable. He agreed with Galt that Canada was the most desirable place for the Irish to go and even consented to accompany Lynch to speak with the various bishops in Ireland.[37] If the mission was successful, a great obstacle to the defunct Irish emigration scheme would be removed.

Lynch's expensive publicity tour, impeccably arranged by Galt, commenced in February 1882. Lynch was encouraged by the friendly conversations and was confident that Gladstone would not refuse his request for assisted emigration. Galt, however, felt that the bishop was too optimistic. "I must report that I fear he is *sanguine*," he confided to Macdonald, but quickly conceded, "Still it is a great favour for the future to hear these men openly identified with Emigration to Canada."[38] Active support from the Irish clergy for a plan to remove a large segment of their parishioners at a time when Irish discontent was at a feverish pitch was most unlikely.

Of greater consequence to Lynch's undertaking was a diplomatic blunder committed by Sir John A. Macdonald. In mid-April Galt arranged an interview between Lynch and Colonial Secretary Lord Kimberley. The reception was decidedly cool and when the negotiations reached an impasse, Kimberley asked Lynch to wait outside his office while Galt was to remain behind. He then read a speech made by Macdonald in the House of Commons in reply to a motion spawned by the strongly unified Irish voice in Canada, which condemned imperial policies in Ireland and advocated Home Rule. Although Macdonald had watered down the resolution considerably, he did allow the measure to pass simply because of the formidable Irish vote in Canada. Kimberley, deeply offended by the obvious colonial interference in British domestic affairs, angrily informed Galt that the cabinet would resent Macdonald's blatant political action. Galt tried to soothe Kimberley's wrath but to no avail.[39] The resolution could not have come at a more unfortunate time. A few days later the chief secretary for Ireland and his assistant were brutally assassinated by Irish extremists. The bishop's meeting with Gladstone had to be postponed indefinitely and Galt would have to remain in London to try to salvage the torpedoed mission. "I may feel it my duty to remain longer here," he informed Macdonald, "I shall in this respect do what I think the public interest demands though I shall be very reluctant to put off my departure."[40] The Irish resolution had seriously damaged the emigration plan and any thought about assisted emigration would have to be put aside for some time. Without a cordial understanding of Canada's needs, the British government could not be expected to assist emigration to Canada, especially Irish emigration, when bloody revolution threatened to erupt in Ireland.

Galt's work in London was also frustrated when he became ensnared in an acrimonious debate over the suitability of the southern plains for agriculture. Without systematic records, the assessment of the southwestern portion of the prairies still depended upon the viewpoint of the observer and the time of his visit. In the summer of 1882, for example, Alexander Stavely Hill, a noted British parliamentarian about to make large investments in ranching, toured the region and commented on the lack of water west of Fort Walsh; yet, only a few years earlier Charles Tupper, the Canadian minister of railways, pronounced the territory as "the garden of the world."[41] Another optimistic, even reckless statement came from John Macoun, a self-taught biologist and sometime surveyor for the CPR. Macoun, who probably observed the region during a particularly wet and verdant season, was convinced that the interior prairies were habitable. In his lengthy *Manitoba and the Great North-West* (1882), a work ostensibly scholarly but virtually propagandistic, Macoun derided the popular distinction between good and bad lands and brashly proclaimed that all were fertile and suitable for settlement. While the CPR and government officials eagerly accepted and propagated Macoun's highly optimistic conclusions, a very hostile reaction came from H. Y. Hind, who as one of the leaders of the Canadian exploration expedition of 1857 had declared the southern region to be an extension of the "Great American Desert" and thus unfit for cultivation. With all the bitterness of a man whose teachings have been maligned, Hind rushed *Manitoba and the North-West Frauds* (1883) into print, a hastily assembled collection of letters that charged Macoun with deliberately applying falsified Manitoba data to the entire Northwest, thereby totally misleading countless settlers. Government officials, "among whom there appears to be none more unscrupulously guilty than the High Commissioner in London,"[42] were culpable because with their personal interests in the Northwest they had without question accepted Macoun's word. Even worse, they had refused to heed Hind's denunciations of Macoun's findings.

The Macoun-Hind vendetta was complicated by a bitter propaganda campaign waged against the CPR and covertly sup-

ported by the Grand Trunk. When the CPR, in its desire to be
economically viable, extended its network of tracks to the industries of Ontario and Quebec, the Grand Trunk countered this
violation of its territorial influence with a vindictive verbal onslaught designed to destroy the CPR's credibility in the British
financial world. Launched in the fall of 1881 with a derogatory
pamphlet, the crusade was in full swing by the following summer.
One English periodical, suggestively named *Truth*, regularly featured unfavourable reports on the Northwest. One issue advised
its readers that it was more profitable to invest in icebergs than in
the frozen wilderness of Canada. Insinuating that Canada's railway boom was merely a "bubble" certain to burst any day, another
article predicted that both the CPR and the Canadian government
would bankrupt themselves in their foolish attempt to build a
railway across the icy Canadian Shield, the desolate prairies, and
the impenetrable Rockies. Obvious in the cynicism was the implication that the financial security of the railway was based on
barren territories, and on a land grant entirely worthless because
the road would never be built.[43] The arguments were vindictive
and circular and could only damage the reputation of the CPR and
western Canada's resources.

At first, George Stephen, who was in London promoting his
railway and the Northwest, shrugged off the malicious propaganda. The caustic remarks had not affected a CPR bond issue for
sale in Montreal in the spring of 1882 and even a good number of
Englishmen had purchased the securities. The CPR president was
confident that he would not have to appeal for funds on the British
money market. He nonchalantly predicted that the propaganda
could only awaken British interest in Canadian affairs. His biggest
complaint at this time was not the virulent denunciations of
western Canada but the frustrating apathy of the British toward
Canada in general and western Canada in particular.[44]

Stephen's assessment, while astutely aware of the public
indifference, overlooked a serious immediate consequence—the
deteriorating relationship between himself and Galt. Stephen,
who tended to see matters strictly in black and white, had never
fully respected Galt; he had always disliked him for his moodiness
and reluctance to support the Irish emigration scheme. He also
suspected Galt's loyalty to the Conservative party, an increasingly

sensitive issue as Liberal opposition to the CPR was mounting. Worst of all, Stephen distrusted Galt's long-standing connection with the Grand Trunk. In a lengthy, angry letter to Macdonald he charged that the high commissioner was still in league with the railway and thus partly responsible for the unfavourable publicity. At the same time he gloated that Galt was afraid of losing his post because the Grand Trunk had gone too far in publishing a series of especially vitriolic pamphlets under the pseudonyms of "Diogenes" and "Ishmael:"

> The Diogenes pamphlet has evidently scared him [Galt]. ... The disreputable method adopted by the subsidized Grand Trunk scribblers to discredit the country, the Gov. Genl. and the C.P.R. Coy will end in nothing but mischief to the G.T.R. Galt having done his friends Baring [and] Glyn a service and placed himself under obligation to them and the G.T.R., it is not to be expected he would be violently agitated if we got into trouble.[45]

Stephen was furious especially because Galt had dared to suggest publicly that the CPR must eventually come to London for funds. Since Stephen had no intention of doing so, he was deeply offended by the attack on his financial prowess. "As to [Galt's] judgment in our financial requirements long experience has taught me that his judg[ment] on such questions is worse than useless. It is simply an impertinence for him to ... say that *he* forsooth, *thinks* we are *mistaken* if we do not need to come to London for money," he fumed. "What does he know about it? ... It makes me mad to have a fellow pretending to advise us for our own good who would gladly see us 'busted'." Stephen's wrath certainly would have intensified had he known that Galt's position ultimately proved to be correct. Meanwhile the childish bickering between the two Canadians in London only served to hamper their effectiveness in promoting assisted emigration.

Stephen was very wrong about Galt and quite unfair as well. To be sure, Galt had openly criticized the CPR but only because he still believed the route north of Lake Superior to be a foolish waste of money and energy. This was an honest criticism, even if ill-judged, but it was not animosity. The thin-skinned Stephen, however, disliked even the mildest criticism. In a reply to Macdonald's attempt to soothe him, he angrily scribbled, "I agree with what you say about Galt but in regard to us, individually, he is controlled by another element of his character...envy."[46] The remark carried some truth in that Galt had always longed to be part of the transcontinental venture, but it was unfair in assuming Galt wanted to destroy the project for selfish reasons. Nothing was further from the truth, for as Stephen himself noted, "[Galt] would like to see the C.P.R. a success for the sake of the venture he has embarked on." Stephen's rash and contradictory statements failed to recognize that if Galt planned to operate a coal-mine in the Northwest, the CPR would become its largest consumer, as would the settlers attracted by the railway.

The conflict between the two men grew even more bitter after Galt returned from a prolonged visit to the Northwest in the summer of 1882. Galt openly stated that the area west of Moose Jaw was semi-arid and unfit for agriculture.[47] It was a reaffirmation of the assessments of Palliser and Hind and an appraisement shared by government surveyor George M. Dawson, who had recommended the area be utilized only for ranching. On the basis of these views Galt scrapped his own plans for a colonization company north of Blackfoot Crossing.[48] As it happened his position was ultimately confirmed as very extensive irrigation works were needed to make the soil suitable for crop production.

Because the CPR planned to run its line straight west of Regina in the area claimed by Galt to be semi-arid, where much of the land grant to the CPR was located, Stephen was furious. He vented his anger in several bitter letters to Macdonald. "It is a thousand *pities* [Galt] could not have been sent somewhere if he would not do much good, would do less mischief," he scrawled indignantly, "He is in a frame of mind that makes him dangerous."[49] In a seemingly endless stream of letters, Stephen tried to convince the prime minister that Galt was purposely creating a false image of the southwestern plains. Stephen also automatically linked Galt with the anti-CPR propaganda campaign. Late in December 1882, for example, he impetuously fired off a flurry of angry telegrams that accused Galt and C. J. Brydges, the Hudson's Bay Company land commissioner, of having written a *Daily News* article labelling a three-hundred-mile belt of land west of Moose

Jaw as barren. Stephen insisted that Macdonald order Galt to retract the statement.[50] Since there was no evidence for Galt's complicity, Macdonald merely asked Galt to send the *News* a second article refuting the original. Galt responded by writing a bland letter to the editor, an insensitive move which infuriated Stephen even more.

Galt's cool rebuttal revealed his tenuous position. As high commissioner he should not have become entangled in a war of words, but should have tried to pacify the rivals. Characteristic-ally, however, he wanted to speak his mind and felt it his duty to warn settlers away from a particular section of the Northwest. Since he believed this certain part of the prairies to be unfit for crop farming, he could not strongly denounce the article in the *Daily News*. To complicate matters further, Galt was so closely associated with the financial backers of the Grand Trunk that he could not act as a mediator between the two combatants. Al-though he told the prime minister that "the Grand Trunk and CPR fight seems to me to be absolute lunacy on both sides," and wisely noted, "the end of such affairs is inevitably coalition and surely they had better come to terms now,"[51] there was little he could do. In fairness to Galt, Sir John Rose confided to Macdonald that, in his opinion, Stephen's stubbornness rather than Galt's imprud-ence endangered the delicate talks in progress to consolidate the landholdings of the CPR, the Hudson's Bay Company, and the Canadian North West Land Company in order to resuscitate the lagging Irish emigration scheme. Still, Rose conceded to Macdon-ald, "the very appearance of antagonism is injurious."[52] Perhaps to spare Stephen's feelings and to create harmony among the pro-moters of western Canada, Galt could have been more circumspect in his remarks. His identification with the detractors of western Canada, inflamed by his outspokenness, jeopardized his position.

Galt's bluntness soon led him into still greater difficulties. In January 1883 he made two speeches in Scotland explaining his grand design of imperial federation. Still a visionary, preoccupied with broad concepts, Galt wanted to extend the principles of Canada's national policies to embrace the whole empire, to create a commercial and political union through preferential trade agree-ments and a federated parliament. As in Macdonald's national programme, Galt saw the Northwest as the linchpin in the scheme.

He believed that this vast empty expanse could relieve Great Britain of the burden of massive food importation and house the surplus population of the British Isles. This comprehensive plan leading to a self-sufficient empire was the new basis for Galt's old argument that, because Great Britain had as large an interest in western development as Canada, it should help finance subsidized emigration. Speaking to the Greenock Chamber of Commerce, he pointed out that assisted emigration was a natural component of imperial unity. He asked his audience whether it was possible "as men of business, desiring to see [Canada] prosper, looking in the most selfish light possible, that you can look with indifference to the two points—to the one either that your population should flow away to and build up a foreign country...like the United States of America, or that you should hesitate for one moment in extending to your colonies the support which they desire, in furnishing them with this surplus labour, which is a burden to you?"[53] Expanding on this theme of imperial unity in a speech at Edinburgh, Galt actually suggested that Home Rule was the best solution to the Irish problem. While the comments on imperial federation and preferential tariffs were merely academic, the criticism of Britain's Irish policy angered several members of the British press and government.

Galt's reference to Irish Home Rule also irritated Sir John A. Macdonald because he believed that the speeches seriously damaged Canada's efforts in England. Once again Galt had confused the public and private roles of the high commissioner: by commenting on the internal politics of the host country he had committed a serious diplomatic blunder.[54] Galt, however, vigorously defended his remarks. He had deliberately mentioned Home Rule to clarify Macdonald's own speech in Canada's House of Commons the previous year. While the prime minister's statement had scuttled Archbishop Lynch's mission, Galt argued that in the end any advocacy of Home Rule would be beneficial. "There is no doubt your address last session and my recent utterances have gained us the friendliness of the Irish party and we shall no longer meet their hostility and preference to the U.S. in the House and in Ireland,"[55] he optimistically informed Macdonald in March, and denied that his remarks had provoked any coolness in official circles.

Surprisingly enough, Galt's assessment was correct. As he had done so often in the past, he sensed a shift in public attitudes. In this case it was a growing appreciation of the empire's value. In the early 1880s the strident nationalism emerging in many countries, coupled with increased world industrialization, challenged Britain's long-standing supremacy in world affairs. Increasingly vulnerable to economic competition, and feeling the pinch of over-population and diminished food supplies, the British were beginning to view the empire as a treasure house of resources and a future home for the unemployed. In the turmoil of the age, the colonies represented stability and loyalty. The telegraph and steamboat had conquered the geographically dispersed vastness of the empire. The exciting concept of an empire built upon the reciprocal relations between the mother country and the large settlement colonies increasingly questioned Gladstone's time-worn Little England doctrine. Galt's call for imperial federation, still premature, was a presage of a future debate.[56]

The appointment of Lord Derby as colonial secretary early in 1883 signalled the advance of the new imperialism. In the first meeting with Derby, Galt sensed sympathy for his cause and believed that a new era had begun in colonial relations.[57] Derby openly supported the principle of assisted emigration and asked Galt to submit a memorandum on the subject. Galt cautiously responded, suggesting an amendment to the Poor Law to provide emigration loans for those temporarily on relief.[58] Derby rejected Galt's timid proposal in favour of the old Irish emigration scheme. A new twist was added to the plan. After several years of negotiations, the CPR, Hudson's Bay Company, and the Canada North West Land Company, all anxious to stimulate lagging land sales, agreed to pool their properties and form a new company to execute Galt's idea of preparing the homestead before the settler arrived.[59] The British government, impelled by the resurgent interest in Britain for the vast prairies, pledged a one-million-pound, interest-free loan to transport ten thousand Irish families to Canada and make ready their land.[60] Finally, after three years of frustrating, difficult talks, the imperial government had accepted a scheme to subsidize large-scale emigration to the Northwest.

Surprisingly, however, Canada torpedoed the proposal by refusing to guarantee the repayment of the imperial loan.

Obviously Galt, who disliked the whole concept, had captured the ear of the prime minister. He had always argued for development by private enterprise because he believed that only businessmen, driven by the profit motive, could ensure the efficient operation of any subsidized emigration scheme. Accordingly, the Canadian proposal called for the companies to guarantee the repayment of the imperial loan. While Britain insisted that the arrangement be made between the two governments, Galt maintained that the Canadian government should not be involved at all. Moreover, he did not relish the thought of a "systematic and continuous flood of poor Irish being poured into Canada," and so suggested that English and Scottish emigrants be included "to leaven the Irish element."[61] Macdonald was in full accord with Galt's objections, favouring free enterprise as a way of developing the Northwest at minimal cost to his government. He also feared the political impact of a massive influx of volatile, destitute Irish families. By using various stalling tactics, he delayed making the final decision, and after a summer of fitful negotiations he allowed the scheme to die. Ironically, in the end Canada scuttled the Irish emigration plan, an idea it had so eagerly supported only months earlier.

From Galt's point of view, affairs in London had improved greatly and he even began to enjoy his work. If only the Canadian government would increase his salary so that his family could return to London! He would then be willing to retract his long-standing resignation and remain in London.[62] In April 1883 Macdonald wired that Galt would be replaced by Charles Tupper. The relationship between the two men had cooled decidedly: Macdonald was annoyed that Galt billed the Canadian government for his western Canadian trip the previous summer. Even though he had filed a few official reports, Galt's main preoccupation had been his private mining and land enterprises.[63] More important, however, was that Macdonald could no longer tolerate Galt's overriding concern with broad, theoretical principles at the expense of careful and discreet diplomacy. Galt had become a liability, in the first place because he was identified with the competitors of the CPR and the detractors of the Northwest, and secondly because he had spoken out against the British government on a domestic matter. Therefore, Macdonald, weary also of Galt's litany of frustrations and discomforts, finally asked Galt to return home; he had lost confidence in Galt's entrepreneurial skill. Galt had failed in his most important mission, to initiate a large flow of immigrants at the least expense to the federal government.

Galt received the sudden "permission" to retire with bewildered regret. After four years of frustrating negotiations his efforts were finally beginning to bear fruit. Yet he had to admit that on balance the years had been a disconcerting experience of unfulfilled ambitions. Foremost of his complaints was the low salary that made it impossible for him to keep his large family in London and live the diplomatic lifestyle. Because his personal financial position was precarious, he was unable to make up the difference from his own funds, a tradition common among diplomats. To a person motivated by the search for profit it was an intolerable situation that depressed his spirit. This dejection was aggravated by his loneliness in London, a feeling he expressed very poignantly in a letter to his wife one Christmas. He simply described a scene in the city:

> A dull room in a dull street in a cool, moist day in London—gas lighted. An old man sitting in a faded armchair before the fire—wrapped in a warm dressing gown—a silk cap on his head and his feet in slippers. On the table beside him a testament and a photograph album and some newspapers.[64]

There he sat, in a melancholy mood, imagining where he wanted to be, in Montreal amid the bright Christmas activities of his family. The key to understanding Galt's activities as high commissioner is his almost constant mood of depression engendered by London town and society. The campaign to enlist support for western Canadian development needed a spirited, optimistic supersalesman. The British bureaucracy and press had to be roused from lethargy. Galt could not muster the required buoyant enthusiasm because the job just did not give him satisfaction.

Galt knew that his mission had not been a complete failure because his mandate had entailed much more than emigration. Despite the objections of the imperial government, the post had become ambassadorial in context: he talked with foreign governments, completed financial arrangements for Canada, worked to increase exports, arranged for Canadian participation in conti-

nental exhibitions, handled matters of defense, and even supervised such routine matters as the production of Canadian coins by
the British mint. Although he failed to secure full diplomatic
recognition, his painstaking efforts in all these areas had elevated
the office of high commissioner to one of considerable influence
and prestige. To mark this position he insisted on direct access to
the British foreign office, bypassing the governor-general and
colonial secretary. He had secured for Canada a senior position in
the empire and a distinct voice, especially in commercial affairs.
His inability to conclude agreements with France and Spain was
due to external factors only: Canada, at the end of his tenure, was
practically free to negotiate her own commercial treaties. He had
also won for her the right to be represented at international
conferences. Standing at the end of his term he saw the culmination of ideas he first expressed in the 1850s. Ever since then he
had patiently but passionately explained to anyone who would
listen that a new federated Canada must have full economic
sovereignty. That right, he knew, was virtually achieved.[65]

Despite this notable accomplishment, Galt was disappointed
that he had not realized one of the primary goals of his mission, the
inauguration of wholesale emigration. He felt all the more bitter
because he could not understand why imperial officials were
reluctant to exploit the abundance of Canadian land to relieve the
over-populated British Isles. While the flow of settlers to Canada
increased during his London stay, he had not overcome the strong
competition from other countries, notably the United States. As
long as the American plains offered more attractions than western
Canada, the latter needed subsidies to lure large numbers of
homesteaders. It was maddening to him that government leaders
did not accept this idea. Why, he often asked his audiences, did
they not realize that an emigrant to Canada remained within the
empire and thereby strengthened its spiritual and economic
coherence? He had faced a complex and delicate situation. Surely
the turbulent state of Irish politics, the indifference of imperial
politicians and financiers, as well as the reluctance of Canadians to
pay for the high cost of development, militated against large-scale
emigration, particularly a massive transplant of Irish to Canada.
The problem required the tactful, yet enthusiastic touch of the
skilled diplomat; Galt was a blunt, outspoken businessman with a

pragmatic outlook who rebelled against polite and drawn out negotiations. In his world, efficiency and profitability took precedence over political considerations. He wanted to dispel indifference and studied delays with belligerent attacks, but the prime minister reined him in tightly. "I think the diplomacy of the High Commissioner must curb the patriotic impetuousity of A. T. Galt,"[66] Macdonald once advised him. That was impossible and so Galt's usual buoyant optimism, which had made his previous endeavours so successful, was deflated. Without it he failed to kindle the interest of politicians and businessmen in the costly task of "civilizing" that lonely, desolate wilderness he had visited in the summer of 1882. So he returned to the private world of business where he felt at home, where he knew he could find some financiers, Canadian or British, willing to invest in the latest techniques designed to wrest from the land its great treasures. In a more limited way he could still have a hand in utilizing the enormous unexploited resources of the Northwest. He could still help transform the somnolent primitive land into a bustling technological society.

Part 2
Techniques of growth

Railways are the very first prerequisite of a new country. Settlement and development cannot go on without railways. In this western world it has been shown that railways must precede, and not follow settlement. Whether it be mining, lumbering, agriculture or any other resources for which a region is principally noted, railways are necessary before this latent wealth can be developed to any extent.

The Commercial (Winnipeg), 12 May 1890

4

Fuel for progress

Aeons ago the great expanse of Alberta was the swampy, western hinterland extended from one arm of the Arctic Ocean. The climate was warm and the humid, tropical atmosphere supported a luxuriant growth of cycads, ginkgos, ferns, and conifers. After the large leaves dropped into the stagnant brown waters, they were preserved in the acid bog. Later, gravel and mud, washed down from the surrounding highlands, covered the dense brown mass, sealing off the air. Relentless pressure squeezed out moisture and concentrated carbon. As the ages slipped by, the compressed vegetation gradually changed from brown to black, and the peat converted to coal. On the surface, the seas retreated, the Rockies thrust up their craggy tops, muds turned to shale, glaciers advanced and polished the surface, then withdrew and deposited rubble and rich soil. Eventually the tan-yellow grasses, the aspen forest, and the birch-clad foothills concealed the slow but relentless dynamics that had produced the great coal reserves. The vast fuel deposits lay undisturbed for countless ages. The red man had little use for the "rocks that burn," and so he rarely dislodged them. Even white explorers, including Umfreville, Mackenzie, and Fidler, only casually noted their sightings of exposed coal-beds in river valleys. Later, David Thompson and Alexander Henry, Jr. mentioned in passing similar outcrops in the Edmonton and Saunders areas, while Sir James Hector, a member of the Palliser expedition, simply recorded the presence of coal east of the Yellowhead Pass. The prairie people simply had no need for coal. And, because transportation costs to world markets were too high, no one bothered to pin-point the location or to measure the extent of the coal reserves.

This lackadaisical attitude was shattered completely in the 1880s. Canada's national dream of expansion, and the vision of open prairies civilized by millions of settlers, hinged on the construction of a transcontinental railway system. The proposed railway, in turn, depended upon a cheap and abundant source of energy. On the treeless prairies the only feasible form of energy was coal, but the nearest collieries were a long and expensive haul away in Pennsylvania. Consequently, the old reports of extensive coal deposits near the Rockies took on new meaning. The railway gave this resource a commercial value and demanded its exploitation.

The Canadian government, which clearly recognized the importance of coal for western settlement, equipped several scientific expeditions to determine the location and size of the reserves. Since the favourite route through the Rockies was the Yellowhead Pass, the surveys were limited to the area west of Edmonton. In 1872 Sandford Fleming, the chief engineer of the Pacific railway, and his close friend and secretary, Reverend George M. Grant, travelled to the Pacific Ocean by way of the Yellowhead to confirm the suitability of that path for rail traffic. Grant recorded in his memoirs that the Hudson's Bay Company smith at Edmonton used coal mined from the nearby river bank. Several days later, at the Pembina River crossing, the party cooked their supper on coal taken from a ten-foot seam on the east bank of the river. Grant also recounted that during the meal, the metis guides told about thick outcrops of coal along the North Saskatchewan near Rocky Mountain House, and of an eighteen-foot seam on the Brazeau River. Grant duly noted the tremendous importance of the coal discoveries and stressed the significance of their proximity to rivers. "Here then," he wrote with obvious excitement, "is the fuel for the future inhabitants of the plains, near water communication for forwarding it in different directions."[1]

During the next few years the Geological Survey of Canada chartered several prospecting expeditions. The most noteworthy was that of Alfred R. C. Selwyn, who canoed up the North

Saskatchewan in the summer of 1873 to search for the coal deposits so vital to the proposed railway and future settlement. Selwyn discovered several large outcrops along the river bank and, at one point about eighty miles downstream from Rocky Mountain House, measured a seam that towered twenty feet above water level. With the boundless optimism so characteristic of the time, he concluded, "There can be no question that in the region west of Edmonton, bounded by the Arthabaska [sic] River and on the south by the Red Deer River, there exists a vast coal field covering an area of no less than 25,000 square miles and beneath the area we may expect to find workable seams at depths seldom exceeding 300 feet, and often ... very favourably situated for working by levels from the surface."[2] Not only was coal available in large quantities but exploitation would be relatively easy, and therefore inexpensive. Elated by Selwyn's positive assessment, subsequently confirmed by his colleagues, expansionists confidently proclaimed that the area west of Edmonton could amply meet the fuel needs of the Pacific railway.

The federal government, intent on prospecting for coal only near the transcontinental route, did not explore areas farther south, but here, too, the existence of coal was well known. Coal may have been found in the Canmore-Bankhead district as early as 1845, but definite reports did not come until later. In 1861 a group of gold seekers, led by J. J. Healy, a Montana trader, discovered a rich seam of coal on the banks of the Waterton River.[3] Four years later, George M. Dawson, a young, brilliant, hunch-backed geologist from Montreal working with the International Boundary Commission, collected a number of mineral samples and determined that large coal-seams lay under the treeless prairies. As a result of subsequent research, Dawson published a report in 1875 that reaffirmed his earlier findings of an abundant supply of fuel in the far southwestern corner of the territories.[4]

The first commercial coal-mine in the Northwest was opened in this area. The operator was Nicholas Sheran, a colourful Irish Roman Catholic adventurer from New York. Sheran, a Civil War veteran who had served with the émigré Irish Brigade, claimed he had once suffered a shipwreck in the Arctic and lived three years with the Eskimos. In the late 1860s he moved to Montana where he worked for the Healy brothers, whisky runners and builders of several fortified trading posts, including the notorious Fort Whoop-Up. In 1870, roaming northward into Canada in search of gold, Sheran found coal at the junction of the Oldman and St. Mary rivers. He produced some coal at this location, but when the seam petered out in 1872, he moved to a richer site farther north on the west side of the Belly River at the base of Indian Battle Coulee, a spot called *Sokohotoki* (the place of black rocks) by the Indians and Coal Banks by the whites.[5] Sheran shipped coal from here to the North West Mounted Police posts at Forts Walsh and Macleod and later supplied the fuel-starved community of Fort Benton, Montana. In 1875, T. C. Powers, a Fort Benton merchant, bought a load of coal from Sheran at five dollars per ton and transported it by bull-train to Fort Benton where it fetched twenty-five dollars a ton. This astronomical price, caused in part by the high cost of transportation, was still lower than that of inferior Mississippi coal or cottonwood,[6] and indicated the tremendous value of Alberta's coal deposits.

In 1879 Elliott Galt, the eldest son of Sir Alexander, touring the Northwest as assistant Indian commissioner, visited Sheran's mine at Coal Banks and gathered a few samples of coal for further analysis. When the coal proved to be of superior quality, Elliott easily persuaded his father to organize a company to mine this valuable resource. Sir Alexander, who had always been keenly interested in the development of the resources of the Northwest, shrewdly calculated that a colliery on the fuel-scarce prairies could be an extremely profitable endeavour. He envisioned that floods of settlers, accompanied by an extensive railway network and local industries, would be voracious consumers of energy. Galt thought the potential demand was so great that he lightly dismissed the threat of competition from the recently opened coal-mines on Vancouver Island. Belly River coal promised to be a lucrative investment, and Sir Alexander launched an enthusiastic campaign to promote the exploitation of the coal-seams. Throughout the winters of 1879 and 1880, while in London as high commissioner, he conferred with influential British businessmen in the search for capital to finance his Coal Banks project.

As long as the projected CPR route followed the North Saskatchewan River, Sir Alexander Galt made little progress. Despite the promise of large profits, his plans found few supporters because of several seemingly insurmountable obstacles. How could any financier be convinced of the value of an unproven coal-mine somewhere in the unpopulated Canadian Northwest? How could any investor be expected to risk his funds on a colliery more than three hundred miles from a railway which was yet in the planning stages? The cost of building a branch from the Pacific main line to the south was staggering, and would never permit a Coal Banks colliery to compete with the mines west of Edmonton, which were not encumbered by high transportation costs. The Canadian government recognized this obvious fact and consequently sponsored very little prospecting in the southern country. In 1880 Galt's proposal, even when linked to a colonization-railway scheme, appeared nebulous and premature; the development of Coal Banks would have to await the overflow of settlement south and west of the railway along the valley of the North Saskatchewan River.

In the spring of 1881, a technical decision made by a small group of men suddenly and dramatically altered Galt's prospects. For various reasons, the promoters of the CPR fancied a more southerly route for the railway, and eagerly seized John Macoun's enthusiastic, almost fanatical generalizations about the prairie climate as justification for the change in plans.[7] The railway tycoons decided to head straight west of Regina. The federal government agreed. Therefore, instead of following the North Saskatchewan, the CPR crossed the southern prairies.

This abrupt shift in route, executed for business reasons, had an immeasurable impact upon the future development of western Canada. No longer would the streams of traffic flow along the rivers, but rather follow the arteries of steel. The fever of speculation that had boomed the communities along the North Saskatchewan suddenly cooled, and settlements like Battleford, Edmonton, and Lac Ste. Anne either stagnated or withered away. The attention of developers swung to the south where the CPR was creating new towns strung like beads along the railway tracks. No longer would the fur trader or settler or even geography determine the location of a settlement: that choice belonged to the directors of the railway. Technology would shape western Canada .

The change in routes also affected the future of coal-mining in the Northwest. High transportation costs devalued the reserves west of Edmonton and inflated the worth of southern coal. The dominion government, still eager to locate cheap fuel for the CPR, switched prospecting missions to the south. In the summer of 1881, George M. Dawson, working at this time for the Geological Survey of Canada, discovered that a gigantic treasure of coal lay buried beneath most of southern Alberta. He reported that one particularly large deposit stretched for nearly two hundred miles: westward from Medicine Hat to the foot of the Rockies, and eighty miles northwestward from the United States border to the Bow River. The seam, which varied in thickness from one to seven feet, increased in quality from a low-grade lignite at "the Hat" to a good bituminous coal at the St. Mary and Belly rivers. Among the many samples Dawson examined was one from a four-foot seam at Coal Banks; it was excellent lignite, capable of being coked, and containing little water and other impurities. The explorer noted that the seam undulated only slightly and was clearly visible in many places along the river banks.[8] This meant that recovery techniques would be relatively easy and inexpensive.

The following summer Dawson eagerly resumed his investigation. After exploring the Kicking Horse and Crowsnest passes he was convinced that the Alberta coal reserves were "practically inexhaustible."[9] To support his optimistic conclusions he reeled off a staggering list of statistics. At Coal Banks alone, for example, ninety million tons of coal were readily available. The scientist could hardly conceal his excitement when he wrote that the figures were so large and mind-boggling that they were meaningless. And, as he was quick to point out, he had not even included in the estimates the extensive seams of even better coal in the foothills and Rockies.

Dawson's report, muted in tone by his scientific mind, was received ecstatically by government officials. Edgar Dewdney, the lieutenant-governor of the territories exclaimed, "The District of Alberta is one huge coal bed, and every settler in that district will have good coal almost at his door, and it only remains for the companies taking out the coal, to work the mines with improved machinery, and on an extensive scale, to ensure to the whole of the Territories a good coal at a very reasonable rate."[10] Dewdney's voice was prophetic, heralding the arrival of technology in the Northwest. The sheer abundance of fuel guaranteed the construction of the railway, which made the settlement of the prairies practical.

The glowing reports and the change in the CPR's route greatly enhanced the value of the coal sites that Sir Alexander Galt had prudently reserved on the Bow and Belly rivers. As a shrewd businessman he recognized that the railway made coal-mining there economically feasible. Was he also aware, however, of his precarious situation? Did he realize that his colliery would always be subservient to the dictates of the railway company? And, even if the Northwest was settled quickly, that the CPR would have to buy as well as move the coal?

Despite his sudden change in fortune, Galt did realize that the road to coal profits was not without obstructions. His previous work, both as promoter and high commissioner, had taught him a harsh truth. Before the West could be settled in any extensive manner, enormous amounts of money were necessary to build railways, telegraphs, and steamboats, to construct coal-mines, lumber mills, and brickyards, and to establish banks, warehouses, and retail stores. Canadians could provide much of the required capital themselves but the bulk of it would have to be imported from Great Britain. Even though the resources of the prairies were incredibly abundant, and their exploitation promised rich returns, overseas investors remained aloof. When Canadians excitedly explained their vision of bustling, civilized prairies, the British listened politely but without enthusiasm, without the same insight.[11] Clearly the flow of capital to utilize the natural resources of the Northwest was not to be an automatic spill over of excess money; instead every investment dollar would have to be wrung out of the pocketbooks of tight-fisted businessmen. Clearly too, the federal government must assure easy access to these resources and minimize costly restrictions. Civilizing the West was a process that required modern technology, backed by overseas capital, enthusiastically supported by friendly politicians, and skilfully promoted by Canadian entrepreneurs.

5

They shall have Dominion

The commencement of CPR construction on the Canadian plains in 1881 signalled the beginning of a new era of change in the Northwest. As the army of railworkers relentlessly churned up the prairie grasses to throw down mile after mile of track, an aura of restless optimism arose among westerners that touched every facet of prairie life. Far in advance of the end-of-steel, speculators feverishly hiked prices in covetous anticipation of fabulous profits. Meanwhile, in its wake the immigrants came, loaded with tents, tools, and cattle, eager to forget their memories of difficult times, cheerfully enduring the hard seats of the crowded CPR cars. The laying of tracks—which was always hurried and often wasteful, using temporary wooden trestles to be replaced only days later with permanent structures—drew enormous amounts of capital to the Northwest. This phenomenon in turn fueled unprecedented regional economic growth that drove the expectations of businessmen and settlers to dizzying heights. Tales of astonishing profits fanned the heated economy into a wild and unchecked boom. Throughout the fall and winter of 1881, as the stockpiling of CPR materials grossly inflated prices, a rash of speculation raged in Winnipeg, especially in real estate; the town became a carnival of land sales, with men winning and losing fortunes amid the gaiety of easy money and the flow of bubbling champagne. The instant affluence generated limitless opportunities for those willing to risk their own or everybody else's money. Thus the driving spirit, which came to dominate the thoughts of western Canadians for some time, was an obsession with the quick accumulation of great wealth and the acquisition of extensive property. The railway was the symbol of this new and reckless society; it promised both investor and immigrant access to the great resources of the Canadian plains. The frenzied enthusiasm engendered among the prairie newcomers was transferred to central Canada, where ambitious men hatched countless schemes for railways, steamboats, lumber and flour mills, warehouses, and land companies. All these plans were designed to exploit the abundant wealth of the prairies.

This frantic activity also affected Sir Alexander Galt. The immense coalfields of southern Alberta became more than ever a timely opportunity for new investment. The noisy trains scurrying across the prairies, the howling sawmills spewing out railway ties, and the restless settlers turning the prairie sod demanded prodigious amounts of coal. By the fall of 1881 Galt's proposal for a colliery in southern Alberta had become a viable project and the task of securing financial backing was relatively easy. Also, Galt's position as high commissioner provided him with many rich and influential friends in London. He could show them the glowing reports of government surveyor G. M. Dawson, an assessment amply confirmed by Captain Nicholas Bryant, a mining engineer and operator of the Londonderry Iron Mines in Nova Scotia whom Galt had hired in the summer of 1881 to determine the feasibility of mining coal in southern Alberta. Of greatest value, however, were the tales of economic boom emanating from the Northwest. Undoubtedly Galt told British investors how he personally had realized fifteen thousand dollars on a number of Winnipeg lots that his son Elliott had bought and sold for him. Elliott, intent on amassing a fortune of two hundred thousand dollars for himself, had already sold twelve of his own plots at a profit of one thousand dollars each.[1] Clearly, a coal-mine straddling the transcontinental, supplying a growing energetic population, would be a safe and extremely lucrative investment.

In an informal, almost casual, way Galt assembled a close-knit group of wealthy and influential men to back his venture. The most prominent of these was William H. Smith, owner of the well-known news agency and bookselling firm, W. H. Smith & Son, and until the most recent election, first lord of the admiralty. A dynamic entrepreneur, William Smith had become a partner in his father's firm and, with the help of his friend, William Lethbridge, had revitalized the newsagency. They had acquired a monopoly on book sales in virtually all the railway stations in England. In addition, they conceived the idea of leasing blank station walls for advertising space. Smith extended his financial interests to Canada and procured substantial holdings in the Northern Railway of Canada. He visited the country in the summer of 1872 and talked with the most notable railway, banking, and government officials. Afterward, he travelled through the United States to the Pacific coast, where he incidentally met Sandford Fleming, who was returning from his cross-Canada trek. Fleming aroused Smith's interests in the Northwest, and so when Smith first met Galt at a state ball in the spring of 1881 he had a keen and sympathetic understanding of the Canadian investment climate.[2] Smith's close friend and senior employee, William Lethbridge, also agreed to join Galt's mining venture. In fact, Lethbridge soon became the most active and enthusiastic member of the group.[3] Smith attracted still another very good friend and a fellow member of parliament, William Ashmead-Bartlett Burdett-Coutts, a wealthy American residing in England who had recently married the elderly Angela Burdett-Coutts, the richest heiress in England, admired for her devotion to charities.[4] These three men and Galt each pledged two thousand pounds for the preliminary expenses of establishing a mining company. The high social and secure financial position of the three British investors linked with Galt's connections meant that the colliery was to be soundly backed, a provision that proved to be the key to Galt's success in the isolated Northwest. When it became necessary to increase the capitalization of the company substantially, the help of the largest and most prestigious British firms could be enlisted.

Galt also recruited several prominent Canadians for his western project (*see* Appendix I). The most colourful of them was James Wellington Ross, a flamboyant real-estate speculator, vice-president of the promising Portage, Westbourne, and North-Western Railway, and a member of parliament for Lisgar, Manitoba. Ross was also a solicitor, and had assembled a huge fortune in land, principally in the brand-new town of Brandon, Manitoba, and during the heady days of the railway boom. Like so many other western speculators, he moved westward in advance of the CPR, amassing land along the right-of-way, selling at tremendous profit, and gaudily flaunting his newly acquired wealth. At the time of the colliery's incorporation, Ross suffered a temporary reversal as the great land sale he staged in Edmonton fizzled and the Winnipeg land boom collapsed; he recovered quickly, however, and his name remained synonymous with land speculation.[5]

Other Canadian backers, while not as flashy as Ross, were nevertheless prominent and influential citizens with a considerable interest in western Canadian development. A long-standing friend of Galt, C. J. Brydges, the land commissioner of the Hudson's Bay Company, and his colleague, John Balsillie, linked the proposed mining enterprise with one of the largest landholding companies of western Canada. This connection was extremely useful in the future when Galt began to assemble lands in southern Alberta. Other investors tied the planned colliery into the Canadian banking and insurance world. James Gibbs Ross, a Scottish immigrant, had expanded his grocery business into a large lumbering and shipping firm. He was also the president of the Quebec Bank, a director of the Guarantee Company of North America, and in 1884 was named a senator. William Miller Ramsay, also a Scottish immigrant, was the manager for Canada Standard Life and a director for Molson's Bank. In addition, Ramsay had married into the wealthy Torrance family of Montreal merchants, to which Galt was also related by marriage.[6] The striking characteristic of this group of Canadians was their lengthy mutual friendship with Galt and each other, a relationship that gave them considerable financial and political power.

On 25 April 1882 this group of friends and associates incorporated the North Western Coal and Navigation Company Limited (NWC&NCo). Initially they capitalized the company at fifty thousand pounds and sold five hundred shares with a par value of one hundred pounds to themselves and friends. They also issued nine deferred shares of one hundred pounds each to Galt and Lethbridge "for services rendered, liabilities undertaken and expenses incurred by them as founders of the Company."[7] The articles of association not only permitted the company to engage in all the activities associated with mining, lumbering, and steamboating, but also allowed it to build a town complete with houses, stores, churches, a school, and a hospital. Significantly, the firm could promote or assist emigration to whatever lands the company might in future possess. Lethbridge was named the first president while Smith, Galt, Burdett-Coutts, and Ramsay were elected to the board along with Smith's solicitor and friend, William Ford, and a London banker, Edward Crabb.

When the incorporation procedures were completed, the company moved to obtain legal rights to a number of coal sites. This was relatively easy because the dominion government, which controlled the natural resources of the territories, was anxious to encourage the rapid development of the immense western Canadian coal reserves. The predominant attitude of the nation's leaders was dictated by two considerations—the belief in the abundance of coal and the urgent need for inexpensive energy. Dawson's enthusiastic reports left no doubt on the first point. Had he not calculated that, on the plains alone, companies could mine a million tons of coal per year for the next three hundred years and still leave the foothills reserves untouched? Had he not concluded that "The coal deposits have proved to be wide-spread and practically inexhaustible"?[8] The terms "limitless" and "inexhaustible" became stock words in the reports of all government officials and the excited promoters of the territories saw no end to the resources of the Northwest.[9] The Canadian government, equally obsessed with western development, was delighted with the solution to the crucial fuel problem and Macdonald, who was also minister of the interior, wrote in his annual report, "The supply of fuel for the use of settlers in the North-West Territories is a question having a very important bearing upon the development of that country."[10] Prairie coal was the power for a great agricultural future: it would warm the homes of pioneers and stoke the engines of the transcontinental trains. Because the Northwest contained an abundance of coal and because government policy stressed rapid resource utilization, stringent regulations, in Macdonald's opinion, were unnecessary and undesirable. The key to the government's management of western Canadian resources was speedy development by privately owned corporations unhindered by bureaucratic restrictions.

Early in 1881 the federal government affirmed this policy by amending the Dominion Land Act of 1879 to give the cabinet power to draft coal-mining provisions. While the concomitant amendments to the act were hotly debated for several hours, the coal clauses received little attention,[11] an indication of the relative unimportance attached to the regulation of the industry. In December of 1881 the cabinet issued a few rules: essentially coal lands could be leased for twenty-one-year periods at an annual ground rent of twenty-five cents an acre and a royalty of ten cents per ton of coal; active work had to be commenced within one year and actual mining operation within two years of taking up the lease; finally, no one was allowed to hold more than 320 acres of coal lands.[12] A minimum number of regulations were established to encourage maximum utilization of the coal reserves.

The lenient coal-mining laws offended the conscientious Edward Blake, the leader of the opposition in the House of Commons. Echoing a habitual Liberal complaint, Blake deplored the lack of stringent controls on mineral development in the Northwest; he feared that large corporations would form a coal monopoly and thereby cheat the settlers out of inexpensive fuel. He introduced a motion in the house that would effectively tighten the provisions and prevent big companies from taking control over the richest seams. He argued that the development of the western coal resources on a competitive basis was already being stifled. As an example he pointed out that, while the application filed by William Lethbridge covered no more than the legal 320 acres, the request was for four different sites undoubtedly comprising the most valuable and those located most conveniently to water transportation. Blake charged that it was "a mistake to put in one man's hands different areas in different places.... This is, in point of fact, the leasing of four separate coal areas and may be the erection of a practical coal monopoly of the coal supply there."[13] Blake asked the prime minister that if Lethbridge could lease four different locations, what would prevent any number of individuals in his company from each leasing a further scattered selection of 320 acres and thereby commanding all the coal reserves? Since an inexpensive fuel supply on the prairies was so crucial, Blake concluded that monopolistic control over the resources had to be prevented at all costs. In his motion he proposed that the valuable coal-seams be advertised and short-term leases on small plots be sold by auction or tender.

In reply to Blake's accusations, Sir John A. Macdonald tried to belittle the fears of fuel shortages, coal monopolies, and high prices. First of all he pointed to the excellent reputation of William Lethbridge, so far the only serious applicant for a coal lease. "Mr. Lethbridge is a gentleman possessed of great wealth and of the highest standing, and he is resolved to push this industry, not as a matter of speculation, not to sell the mines, but to send out his labourers and overseers and to put steamers on the Saskatchewan to carry coal to market. I would be glad if we could get others like Lethbridge here," he assured his listeners, "There is no fear of monopoly in that market."[14] According to Macdonald, the coal resources of the Northwest were so vast as to preclude monopolistic control, and he told the house that Dr. Alfred Selwyn, the director of the Canadian Geological Survey, thought it "absurd to ask for any royalty at all, that [coal] is so plentiful it will have no special value, and that the land containing it should be sold as common agricultural land under the regulations for the sale of other farm lands so that the person who gets it may work the coal on his own estate without paying any royalty." The prime minister smoothly echoed the optimism of the day and exclaimed, "...the supply is without limit, and, therefore, is of no special value." He then went on to argue that undue competition and short-term leases would seriously hamper explorations in the remote and vast territories where mining and marketing operations were very expensive, and that excessive government restrictions would choke off future mining enterprises. Government regulations, for instance, had delayed the Lethbridge plan already for one year and more stringent controls might kill the project altogether.

Blake did not appreciate Macdonald's cavalier attitude and, in reply, once again voiced his concern that the loser of a lax mineral-resource policy would be the settler. His incisive mind grasped a glaring inconsistency in Macdonald's twofold argument and, not without some sarcasm, he pointed out:

> With one breath he tells us that the country is one mass of coal lands, that you could not walk over it without finding

coal land, every man has a coal mine on his farm. (Macdonald interrupts: "In the ore country.") The hon. gentleman then went on to say that even if a coal mine should be found, experienced coal miners would have to be sent out in a proper way at great expense, that it would take [a] whole summer to work and examine and ferret over the land, and if you did hit upon a coal mine, you were so deserving of commendation for your discovery, your expense, and the trouble you have gone to, that I almost expected him one moment to say that we ought to give him a handsome premium for finding the coal mine, and give him the coal mine into the bargain.

Blake's cutting remarks merely sliced thin air: his motion was defeated.

The debate clearly established the position of the government and opposition parties. Both agreed that the royalties were set high enough because for some time the market for western coal would be confined to the region, and the settlers would ultimately pay the tax. The basic disagreement arose over the control of the industry: the government was willing to make generous concessions to private industry in order to encourage the development of the abundant resource; the opposition, concerned about the individual settler, opposed lax regulations for fear large corporations would monopolize the industry.

That Blake's misgivings were not entirely groundless became apparent that summer as four directors of the NWC&NCo each applied for separate mining leases. Originally Lethbridge, as Blake reported, had applied for mining leases of eighty acres each at four different locations, two at Coal Banks, one at Woodpecker, and one at Blackfoot Crossing. In June Alexander Galt petitioned the cabinet to separate the application and accordingly one site each was granted to Lethbridge, Smith, Burdett-Coutts, and George Bompas. Although only one order-in-council embraced all four applications, the size of each lease was increased to 320 acres,[15] clearly violating the spirit of the regulations. Galt also wrote a second application requesting another 320 acres near Grassy Lake, just south of the junction of the Bow and Old Man rivers.[16]

The directors of the NWC&NCo did not lease these lands merely for speculation or only to exclude possible competitors.

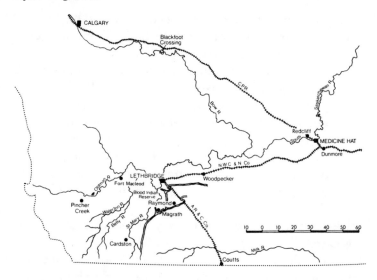

Map I   The Lethbridge Area, 1900
The scale is in miles.

Earlier, Galt had written Macdonald to explain that all five locations would be explored in the summer, the best site selected, and the remainder discarded.[17] With the legalities out of the way, Galt proceeded to develop the properties; late in the spring he sent out a crew to determine the most suitable location for the first colliery.

Even though the NWC&NCo had by no means tied up all the coal-seams in the Northwest, its tactics exposed the threat of a coal monopoly; consequently, the federal government moved quickly to tighten regulations. To prevent lessees from combining into large companies with vast tracts of coal lands and thereby reducing government revenue, Macdonald recommended to his cabinet that the leasing policy be ended. Accordingly, the cabinet approved a regulation which set aside from public sale and settlement a number of valuable coal areas that were also close to transportation facilities. The first four areas so designated were on the Souris, Bow, Belly, and Saskatchewan rivers. The coal lands, totalling about seventy-five townships, would be surveyed as soon as possible and the coal sites sold by tender or public auction but, contrary to Blake's suggestion, the minister of the interior retained the right to sell lands at any price he chose. Lastly, a provision was included for those who already possessed leases to convert these into freeholds at a price to be determined by the minister.[18]

The government had moved ostensibly to fill a gap in regulations, but whether the change was an improvement is questionable. Royalties were abolished entirely. The government, through the mechanism of sales, could control the allocation of coal-seams, but it did not specify the amount or price of coal land any company could buy. Therefore, the government could still make special concessions to individual corporations, as it eventually did in the case of the Lethbridge holdings. Moreover, because the sites were sold without a minimum time limit on the start of development, certain valuable coal lands were alienated from the Crown and the public lost control over the direct utilization of this natural resource.

Meanwhile, Sir Alexander Galt authorized Captain Nicholas Bryant to hire a small prospecting party to recommend the most suitable site and begin developmental work. Since Bryant was an expert in iron-mining rather than coal-mining techniques, he persuaded William Stafford of the Acadia Coal Company of Nova Scotia to accompany him. Late in May 1882 Bryant, his wife, and daughter, two male cousins and a nephew, with Stafford and his son, started the long and difficult journey to the far end of the Canadian prairies. They travelled most of the way by train but at Bismarck, North Dakota, they boarded a small crowded river boat and slowly steamed up the Missouri to Fort Benton, arriving there on the fourth of July. After purchasing cooking and camping provisions, buffalo robes for blankets, and a wagon and team of horses, the group followed the deeply rutted Whoop-Up trail across the grey-yellow prairies into Canada. For the next three months Bryant and his workers explored the valleys of the Bow and Saskatchewan, wandering as far east as Medicine Hat and as far south as Coal Banks.[19]

Meanwhile, Sir Alexander Galt crossed the ocean from England to inspect the company's coal sites in western Canada and to determine the location for the corporation's land settlement plan. The coal-mining scheme included a million-acre land and colonization project, which Galt wanted to establish near the CPR. He hoped that the NWC&NCo could receive some of the land as a government subsidy for building a branch line from the trans-continental railway to the proposed settlement.[20]

Galt broke his journey at Montreal to tend to several personal business affairs that had seriously deteriorated during his absence in London. He also wanted to confer with CPR officials in the hope of gaining a special rate for transporting the heavy mining equipment to the western end-of-steel as well as a fixed tariff for hauling his coal to market. The railway men refused to play ball, however, and the disgruntled Galt complained to Prime Minister Macdonald:

> The C.P.R. have for the moment blocked Lethbridge & my plans about the coal by refusing to name a rate for transport. We dare not get our friends here into an expenditure of £30,000 to £40,000, and then find ourselves at the mercy of the Railway.[21]

It took several meetings with Stephen and his officials for Galt to work out a satisfactory arrangement.

Early in August, Galt and his son, Elliott, began the western tour. They were accompanied by C. J. Brydges and a Hudson's Bay Company surveyor. The party travelled by CPR as far as the Assiniboine River and then trekked the remaining seven hundred miles across the dusty prairies by buckboard. The sixty-year-old Galt found the trip difficult and tiring. He caught a severe cold and almost turned back. "Our journey across the plains was rather monotonous," Galt complained to his wife, "Not a tree for hundreds of miles—great scarcity of water & firewood."[22] At the end of the month the party reached Blackfoot Crossing, the large, bustling tepee village of Crowfoot and his band. This is where Galt hoped to build the colliery and establish the headquarters of the land company. He was deeply disappointed, however, because three test audits had uncovered coal that was dirty, slow to ignite, and liable to crumble when exposed to air. Moreover, the surrounding countryside was not suitable for agriculture. There-fore, Galt was forced to scuttle both parts of the Blackfoot Crossing development scheme.[23]

From Blackfoot Crossing, Galt travelled to Calgary where he parted company with C. J. Brydges. With his son and Major Crozier of the NWMP, he moved on to inspect the NWC&NCo sawmill near Beaver Creek in the Porcupine Hills about twenty miles west of Ford Macleod. Because nineteenth-century collieries with their labyrinthine underground passages devoured enormous amounts of support timbers, William Stafford had erected a portable sawmill at the company's timber limits in these tree-clad foothills. He had laboriously hauled the heavy equipment from Fort Benton with the company's own bull-train and throughout the summer had cut mine props and building materials for Fort Macleod.[24] By developing this important supply of timber as well as maintaining the means of transportation, Galt not only saved the company money but revealed his intention to control as many facets of the NWC&NCo's operations as possible.

Satisfied with the wood-cutting operations, Galt next visited the coal leases at Coal Banks. Here the news was encouraging, and in consultation with Bryant and Stafford, he chose this site as the first property to be developed. Accordingly, in December 1882, a small crew of Nova Scotian miners dug two short drifts from the river flats into the banks and during the winter extracted twenty-two thousand tons of coal, most of which was sold in Fort Macleod.[25]

Meanwhile, Galt had returned to London by way of Fort Benton, Helena, Chicago, and Montreal. It was a long trip and he had much time to ponder a nagging doubt—was Coal Banks really the best spot for a coal-mine? It undoubtedly had the highest quality coal yet uncovered in southern Alberta and an abundant supply of wood less than fifty miles away. But Galt's plan had been to develop the site sometime in the future when the region was more settled. Now that he knew the other locations contained inferior coal, this option was no longer available. Unfortunately, however, Coal Banks suffered a major flaw—it was remote from the transcontinental. To be economically viable a colliery at Coal Banks had to extend its market to embrace the entire Northwest, particularly the CPR. To survive the competition that was certain to appear shortly, Galt had to replace the expensively slow bull-trains with a more efficient and faster transportation technique. No matter what he chose, it would be expensive, and so he was disappointed that yet another costly obstacle blocked the immediate production of coal.

The problem was essentially Galt's. As the only board member familiar with the Northwest, he had become in practice the company's agent and manager. He sold all the shares, consolidated all the directors' timber limits and coal leases under the company's name, and converted the leases to freehold.[26] Galt also engineered the pruning of C. J. Brydges from the board of directors when he failed to pay up his shares.[27] Faced with the transportation problem, Galt could connect the mine to the CPR main line with either a railway or a steamboat with a fleet of barges. On the one hand, a railway, while more efficient in the long term, required much planning, involved considerable bureaucratic red tape, and meant an enormous capital outlay. On the other hand, a steamboat, while it could be built quickly and cheaply, could only be used in the summer. The choice was cruelly difficult, but eventually and reluctantly Galt elected transportation by water. He was worried about his own precarious financial position and afraid the whole scheme might fail. His investment in the NWC&NCo, which was really more than he could afford, represented a desperate bid to gain financial security in his old age. He needed quick returns. The steamboat could easily bring the coal to market next summer and immediately earn profits for him and his partners. It was also clear that the coal had to be marketed soon so that the reputation of the NWC&NCo might be established before competitors entered the field. It was a difficult decision, burdened by the haunting thought that another summer or two of prospecting might discover a much better location. There was no time, however, to begin all over again. He pushed the doubt out of his mind and resolved to make a vigorous presentation to the shareholders in favour of Coal Banks and the steamboat.

The plan to build the steamer, grudgingly approved by the London board, was carried out by Galt's eldest son, Elliott, who had become in effect the NWC&NCo's local manager. Probably to Galt's immense satisfaction, Elliott had inherited his father's flair for spotting profitable opportunities and optimistically devising expansionist schemes. The elder Galt had always hoped great things for his son and had carefully groomed him for a business career. Elliott was sent to Bishop's College School in Sherbrooke and Harrow in England, climaxed by a tour of European cities to meet prominent businessmen introduced to him by the local embassies. Well over six feet tall and lean, Elliott was a splendid graceful athlete with a love for scholarship nourished by much reading. Unlike his father, he was reserved, even shy, perhaps overly polite; he was soft-spoken and loathe to criticize others. His greatest strength was a meticulous attention to detail; all his proposals were carefully and clearly composed and punctiliously executed.[28] Given the same chances, as a promoter the patient Elliott Galt might well outperform both his father and grandfather. The relationship between father and son, however, while close, was strained. Living up to the very image of the stern Victorian *paterfamilias*, Sir Alexander ruled his family with a tight rein; moreover, he had serious reservations about his son's strength of character. In one instance he refused to give the twenty-two-year-old Elliott part of a bequest because he felt that the easy acquisition of wealth could only create desires for more money and therefore corrupt his son. "My constant prayer to God is that you may be preserved from the great danger of acquiring the habit of considering only your monetary enjoyment," he lectured his son, "The dealing with this money will distract your attention from what is now to you of more importance—a strict attention to your office duties."[29] Finally, in 1879 the elder Galt decreed that Elliott's "life of self-indulgence" and "great temptation" had to end, so he asked the prime minister to give his son a position away from his friends.[30] Accordingly, at the age of twenty-nine, Elliott became the secretary to the Indian commissioner, a task that, to everyone's surprise, he performed well.

Exposure to the exhilarating spirit of western development awakened Elliott's latent entrepreneurial instincts. He alerted his father to the coal resources, wrote him about grand plans for steamboats and gristmills, and above all pointed to lucrative land speculation.[31] He bought land for himself and his father in Winnipeg and, with his immediate superior, Edgar Dewdney, invested in a Regina land syndicate.[32] For the federal minister of justice, Sir Alexander Campbell, he created a partnership to buy some good but inexpensive land in Manitoba, and arranged for an English investment house to buy the land at a healthy profit.[33] Within a few years Elliott was deeply involved in the tangled web of land jobbers and syndicates that spread across the prairies in advance of the railway. Probably, it was he who brought the new wealth of Winnipeggers James Wellington Ross and John Balsillie into the NWC&NCo. In February 1883 Elliott resigned from his government post to serve as the full-time manager of the coal corporation.[34] With his keen eye for profit and his strong sense of dedication, he became a capable steward of the company's properties. He also served as his father's trusted right-hand man.

Early in 1883 the NWC&NCo authorized Elliott Galt to hire a crew of experienced Mississippi shipwrights to build a stern-wheel steamer and four barges. To save on transportation costs the barges were to be built at Fort Macleod and the steamer at Coal Banks. Working over four hundred miles from the nearest railway, the shipbuilders faced enormous difficulties. Since the rivers were frozen, all the lumber had to be hauled by laboriously slow bull-trains from the company's sawmills to the construction sites. With luck, a bull-train, usually made up of sixteen oxen and three wagons each, could carry forty-five tons for about twelve miles in a day. Such luck was scarce, however, as strong winds, howling across the bald prairies, dumped tons of snow on the difficult trail, halting the slow-moving wagons despite the cursing drivers; the crossings over treacherous river ice often proved disastrous as wagons broke through and were lost. To minimize the high cost of transportation, the trains returned with coal which, sold at $12.50 a ton in Fort Macleod, realized a good profit.[35] Still, lumber remained so expensive that the workers built only a tiny shack at Coal Banks in which to cook and eat; they slept in a crowded tent despite temperatures that plummetted to thirty below zero. The isolation also meant that the men made do with primitive tools and inadequate materials, resulting in inferior workmanship that often caused costly breakdowns later.

In spite of difficulties, the work progressed rapidly. The first barge was completed by April and was loaded with wood to be floated down river to Coal Banks. Nature still had the upper hand, however, because the vessel ran aground only five miles from its starting point. The accident was an ominous portent of future shipping problems. With great difficulty the crew freed the barge but she floundered on sandbar after sandbar. Finally near Fort Kipp the exasperated men threw the lumber overboard and allowed it to drift downstream on its own accord.[36] On 2 July 1883 the steamer's hull was launched at Coal Banks and floated downstream to Medicine Hat to receive its machinery.[37] Elliott Galt had purchased the gear at Pittsburgh and shipped it by rail to Swift Current. Horses and wagons carried it the remaining 350 miles to Medicine Hat. After the engines were installed, the top deck and pilot-house were added. When finished in the middle of August, the ship, christened the *Baroness* after Baroness Angela Burdett-Coutts, measured 173 feet in length, thirty feet in beam, weighed 320 tons gross but drew only eighteen inches of water.[38] Technology had come to the far Northwest, a product of the collective skills and perseverance of the company's workers, who had overcome the obstacles imposed by weather, distance, and isolation.

Meanwhile other workers continued to develop the colliery and lay the foundations for a village. William Stafford travelled to Nova Scotia early in 1883 to recruit miners, who soon began to trickle into the fledgling settlement. That summer he built a home for his wife and nine children, and another one for Captain Bryant's family.[39] Surrounded by a motley assortment of shanties and bunk-houses, the two dwellings lent the appearance of permanence to Coal Banks. In August, Elliott Galt engaged another twenty-two men to lay a short rail line from the mine entrance to the river edge and increase production to an average of eighty tons per day. He also hired twenty men for the sawmill in the Porcupine Hills and yet another crew to build a coal and lumber yard at Fort Macleod. A third group was to erect coal-sheds at Medicine Hat.[40] Even at this early date the influence of the company had spread over a large area and had begun to stimulate the economic activity of the entire region.

Sir Alexander Galt, whose resignation as high commissioner had finally been accepted, spent several months in the Northwest that summer. He came partly as an agent of the Canadian government to look after the Jewish refugees settling in Winnipeg, but he also wanted to inspect the colliery and participate in the *Baroness*'s maiden voyage.[41] After a two-day shakedown cruise, the steamer sailed to Coal Banks loaded with cargo for Fort Macleod, and returned with 200 tons of coal. To Galt's intense disappointment no more coal could be shipped that season because of low water levels.

In spite of the hard work and material achievements, the first year of operations had been a dismal failure in financial terms. Only the sawmill had earned money for the company, and that solely because Elliott Galt had won a seventy-five-thousand-dollar government contract for the construction of police barracks at Fort Macleod, Medicine Hat, and Maple Creek. It was the only, and tenuous, reason keeping the impatient and disgruntled financial backers loyal to the project.

Even more ominous was the threat of competition. Sheran's mine at Coal Banks and that of H. A. Kanouse, several miles upstream on the north bank of the St. Mary, were expanding and shipping a good quality coal to Fort Macleod. Neither of these collieries were a real danger to the NWC&NCo because their limited funding restricted them to the local market. More menacing was a large Winnipeg firm developing a coal-seam on the Saskatchewan River near Medicine Hat, merely a short spur line away from the CPR. Also enjoying the proximity to the transcontinental were several smaller collieries around Medicine Hat. Most inauspicious of all were the discoveries of valuable seams of good quality anthracite by CPR construction crews. A promoter named James Anderson had just formed a company, reportedly capitalized at one hundred thousand dollars, to mine the anthracite near Banff.[42] A colliery located on the CPR and producing a superior coal could be fatal to the Galt interests. Therefore, if they wanted to secure a substantial segment of the Northwest fuel market, the NWC&NCo would have to solve their transportation problem immediately.

Low water had foiled the *Baroness*. Would this happen again next season? Even if conditions were favourable, could she haul enough coal next year to assure the CPR a constant supply of fuel at a competitive price? These were distressing questions troubling Galt. Was the best answer not a branch line to the CPR? Surely Galt's past had demonstrated his great ability to promote and build railways, especially with government assistance? Financing railways was the essence of his business mind. Not surprisingly, therefore, Galt had written a memorandum to Prime Minister Macdonald concerning a branch line as early as June 1883, even before the *Baroness* was launched.[43] During the summer he visited Macdonald several times and obtained a letter from the prime

minister supporting the project in principle.⁴⁴ At the end of
August, Galt wrote Macdonald an enthusiastic letter that underscored the value of the colliery to the Northwest and the CPR as
the basis for government support of the proposed railway:

> I think you will share my gratification at my receipt last night
> from Stephen [president of the CPR] of the following mes-
> sage.
> "Coal done splendidly. Go ahead with your railway.
> Made trip from Winnipeg to Calgary in 33 hours."
> The satisfactory result of the test of our coal has a public
> importance in two ways. First—with reference to the general
> fuel question for the whole N[orth] W[est] and secondly in
> the benefit it will be to the C.P.R. as removing the objection of
> the excessive cost of fuel to which they would be exposed in
> working the line in the West. Stephen, I am sure, thoroughly
> appreciates the importance to them and the help it will be in
> the further issue of their stock. You really must give us a
> helping hand, especially as you know I will ask nothing either
> unreasonable or likely to produce political difficulties.
> I want to get the Railway so far on its legs—before the
> Session as to enable the rails etc., to be bought & shipped
> early in the spring. I think this can be done without in any way
> compromising the Government.
> The decision of the modus operandi I reserve until you
> are in Ottawa.⁴⁵

Now that Galt and Stephen were talking business, their
animosities were set aside. Stephen's railway was beginning to
experience considerable financial difficulties and the alternatives
to Galt's coal were heavy investments in company-owned collieries in Alberta or extensive storage facilities at Fort William for
Pennsylvania coal.⁴⁶ Neither option was desirable and so the CPR
president welcomed Galt's proposals. "Galt was in today full of his
coal," Stephen informed Macdonald, "If only half he hopes from
their deposits are realized, the fuel question may be dismissed as of
no account.... We'll be glad to see his line open and carrying coal to
the railway."⁴⁷ Stephen contracted to purchase twenty thousand
tons of coal at five dollars a ton, delivered at Medicine Hat. He

agreed to transport all the necessary railway equipment to Medicine Hat at a low rate and approved an integrated rate structure with the proposed railway. In addition he promised to lobby government members in support of Galt's railway charter.[48] Clearly the CPR wanted Galt to succeed.

With CPR co-operation assured, Galt canvassed his friends in the federal cabinet for special concessions. He sought a free grant of land for the right-of-way and stations, the right to buy 6,400 acres of land at one dollar per acre for every mile of railway built, and the right to purchase fifteen thousand acres of coal lands. Galt justified these privileges on the ground that the proposed railway would speed the development of southern Alberta. "The construction of the proposed railway, while developing the entire McLeod [sic] District, by promoting its settlement and affording to an important section of the Northwest rail facilities, which cannot otherwise be obtained, will at the same time ensure a supply of excellent coal, at reasonable rates, to the settlements as far east as Winnipeg, and will also bring to the Canadian Pacific Railway the cattle and mining traffic of Montana,"[49] he wrote. While this argument was undoubtedly valid, the primary, though unstated, reason for requesting the subsidy was to alleviate the heavy financial burden of building the railway. Without generous government aid, Galt simply could not promise investors good profits.

Sir Alexander's request went far beyond government policy land regulations. In 1879 parliament had set aside the odd-numbered sections in the Northwest to be sold to the projected Pacific railway at one to six dollars per acre. J. S. Dennis, then deputy minister of the interior, had argued that these lands should also be made available to other colonization companies, to stimulate the settlement of other areas of the territories and thereby increase the value of the government's even-numbered sections. Following this recommendation in the summer of 1880, the government permitted the Manitoba and South-Western Railway as well as two other railway colonization companies to purchase 3,840 acres per mile at one dollar per acre plus survey costs. A few months later the CPR was given a free grant of land.[50] This subsidy was not extended to the smaller companies, however; in fact, an order-in-council on 4 June 1883 raised the price of land for railways to $1.50 per acre.

If these regulations were to be strictly enforced, Galt's application was clearly unacceptable. Not only did he ask for nearly twice the allowable amount of land but he wanted to pay the old price of one dollar per acre; moreover, his railway did not even technically qualify for the subsidy because it was a resource transport system rather than a colonization road. Mere regulations were not to stand in Galt's way, however, because Prime Minister Macdonald, who was also the minister of the interior, liked the proposal in principle and believed that Galt warranted special privileges. Upon Macdonald's recommendation, in October 1883 cabinet passed an order-in-council subject to parliamentary approval, which not only granted Galt's company a subsidy of the regular 3,840 acres per mile but, notwithstanding the June order-in-council, allowed the NWC&NCo to buy the land at only one dollar per acre plus survey dues. The cabinet also authorized the sale of ten thousand of the requested fifteen thousand acres of coal lands at ten dollars per acre. The other requests were refused.[51] The terms, although less than asked, were still more than generous and enabled the NWC&NCo to expand from a coal-mining company to a rail and land enterprise.

Toward the end of 1883 Galt sailed to London to place before his friends, as he put it to Lethbridge, "the most complete project on a small scale you have ever been asked to join."[52] He wanted them to form a new company, the Alberta Railway and Coal Company, which would build the 110-mile railroad at a cost of eleven thousand dollars per mile. This new company would absorb the land assets of the NWC&NCo and use them as security for the bonds and stocks needed to finance the railway. Furthermore, the colliery would be expanded. Galt also confided to Lethbridge that, as architects of the NWC&NCo, the two of them could convert their NWC&NCo founders' shares into preferred stock of the proposed company and realize substantial profits. Galt brimmed over with enthusiasm. He calculated that the CPR agreement would net the NWC&NCo a tidy profit of $3.50 per ton of coal.[53] Adding this to the cabinet concessions, he could only conclude that the company's success was guaranteed; therefore, he was fully confident that the London financiers would gladly provide the funds for the greatly expanded project.

Yet Galt, ever impatient, had been too optimistic, and he was forced to revise his timetable. To his annoyance, the wheels of government turned very slowly and the hopes for immediate parliamentary approval of the cabinet concessions grew dimmer every week. Prime Minister Macdonald was too preoccupied with the CPR, whose government-backed shares were falling in price on the New York market, to busy himself with Galt's concerns. The decline in CPR securities was symptomatic of a wide-spread economic slump that was deepened by the sudden bankruptcy of the Northern Pacific in the United States. This failure eroded the credibility of all North American railroad stock. Under these adverse conditions Galt found it impossible to float yet another railway bond issue, especially when parliament had not yet approved the land subsidy. Deeply dejected, he wrote Macdonald:

> I have had infinite worry about my Railway and now had finally to postpone it for a few months. We must get the Act first and it is also desirable to show by actual results that the Coal can be got out for what it will be sold at. We have therefore ordered Elliott to build another steamboat & more barges so as to get down say 25,000 tons next spring.[54]

Casually, yet in a tone tinged with despair, he added that if the rumours of still greater CPR bond guarantees by the government were true, could Macdonald not "make them build my little road on the ground of fuel supply?"

Backed to the wall, Galt stubbornly turned to steamboating once again. He could not afford to lose another production season, so he ordered Elliott to import Minnesota oak for a second steamer. Built entirely at Medicine Hat and launched on 15 April 1885, the *Alberta* measured one hundred by twenty feet and weighed 150 tons gross. A third steamer, the *Minnow*, only thirty-five feet long, ten feet wide, and powered by a tiny five-and-three-quarter horsepower engine, was built in Winnipeg and shipped in one piece by railway flatcar to Medicine Hat. The rationale for spending forty thousand dollars on ship construction[55] was extremely weak because the delay in railway plans had caused the CPR to cancel its agreement with the NWC&NCo. The railway needed an assured supply of fuel and the general manager of the CPR, William Van Horne, did not think the steamboats could deliver it. So he promised to buy only a paltry five thousand tons at six dollars per ton delivered at Medicine Hat.[56] Despite this serious setback, Galt had to move ahead. He could not wait another year. His railway plans required much greater capitalization than before, and in order to attract new investors he had to prove that Coal Banks coal was not only valuable but marketable.

Sir Alexander remained in London trying to strengthen his position. On 19 April 1884 he incorporated the Alberta Railway and Coal Company (AR&CCo), capitalized at 1.5 million dollars in shares of one hundred dollars. The AR&CCo proposed to build the railway from Medicine Hat to Coal Banks and, if two-thirds of the shareholders approved, to assume all the assets and liabilities of the NWC&NCo.[57] The AR&CCo's board included most of the directors of the NWC&NCo but it also introduced new names, including that of Peter Redpath of Montreal and Robert Gillespie, Galt's former employer at the British American Land Company. Also on the board was Alexander Stavely Hill, the prominent British barrister and politician with considerable financial interests in the Northwest, including the large Oxley Ranch.[58] Hill's presence on the board greatly strengthened the company's position because, as a staunch Conservative, he was a close friend of Sir John A. Macdonald. Thus Galt's venture had matured into a sizeable endeavour backed by an increasing and impressive group of investors.

This success buoyed Galt's hopes; he could feel his luck turning. Coincidentally, on the day of the AR&CCo's incorporation, Canada's legislature passed the railway charter.[59] Debate had been mercifully short and only the irrepressible Edward Blake had observed that the bill's title mentioned the road's point of origin, Medicine Hat, but not its destination. "To a point named in the Bill,"[60] was the terse reply of M. C. Cameron (Victoria), the bill's sponsor, accompanied by Macdonald's rendition of "All around the hat." With the railway charter approved, all that Galt had yet to gain was approval of the land subsidy.

That spring, however, Galt's optimistic hopes for substantial coal sales were cruelly dashed again. The steamboats failed once more. The shipping season lasted less than seven weeks; the *Baroness*, flagship of the little fleet, completed only nine trips, while the *Alberta* finished eight; in all, they delivered merely three

The NWC&NCo's second steamer, the *Alberta*, was built
in 1884 just west of the CPR trestle in Medicine Hat.
(Glenbow Archives)

thousand tons of coal to the CPR. The Belly River was unsuitable
for navigation because water tumbling from the melted snows of
the Rocky Mountains usually crested in June and fell again so
quickly that by July the river was shallow and dangerous. The
shifting sandbars of the low river proved too great an obstacle for
the captains who wasted too much time freeing their ships from
the sandy barriers. Ironically, at high river the stern-wheelers
were underpowered: for example, if all went well, the *Baroness*
could race down river from Coal Banks to Medicine Hat in one day,
but needed five days of hard steaming to return. Meanwhile, the
ships burned so much coal that refuelling stops were necessary
along the way. One crew member recalled the difficulties:

> I was thinking of the time in 1884 . . . that I made the return
> trip from Lethbridge to Medicine Hat as a hand on one of the
> river barges that was hauling coal down to Medicine Hat and
> what a terrible trip it was and took us nearly two weeks. The
> river was dropping awfully fast and we were continually

getting stuck on sand and gravel bars. We finally got down to Medicine Hat. Our main concern was to get the boat back to Lethbridge and, as the river was still dropping, we were unable to take on much freight. The return trip was even worse as we had to buck the current. The boat hands were out in the water most of the time with poles prying the boat off the sand or gravel bars. It was hard, gruelling work and we often lay down to sleep for a very few hours in our wet clothes. We were continually running out of fuel for our boilers, and as there were seams of coal along the river banks we dug out coal and packed it in sacks down to the boat.[61]

Galt spent a lonely anxious week at Medicine Hat early in May vainly waiting for the steamboats to arrive laden with coal. He had much time to ponder his depressing situation. The expensive steamboat gamble had collapsed. Although he was still convinced that the effort had been necessary to prove that Coal Banks coal was worth the cost of exploitation, he knew that his English friends were thoroughly disillusioned. For several years they had poured money into the western enterprises and had seen no returns. How could he possibly ask them to invest still more money in a highly dubious railway venture at a time when the CPR was headed toward financial disaster and some American railways had foundered?

Complicating this nagging question was his own desperate financial problem. As the general euphoria sparked by the construction of the CPR had dissipated in the chill of continent-wide depression, Galt himself was near bankruptcy. The end of the Winnipeg real estate boom left him and Elliott with worthless properties, burdened with debts amounting to thousands of dollars, and without any means of even paying the accumulating interest costs.[62] Much of his time, he complained to his wife, was spent frantically shuffling around his assets in order to ward off impatient bankers. "The truth is my own position is such that I must endeavour before the New Year to devise some mode of ... [resolution] or I do not see how I can get on much longer," he confided to Amy, "It seems a little hard to have to struggle against adverse fortune when one is getting old but I should be very thankful that my energy and physical ability are not yet unequal to the strain and I comfort myself with the belief that it must be all wisely ordered."[63]

While still dolefully ruminating at Medicine Hat, Galt re-solved to re-enter politics. It is unlikely that he hoped to solve his business problems with a parliamentary seat because he had enough friends in the cabinet to plead his cause. To Macdonald he explained that he could make a positive contribution to the two most important issues facing Canada—the CPR and the North-west.[64] Unstated, however, the decision also expressed a desire to escape from a seemingly hopeless, dreary situation. So when Macdonald summarily rejected his overture, he was deeply hurt. "I may be somewhat erratic," he shot back angrily, "but have a good mind yet and I think I can be of service."[65] For someone with a political career nearly as long as that of the prime minister himself, the realization that he was no longer considered an asset to the party was a heavy blow.

The cold rebuff shocked Galt into action and he was deter-mined to make one last-ditch stand. For expediency's sake he decided to reduce the scale of operations and seek more govern-ment assistance. He again appealed to Macdonald. Would the prime minister permit an alteration in the railway charter to allow for a less expensive narrow gauge railway? "If we can't get a first class road, we must be content with a cheap one—anything to get the coal to market," he explained, "I shall have to get your consent to substitute a cheap narrow gauge line for the other . . . we must get the Coal out."[66] But, even with the savings realized by nar-rowing the gauge, Galt could never raise the funds to buy the lands permitted under his railway charter. At one dollar per acre plus survey dues, the 3,840 acres per mile amounted to a stagger-ing sum of nearly a half million dollars. Therefore, he had to rearrange the terms of the land subsidy. In a series of difficult negotiations with the prime minister and senior government officials, Galt outlined his proposal. He offered to relinquish half of his land subsidy provided that the government converted the remaining half into a free grant. He argued that such a move would cost the government very little as the proposed railway would automatically increase the value of all government land in the vicinity. At the same time, he declared, the road would open a valuable coalfield and provide inexpensive transportation for the coal so desperately needed in the Northwest.[67] Once again the official submission did not mention that the primary motive for government subsidies was not the public good but attractive profits for reluctant foreign investors. Surely Macdonald understood this, but he believed that Galt's colliery was an important part in the machinery of national policies. While he no longer trusted Galt as a politician, he still admired him as a skilful entrepreneur; therefore, he verbally assured him of government support.

Armed with Macdonald's promise, the aged Galt wearily returned to London in August 1884, once again in search of capital. The obstacles seemed insurmountable. Both Lethbridge and Smith had lost all confidence in Galt. "[Galt] is a good fellow," Smith told a friend, "but I would as soon trust a dreaming gushing young lady in business matters."[68] Both Smith and Lethbridge had guaranteed the bonds for the construction of the useless steamboats and idle colliery. They wanted to quit, and refused to discuss further expansion. In retaliation, resilient as ever, Galt persuaded his former partner, the brilliant railway builder Colonel C. S. Gzowski to lend his prestige to the enterprise by acting as consulting engineer. Gzowski helped Galt convince Burdett-Coutts to invest another ten thousand pounds, on the condition that the others did the same. Next Gzowski won over Smith and then induced Lethbridge to come to London for a meeting of the five men in the colonel's rooms. With the ground prepared by Gzowski, Galt unfolded his plans for the railway, and after a lengthy and heated debate talked the partners into pledging ten thousand pounds each toward the cost of building the railway. The deciding factor in their decision was Gzowski's endorsement of the project and his willingness to serve as consulting engineer and professional advisor; he had to approve all plans, specifications, and expenditures. Galt no longer had a free hand in his western enterprises.[69]

Still, the future looked bright. Charles Tupper, the Canadian minister of railways and canals as well as the high commissioner in London, strongly recommended Galt's case to his colleagues[70] and on 27 September 1884 the cabinet granted 1,920 acres of land per mile at the survey cost of ten cents per acre to the NWC&NCo.

The government also permitted the company to reduce the track gauge to three feet as long as it furnished good facilities for passengers and freight.[71] By mid-October Galt finished the tedious negotiations of details. In the end he had won for himself a $550,000 contract to build the railway. The AR&CCo directors, the prospective owners of the road, bought about $225,000 worth of bonds and promised to buy another $150,000. The CPR pledged to accept $50,000 in coal as payment for transporting all the railway equipment to Medicine Hat. Galt was confident that the remaining bonds could be sold easily to the public. The final contracts were signed on 14 October 1884, one day after Elliott had commenced construction work.[72] On 30 October 1884 Sir Alexander sailed home.

It was a happy voyage. The satisfactory conclusion of two months of strenuous negotiations was a tremendous relief to the weary Galt. The success of the coal-mining venture was assured; if no bad luck intervened, he would personally earn fifty thousand dollars from the railway contract, enough to abolish his financial difficulties. At the same time, the railway was bound to increase the value of the coal-mining interest. He wrote Amy a jubilant letter in which he revealed that his pious trust in a provident God was closely linked to practical business sense:

> I cannot refrain from writing you again by the Oregon to tell you of my great thankfulness to God that it has pleased Him to bless my efforts here, and to relieve my mind from the great weight of anxiety with which I have looked forward to the future not only on account of the dishonour which attaches to all who are unable to meet their obligations but also for the trouble and possible privation, which I dreaded was impending over you and all I love.
>
> My trust has been in God's mercy and it has been signally shown to me in turning circumstances that seemed most untoward into the means whereby I have now bright hopes of extrication from my difficulties. The failing of our navigation last summer, was a severe trial, but without it, I never could have succeeded in inducing my friends here to undertake the Railway—And again the very difficulty in raising money, which seemed to threaten failure has obliged them to make

arrangements with me which I now regard as guaranteeing an early escape from pressing pecuniary anxiety.[73]

Although the profits for his company were assured, Galt discovered an avenue to still greater returns. At the same time that he was negotiating his railway deal in London, the Canadian cabinet had granted the Manitoba and South-Western Colonization Company, the Manitoba and North-Western, as well as the Qu'Appelle, Long Lake, and Saskatchewan Railroad and Steamboat Company free grants of 6,400 acres of land for each mile of railway constructed. This radical change in government policy had come about through public and business pressure. Disenchanted with the failure of colonization companies to effect large-scale immigration, various spokesmen used the CPR and NWC&NCo land grants to argue that railways and land subsidies were logical complements in any settlement policy.[74] "Surely there is land to spare in the Northwest, which cannot be put to better purpose than the development of the country, "so the Winnipeg *Daily Free Press* summed up the argument; generous subsidies were justified because "farming cannot profitably be carried on at any distance from a railway."[75] This was precisely the principle that Galt had advocated throughout his entire career, and his company had been the first small western railway to receive a free land grant.[76] With the precedent established by him, other companies, all of which faced financial difficulties, demanded similar treatment. When the cabinet concurred, Galt requested that his subsidy be increased to 6,400 acres per mile as were the others. As an inducement to the government, he promised to complete the railway one year earlier than projected and bring the coal to market by the fall of 1885.

Galt's petition was introduced to the cabinet by Sir David L. Macpherson, the old and doting minister of the interior. As a former business associate in Gzowski and Company and the Toronto Rolling Mills, Macpherson was Galt's personal friend. He could do little for his former crony, however, because his fellow ministers refused to grant such a large subsidy to a narrow gauge road. Macpherson withdrew the measure to await the prime minister's return from a business trip.[77] Macdonald's personal intervention was necessary to ram the order-in-council through the cabinet. Still, all that he could get for Galt was a grant of

3,840 acres per mile, consisting of all the odd-numbered sections in six-mile belts on both sides of the railway.[78]

Late in March 1885 the government introduced an omnibus bill covering the land grants for the three railway colonization companies, as well as Galt's resource railway. The legislation aroused immediate and acrimonious dissent from the opposition benches, whose members were eager to pounce on a government beleaguered by the economic crisis and the faltering CPR. The chief critic was Edward Blake, and his hard-hitting speech, as always based on thorough knowledge and keen insight, singled out the NWC&NCo as an example of excessive government assistance to private enterprise. Although Blake confessed he approved of the principle of subsidies to branch lines, he denounced Galt's grant as exorbitant, particularly because his company had already raised the needed funds on the basis of the smaller land grant. With the land valued at two dollars an acre, he reckoned that the subsidy covered the entire cost of construction and thus opened the way for inordinate profits once the road was in operation. He also pointed out that the public was being asked to subsidize an inefficient narrow gauge railway, subject to extra trans-shipping expenses, which undoubtedly were to be passed on to the consumer. In fact, Blake questioned the need of an expensive branch line at all when the CPR crossed several good coal-seams. Furthermore, Blake still feared that the NWC&NCo could establish a coal monopoly in the Northwest with resultant high prices because the company controlled not only ten thousand acres of coal lands, but also the only access to this area; therefore, if Galt chose to charge very high rates for coal shipments, no one in the region could compete with him.[79] In sum, Blake cogently expressed the feelings of critics of the bill, that the public was being asked to bear the cost of resource development while the company reaped the profits. The members of the opposition loudly demanded that the government assure the people that the enormous resources of the Northwest were to be exploited not for the benefit of a few foreign investors but for the advantage of the Canadian public.

The government side of the house, of course, viewed the matter from a different perspective. The buoyant spirit engendered by the start of CPR construction had dissipated with the collapse of western Canada's economic boom and the onset of a general depression. The CPR, the very keystone of the government's national policies, was close to collapse; the happy vision of a settled West threatened to become a nightmare of failure. More than ever before the government felt compelled to grant generous concessions to lure development capital to the prairies. As the prime minister pointed out in the debate, the unparalleled shrinkage in railway money in North America had dried up all financial interest in western Canada; the government, therefore, had to do all it could to revitalize investments in the West so that the bountiful resources, which were worthless without improvements, could be fully utilized. Galt's case was justified by government members on this basic premise, and the fear of a coal monopoly could be dismissed by them on the grounds that the reserves were so plentiful that competitors were bound to appear. The cheapest incentive available to the Canadian government was land, and so convinced of abundant western resources and deeply committed to the development of these riches, it was willing to grant liberal bonuses to ensure their exploitation.

Galt, aided by his allies in the cabinet, took full advantage of the government's pessimistic mood. By confidently promising success in an era of failure, he wheedled more out of the government than he needed. Although he had already decided to start the railway with the smaller land grant, his promoter's instinct compelled him to grab the largest gain possible. The obsession with making money, which dominated his commercial activities, clashed harshly with his pious custom of seeking God's guidance in all his business endeavours. This over-emphasis upon monetary profit, so common of the age of capitalism, distorted the biblical teaching of responsible stewardship for the community at large. Although Galt had resolved to fulfil his obligations to the Canadian public, he was equally determined to seek the greatest financial return possible.

In the meantime the work on Galt's railway had continued. As always, construction activity triggered an economic boom; it transformed Dunmore, the sleepy CPR station just east of Medicine Hat, into a bustling construction camp. Since it was to be the junction of the two railways, a crew of twenty-five men were busily engaged in the construction of a siding, round-house, car

shop, coal-transferring facilities, and a rooming-house. Ties for
the new road arrived daily from the company's new timber berth
west of Banff, along with fifty thousand surplus ties purchased
from the CPR.[80] By March some seventy-five thousand ties were
stacked in massive piles in anticipation of the rails, bought in
England and already in Canada awaiting the spring breakup of the
Great Lakes.[81]

Coal Banks, already popularly known as Lethbridge, was the
centre of the railway fever. C. A. Magrath, a government surveyor, laid out the town-site high on the benchland about three-
quarters of a mile from the river. Captivated by the spirit of the
open expansive prairies, Magrath drew wide streets and reserved
a large square opposite the projected railway station as a parkland
core for the business district. Since the company owned the entire
town-site, the community was spared the frantic transactions and
soaring land prices caused by avid speculators; at the same time the
brisk flow of applications for town lots restored the confidence of
British investors. Eager buyers scurried to procure choice properties. By May seventy lots had been sold, and two months later all
the commercial real estate around the square was taken. Some
merchants simply pitched tents to serve as stores and warehouses,
while one enterprising individual erected a ramshackle hotel complete with billiard room and saloon. Elsewhere workers prepared
the town for the arrival of the railway; they hurriedly constructed
two large water-towers to serve the engines and the community
and built several cottages and a boarding-house to accommodate
the impending influx of miners and railroaders.[82] Coal Banks
was astir in lively anticipation of the opening of the colliery and
railway.

Fort Macleod also shared in the excitement created by the
large influx of capital. Convinced that the NWC&NCo planned
eventually to lengthen its rail line through the town to the
Crowsnest Pass, the editor of the *Fort Macleod Gazette* urged his
readers to raise money for a bonus for the company as an inducement to build the extension immediately. With the railway and
enthusiastic management, so the editor grandly prophesied, Fort
Macleod would soon outstrip Winnipeg and become the "Queen
City of the West."[83] Surely the telegraph-line being strung from
Dunmore to Fort Macleod was an obvious harbinger of progress,

signalling the end of isolation. Soon the settlement would be linked into the mainstream of Canadian civilization. In their intrepid optimism, however, Fort Macleodites failed to attach any significance to the fact that the NWC&NCo had not only leased the entire telegraph-line from the government, but was operating the ferries at Coal Banks, Fort Kipp, and Fort Macleod.[84] The Galts, through their company, were assuming control over transportation and communication in the Southwest; the old ranching centre was falling into the orbit of a new and aggressive corporation. No one recognized the symbolic significance in the constant flow of logs that day after day floated past the community en route to the new town-site at Coal Banks.

All this activity stopped abruptly in March when violence erupted hundreds of miles away from Coal Banks. For a time all attention was focused on Duck Lake, Battleford, and Frog Lake, where the Indians and metis of the Northwest reacted desperately with rifles and bloodshed against the indifference of the Canadian government to their needs and fears. As a nomadic people accustomed to the freedom of the plains, they had lost their livelihood, the buffalo, and so they had become hopelessly dependent upon the foreign and frightening technological society invading their hunting grounds with fences, railways, and laws. As the alien surveyors divided the open range into little squares without regard for natural trails and existing plots, the native people rebelled against the degradation of being treated as obstacles in the way of the westward march of the Canadian people.

The insurrection temporarily clouded the economic future of the Northwest because it made the region a poor investment risk. Galt's fickle backers in London once more withdrew their support. "The effect on my English friends has been disastrous as preventing our raising money which we had every hope of doing with the land grant," Galt complained to Macdonald, "Now they write me they must stop the effort to get more capital subscribed until they see this miserable business closed."[85] The precariousness of the situation was aggravated by adverse publicity originating with the CPR. Not only did the company severely criticize the narrow gauge railway as economically unfeasible, but it announced tentative plans for a colliery in the Kicking Horse Pass.[86] Galt, very much distressed by this unexpected quirk of events, rushed to soothe his anxious partners with a promise of further government subsidies. He hoped to secure a government-guaranteed loan of one hundred thousand dollars on the basis of a government freight and mail contract held by the NWC&NCo. Frantically, he then turned to the prime minister and pressed him to approve such a loan quickly so that he could use it to pry more money out of the reluctant shareholders. If a guarantee was not forthcoming soon, Galt warned that the AR&CCo might not be able to complete the railway by the end of the year. A failure to honour the contract would jeopardize the NWC&NCo's land grant.[87] Unimpressed by Galt's desperate pleas, Macdonald and the cabinet refused to guarantee the loan.

The setback was only short-lived, however, because the NWC&NCo ultimately profited from the insurrection. Immediately after the outbreak of the rebellion, Galt wired Macdonald offering to lease his steamboats to the government.[88] Three days later he convinced Adolphe Caron, the minister of militia, that troops and supplies could best be carried across the vast and sparsely-populated prairies by utilizing the rivers. Once again he spoke too optimistically about the steamers. "With exertion," he promised to deliver the boats, still beached at Medicine Hat, to a spot near Swift Current within the week and to Prince Albert four days later.[89] Instead he launched a comedy of errors. Although Elliott Galt hastily mustered the crews in Winnipeg and rushed them to Medicine Hat by special train, he was too late. The water level had already fallen and only the little, shallow-drafted *Minnow* made it to Swift Current.[90] At that point her crew refused to travel further without a military escort. The local commander, Major General J.W. Laurie, replaced them with volunteers and dispatched the *Minnow* northward to relieve another large steamer, the *Northcote*, which was struggling her way to Clarke's Crossing near Saskatoon.[91] The *Minnow*'s captain, a drunken incompetent, chose to take in tow a private barge which Laurie then filled with oats. Burdened by this load, the *Minnow* reached Clarke's Crossing fully five days behind the *Northcote*. Meanwhile the two larger steamers lanquished on the sandbars of the South Saskatchewan until early May when meltwater from the Rockies freed them. Their work consisted largely of running up and down the North Saskatchewan, sometimes as far west as Edmonton,

The first locomotive into Lethbridge. (Glenbow Archives)

carrying supplies. Once the well-armed militia had managed to blunder its way to victory, the Galt steamers carried the wounded down the Saskatchewan to Grand Rapids near Lake Winnipeg.[92] The uprising was over and, as far as many people were concerned, the development of the Northwest, briefly interrupted, could be resumed again.

The steamboating enterprise proved to be lucrative for the company because the government leased the boats for five hundred dollars per day and paid for all expenses. Although the administration procrastinated payments, by July it had remitted thirty-six thousand dollars and agreed to negotiate for the remainder.[93] The unexpected income was a boon to the company's precarious financial position and it helped to secure the completion of the railway. "No doubt the steamboat business has been a perfect Godsend and a set off against the rebellion,"[94] Galt confided to Lethbridge and, although he quickly added that the human cost was deplorable, the implication that the rebellion had been good for business was clear.

Meanwhile, construction work on the Galt railway continued,

even if spasmodically. Rumours abounded everywhere that the southern Indian tribes planned to join the rebellion. Consequently, the main contractor, Donald Grant, a former CPR contractor and survivor of the Sioux wars, adamantly refused to come to Canada until the insurrection was completely quashed. Galt applied for military protection, but that request was refused.[95] He did, however, receive a NWMP guard for his construction crews. Under these conditions W. D. Barclay, the assistant chief engineer of the CPR, agreed to supervise the grading of the road-bed. He started two crews, one at Dunmore, the other at Woodpecker. The work progressed rapidly and by the end of June grading was complete. By then the war was over. Donald Grant came to Canada and in forty-nine working days laid the 110 miles of track. On 25 August 1885 the first train puffed into Coal Banks.[96]

Although the tracks were laid, the road did not go into operation until the first of September and was not officially opened until the twenty-fourth. At four that afternoon a group of dignitaries, including the governor-general, the Marquis of Lansdowne, the Anglican Bishop of Saskatchewan, Reverend John Maclean, and the general superintendent of the CPR, J. M. Egan, arrived in Coal Banks, now officially renamed Lethbridge, by train. They were welcomed by a large crowd of townsmen and miners. After a short address by Galt, Governor-General Lansdowne confidently declared that the Galt colliery and railway had solved the pressing energy problem for the North West Territories. In his speech he expressed the exuberant hopes of all westerners by boasting of the "inexhaustible supply of the best class of fuel."[97] He boldly prophesied that, "from these cliffs we shall be able to draw without stint the materials which will supply us sources of heat and light for generations to come." In a similar vein Lansdowne grandly described his vision of a future Lethbridge, a large industrial metropolis built on the coal-mines, augmented by smelters and foundries, providing work for thousands of labourers. After these grandiose predictions he officially opened the railway. Afterwards the party visited the inclined railway that brought the coal up from the river to the railway terminal, and then inspected the coal transferring facilities. In the evening Galt hosted a banquet in the company boarding-house at which many speeches once again lauded the enterprise of and the beneficial effects upon the surroundings of the NWC&NCo.

Steel rails finally tied the colliery securely into the CPR system. For five difficult years Sir Alexander had persisted against almost overwhelming odds to develop the Coal Banks reserves and bring the valuable resource to market. The chief obstacle had been the London investors and Galt once again discovered that foreign capital did not flow automatically into the Canadian economy. He had started the project under the favourable conditions of a heated railway boom, but within a few years the economic winds shifted and a cold indifference settled like snow among British investors. With other Canadian entrepreneurs, he found himself begging for western development funds. The struggle had been a long de- pressing experience in which he had received little encouragement from his friends and associates. When he had finally secured the enlarged land subsidy, for example, the company directors had muttered only about the added cost of the quickened pace of construction. When he demonstrated that these additional lands increased the firm's assets by almost two hundred thousand dollars, or almost half the cost of the railway—which meant that the company's bonds, bought by the founding members at seventy- five percent, jumped to ninety percent of their value—the bond- holders only grumbled about the twenty-thousand-dollar loss on operations in 1884.[98] Right up to the completion of the railway, his London partners questioned the expenditure of every penny: they complained when he ordered heavier and better quality rails; they balked when he bought an extra locomotive and several cars; and they fretted when the Bank of Montreal refused to honour their overdrafts. Governed by the desire for quick returns on their investments, the London shareholders stressed the steamboat failures rather than the rapid completion of the railway. Un- familiar with the Canadian scene, they cautiously distrusted Galt's sweeping visions which transcended the timid plans for a small colliery to embrace a bold but costly railway and land development scheme. In sum, all along the way, Galt had to fight his London associates in order to satisfy his expansionist urge.

Galt moved too quickly and too far for his hesitant backers. The visionary streak in his character, his impatient impulse to change the natural environment to suit human needs, compelled him to defy all obstacles to reach his goals. His career was devoted to land and railway schemes, designed in large measure to create a strong and dynamic Canada, an independent northern nation prospering on abundant natural resources. He wanted to play a prominent part in Canada's strategy to stimulate the economic growth of the Northwest. Despite frequent illness and financial problems, he overcame the disappointments of the floundering steamboats and recalcitrant partners to construct a railway built, first of all, to provide dependable transportation for his coal, but also to aid the settlement of western Canada and to develop its great wealth for the benefit of the nation. As one of the architects of Canada's national policies, Galt saw his Coal Banks project, however small, as an essential contribution to Canada's quest for a dominion from sea to sea.

This altruistic dream was undeniably tempered by a large dose of pragmatic self-interest. A strong desire for profit was always present in Galt's thoughts. The Coal Banks enterprise was devised to a large extent to extricate him from his financial difficulties. The short-range need for cash and the dreadful fear of imminent bankruptcy inspired the ill-conceived steamboat venture with its large losses, wasted efforts, and squandered materials. Likewise, Galt wrung every possible concession from the federal government, relying upon his many influential friends within the administration. Indeed, without a willing government, eager to minimize regulations and generously support private enterprise, Galt's scheme would have been delayed at least for several more years.

The pragmatist and visionary worked hand in hand to make Galt above all an agent of change. As high commissioner in the placid sluggish realm of diplomacy, he could not implement a massive transplant of immigrants; but, in the seething world of finance, with its restless gambling spirit, he vigorously attacked the challenge of utilizing Canada's natural resources. While often discouraged by unfavourable turns in events, he nevertheless felt at home in a transitory environment. His ambition was to reconstruct and civilize what he thought was a bleak and unproductive wilderness. As entrepreneur, Galt was in fact a technician of finance whose essence was to innovate and to introduce growth and expansion. His enthusiastic determination injected life into an economically stagnant region; and, at the same time his stubborn optimism brought an end to an old and simple way of life. The railway that he built symbolized the beginning of a new and technological society: the hissing, clangorous locomotive replaced the squealing bull-train; technology and the ethos of progress arrived with the railway.

6

The ties that bind

The change was drastic and swift. The tools provided by the latest technology enabled men to alter their environment more quickly and profoundly than ever before. Where just months ago the tan-yellow grasses swept without interruption toward the horizon, dense clouds of white smoke, spewing from colliery stacks and locomotives, broke the clear blue sky. A new town, Lethbridge, had sprung up on the grassy plateau that overlooked the wide valley of the Belly River. To keep pace with the rapid influx of miners, railroaders, merchants, and their families, more than two hundred buildings, ranging from small shanties to large ware-houses, had sprung up south of the railway tracks. Lethbridge buzzed with intense excitement. Merchants of all descriptions conducted a lively trade from their hastily constructed offices and stores. Several ramshackle hotels, bunkhouses, and boarding places furnished lodging; a few billiard rooms provided entertainment; and half a dozen saloons openly dispensed illegal liquor. Thrice weekly a stage-coach carried people to Fort Macleod, and every day a passenger train whisked persons to their connection with the CPR. The town even boasted a newspaper, the *News*, which enthusiastically called for schools and churches to serve a population that undoubtedly would double within the year.[1]

The nucleus of the town was the railway station and the coal-mine. At the side of the bluff on the bottom lands of the Belly River, miners burrowed ever deeper into the river bank to extract the coal that made it all possible. The colliery complex included engine- and hoisting-houses, machine and repair shops, offices for the storekeeper and superintendents, as well as an assortment of decrepit shanties. The company also operated a ferry service across the river and a sawmill, which had been hauled in from the Porcupine Hills. A ceaseless line of grimy coal-cars lumbered up the inclined railway, then rumbled onto a wooden trestle, and dumped their dusty black loads into waiting railway cars. From nearby came the metallic sounds of the maintenance shops and the noise of bellowing cattle corralled in the stockyards awaiting shipment eastward. In front of the station, on the town square, swearing teamsters loaded bull-trains for outlying points. An exciting surge of prosperity and progress radiated from the station-colliery complex and stimulated the entire community.[2]

If the station-colliery was the settlement's nucleus, the railway functioned as its umbilical cord. Six locomotives and more than a hundred railway cars maintained the lifeline between Lethbridge and the CPR main line at Dunmore. The trains not only imported the necessities of life—clothing, tools, hardware, and food—but they also exported the coal that paid for these essentials. If this vital artery were cut, the colliery would slowly grind to a halt and Lethbridge would die. The narrow gauge line, therefore, was a costly but indispensable part of the NWC&NCo's corporate structure, absolutely fundamental to town and company. In addition to the tracks and rolling stock, the company had built stations and maintenance shops at Woodpecker, Grassy Lake, and Winnifred, as well as an expensive inclined trestle of wood, running parallel to the CPR tracks at Dunmore, with eight coal-shutes to facilitate the trans-shipment process. Coal could also be stored at Dunmore in ten holding bins containing one hundred tons each. By the end of 1885 the company had spent nearly seven hundred thousand dollars on the railway facilities alone; the shareholders were expecting dividends.[3]

By mid-November, after only eleven weeks of operation, these expectations seemed to be met. Total earnings for the railway during this period were $16,000 for ordinary and $23,000 for coal traffic, while its average running expenses were only $1,500 per week and interest on its bonds an additional $1,000 per week.[4] Thus the road had earned a profit of $11,500 or an average

In the late 1880s the NWC&NCo used this inclined
railway to haul coal from the river valley to the plateau
above. (Glenbow Archives)

NWC&NCo miners, wearing uncharacteristic headgear,
ride the inclined railway. (Glenbow Archives)

of over $1,000 per week. The initial success of the railway was reflected in the value of its shares; the company was beseiged with about £30,000 worth of offers for only £22,000 in outstanding shares. As a result Galt planned to increase capitalization to £150,000 in order to permit further expansion in operations.[5]

Beneath the bright flush of triumph, however, some serious disappointments emerged. The CPR, which used Galt coal extensively on its prairie run, temporarily closed off the mountain section and so dramatically cut consumption. To aggravate the problem, a spell of mild mid-winter weather also reduced domestic use. The slump in sales hit the NWC&NCo so badly that Elliott Galt even asked the CPR to pay cash for its coal purchases even though they had a large credit for freighting the Dunmore railway equipment. He should have known better: Van Horne gave short shrift to the request and added sarcastically that, as soon as the freight credit was used up, "you ought very soon to be gorged with money and be able to help us over a shoal place now and then."[6] Not until the return of cold weather and an increase in CPR traffic did production recover to an average of 200 and a high of 300 tons per day. The resurgence was only temporary, however, because in mid-March the Pennsylvania coal producers drastically slashed their prices. The CPR immediately informed Galt that unless he too reduced his prices they would buy only American coal. Galt was stunned because his colliery could not survive without the CPR contract. The only way to meet the CPR's ultimatum was to cut his prices by half to $2.50 per ton and at the same time increase the output of the mines.

Both Galts worked feverishly to ward off the menace of American competition. Elliott rushed off to Pennsylvania to buy several coal-cutting machines. Although expensive, the modern compressed air machines, highly suitable for Lethbridge's level seams, promised to reduce wastage greatly and substantially increase production.[7] Meanwhile, the elder Galt was utterly ruthless to the men who cut and hauled the coal. He instructed his mine manager, William Stafford, to stockpile as much coal as possible at Dunmore and then close the colliery and discharge all the miners. Stafford was to give all the unmarried workers tickets to Dunmore and gradually rehire the married men with families at a seventy-five percent reduction in wages. "Don't hurry to engage the men," Galt cautioned Stafford, "we can afford to make good terms."[8] Drastic action was necessary, he told the manager, because "the coal must be produced as cheaply as possible in order to enable us to exclude American soft coal from the market." Still, Galt's lack of compassion caused considerable hardship and the local press complained about the many vagrants in the area looking for work.[9] The incident clearly showed that Galt considered himself to be the master of his collieries, able to lay off "obstreperous men"[10] as he pleased. For the community, it was a hard lesson. The people learned that they were totally dependent upon a coal-mine, which was ruled in turn by economic forces over which the mine managers had no control.

By reducing the cost of labour while still increasing productivity, Sir Alexander managed to undercut American coal production. By the end of April he secured a new one-year contract with the CPR in which the railway agreed to use Galt's coal exclusively between Winnipeg and the Rockies. Although the price the CPR was willing to pay had dropped considerably from the 1885 level, Galt, always the optimist, believed the NWC&NCo would earn about fifty cents per ton. Meanwhile he planned to sell coal for domestic use in Winnipeg for $6.50 per ton.[11] Mining resumed only sporadically throughout the summer, but more regularly during the fall, so that by December 1886, three trains were hauling away 300 tons daily.[12]

The good fortune was short-lived, however. Beginning in the second week of January 1887, a series of vicious snowstorms blanketed the prairies, crippling the railways and cutting the lifeline to Lethbridge. Nature had not yet been conquered. Elliott Galt, on his way to New York early in February, was imprisoned for five days in his own railway car while the train inched its way through fifteen-foot drifts; in one particularly bitter day the crew of thirty men, aided by a snowplow and three locomotives, fought for the entire day in forty-below-zero temperatures and driving winds to move half a mile. The light-weight trains simply could not clear the tracks and the younger Galt cancelled his trip in order to work on the railway. The storms continued through February into March, and the track was not cleared until 20 March when the rapidly melting snows seriously undercut the road-bed and tore out some tracks. On 22 March, for the first time since January, the trip from Lethbridge to Dunmore was made within one day. Seventy-nine days had been lost because of the storms, and little coal was sold. Despite the lack of revenue, Elliott Galt still had to meet the pay-roll and other expenses: he barely managed.[13]

No sooner had the snow melted than Elliott Galt encountered labour difficulties. The miners laid down their tools to back up their demands for higher wages. Since the CPR's coal supplies were dangerously depleted and the NWC&NCo's cash reserves uncomfortably low, neither company could afford a work stoppage and so Galt settled quickly. Encouraged by their success, the miners repeated their action two months later in June, but this time they miscalculated. The coal shortage had eased and the company could afford to wait. Elliott closed the mine for two weeks and imported a crew of miners from eastern Canada and Ohio. The workers tried to prevent the strike-breakers from entering the mine, but a detachment of mounted police rushed in from Fort Macleod, guarded the company's properties, and prevented any outbreak of violence.[14] While the *Lethbridge News* made little comment on the strike, the *Fort Macleod Gazette* applauded the company's action, reflecting the prevailing attitude that the owner and not the miners' union was the proprietor of the colliery, and that Elliott Galt had justifiably thwarted the "tyranny" of the workers and rightfully refused their "unreasonable" demands.[15]

In two years, the utter dependence of the region upon the NWC&NCo was revealed. During the snowstorms the community of Lethbridge and Fort Macleod experienced shortages of essentials; by February, Fort Macleod was out of coal and feed, and other supplies arrived only sporadically.[16] The effect upon Lethbridge was even more devastating because the settlement's entire economy depended upon the company's pay-roll. Whenever the demand for coal fell, the colliery was closed and the miners were summarily dismissed. These massive layoffs, even if temporary, caused great duress as lines of credit between miners and local merchants, and those of retailers with out-of-town wholesalers, stretched dangerously to the limit. The town's spirit of subserviency was clearly illustrated in the deferential editorials occasionally published by the *Lethbridge News*. One such article uncritically applauded the company's efforts in Lethbridge:

The money which they have put in the development of this western country, and their enterprise has in this way been a benefit to everyone here. Liberal in all their dealings, and displaying none of that selfishness which is generally characteristic of large companies, they merit the confidence and good will of the people of the district, and this they enjoy to the fullest extent.[17]

The first two seasons of operations demonstrated to the Galts that the market for their coal was too small. For a few months in the early winter the colliery reached top production but in the summertime, when few people thought of ordering and stocking coal for the winter, the output was minimal. Dr. Alfred Selwyn, the director of the Geological Survey of Canada, stated that while Lethbridge had good coal, "The population of the country is so scattered ... at present and the means of transportation so costly and difficult, that were it not for the C. P. R., which uses immense quantities, the company could not afford to work the mines."[18] Unfortunately, the CPR was not an "immense" consumer of coal because a small population also meant limited traffic, especially in the far West where the bulk of Galt coal was burned. C. A. Magrath, the land agent for the NWC&NCo, outlined the problem more explicitly than Selwyn:

Lethbridge in the earlier days depended entirely on the Company's coal and railway pay sheets. The construction of the Canadian Pacific Railway had not brought to the west the anticipated prosperity. Our coal miners were busily employed for a couple of months in the winter only; in the summer it was a matter of a couple of days work weekly.[19]

The flood of settlers so confidently expected in the heyday of early CPR construction had not materialized and the NWC&NCo suffered for lack of a market. The annual report for 1886–87 revealed a loss on operations of £4,173.[20] After two years of production the company was not selling enough coal to pay for its large investments. Once again Sir Alexander had to seek a solution in expansion. As he had found so often before, survival in business required constant growth and enlargement.

To make the colliery a profitable operation, Galt had to break out of the confines of the small western Canadian market. As early as the beginning of 1885 he conceived of a plan to build a railway from Lethbridge to Fort Benton, Montana, at $7,000 a mile. The price was relatively high because the line would have to cross two wide rivers, but Galt believed that the expense could easily be recovered because the railroad would carry his coal to the smelters of Montana. He could also transport American cattle to the CPR. The feasibility of the project was confirmed by William Barclay, the CPR engineer, who made a preliminary survey of the route.[21] It was a bold plan, but it would launch Galt into another four years of frustration and disappointment.

Initially Galt was very successful and enthusiastic. He enjoyed the game of railway promotion and by the end of 1885 he had created the financial structure for the scheme. Using the pattern of his earlier international enterprise, the Montreal to Portland railway, Galt envisioned a new Canadian corporation, in no way associated with the NWC&NCo, to build the Alberta portion of the railroad. The principal backer was Sir David L. Macpherson, a former associate and close friend of Galt and, at that time, minister of the interior.[22] Another former business partner to become involved was Walter Shanly, member of parliament, a noted railway engineer and former manager of the Grand Trunk Railway. Galt also attracted an expatriate Canadian living in New York, Sir Roderick Cameron, whose wealth was based on a prosperous shipping firm of packets sailing to London and Australia. Cameron also had extensive land holdings in the Lethbridge region. Lastly Galt won over his brother-in-law, William M. Ramsay, a director of the NWC&NCo, the Intercolonial Railway, Molson's Bank, and the manager of the Canada Standard Life Assurance Company.[23] Once again Galt had gathered together an impressive group of investors to provide financial prestige and stability for the endeavour.

For the American part of the railway, Galt found an equally powerful group of financiers from the United States. The leader of the group was William G. Conrad, a very wealthy and powerful Fort Benton merchant, who had bought out George Baker's share in the thriving I. G. Baker firm in the early 1870s. Conrad became the dynamic personality in the Baker company and under his

The bottom of the NWC&NCo's inclined railway, the rails curving from the left to the mine mouth on the right. (Provincial Archives of Alberta)

shrewd leadership the firm expanded so rapidly that by 1878 it handled 2.5 million dollars of merchandise. Conrad's competitor and friend, Thomas C. Power, also became involved in the Canadian railway. Power had arrived in Fort Benton in the summer of 1867 fully qualified to revitalize the decayed commercial empire of the American Trading Company. As early as 1875 he had recognized that a fuel-starved Montana could pay for the empty bulltrains heading southward from Fort Macleod to Fort Benton; he bought coal at Nicholas Sheran's mine for five dollars and sold it in Montana for twenty-five dollars a ton. Power was a leading figure in the Republican party and eventually became a senator. These two men, Power and Conrad, virtually controlled Fort Benton's economic hinterland, and their profits from the fur and Indian trade, associated wagon and boat cartage endeavours, and fat government contracts, were channelled into mining and milling, retailing and merchandizing, as well as banking. Aided by Conrad's Democratic connections, the two men received government contracts from both parties; their influence even extended to the Canadian government, which gave them large contracts to supply the North West Mounted Police and other government agencies. With the completion of the CPR to Medicine Hat in 1883, their freighting business collapsed and the pair lost their financial control over the southwestern Canadian territories; Power sold his interests to the Hudson's Bay Company, but the I. G. Baker stores continued to operate in Canada. William Conrad was especially pleased to support the proposed railway because a mountain range separated the most northerly American transcontinental, the Northern Pacific, from Fort Benton.[24] He and other merchants naturally looked northward for a supply and trade outlet; they listened eagerly as Galt unfolded his plans for a railway to replace the obsolete Whoop-Up Trail; and quickly seized the opportunity to re-establish their commercial ties with the developing Canadian Northwest.

Behind these two Montana men stood the ambitious Samuel T. Hauser, president of the First National Bank of Helena. Hauser, who later became governor of Montana, had earned his wealth during the early gold rush days in California and Montana. In 1879 he backed Power and Conrad to establish the Benton National Bank, whose profitable financial network at one time furnished the funds for the dominion government's activities in western Canada. Hauser had financial contacts in New York and Montreal as well as Europe, and was involved with the Northern Pacific Railroad. In fact, he was interested in Galt's proposal because the Northern Pacific, which kept a vigilant eye on the western Canadian coalfields, was not permitted to build branch lines. Hauser planned to circumvent this regulation by building Galt's railroad as an independent company and gain the traffic of the Canadian prairies and Pacific coast for the Northern Pacific Railroad.[25]

The association with the Northern Pacific was the fatal flaw in Galt's proposal. George Stephen of the CPR, always watchful of his arch-rival, quickly killed the Montana project. He had undertaken the very expensive rail line north of Lake Superior on the condition that no competing firm be permitted to build a branch line south of the CPR main line unless it ran in a west of southwesterly direction and did not come within thirty miles of the United States border. The Dunmore to Lethbridge railway had been permitted because it ran straight west and did not come within thirty miles of the boundary; the Montana scheme obviously violated the monopoly clause. Nevertheless, Galt argued that because the Dunmore-Lethbridge-Fort Benton system first went one hundred miles west before dipping south into the United States, it would never drain CPR traffic to the Northern Pacific but would instead feed cargo into the Canadian system. In other words, Galt wanted to reverse the old Whoop-Up Trail and make Montana an economic colony of Lethbridge and central Canada. Once again, Galt saw matters in the broadest possible perspective, and he was so confident of his argument that he even asked George Stephen to invest in the project. It was a foolish request. Stephen's fear of a rival branch line to the United States bordered on paranoia, and he brusquely refused to join the scheme.

Galt's plan also ran afoul of the aggressive ambition of another enemy of the Northern Pacific—J. J. Hill of the St. Paul, Minneapolis and Manitoba Railroad. That ebullient railway magnate was casting a covetous eye on the rich natural resources of the northern reaches of Montana. Ever since Hill had built a fortune as a coal dealer in the St. Paul region, he had cultivated a keen interest in coal resources. For Montana he envisioned a conglomerate scheme of coal-mines, high-grade metallic ores, hydro-electric power, and railways. To put it all together, he created the Montana Central Railroad as a connector between Great Falls and Butte, Montana. Sometime in the future he planned to extend his Manitoba railway to Great Falls and tap the wealth of Montana. He could not afford to tarry, however, as the Northern Pacific threatened to move into the Butte area from the south, and Galt loomed in the north. Galt could be disarmed rather easily. A note to a close friend and business ally, George Stephen, settled the matter. In his reply Stephen assured the worried Hill that the CPR monopoly clause would kill Galt's charter, and that if anyone were to build to Montana, it would be the CPR.[26]

Galt's proposal, therefore, antagonized too many rival interests. In May 1886 the Canadian government withdrew Galt's bid for a charter from the legislature.[27] Without CPR approval, the Macdonald administration would not consider Galt's proposal and without Stephen's support, Galt did not have the political clout to force the issue. He could not even appeal to the Liberal opposition because he dared not antagonize his largest customer by far, the CPR.

The House of Commons, then, did not even consider Galt's railway charter, but did make him a pawn in an acrimonious political debate. Early in May the Liberal party launched an all-out attack on the Conservative government. In a lengthy and angry tirade, John Charlton, the wealthy lumberman from Ontario, denounced several Conservative members for lavishly bestowing upon their friends lucrative timber limits, coal reserves, and ranch leases, as well as generous rail subsidies. When he referred to the coal lands, Charlton charged that some members had obtained valuable coal properties for their friends without any competition and thereby created a coal monopoly in the Northwest. He summarized his argument:

> The policy of the Government with regard to the coal lands of the North-West was not one in the interest of the settler. It was not to the interest of the settler that a coal mining monopoly should be granted, and that the Government should second efforts to take the coal lands of the North-West and put them in a few hands who might monopolize the business of mining and compel the people to pay so much more for their fuel, which is so necessary in a cold climate like that.[28]

Charlton received support from several Liberal members; at one point, James Lister, the representative for West Lambton, shouted that the government "has given away recklessly coal lands, the fuel that ought to be preserved for ourselves and future generations. Not only that, but it has placed its hands in the public Treasury to pay out money to one of the greatest monopolies in the North-West, Sir A. T. Galt's coal monopoly."[29] Probing for any chinks in the government's armour, Charlton and his friends once again dredged up the charge that Galt had received undue government assistance to establish a coal monopoly.

The general allegations of corruption and the implications of gross misconduct were neatly fielded by the new minister of the interior, Thomas White. He carefully listed the basic charges and then coolly dismissed them one by one. He demolished the coal monopoly charge by simply pointing out that the introduction of Galt coal into Winnipeg had dropped the price from seventeen to seven dollars per ton, and that closer to the mine, the price was reduced by a third; therefore, even if the government had favoured the Galt enterprise, the object of providing cheaper fuels for prairie settlers had been attained. White also used the old argument that competitive bidding for Northwest coal leases was unnecessary because of the extensive deposits, and he pointed out that anyone could obtain coal lands under the government's regulations. The quarrel continued into the early morning hours as member after member rose to attack or defend the administration's position. Not until 5:45 A.M. did the House of Commons defeat Charlton's motion for an investigation into the charges of government misconduct. The debate only served to show that while the opposition was growing in strength, the government's stand, based on the abundance of resources and the dearth of developers, was still unassailable.

Although in 1886 Galt was the largest solvent producer of coal in the territories, the Liberal charge of monopoly was not completely justified. To be sure, he had complete control in the vicinity of Lethbridge because he had deliberately set a prohibitively high tariff on his railway to preclude any competitors from shipping coal by way of his railroad.[30] Elsewhere along the CPR, however, any promoter could compete. Several companies did, but by 1887 none were successful. Close to Medicine Hat, for example, the Saskatchewan Coal Mining and Transportation Company developed properties, but succumbed to a plague of labour difficulties and financial problems, and sold its properties to a relatively small group of Toronto investors called the Medicine Hat Railway and Coal Company, which planned to build a railway just southwest of Redcliff.[31] Two townships to the east, the Bow River Coal Mine, Railway, and Transportation Company, a consortium of British, Montreal, and Toronto financiers, announced plans for a short railway from its mine to Medicine Hat.[32] Further west, just outside of Cochrane on the CPR main line, C. W. Moberly, the former CPR surveyor, and his associates spent $14,000 on a shaft that constantly flooded while still further west, near Midford, a Major Vaughan carried out a very small operation.[33] Despite ambitious plans not one of these efforts produced any significant amounts of coal during 1886 and were not likely to do so in the near future.

The real threat to Galt's operation came from Kicking Horse Pass where C. W. Moberly had uncovered the rich anthracite deposits near Banff, the immense value of which was confirmed by George M. Dawson and C. D. Wilber, a Chicago mining expert. In October of 1886, McLeod Stewart, then the mayor of Ottawa, formed the Canadian Anthracite Company to exploit the reserves. Throughout the summer a ninety-man crew drove a tunnel into the mountain to reach the valuable coal, laid out a town-site in the beautiful mountain valley below the mine entrance, erected freight sheds, a spur line to the CPR, and a telephone connection to Banff. The company's prospectus, published in 1885, glowingly promised sales of 250,000 tons of coal per year to the CPR towns along the railway, and to the Pacific naval stations of the British admiralty.[34] Stewart ran into a serious problem, however, when George Stephen refused to sign a large, long-term contract because it was CPR policy to buy its coal as cheaply as possible. Despite the presence of one CPR director, Sandford Fleming, as one of Stewart's associates, the president decided to act in the best interests of the railway. To Stephen this meant buying coal from Galt.

When McLeod Stewart complained to Sir John A. Macdonald about his failure to secure a CPR contract,[35] the prime minister demanded an explanation from George Stephen. In a carefully phrased reply, the railway president tried to justify his policy on ostensibly humanitarian grounds. "Perhaps I ought further to say that, in dealing with Galt, we departed from sound business principles and made a contract with him for five years supply, and upon terms we should never have thought of except that, he being the 'pioneer collier,' we wanted to get the business started. I fear, if we had not done so, it would be a 'cold day' now for the Galt coal mine."[36] Stephen's excuse was pure hogwash. Galt had indeed secured a five-year contract to sell a small monthly amount of coal to the CPR at five dollars per ton, delivered at Dunmore. "Even at that price," wrote Thomas Shaughnessy, the assistant general manager of the CPR, "we were saving very considerably, as all our coal was coming from Port Arthur."[37] Here, indeed, was the key to the coal situation in the Northwest. Stephen was more than willing to support a prairie coal-mine, but only if that colliery would sell its product more cheaply than Pennsylvania anthracite. Although the CPR was a prime beneficiary of the national policies and enjoyed the security of a railway monopoly in western Canada, Stephen refused to pay out an extra dime to foster a native coal industry.

When in March 1886, for example, Pennsylvanians reduced their coal prices, the CPR forced Galt to negotiate a new one-year contract for coal to be delivered at Dunmore at $2.50 a ton, that is, half the very reasonable price they had paid before. In April 1887 the price of American coal rose by thirty-five cents and Shaughnessy immediately ordered 10,000 tons of Galt coal, but only at two dollars a ton. A month later he ordered another 8,000 tons. At the same time, the CPR general manager increased the standing order by nearly 900 tons per month and served notice that his company reserved the right to add occasional orders at any time. Lest Galt think the CPR was loosening its grip, Shaughnessy reminded him that snowstorms were not a valid reason for failure to deliver the coal on schedule.[38]

No other company could match Galt's record. How could the Canadian Anthracite Company, for example, hope to sell its product in Winnipeg for $10.00 while the Americans placed theirs at $8.75 and Galt sold his somewhat inferior coal for $6.75 a ton?[39] Galt's mine only survived the cutthroat competition because he used coal-cutting machines, reduced his labour force, and slashed the wages of the remaining miners by seventy-five percent. He drove the Americans out of the region east of Winnipeg by selling his coal at break-even prices. In fact, the NWC&NCo lost £4,000 in 1887.[40] Unfortunately, with these tactics Galt also killed all western Canadian competition. No one could duplicate his extremely efficient operation, but more importantly, no one had his financial resources. Even if his coal-mine and railway did not earn any profits, Galt could always assuage worried investors by pointing to the potential earnings of the land grant. No other western Canadian coal-mine operator enjoyed this great advantage and therefore none could compete as effectively as the Lethbridge colliery.

In sum, the basis of the western coal problem was that the CPR, in its relentless search for the cheapest possible supply of fuel, took advantage of the geographical isolation of western Canada to drive down coal prices. The transcontinental railway, so heavily subsidized by the Canadian people, placed profits above national interests and dictated what it wanted to pay. In this cold-blooded quest, it deliberately stifled the growth of a vigorous, competitive coal industry in western Canada. The principal bene-ficiaries of this ruthless policy were the shareholders of the CPR; its chief victims were the coal-miners grubbing in the dark wet mines for less than fair wages.

In this way, Sir Alexander Galt, who was an architect of this heartless system, had become hopelessly ensnared in the intricate web of financial techniques. To his mind, the only escape from the CPR stranglehold was expansion to Montana. And so, at the NWC&NCo's 1887 annual meeting held in London, Galt first apologized for the previous year's weak performance but then pleaded with the directors for still more money for the enterprise. With consummate skill he spoke of even more land grants, of a huge coal-mining complex as the basis for a large industrial metropolis. Let them consider the potential value of the lots they held in that yet undeveloped city. Would failure to act at this instance not mean a loss of all this wealth? More directly to the point, however, Galt reasoned that the NWC&NCo could only earn substantial profits if it destroyed the consumer monopoly held by the CPR. The logic of Galt's argument could not be denied and the directors agreed to back the Montana railway.

Early in the summer of 1887 Galt once again applied for a charter to build a railway to the United States. Not unexpectedly, Stephen fought the move. Not only did he distrust a precedent-setting breach in the monopoly, but he also feared that Galt, with an alternative market at his disposal, would force the CPR to pay higher fuel prices. As a result, in June the government withdrew the legislation.[41] The CPR had once again withstood the attack on its monopoly. It would not be able to do so much longer, however, because Galt's Montana scheme was but one example of the rapidly mounting political and economic pressures in western Canada for repeal of the monopoly clause.

The recurring withdrawals of Galt's railway charter angered many westerners and they loudly voiced their discontent, adding these actions to their long list of grievances against the CPR. The *Fort Macleod Gazette* was typical of the growing resentment in the Northwest against the CPR monopoly. The editor sharply re-buked the CPR, which was heavily subsidized with western lands,

for charging exorbitant freight rates that enriched eastern capitalists but choked western economic growth. The NWC&NCo
was a good example of this discriminatory policy, he charged,
because the company could not increase production without a
railway to Montana. For the colliery to survive, the government
had to repeal the monopoly clause and permit the rail connection
to the United States, which was so vital to western Canadian
development. The *Gazette* went even a step further and suggested a
removal of all tariffs between Canada and the United States. Such
a policy would greatly benefit southern Alberta and the
NWC&NCo, which could then compete with American coal unhindered by high tariffs and monopolistic freight rates.[42] The Fort
Macleod newspaper had adopted the Liberal party's platform of
commercial union with the United States, a policy gaining favour
in the Northwest but radically opposed to the Conservatives'
national policies.

The position of the *Lethbridge News* was more complex than
that of the *Gazette*; the tone of the *News* was therefore more muted.
Lethbridge was Sir Alexander's town and Galt had always been a
strong defender of the National Policy. While the newspaper conceded that the CPR monopoly and high American tariffs shut
Galt's coal out of the Montana market, it voiced the opinion that
commercial union was not the panacea for the economic ills of
western Canada. Closer economic ties, the Lethbridge editor
asserted, would eventually make Canada an economic adjunct of
its much larger neighbour; it would destroy the imperial connection. "With commercial union in force, and unrestricted railway
connections with the United States, it is certain that our Northwest merchants would purchase a large if not the largest portion
of their stock from St. Paul, Chicago, and other American wholesale cities."[43] Put in emotional and patriotic terms, the removal of
tariffs between Canada and the United States was unacceptable to
the nationalistic and imperialistic sentiments of the *News*; placed in
pragmatic and economic perspective, however, a rail connection
with Montana was essential to the vitality of the NWC&NCo and
Lethbridge. Reflecting Galt's personal situation, the *News* recon-
ciled these two opposing concepts in a self-centred and rather
tortured way: only the Montana railway should be exempt from
the monopoly clause but the tariff structure must remain intact.

Since Montana suffered from chronic fuel shortages, Galt could compete with American coal producers despite high tariffs. In this very restricted sense, Lethbridge could remain within the national economic context of the Canadian imperial system because Montana would become the hinterland of Lethbridge. Galt's project, according to the *News*, would not disrupt the east-west pattern of Canada's economic nationalism, but retain the strong financial and emotional ties with Montreal and London.[44] In this way, the *Lethbridge News* echoed Galt's justification of the link to Montana while still adhering to the principles of Macdonald's national policies.

The heated discussion between the *Gazette* and the *News* echoed a national debate. Many westerners heartily endorsed any attack upon the transcontinental railway, and Manitobans in particular pressured their government to break the CPR stronghold over the western economy. The Manitoba government, buckling under this pressure, approved a rash of railway charters that deliberately violated the monopoly clause, while the federal government, motivated by a desire to maintain national economic unity, promptly disallowed them. Sectional interests triumphed, however, because Premier Norquay, besieged by farmers wanting low competitive freight rates and weakened by a recent provincial election, resolved to build the Red River Valley Railway to link Winnipeg with the Northern Pacific as a public work. A hail of legal injunctions by the CPR, a lack of interest among British and American investors, and a political scandal upset the plan, but Norquay had made his point. The tide of anti-CPR feeling would not be turned, especially in the fall of 1887 when, after several years of crop failures, the prairies grew a bumper crop too large for the CPR to transport. The federal government, weary of the continual struggles with Manitoba and very concerned about the grain blockade, relented and offered the CPR compensation for the loss of the monopoly. After a set of lengthy and complex negotiations, the three parties agreed to repeal the monopoly clause.[45] Branch line construction to the south could begin.

Galt's reaction to the expected repeal of the monopoly clause was immediate, and on 27 March 1888, Donald W. Davis, the member for Alberta, reintroduced a bill to incorporate the Alberta Railway and Coal Company of which he was a director. The company proposed to build a railway from Calgary through Lethbridge to the international border where it was to meet an American line running to Butte, Montana.[46] Galt was so confident that the bill would pass that he withdrew all the town lots from sale in anticipation of the impending land boom in Lethbridge.[47] The wait was longer than he had expected; in May the bill was withdrawn for the third time.[48]

This time the opposition demurred and demanded to know why these railway bills kept appearing and disappearing. In reply, Sir Hector Langevin explained that the Senate had tacked a number of amendments to the CPR legislation and returned it to the House of Commons. Since parliament was scheduled to prorogue in a few days, there was not enough time to repeal the monopoly clause; therefore the branch line charters could not be passed this session. This facile answer angered John H. Wilson of the Elgin constituency because the CPR monopoly would choke western economic growth for yet another year. He also demanded to know if the backers of the Alberta Railway and Coal Company could be patient and retain their interest in the project until the next session.[49]

The same question was also on Galt's mind. In order to retain the support of his financial backers, he asked Prime Minister Macdonald to seek an order-in-council approving the railway charter as well as the seemingly automatic land subsidy. Galt argued that this irregular procedure was justified on the grounds that the third postponement of the railway legislation jeopardized the negotiations for the financial arrangements as well as the proposed merger of the Alberta Railway and Coal Company and the NWC&NCo.[50] Macdonald granted Galt's request and he instructed Edgar Dewdney, the minister of the interior, to seek cabinet approval-in-principle of the railway charter and its land grant.[51] Cabinet concurred and committed the government to subsidize the Montana railway with 6,400 acres per mile and free titles to the right of way and station sites. As soon as the company widened the Dunmore section to standard gauge, it would receive an additional 2,560 acres per mile for that railroad.[52] Provided parliament agreed, the second land subsidy would nearly double the land holdings of the NWC&NCo and transform it into a large colonization company.

Parliament agreed to co-operate, but not without dissent. On 8 February 1889, when Walter Shanly, a director of the proposed Alberta Railway and Coal Company (AR&CCo), introduced the legislation to authorize the Montana railway charter and land grant, he encountered bitter opposition. James Trow of South Perth led off the attack by accusing the government of subsidizing a coal monopoly in western Canada. He charged that while it cost the NWC&NCo four dollars a ton to mine coal and deliver it to Calgary, the company extorted eight dollars a ton from consumers there. He went on to complain that in Winnipeg, which was so much farther away from Lethbridge than Calgary, the same price prevailed. Obviously, monopolistic conditions had created artificially high prices all along the CPR tracks. Robert Watson of Marquette also took up the theme of high prices. He observed that the company was taking undue advantage of government concessions because it earned about four dollars in Calgary and two dollars in Winnipeg for every ton of coal sold. In the latter city alone, Watson calculated, Galt sold at least twenty thousand tons of coal yearly and thus realized tremendous profits. "There is no doubt it is of immense importance that we should have cheap coal in Manitoba and the North-West, and that cheap coal we cannot have so long as there is a coal monopoly," Watson thundered, "and there is a practical monopoly existing today because the Galt Coal Company have the only railway that can carry coal from the mines where good coal is turned out, to the line of the Canadian Pacific Railway."[53] He suggested an amendment to the bill, which would empower the government to control the freight rates for coal on the Galt railways. "The principal traffic on the railroad is and will be coal," he correctly pointed out, "and while I do not object to the Government giving a land grant to aid in developing the coal-mines, I contend that they should limit the company to charging a certain rate on the coal."[54] According to Watson, then, the Canadian public had built a railway largely for the benefit of the company, hence the government had the right to set the tariffs on the road. Or, as his colleague and ardent free-trader Sir Richard Cartwright put it, the Galt collieries were subsidized, therefore the free enterprise tenets of supply and demand no longer applied and government control of coal prices was legitimate. In other words, the opposition believed that subsidies should benefit the public as well as the companies; no corporation, which had been assisted by the dominion government to exploit the public natural resources, should be permitted to charge all that the traffic could bear.

Criticism also came from the government benches. Nicholas F. Davin, the Conservative member for Assiniboia-West, presented the most cogent argument against the NWC&NCo and the policies of his colleagues. He felt that Galt's company definitely had a monopoly on the coal supply in the Northwest. "I am sorry to say I cannot agree with my hon. friend [Shanly] that the Galt Mine has solved the fuel question in the North-West," he said. "The fuel question in the North-West cannot be said to be solved when, in the capital of the North-West, the lowest price charged for soft coal is $8.50 a ton."[55] He continued by pointing out that 400 miles farther from the mine, at Winnipeg, the coal cost only eight dollars, and he angrily charged that "[the Galts] will put on the very last cent that they can put on . . . and when you pay $9 for soft coal and $13 for hard coal, you are burning gold, and you cannot be said to have solved the fuel question." The problem according to Davin was much more serious than simply the coal monopoly, and in emotional words he incisively criticized the government for favouring eastern Canadian and foreign businessmen rather than local western developers:

Our system has been to skim the cream and let it go into the pockets of the Canadian capitalist, or the English capitalist, or the Scotch capitalist, as the case may be. Our system has been not to strengthen the young territory, to coax it into vigor and leave it what native energy and physical resources might properly belong to it; on the contrary, we have taken away the strength that should be there, the milk that should have been there to nourish it, and then we have left it to fight the battle of life and struggle into existence as best it could. What is the result? The result is that we find rich men, rich companies, have hold of the North-West here and there, they have in fact, pecked the eyes, to some extent, out of the North-West. We find the country full of interests of persons hundreds of thousands of miles away from the country; and when you come to a town like Regina, or any other town along the line of railway, you find a lot of struggling men, whereas, if you had pursued the system you ought to have pursued, of allowing the wealth of the country to remain in the country, while it was young, you would have in all those places at the present moment rich men to help them forward, and you would have had the profits of their early enterprise helping to build the country up.

Davin concluded by stressing the short-sightedness of Canada's railway policy and argued that the territorial assembly with its local insight into peculiar western problems should control the disposition of the natural resources of the Northwest. While Davin heartily endorsed the concept of western development, he had perhaps unwittingly laid bare the fundamental problem—to what extent should the government subsidize private enterprise to utilize the resources and realize maximum benefits for the people, and at the same time ensure attractive profits for the companies?

The government, of course, was still committed to a policy that encouraged, by means of subsidies and minimal regulations, the construction of railways in undeveloped areas. In defense of Galt's bill, Shanly deftly evaded the issue of the coal monopoly by confessing he had never heard any complaints of exorbitant prices. In any case, so he stated, the price of coal was irrelevant to this particular bill because not the NWC&NCo but the CPR set the freight rates, and the coal agents set the price of fuel. Shanly also cleverly played upon the general abhorrence of government price controls in the then prevailing free enterprise philosophy by asserting that the colliery and railway were one and the same corporation; parliament, therefore, might as well fix the price of coal as set the freight rates. Lastly, Shanly vigorously defended the land subsidy policy because of high construction costs in the isolated Northwest. In the case of the Galt company the grant was well deserved because that concern was successful in attracting money to the Northwest:

There is no other instance in the North-West Territories so forcible of what capital can do as is there presented [in Lethbridge]. An enormous capital has been there expended by this company, every dollar of which has come from abroad; the lands already sold have not diminished that capital burden to the extent of five cents in the dollar.[56]

Other government members helped Shanly justify the land grant. Thomas Daly, the member for Selkirk, explained that high coal prices were caused by several reverses, like the snowstorms the company had suffered in the past, but he was confident that the widening of the Dunmore line would reduce the high price of coal. The most stirring appeal came from Peter White, the future speaker of the House, who expressed the preoccupation of the government with western development and its urgent desire to attract investment dollars:

> I have had the opportunity of visiting the coal mines of the Alberta Coal Mining Company [actually the NWC&NCo], and of passing over the railway they have built from Dunmore to Lethbridge. Any gentleman who has visited that locality and has given attention to the large amount of money that that company has expended in the construction of that road, which runs through a country that is almost totally uninhabited, and which has no trade except what is derived from the carriage of coal, anyone who looks at the large amount of capital that has been expended in developing the coal mines at Lethbridge, and who had knowledge of all the circumstances in connection with the opening of those coal mines and the difficulties the gentlemen engaged in that enterprise have had to encounter, would not deny them the privilege of obtaining a larger market such as they are likely to get under the operation of this Bill now before the committee.[57]

All the speakers, most of whom were businessmen, echoed the popular sentiments of the day. In the last decades of the nineteenth century, men exalted the technology that enabled them to so rapidly exploit the natural resources for the sake of material prosperity. Even Nicholas Davin, while he deplored the coal monopoly, was forced to admit that Galt's endeavour was beneficial to the region. In very laudatory terms he acknowledged the utility of the NWC&NCo to the Northwest:

> Anyone who visits Lethbridge will see that the Galt Company has been a great blessing to it, and to the North-West generally. The growth of that town and the population which the Galt Company has brought in, and the general rush forward which that Company has given to that territory, must make every North-West man feel grateful to the Galt Company for what it has done.[58]

In sum, all members of parliament endorsed the development of the Northwest; they only disagreed on the size of the subsidies to particular companies. While the Liberals distrusted Galt as the only effective supplier of coal in the Northwest, the Conservatives were happy to grant him generous concessions. In March of 1889 parliament approved Galt's railway charter and land grant.

Although none of the legislators really understood the western Canadian coal situation, their accusations of a coal monopoly had considerable foundation. By the spring of 1889 Galt was still the largest producer of coal in the Northwest. Near Medicine Hat, for instance, several mining companies were still struggling to organize profitable establishments. The Medicine Hat Railway and Coal Company, southwest of Redcliff, had stopped production in 1887 because of financial problems and subsequent litigation. While its promoters reincorporated themselves a second time and planned to work the south rather than the north bank of the Saskatchewan, further legal complications thwarted the project and the properties were sold to a small company which planned to supply only the local market. Also on the south side of the river, the Medicine Hat Coal and Mining Company had sunk a shaft but marketed no coal until it could finance a branch line to the CPR, a dubious prospect because of the poor quality of lignite in the Medicine Hat area. Further west along the CPR line other futile attempts were made to mine coal. The Moberly mine near Cochrane was abandoned because of flooding, while the Vaughan mine near Midford was deserted because wasteful mining techniques had caused ruin. In 1887 T. B. Cochrane opened the Bow River

Mine nearby and installed a coke oven, but he too halted production within two years owing to lack of capital. He was unable to float a five-hundred-thousand-dollar bond issue in Great Britain to properly develop the colliery.[59]

Similar financial difficulties hampered the Canadian Anthracite Company. Throughout the winter and spring of 1887 Galt's chief rival for the CPR coal contract, McLeod Stewart, spent large sums of money to raise mine production to 500 tons a day; the company employed over a hundred miners to blast a 300-foot tunnel into the mountainside to reach the valuable anthracite. Since Stewart could not compete against Galt on the prairies, he concentrated instead on the traditional markets of the Vancouver Island collieries. In the fall of 1887 he made several large trial shipments of coal via Vancouver to San Francisco.[60] Government officials were ecstatic about this wedge into the American fuel market and William Pearce, the inspector of mines, wrote in typical western style that this vigorous company would soon be shipping "an incredible amount" of coal from the "almost unlimited supply of anthracite of first class quality."[61] The exuberance was ill-founded, however, because in July 1888 the colliery suddenly ground to a halt; the company summarily dismissed 200 miners and retained only a skeleton crew to continue the work of exploration and development.[62]

Unlike the other coal-mines, that of McLeod Stewart was not a small operation. Among his associates were such prominent men as Sandford Fleming of the CPR and W. B. Scarth of the Canadian North West Land Company. Nevertheless, the firm ran out of capital and Stewart sought in vain for new investors. His failure to attract more capital was endemic to the western Canadian coal-mining industry. With the high overhead cost of mining the very faulted coal-seams of the Rocky Mountains, Stewart could not compete with the artificially low prices of the Lethbridge collieries. In the first quarter of 1888, for example, Galt was selling more than 4,000 tons of coal per month to the CPR at an average price of $2.75 a ton delivered at Dunmore.[63] Stewart could not place a ton with the transcontinental and his prospects were dim. As long as the CPR strictly maintained its businesslike policy of buying fuel as cheaply as possible, no one, apart from Galt, could develop Alberta's coal-seams.

By 1889, therefore, Galt had created a coal monopoly west of Winnipeg simply by ruthlessly slashing his prices in order to secure the CPR prairie coal contract. Lower production costs were part of his success but so was the existence of the Lethbridge-Dunmore railway. Galt could offset the losses on coal sales with revenues from the transport of supplies and coal. Moreover, he could use the railway's large land grant as an enticement to investors. As a result, he was able to construct a well-financed and efficient coal-mining operation that drove the Americans out of the western Canadian market. However, Galt's ability to meet the stringent demands of the CPR also greatly retarded the birth of a viable and competitive coal industry in the Northwest.

The generous land concessions and the virtual coal monopoly in the western fuel market did not produce instant wealth for Galt, nor did it bring him peace in his old age. To become a lucrative investment, the colliery had to escape total dependence upon the CPR. Galt still had to build a railway to Montana, but in his search for funds he encountered only frustration. In March 1889 he travelled to New York to issue the stocks for the Montana company, but the market, perhaps upset by the Boulanger crisis in France, failed to absorb the new securities.[64] Two months later he tried to float the bonds for the Canadian section and, to bolster his position, he asked the government to increase the land grant to ten thousand acres per mile.[65] It was to no avail and by June when Sir Alexander and Elliott left for the annual meeting of the NWC&NCo in London, few sales of stocks and bonds had been made. The depressive economic conditions, which had plagued him during the Dunmore negotiations, had not yet lifted and investors were still reluctant to place their money in North American railways. Galt had planned to build the road completely separate from the corporate structure of the NWC&NCo but eventually the lack of capital forced him to return to his London associates.

For ten years the aging Galt had fought for his western dream, which appeared to be slipping away from him. This year the confrontation with the directors was especially bitter because they were completely hostile to Galt's expansion plans; they were unwilling to commit further funds or approve the amalgamation between the NWC&NCo and the AR&CCo. Their reluctance depressed and sickened the seventy-two-year-old Galt and he lost his temper at one particularly fruitless meeting. He confided to his wife, "In any case I attributed my complete recovery to a meeting of our Coal Directors on Thursday at which I got so much enraged at the persistent difficulties raised by Mr. Ford, that I told them I would take no more trouble about it but left the whole responsibility of failure on their shoulders—I took my hat and walked out of the room."[66] The typical temperamental outburst not only improved Galt's ailing stomach but shocked the startled directors into action. The next day, they invited Galt and Lethbridge to a special meeting where they requested Galt to outline his case once more. Skilfully employing all the talents gained from a lifetime of explaining intricate financial structures, Galt once again demonstrated that the colliery could only survive if a railway provided access to the smelter and railway market of Montana. As he had done so often before with his meticulously executed presentations, Galt persuaded the financiers to approve the plan despite threatened resignations from a few directors.

Although Galt had won the support of his London partners, the venture remained uncertain because of the continued scarcity of investment capital. Throughout the summer he worked hard to round up the necessary funds, but with the depression hanging like a pall over the North American railway world, no one appeared eager to back yet another potential failure. Late in September, Galt travelled to New York and wheedled some token support from the financially troubled Northern Pacific, which was still seeking more connections with western Canada.[67] But the bulk of the money still had to come from the London money market; so in October Galt crossed the Atlantic for the second weary time that year in the frustrating search for capital.

Before he left for London, Galt announced a number of alterations in his plans. The changes reflected both the scarcity of investment capital and the vagaries of railway politics in Montana. Samuel Hauser had become disenchanted with the Northern Pacific's precarious financial position and had switched his allegiance to the daring enterprises of J. J. Hill. In 1887 Hill had completed the western extension of the St. Paul, Minneapolis, and Manitoba Railroad to Great Falls and was using his Montana Central to run his trains as far as Butte.[68] With the switch in alliances there was little sense for Galt to continue his road beyond

Great Falls and he shortened his project accordingly. More significantly, Galt decided to construct another narrow gauge railway and postpone the widening of the Dunmore line indefinitely.[69] Once again economic conditions dictated stringency; in Galt's pragmatic opinion, a narrow gauge railway was better than no road at all.

The reduction in the gauge could have a serious effect upon the company's land grant; according to the precedents, the subsidy for the widening of the Dunmore section had to be repealed and the grant for the Montana part reduced accordingly. Galt, however, visited Sir John A. Macdonald and persuaded him to allow the company to retain the full land grant on the grounds that the coal was of benefit to Canada and that he was building 125 miles in Montana without any subsidy at all.[70] Once again Macdonald was swayed by his friend's desperate pleas and he wrote, "I shall endeavour to secure for you the full grant of 6,400 acres with good hopes of success."[71] It was a remarkable promise to make since the actual colonization companies had to build expensive standard gauge roads to earn 6,400 acres per mile while Galt's, which was essentially a resource railway, was to earn the same amount for less expenditure. Undoubtedly the prime minister considered land grants, which involved no direct monetary outlay, to be a cheap subsidy to assist a coal-mining company—a privilege, incidentally, extended only to Galt's enterprise.

Armed with Macdonald's liberal assurance, Galt arranged the final details of the project in London. He lined up very impressive backing for the Lethbridge scheme including the large banking firm of the Barings as well as Glyn, Mills, Currie, and Company. In addition he successfully solicited support from three important London trust companies, the Industrial and General Trust Limited, the Trustees' Executors and Securities Corporation, and the U.S. Debenture Corporation.[72] Galt had managed to turn the small Coal Banks venture into a large, well-financed concern.

Just when success seemed assured, Galt ran into a difficulty that nearly ruined the delicate financial structure he had erected. Suddenly, Lord Revelstoke, the head of the Barings, pulled his substantial pledge out of the proposed railway's fund because George Stephen had told him that the Montana railway would seriously interfere with Canada's plans for the CPR. The situation

Shaft 1 shortly after its construction. Stacked in the
foreground is mining timber. (Glenbow Archives)

was an uncanny analogy of seven years previous when Galt had
questioned the suitability of the Palliser Triangle for agriculture.
This time Stephen, obviously afraid that Galt would increase his
prices when no longer solely dependent upon the CPR market,
intimated that he had no confidence in Galt's Montana railway.
Stephen must have disliked the idea of the wily Galt controlling
this very vital link between the CPR and its original parent
company, the St. Paul, Minneapolis, and Manitoba Railroad. Although Stephen and his partner Donald Smith had major holdings
in both the giant railways and Smith owned shares in the
NWC&NCo, the CPR president was terribly uneasy about the
unstated intentions of Galt. Stephen's words carried great weight
in this instance because the Barings, through Lord Revelstoke, had
substantial investments in the CPR. Galt was enraged because he
could not carry the venture without Revelstoke's support. Just
when he had finally won the backing of George Carr Glyn for the
Montana railway, Stephen's remarks threatened to destroy his
credibility. At the same time they jeopardized the critical merger
talks between the NWC&NCo and the AR&CCo. "As far as

S[tephen] is concerned I consider his actions most shabby and uncalled for and R[evelstoke]'s not much better,"[73] Galt wrote angrily and, like Stephen seven years earlier, he sent a flurry of telegrams to Macdonald asking him to disavow Stephen's statements. At first Macdonald hedged and lamely cabled Galt that the cabinet did not want to comment on a foreign railway, but later he relented and grudgingly asked Stephen to disclaim his allegations of government hostility toward the AR&CCo's plans. As a result, Revelstoke repledged his fifty-thousand-dollar investment and Galt quickly rebuilt the financial structure opening the way for commencement of construction.[74]

News of Galt's success travelled quickly and soon Lethbridge was astir with excitement. The citizens of Lethbridge, while keenly interested in the company's activities, were not fully aware of the extent of Galt's difficulties. On the surface they could see the preparations for greatly increased production, which was expected to soar to 1,000 tons per day; crews were laying more track and sinking a mine shaft from the benchlands just north of the town to the coal-seam directly below, while underground miners were excavating new levels and rooms.[75] Yet, as the local press indiscriminately leaked rumours and facts, mixing the good news with the bad, the spirits of the town's businessmen vacillated back and forth from quiet despair to jubilant optimism. By the end of October confidence was triumphant; the town's newspaper carried stories of Galt's successes and reported that local merchants had received contracts for timber supplies. Lethbridge buzzed with enthusiastic buoyancy; the colliery was expanding, the railway was to be a reality in 1890.

Bit by bit the *Lethbridge News* revealed the plans for the railway. Late in January of 1890, W. D. Barclay, the chief engineer for the project, arrived in Great Falls and announced that the final route had been determined and that detailed surveys were to begin at once. The tracks of the American section would leave Great Falls and head northward to Leavings, cross the Teton River near Choteau, bypass the west side of the Sweet Grass Hills, and proceed northward to the international boundary. The plans further called for the railway to cross the border at a new town to be called Coutts, where the company planned to deposit on the hot and desolate plain a round-house, custom's post, and other servicing facilities. From the border to Lethbridge the projected line of the Canadian section traversed the empty plains virtually in a straight northwesterly direction to Lethbridge. Even though the road crossed the deep valleys of the Teton, Marias, and Milk rivers, the maximum grade never exceeded one percent and grading across the slightly undulating prairies was expected to be relatively simple. Hauser's Fort Benton Construction Company was awarded the contract for the American section while Donald Grant and Company won the tender for the Canadian part. Early in February, Elliott Galt ordered rails from the Illinois Steel Company, locomotives from Baldwin's Locomotive Works, and cars from Wells and French; he also sent a crew to the Sun River area to cut wood for ties.[76] The railway was rapidly becoming a reality.

Events were moving quickly to a conclusion. In mid-February, Sir Alexander concluded the marriage arrangements between the NWC&NCo and the AR&CCo. The complicated negotiations, which had taken him two years to complete, signalled the end of the NWC&NCo. All its assets and liabilities were to be transferred to the Alberta Railway and Coal Company, which was to assume control over the Lethbridge to Dunmore line, the collieries, all coal properties, and land grants. Although the merger was approved by the shareholders, parliament still had to sanction the move and, for the time being, the companies retained their individual identities. The only immediate difference that Lethbridgeans could notice then was a slight lowering in the freight rates and the inauguration of a completely separate passenger train service.[77]

Late in March, parliament approved an amendment to the AR&CCo's act of incorporation. The company was permitted to reduce the gauge of the Montana line to three feet.[78] No mention was made in the act of the land subsidy; in fact, a separate amendment corrected a previous error giving the grant to the NWC&NCo instead of to the AR&CCo.[79] Parliament was not asked to approve the retention of the full land grant and this probably explains why there was no debate whatsoever on the bill that permitted the reduction in gauge. Officially, therefore, the AR&CCo was to receive the third subsidy of 413,568 acres of land for 64.62 miles of narrow gauge railway at 6,400 acres per mile.[80] At the same time, the NWC&NCo retained the second subsidy of

280,320 acres of land for 109.5 miles at 2,560 acres per mile originally granted for widening the Dunmore to Lethbridge railway, although the work was postponed indefinitely.

Simultaneously with parliamentary approval of the narrow gauge came assent for Galt's application for a charter to extend the NWC&NCo's line via Fort Macleod and the Crowsnest Pass to a point at least seven miles into British Columbia.[81] The pass was being recognized more and more as a valuable source of minerals. Every summer since 1887 William Fernie of Fort Steele and Colonel Baker, a member of the British Columbia legislature, had employed prospectors to survey their ten-thousand-acre tract at Elk Valley. By 1889 they had bored several tunnels into a twenty-five-mile-long coal-seam that varied in width from twelve to sixty feet. Its immensity prompted the *Fort Macleod Gazette* to exclaim that the pass had "enough coal to last the world forever."[82] Little development work was done, however, because Colonel Baker, like other western Canadian colliers, found it impossible to secure financial backing from London financiers.[83] Still, the knowledge of the valuable coal deposits and the relatively easy grade through the pass led railway companies other than Galt's to explore the possibilities of the Crowsnest. The *Fort Macleod Gazette* reported in 1889 that the Alberta Colonization Railway Company planned to apply for a charter from Cassils on the CPR through the Crowsnest Pass to the Pacific, and it suggested that the company was an affiliate of the CPR.[84] The paper incorrectly claimed that the Northern Pacific also planned to build through the pass to compete with the CPR, whereas in fact it was the Great Northern that had such designs.

Galt's application for the Crowsnest charter did not necessarily represent a serious intent to build the road. He knew that the CPR was interested in the pass, since several years earlier Van Horne had advised him to build to the Crowsnest instead of to Montana. When Galt dismissed the suggestion, the CPR sent survey crews into the area to determine the feasibility of the route.[85] This activity and the coal discoveries, which threatened his Lethbridge enterprises, spurred Galt into action. "Knowing the parties I have to contend with," he told Macdonald, "I have given notice for a charter through the Crow's Nest Pass."[86] The move displeased Van Horne who suggested that Galt withdraw his charter in order to "avoid embarrassment,"[87] but it was unlikely that Galt planned to do so. His strategy was uncannily predicted by the *Fort Macleod Gazette*, which believed that a widened Dunmore railway extended to the Crowsnest Pass would become part of the CPR system.[88] It is likely that Galt, who controlled the Dunmore-Lethbridge section of any Crowsnest through-line, hoped for a coup similar to that which he executed some forty years earlier against the Grand Trunk. Since the relationship between them had been far from cordial for the past few years, Galt was looking for all the leverage against the CPR that he could muster. A little blackmail was not beyond his nature and as subsequent events showed, Galt wanted some favourable concessions from the trans-continental and his charter through the Crowsnest was the means to attain them.

The turbulence preceding railway construction very much affected Lethbridge. The commencement of the detailed surveys lifted Lethbridge out of its economic doldrums and animated spirits in the town. The symptoms of an economic boom appeared: a cacophony of pounding hammers, soaring land prices, and crowded stores typified the rapid expansion and increased de-mands. Although a number of houses were under construction, only a few were available to renters and so only those with sub-stantial savings could find comfortable accommodations. The scarcity of suitable housing deterred many men from bringing their families to Lethbridge. The town newspaper, swept up in the ebullience of economic optimism, completely forgot the past era of stagnancy and naively assumed that progress was inevitable. "As the *News* has time and again pointed out, the financial strength, coupled with the ability and energy of the Company and capitalists who were, and are, so largely interested in the town, was an al-most absolute guarantee of progress; and the present position and prospects justify this confident attitude."[89]

A superficial look at the company's activities, which so greatly affected the welfare of the community, certainly corroborated the newspaper's optimistic view. To satisfy the demands of the "prac-tically unlimited" Montana market, the company was boring two more shafts: Shaft 2 was projected to reach the "practically inex-haustable supply of coal" within two months while Shaft 3 was scheduled to begin production in the fall. Elliott Galt announced total projected expenditures of $200,000 on colliery expansion, and plans to employ 600 men in the mines and 250 on the railway. Throughout June, three shifts of 300 miners extracted an unprecedented summer month average of 400 tons per day. To help him oversee the expanding coal and rail empire, Elliott Galt appointed G. H. Wainwright as the assistant manager of the AR&CCo.[90]

Meanwhile the railway progressed steadily throughout the spring and summer. A crew of 500 commenced to grade the road-bed for the Great Falls and Montana Railroad, which was the Montana section, while surveyors began to draw the line southward from Lethbridge for the AR&CCo. The surveyors were finished in mid-June and workers began building the Canadian segment. Sir Alexander arrived in Lethbridge at the end of August, accompanied by the railway's consulting engineer, Walter Shanly, who was to make the final inspection before the company accepted the railway from the contractors. On their first trip along the road, the men found that the American section was completed, while the Canadian branch needed a few miles of grading.[91] The smooth progress of construction work pleased the London investors and their satisfaction rose when Galt announced that he and J. J. Hill had signed a contract for delivery of 200 tons of coal daily to what was now called the Great Northern.[92] This agreement, while not exceptionally large, could form a solid basis for establishing the Lethbridge collieries. On 22 October 1890, the first trainload of coal left for Montana; the train, consigned to the Helena Lumber Company, was kept small because incessant rains had seriously weakened the road-bed. Nevertheless, Lethbridge coal was dumped into the cars of the Great Northern for $7.25 per ton.[93] The railway had cut the price of coal in Montana by more than two-thirds.

Lethbridge greeted the completion of the road with a holiday. A committee consisting of the town's leading citizens had planned a full schedule of entertainment, including speeches by company officials and the driving of the last spike by the town's Roman Catholic priest, Father Van Tighem. Flags, bunting, and pennants added colour and cheer to the celebrations, although the "Stars and Stripes" of the I. G. Baker store displeased some patriots. The whole community joined in the day of family sports and evening of dancing. The day was to be crowned with an elaborate display of fireworks, but the usual high winds spoiled the event. The first rocket fizzled, then suddenly shot up and exploded, according to some cynics, near Dunmore.[94]

No one was happier that night than Sir Alexander Galt. Only eleven years after his son Elliott had first visited Coal Banks, unpainted buildings encrusted in coal dust and tall chimneys spewing dark smoke broke the expanse of the yellow grasslands, while beneath the surface hundreds of industrious miners burrowed even deeper into the earth to extract the precious fuel. Although he nostalgically recalled the frustrations and disappointments, he was ecstatic because he had realized his ambition to convert the isolated wilderness into a productive part of Canada. The pilgrimages to London had come too often and were too tiring for the seventy-year-old; the sessions with bankers and investors were so discouraging and often humiliating. Nevertheless, the memories of thwarted efforts dissolved in his moment of triumph. He saw spread before him the largest colliery-railway complex in Canada. To build it, he had drawn upon all the influences garnered over a lifetime as financier, politician, and diplomat; he had utilized his friendship with the most prestigious bankers in England and the most powerful politicians in Canada. He knew that the Canadian people craved rapid economic progress and that their politicians, equally obsessed with industrial growth, were eager to bestow lavish aid and generous concessions to any private developer who promised to lure capital to the Northwest. So he had seized the opportunity and patiently assembled coal properties, timber leases, railway charters, and land grants to create, first of all, a profitable commercial empire, but also important, to change the very face and character of southern Alberta. For Galt, the quest was ended; the sense of relief complete.

The opening of the Montana railway marked a high point in Sir Alexander's life. After 1890 his health deteriorated rapidly and he lost interest in the Lethbridge enterprises. While he retained a number of directorships and presidencies in various companies, the Lethbridge concerns were managed almost entirely by his son, Elliott Galt.

At first the younger Galt's endeavours were very successful. The railway to Montana seemed to have solved the problem of a heavily capitalized industry serving a regional market too small for

efficient operations. Throughout the fall of 1890 production increased steadily, and by the end of the year it had soared to a
thousand tons a day, over half of which was sold in Montana.
Shaft 1 was still the largest producer but the river-bottom mine
was also in use. Early in 1891 Shaft 2, built to the north of Shaft 1,
went into action as well.[95] Lethbridge prospered amid this expansion; in January 1891, for instance, the company paid out $50,000
in wages to 58 mine workers and 398 railway and shop employees.
Several of the miners, who were paid on a contractual basis for the
amount of coal they extracted, earned over a hundred dollars for
the month. In addition to the pay-roll, the company also spent
$15,000 locally for supplies.[96]

With the coming of spring, however, prospects bleakened and
the remainder of the year was a disappointment. The Anaconda
smelting works, Galt's largest customer in Montana, closed and
the Great Northern and Union Pacific, which also owned mines,
began to sell coal at cut-rate prices. Since Galt had to pay protective duties, the American railways presented formidable competition and only the superior quality of his coal saved it from
complete annihilation on the Montana market. Meanwhile, in
Canada Galt faced strong competition from Pennsylvania coal,
particularly in Winnipeg.[97] Consequently, the two shaft mines
closed for the summer while the drift mine operated two or three
days a week. All redundant labour was dismissed and not rehired
until Elliott Galt reopened Shaft 1 in September and Shaft 2 a
month later.[98] The Montana railway had failed to supply a stable
market for the enlarged collieries.

To consolidate and strengthen his precarious financial position, Galt employed a complex financial manoeuvre. In March
1891 he completed the transfer of all NWC&NCo assets and
liabilities to the AR&CCo. The company that had founded Lethbridge ceased to exist and the AR&CCo gained control over the
coal-mines as well as the railways to Dunmore and the American
border. The move also consolidated the land grant under one
corporation.[99] Galt went still one step further and created the
Lethbridge Land Company to buy $800,000 of mortgages on
45,000 acres of land outside Lethbridge and 1,500 town lots that
the NWC&NCo had sold. The new company, with its headquarters in London, was capitalized with only £100 in £10-shares,

but it paid for the mortgages and land with £200,000 in six-percent bonds secured on the properties and redeemable in 1905. Although neither of the Galts were on the board of directors, the Lethbridge Land Company shared one board member with the AR&CCo.[100] It was a transparent attempt to liquidate some of the AR&CCo's assets and buttress its financial structure.

Modifying the company's organization did not brighten the annual report of 1891. Even though the volume of traffic on the railways was still growing, the financial statement claimed that the collieries had suffered a loss that had to be covered by a £35,000-transfer from its land reserve account. To pay the interest on the firm's debentures, the directors borrowed £50,000 and convinced the coupon holders to accept land for twenty to fifty percent of the value of the coupons.[101] Clearly the corporation's extensive landholdings were keeping it solvent.

Coal sales increased slightly during 1892 but the collieries, designed to produce 2,000 tons per day, seldom extracted more than 800 tons. The problem was markets. The sluggish growth of the Northwest's population meant that demand for domestic coal increased very slowly. Moreover, the AR&CCo had to contend with American competition. In an attempt to enlarge its share of the market, in 1892 the company appointed its land commissioner, C. A. Magrath, to travel though Manitoba and Saskatchewan and push coal among fuel agents and settlers.[102] Fortunately for Magrath, he encountered little competition from territorial producers. Practically all the mines along the Bow River had disappeared. There was some activity at Knee Hill (near modern-day Drumheller), while at Edmonton several little concerns produced coal for local consumption. The high cost of transportation made it impractical for these bantam operators to send coal far beyond their mines, and completely impossible for them to ship coal out of the territories. The many failures clearly demonstrated that although the district's coal resources were vast, mining was no easy proposition, highly competitive, and required careful planning, large-scale financing, and the application of the most efficient technology. Even at its slow rate of development, the industry was already outpacing the growth of the western economy. This was particularly true in steam coal production.

Sales to the CPR were still very important to the AR&CCo's

balance sheet. But that market, too, was threatened by competition. The Canadian North West Coal and Lumber Syndicate, which had commenced development work at Canmore in 1890, was replacing some of Galt's coal on the CPR line west of Medicine Hat. More dangerous, however, was H. W. McNeill & Co. Limited, which had taken over the anthracite properties and also controlled a site at Canmore. A well-financed, efficiently managed concern, the McNeill company was concentrating most of its attention on the Canmore site where, by September 1892, it was extracting about 125 tons a day.[103] The CPR watched this development with interest. Not only was Canmore right on the main line at the mouth of the pass through the Rockies, the coal found there was superior to that of Lethbridge. The CPR's vice-president, Thomas Shaughnessy, devoted his personal attention to the railway's fuel supply, and wanted to help the new firm as much as possible. He built a siding to the mine and even guaranteed a large loan for equipment. Moreover, he was prepared to pay a premium for McNeill's coal for a limited time. "The high price was justified," he wrote a fellow executive, "by the importance of having the [McNeill] mine opened and kept open."[104] He quickly added that once the colliery was well established and dependent upon CPR consumption, he would force them to lower their prices, possibly to $3.00 a ton. Because coal from AR&CCo cost $3.50 at Dunmore, the fate of the company was inevitable. For the time being, however, Shaughnessy preferred to keep buying Galt coal. Not only was it cheaper to use on the Medicine Hat-Moose Jaw run, but it could also serve as a back-up should the McNeill venture fail. In April 1892 he warned Elliott Galt that their contract, due to expire in October, would be renewed but quantities would be drastically reduced.

Shaughnessy's notice was a serious blow to Elliott Galt. With the domestic market too small to support expensive collieries and the outlook for expanded sales in Montana bleak, the CPR's cut threatened the survival of his enterprise. To avert the crisis, he completed a complex and risky move. In July 1892 he had petitioned parliament to extend the Crowsnest Pass charter, which his father had obtained in 1890, as far as Hope, British Columbia. Once he received it, Galt planned to use the amended charter to wrangle concessions from his rival, the CPR.

A group of travellers prepare to take the AR&CCo train
from Dunmore junction to Lethbridge. (Glenbow
Archives)

Since the AR&CCo's two railways and the Crowsnest charter occupied a strategic location, Elliott Galt planned to play on the
Canadian transcontinental's fear of American competition to extract some favourable terms. A perceptive editorial in the *News*
speculated that the CPR, the AR&CCo, and the Great Northern
were playing a poker game, and Galt was pitting the two giants
against each other. The weekly's editor, who probably had talked
with Galt, discounted the CPR's claim that it was cheaper to build
an entirely new road than to buy out the Galts. Furthermore, he
pointed out, the Great Northern could purchase a link through the
Canadian Rockies by way of the AR&CCo's railways and charter
and seriously undermine the CPR's position in southern Alberta
and British Columbia.[105] The CPR was, in fact, at that moment
making a strong bid to wrest away from its American rivals,
particularly the Great Northern, some of the oriental traffic. CPR
officials were planning the construction of a branch line from
Moose Jaw to Hankinson in the far southeastern corner of North
Dakota. By connecting this line to a branch of the Minneapolis, St.
Paul, and Sault Ste. Marie, the CPR could shorten the distance

between St. Paul and Vancouver.[106] Any arrangement between Elliott Galt and J. J. Hill could ruin that plan and so the CPR wanted to make a permanent arrangement with the AR&CCo. The transcontinental was not powerless of course because it could always refuse to buy Galt's coal, raise its coal freight rates, and strangle the life out of the Lethbridge operations. Galt's position, therefore, was strong, but he still had to move carefully and not demand too much.

By March 1893 Thomas Shaughnessy and Elliott Galt had worked out a tentative arrangement, which included the sale of the AR&CCo's Dunmore-Lethbridge railway and the Crowsnest charter. The CPR's directors found the proposition premature and too expensive but, because Galt's railway was a crucial part of their expansion plans, they countered with a long-term contract tying the AR&CCo firmly into their empire. They suggested that after the AR&CCo widened its railway to standard gauge, the CPR would lease the road until the end of 1897 when it could purchase the line for $9,000 per mile. Elliott Galt approved the alteration and vigorously defended it before the AR&CCo's directors in London.[107] The scheme promised to rid the AR&CCo of an expensive liability, guarantee a steady income, and most importantly, commit the CPR to regular purchases of Lethbridge coal. The board readily agreed to this measure of retrenchment and by July 1893 Galt and Shaughnessy had worked out the details. The CPR contracted to operate the railway and provide all the rolling stock, pay the AR&CCo forty percent of the gross revenues collected on this section, and purchase 200 tons of coal per day at $2.50 per ton delivered in Lethbridge. The CPR calculated the cost of transporting coal to be sixty-eight cents per ton for its own use and seventy-five cents per ton for public consumption, with the AR&CCo receiving a forty-percent rebate on all coal shipped. The two firms agreed to share all the railway facilities in Lethbridge and if the station or yards needed expansion, the AR&CCo would provide the land and the CPR would supply the labour and materials. Lastly, the CPR gave the AR&CCo the option to extend the railway from Lethbridge to Fort Macleod and lease it out under the same conditions.[108]

Even before the agreement was signed, work on widening the AR&CCo railway had begun. Galt had been building up the road-bed with mine wastes since 1890 and so the job was simplified immensely. He also saved considerably by buying used rails from the CPR. Construction was carried out during the summer and fall and on 28 November 1893 the first CPR train rolled into Lethbridge.[109] Its piercing whistle signalled the beginning of the end of the Galt influence in southern Alberta.

The arrival of the CPR's locomotive was symbolic of the new reality. In the past the Galts had guided the development of the Lethbridge enterprises. They were losing that initiative, and ironically they were losing it because of their own policies. Sir Alexander Galt and his son had established the collieries and the railways primarily for economic reasons and they had used the most modern techniques of mining, transportation, and finance to accomplish these aims. By doing so they became subject to the rules of economics and technology, that is, profitability for the former and efficiency for the latter. These basic considerations, synonymous in purpose, enlarged the modest project into a miniature but always developing empire. While the Galts had designed their colliery to furnish fuel for the CPR and a rapidly growing prairie population, the sluggish influx of settlers onto the prairies made them entirely dependent upon the transcontinental railway. The desire for efficient solutions, the need for immediate profits, and the very urge for survival dictated growth and a railway to Montana, even if it violated the patriotic ideal of an independent Canadian economy. The ties the Galts forged were not those of sentiment but of money and railways. These ties bound Lethbridge into a restless system of global finance and technology. Expansion to Montana, therefore, could not free the Galts from the CPR's sphere of influence. On the one hand, the heavy expenditures on the American railway and the enlarged mines made the Lethbridge collieries even more reliant upon sales to the Canadian railway. On the other hand, in the broad context of North American railways, Galt's little empire was an anomaly. It was not efficient; it was not profitable. Therefore the 1893 agreement, so shrewdly executed by Elliott Galt, was but the first step toward the total integration of his companies into the Canadian railway empire.

The elder Galt was not to witness the culmination of this process. In his last years he was often confined to his bed, suffering from a painful cancer of the throat. Early in 1893 doctors performed a tracheotomy; later that summer Galt lost his voice. A friend noted that it had been "a voice that so often charmed and convinced Parliament and the people of Canada on questions of grave public import."[110] Persuasive speech, backed by a clear analytical mind, had been Galt's greatest asset and had given him power over people. His daughter recalled later that her father dominated people with a quiet charming assurance. From his family he demanded instant and total obedience, yet his children adored him and looked forward to the times he told them tales about Greece and Rome, or his early life in Canada.[111] His soft voice, enriched by a pleasant Scottish burr and supported by the skill of reducing complex ideas into simple terms, impressed his listeners. Galt could win over reluctant investors with an infectious enthusiasm. He knew how to handle people, to lead them deftly through intricate and often boring negotiations, adroitly circumventing the obstacles and ingeniously compromising difficulties. His were the abilities of a master salesman, the talents that had inspired the Lethbridge enterprises.

Galt died on 19 September 1893 at his Montreal home on Mountain Street. A few weeks before his death he wrote on a fly sheet of a book,

> I have much to be thankful for, a long life with many blessings, and I try to accept God's will as my most supreme comfort. No one could have had greater blessings in his family than myself. I do not pray God to prolong my life, but only to support and strengthen me and to let my departure be tranquil.[112]

Galt's contemporaries mourned his death. The Montreal *Gazette* recalled his kindly nature and courteous bearing, while the Toronto *Globe*, which had few kind words to spare during Galt's lifetime, lauded him as a "contributor in many ways to the advancement and development of Canada."[113] *The Gazette* perceptively added that Galt, whose life was railways, had witnessed a phenomenal revolution: at the time he landed in Canada, the country had not a mile of railways, while at his death they spanned the continent. "A man who saw this revolution...," the editor wrote, "might well be hopeful of the land in which it occurred."[114] Galt had always been hopeful for his country and he fervently believed that railways were the instruments to her prosperity. To Canadians he represented the courage and tenacity needed to tame the frontier. The competition with other developing new world countries for the capital and technology to surmount the enormous obstacles of nature in her expansive territories was fierce and discouraging. Galt, however, was one of those innovative technicians familiar with financial institutions, who was able to lure investment capital to the unexploited prairies. His was one of the few government-subsidized firms that met all its obligations; it completed the railways and the collieries deemed essential to the civilization of the Northwest. This was the essence of Galt's work. He initiated a process that tied a portion of the undeveloped West into the political and economic, that is, cultural structures of Canada. In doing so, he unleashed a process that not only profoundly altered the physical environment of southern Alberta, but changed it more rapidly than ever before and would continue to modify it ever more quickly. These unrelenting transformations would persistently influence even the very composition of the town of Lethbridge.

7

Genesis of a coal town

Sir Alexander Galt's technical decision to open a coal-mine in southern Alberta resulted in the birth of the mining town of Lethbridge. As long as the colliery was only in its development stage, the settlement was no more than a mining camp consisting of a dreary assortment of tents, unpainted shacks, and drab bunkhouses huddled on the banks of the Belly River, fully fifty miles from its nearest neighbour. Every summer the operations attracted a few hundred Nova Scotian miners, who left as soon as the colliery closed for the winter. The household of William Stafford, the mine manager, was one of the few that provided some sense of permanency to the settlement. Indeed, when the thirty-six-year-old Mrs. Stafford gave birth to her twelfth child, the *Fort Macleod Gazette* warmly applauded, "the population of the North-west would be rapidly and materially increased by a few more such women."[1] Such women were rare, however, and by the summer of 1885 the population of Coal Banks scarcely numbered fifty people.[2]

The camp's somnolent tranquillity ended abruptly late in September 1885 when Galt completed the rail connection between Lethbridge and Dunmore. The technology of railways made it possible to ship coal all year-round, and so Galt began to recruit workers from all across the continent to run his colliery. Suddenly the town throbbed with new life; the hotels and saloons, which appeared like magic, were crowded and noisy, while town lots sold

Just a few months after the NWC&NCo opened the
townsite, Lethbridge's enterprising merchants
completed these buildings on Round Street in 1885.
(Provincial Archives of Alberta)

briskly to the newcomers. By the end of October Lethbridge
boasted over sixty buildings including six stores, five hotels with
saloons, four billiard rooms, two barber-shops, and a livery stable.
Only the hotel wore a coat of paint. Despite the hasty construction, overall development was orderly because the company, as the
original landowner, had surveyed the site and laid out wide and
straight streets in accordance with prairie custom. The scarcity of
lumber, however, severely limited the erection of private homes
and many miners were forced to live in tents, a hazardous practice
especially in winter-time—at least one child burned to death in a
flaming canvas contraption. Within months Lethbridge had mushroomed from a primitive mining camp to a lively urban centre. As
the *Fort Macleod Gazette* observed, not without some envy, the town
had materialized "like a new born infant city just dropped from the
clouds."[3]

Unlike most mine owners, Galt decided that private enterprise would build and supply the new settlement. Consequently,
he cleared the way for the establishment of a commercial and
social elite, who recognized that the instantaneous creation of a

Among the more ambitious Lethbridge merchants was
Harry Bentley. His store was open for business even
before he had mounted his sign, seen here resting against
his neighbour's building. (Glenbow Archives)

town inevitably produced countless opportunities for rapid social
advancement and quick riches. Indeed, the first citizens to arrive in
the fall of 1885 were ambitious, confident young businessmen
eager to found prosperous enterprises in the new-born community. These men fully shared. Galt's entrepreneurial spirit of
change, embodied in material progress and expansion; they reso-
lutely accepted the challenge of building a thriving and growing
economic foundation as well as a robust society in their adopted
home town. Never content with Lethbridge as simply a dormitory
for the coal-mine, they strove assiduously to construct an industrial and commercial metropolis founded on a seemingly inexhaustible supply of energy. They firmly believed that with dedicated zeal they could make Lethbridge a promised land of unchecked prospects.

A good example of a businessman who started a thriving
concern in Lethbridge was Harry Bentley, an employee of an
Ontario retail firm who had started a store in a tent at Medicine
Hat just prior to the arrival of the CPR. Well before the completion
of the NWC&NCo railway, Bentley borrowed some money from

his employers, loaded up a team and wagon with supplies, and set out for Lethbridge. Upon arrival he found that the town-site was still being surveyed, but undaunted, he pitched a tent and began to sell general merchandise. As quickly as possible he moved his business to a small shack, and soon after the completion of the railway opened a large store facing the town square. Having gained the initial advantage, Bentley built up a busy general store, operated the stage-coach service to Fort Macleod, invested in a large warehouse and hotel, and within a year was one of the wealthiest and most influential men in Lethbridge. Bentley also became involved in practically every social organization in Lethbridge. He served on the town council, and eventually became mayor.

Another budding entrepreneur who chose Lethbridge was John Craig, aged twenty-six, a carpenter's helper who had borrowed enough money to leave his home in Winnipeg to set up shop in Calgary. On the way, however, he met a friend who convinced him to join a gang of navvies working on the NWC&NCo railway. Purely by chance, Craig found himself on the first through-train to Lethbridge. He decided to stay, became a building contractor and casket-maker, and eventually opened a furniture store. Craig was instrumental in establishing a school district in Lethbridge and was elected the first chairman of the school-board of trustees.[4]

Yet another businessman to seek his fortune in Lethbridge was John D. Higinbotham, a twenty-one-year-old druggist, born in Guelph, Ontario. Lured by dreams of adventure in the Northwest, Higinbotham accepted a position as pharmacist attached to the North West Mounted Police post at Fort Macleod. He also became a land agent for the NWC&NCo and in this capacity bought for himself two Lethbridge town lots. In October 1885 he and his brother moved to Lethbridge to establish their own drugstore. They found the mining town to be rough, crude, and teeming with noisy saloons. The nights, especially after pay-days, were filled with boisterous disorder, and drunken brawls were commonplace. "It was a surprise to us," Higinbotham noted laconically, "that any of the eighteen saloons were still standing."[5] For the first few months the two druggists stayed at the Lethbridge Hotel, a large ramshackle wooden structure operated by Henderson and Hogg. Privacy was unknown in this flop-house because the rooms were partitioned off by cotton sheets, seven feet high, leaving a sizeable space at the top. The constant noise and insects falling from the ceiling made sleep virtually impossible. Warm water was non-existent. On the day after Christmas, the guests had to prepare their own breakfast because the cook and his helpers were sleeping off the previous day's revelries. The crudeness of the hotel and the noise of its inmates proved too much for the Higinbothams and they moved to the rear of their store, where each night they were joined by new arrivals and travellers unable to find accommodation in the crowded town.

Medical care was virtually unavailable in these first few months. For a number of days in October one individual claiming to be a doctor examined patients in the Lethbridge Hotel. When his clients found him to be perpetually drunk, his practice faded away and he left town. In the meantime, Higinbotham examined the ill and prescribed medicine. He described the symptoms and remedies in daily letters to the mounted police surgeon at Fort Macleod, Dr. G. A. Kennedy, and if no answer was forthcoming presumed his diagnosis and treatment had been correct. Fortunately for the druggist, late in 1885, twenty-seven-year-old Dr. Frank Mewburn of the Winnipeg General Hospital agreed to become the salaried medical officer for the NWC&NCo. Born in Drummondville and trained at McGill, Mewburn became a very popular physician, especially among the miners and Indians. Although gentle with his patients and quick to forgive accounts owed by the needy, he did lash out at those unwilling to follow his advice with profanities that had, according to a friend, "poetic rhythm...which could be beautiful and yet destructive."[6] Although physically frail, Mewburn worked many hours at his practice and still found time to serve on various civic bodies including the school-board and chamber of commerce. Like Harry Bentley, he served on the town council and also became mayor of Lethbridge.

Some company officials also became involved in the establishment of Lethbridge. The most prominent was Charles A. Magrath, the NWC&NCo land commissioner. Magrath was born in North Augusta in Upper Canada in 1860 and at an early age became a sessional clerk in the House of Commons. Tiring quickly of the long tedious hours at low pay, he joined a government geological survey crew and spent the next seven years, including two winters, under canvas—the last two years in charge of his own crew. He had experienced at first hand the blistering heat and mosquito-infested swamps of the prairies. Yet, Magrath grew to love the lonely land and when Elliott Galt offered him a post with the NWC&NCo in May 1885, he eagerly accepted. Late in July he travelled to the mine-site to lay out the streets and building lots for the proposed town of Lethbridge. For some time he lived in the colliery store-house with the mine superintendent, two accountants, and the master mechanic, but later he moved to one part of a duplex dwelling he built with Dr. Mewburn.[7] Magrath, who established a warm friendship with Elliott Galt, became the unquestioned leader of the community and was the driving force behind the formation of virtually every social and civic organization in early Lethbridge.

Warm and lasting friendships were formed under these pioneering circumstances, a factor which contributed to the social cohesion of the new mining village. This intimate circle of young men with common central Canadian backgrounds embraced most of the town's businessmen, company officials, and professionals. It became a tightly knit clique of dedicated and ambitious men determined to build their careers in the new town. Since they had linked their fortune to the progress of the area, they were the individuals most actively involved in all matters contributing to the survival and growth of the settlement.

The task of building the community was eased considerably right from the start by the presence of the North West Mounted Police. The size of the force stationed at Lethbridge grew every year and by 1888 consisted of nearly a hundred men housed in police barracks just south of the town. While the mandate of the police embraced the immediate territory, they also kept a watchful eye on the mining community. They were able to moderate the exuberance of an immature society where the boisterousness of rowdy miners, railway workers, and cowboys often flared up into noisy brawls. While such frays were common, violent crimes such as murder and manslaughter were rare. The police also fulfilled an active social function. Beginning in 1887 they sponsored annual balls in the barracks dining-hall which was lavishly decorated for the occasion. The first such affair featured the seven-piece police band playing for two hundred guests. The band also performed at concerts, parades, and community sports days.[8]

That the force became an integral part of the community was in no small measure due to the unflagging efforts of Captain Burton Deane, who arrived in Lethbridge early in 1888. Born in India in 1848, Deane was educated in England, obtained a military commission in 1866, served in the Gold Coast, and saw active duty in the Ashanti wars. In 1883 he joined the NWMP and served at Regina until appointed commanding officer at Lethbridge. Deane was not impressed with his new assignment. "The Police Post at that time consisted of nothing more than a number of houses dumped upon the open prairie, forming the sides of a sufficiently capacious square. . . . the Range cattle swarmed all over the place at their own sweet will, and at night they used to come and upset our slop barrels, and pick over the contents making a horrible mess."[9] No trees or shrubs graced the barracks or broke the ever present strong winds. With proper British resolve, Deane attacked the problem in his spare time, occasionally appointing a prisoner to haul water to the trees he was always planting around the barracks. He was very much the haughty British officer, authoritarian by nature with a strong awareness of class and protocol. Happily, his keen sense of humour saved him from heartless legalism, a fortunate trait because his legal powers in Lethbridge were very great. He was at once the town's chief of police, magistrate, and jailer. Moreover, Deane was very active in the Anglican church, founded several clubs, directed a troup of amateur actors who even travelled to neighbouring towns, and organized many local concerts in which he and his family participated. He also joined the local board of trade and helped organize local government for Lethbridge.

Under the protective umbrella of the mounted police the young town quickly achieved the basic stability needed to foster the growth of social institutions. One of the first of these was a tax-supported school. A private school had been opened late in the summer of 1885 by Miss Edith Coe, the daughter of James Coe, an anglicized Huguenot who had migrated to Alberta in the hope of establishing a ranch near Beaver Creek. After a swindler relieved Coe of all his capital, the family moved to Fort Macleod where

James Coe became a NWMP veterinarian. In mid-1885 the Coes moved to Lethbridge. Edith, who had earned a teacher's certificate in Paris, started a private school in one of the rooms of the Miner's Library, a building situated near the town square. Unfortunately, her classes ended abruptly when she married a member of the local NWMP detachment.[10] Her successor was Reverend Alfred Andrews, the Methodist minister, who started another private school in the Presbyterian church. A few concerned citizens collected his teacher's salary through subscriptions, but when this proved to be a haphazard and unreliable approach, they petitioned the territorial government to create a school district with the power of taxation.[11] The request was granted, and the group elected a board of trustees with furniture-maker John Craig as chairman, and mine superintendent William Stafford and company accountant Howard F. Greenwood as members. This first board built a small schoolhouse, costing less than $1,600 and completed in April 1886. They hired B. L. Latimer as the first teacher. By the fall of 1887 the school-board engaged a second teacher, Miss Margaret Duff, to teach the average enrollment of nearly fifty pupils.[12] While the relatively low number of students and the high rate of absenteeism pointed to the sparsity of children in the town, the school itself attested to a sense of continuity among some of its inhabitants.

Concerned citizens also organized churches to minister to the spiritual needs of the mining community. Before the autumn of 1885 itinerant missionaries and preachers occasionally conducted services at the home of William Stafford. One of these was Reverend John Maclean, a Methodist missionary to the Blackfoot Indians, another was a Methodist circuit rider based in Medicine Hat, and a third was M. P. Mackenzie, a Presbyterian student serving Fort Macleod.[13] Father Leonard Van Tighem, a Belgian-born cabinet-maker who had left his home to serve the church in the Canadian Northwest, looked after the Roman Catholics. Educated and ordained into the priesthood at the St. Albert mission, Van Tighem's first charge was at Fort Macleod. In May 1884 the priest visited Coal Banks to say the last rites for an ailing Michael Sheran, owner of a small independent mine. About twenty Roman Catholic miners attended the service held in Sheran's shack. Sheran recovered only to die a year later when Van Tighem made his second trip to the mine. Noting the growth of the Roman

As late as 1888 the Presbyterian church and school stood
isolated, slightly apart from Lethbridge's business
district. The NWMP barracks are in the far background.
(Glenbow Archives)

Catholic population around the collieries he resolved to return on
monthly visits.[14] In keeping with the tradition of very small
frontier towns, these early worship services tended to be ecu-
menical; in some instances, pastors of different denominations
worked together in the same service.

The spirit of interdenominationalism wore off rather quickly,
however, as the population increased. In the fall of 1885 Rever-
ends H. T. Bourne and Samuel Trivett gave the first of many
Anglican services in a saloon called Bourgoyne's Hall, where the
handful of worshippers had to contend with the unpleasant
odours of stale smoke, beer, and whisky. In March 1886, under the
leadership of G. F. P. Conybeare, a lawyer, the Anglicans established the parish of St. Augustine. Denominational exclusivism
deepened when the NWC&NCo offered free town lots to any
group wishing to build a church. The Presbyterians were the first
to take advantage of this proposal and in February 1886 completed
and dedicated Knox Presbyterian Church. A second group of
volunteers completed the Methodist church by July 1886, and the
Roman Catholics finished their building the following year. The

Anglicans, aided by donations from the Galts and Baroness Burdett-Coutts, constructed a small brick church in the spring of 1887. Despite the embarrassment of an incomplete exterior caused by the local brick-maker's failure to supply sufficient bricks, the edifice began service with a concert, which included selections from Rossini played by the NWMP band.[15]

Thus by the spring of 1887 four small churches filled some of the large gaps in the town-site. The structures, totally devoid of beautifying shrubbery, stood starkly alone on their large open lots, a forlorn isolation that aptly symbolized the role of the church in the young, lusty mining community. None of the congregations placed their houses of worship among the miners' shanties or houses near the mine shafts north of the tracks, but built them close to the business centre of the town. While the location of the churches did not necessarily betray a lack of concern for the miners, it certainly revealed which social class in the community supported them most strongly.

The solitude of the church in the earthy brawling town was keenly felt by Father Van Tighem. In 1888 the Roman Catholic population of Lethbridge had outstripped that of Fort Macleod, and so the priest was transferred to the mining community. Van Tighem found his welcome to be less than cordial. "At first I was somewhat lonesome at Lethbridge," he recalled later, "I had left a good home at Fort Macleod and here I barely had a shelter. For awhile I had to sleep and study in the choir loft of the church."[16] Van Tighem's loneliness was short-lived, however, because many of the local miners were of east European and Roman Catholic origin, and so he soon was deeply involved in ministering to their needs. An even greater sense of loneliness was experienced by one of the most colourful individuals ever to arrive in Lethbridge, the Presbyterian pastor, Reverend Charles McKillop. Born in Glasgow, Scotland, but raised by an uncle in various lumber camps along the Ottawa River, McKillop knew the tough life of the lumberjack well, and while working as a lumber camp cook, had earned the reputation as the best wrestler and boxer on the river. In his spare time he read philosophy and ultimately, through self-study, gained admission to law school. There he was converted to Christianity and subsequently enrolled in the Presbyterian college at Montreal to become a pastor. After serving an Ontario congregation for several years, he was sent to Lethbridge. His reception in the mining town was decidedly cool, and he felt out of place:

> No welcoming hand took mine as, tired and travel-stained after a journey of two thousand miles, I stepped out on the platform of the depot. I felt as a stranger in a strange land. I lifted my heart in prayer to my Master to give me courage and wisdom for my work. That night, under the pilotage of a Presbyterian whom I had met on the street, I "roosted" under the roof of what was then known as a hotel. The minister's room was one of two directly over the barroom. One layer of inch flooring was all that separated him from the scenes below. I went to sleep with the clinking of glasses, bits of ribald song, fierce oaths and a jumble of talk all mingled in my ears.[17]

He was rudely awakened by some gunshots, but was reassured by the manager that the boys were only playing a game:

> I soon discovered that in the eyes of the community I was practically a nobody. I had no money to spend; I wouldn't gamble; I wouldn't consort with "sassiety." The big men of the town were familiarly spoken of as "Harry" and "Billy" and "Curly" and the popular women as "Georgie" and "Minnie" and "Annie." These and others like them, whiskey sellers, smugglers, keepers of disreputable houses and gamblers, were the aristocrats of this western village. They dominated society and moulded public sentiment.

They would not shape public opinion for long. McKillop's personality fully matched the roughness of the town and his weaponry extended beyond the spiritual to the physical; his skill in ju-jitsu stood him in good stead when confronted by bullies. One time his black top hat prompted derisive taunts from a group of men idling near a saloon; seconds later they were sprawled in the dust. Through the gritty streets of Lethbridge he marched, a tall intensive figure with a short beard and moustache, curiously dressed in correct eastern ministerial garb, the proper broadcloth Prince Albert coat complete with clerical collar and tall black hat.

Yet, his great physical strength, his commanding stature, and his loud and clear voice demanded respect; and through his sermons, which, while not learned, were clear-cut and direct, he launched a vigorous campaign against all the forces of vice in the small mining town.

The chief sin to be eradicated, according to the clergy, was the drunkenness so prevalent in Lethbridge. The Methodist pastor, Alfred Andrews, voiced the western myth that the territories were a brand new country where people could build a society unblemished by the errors of past generations. Andrews firmly believed that one mistake that could easily be avoided was the abuse of alcohol, the root cause of flagrant prostitution and other immoralities rampant in the mining settlement. The minister argued that the limited permit system then in existence in the territories should be abolished and replaced by total prohibition with heavy fines for violators and drunkards. Government outlets could dispense medical liquor on doctors' prescriptions.[18]

It was an unrealistic solution, because the NWMP could not even enforce the existing regulations. Occasionally they raided the saloons and fined the owners but they could hardly cover the entire American border. Despite their herculean efforts to patrol this vast territory, the police failed to stop the abundant stream of illegal liquor flowing into Alberta. According to Captain Burton Deane, the volume of contraband traffic fluctuated with mine production. In the summer of 1889, when the mines worked only at half capacity, money was scarce and the town was quiet.[19] With the construction and completion of the Montana railway, the local economy recovered and hundreds of single miners flocked into Lethbridge accompanied by gamblers, whisky smugglers, and prostitutes bent on skimming the cream from an affluent society. As crime and violence reached crisis proportions, Captain Deane expressed his concern. "Lethbridge is becoming in Western parlance 'tougher every day'," he wrote, "Gambling is rife with its concomittant evils and cannot be abated."[20] The crime ledger swelled proportionately and in October the NWMP jail was overcrowded. The month's list of indictments revealed much about the problems and needs of a transitory male population: of the twenty men arrested, ten were charged with disorderly drunken conduct, three with indecent exposure, three with selling liquor to the

Indians, two with assault, and two with unspecified crimes.[21]

Alcohol abuse, then, was the most serious problem facing Lethbridge. On one occasion, Reverend Charles McKillop, preaching to an overflowing audience, chose Habbakkuk 11:5, "Woe unto him who giveth his neighbour strong drink," to expose the decadence of the amusement area just south of the mine entrances. He claimed that a personal survey conducted in the summer of 1890 revealed that fifty saloons served the drinking needs of the fifteen hundred men, women, and children residing in Lethbridge. Some of the places he visited were to him "literal Sodoms and Gomorrahs, places that if they were to sink down into the earth, it would be a blessing to Lethbridge, if only the souls of the inmates might be saved."[22] While the minister admitted that a few of the bars were respectable, the majority were "hell dives" where prostitution and gambling were prime attractions, and furthermore, he charged that he could name twenty men who thrived solely on robbing inebriated miners. McKillop was not a fanatical temperance promoter calling for total prohibition; he suggested instead that the saloons be destroyed in favour of licensed bars at the hotels. This moderate position, his intimate knowledge of Lethbridge, and the respect he earned among the miners lent credence to his assertions that the young community had a serious social problem.

The centre of the disorderly conduct described by McKillop was well west of the respectable business centre of Lethbridge. On one of the triangular landspits jutting out into the river valley, the saloon keepers, harlots, and gamblers built a little but thriving empire of vice. Bordered by deep coulees on three sides, the promontory, locally known as the Point, became an enclave of vice conveniently isolated from the reputable segment of the settlement. This prominent point of land, topped by practically the only painted houses in town, became an ironically, but fittingly, garish landmark second only to the black tipples and smokestacks of the colliery. By 1890 six brightly painted, two- and three-storey brothels, a cluster of saloons, and the company's bunk-house huddled together on the Point, catering not only to the local miners and railroaders but enticing men from miles around.[23] Frequently the intemperate carousing erupted into violence, especially so on pay-days when the workers were determined to squander their earnings in one wild drunken week-end. The tensions created by the dangerous underground labour, the boredom of the small isolated town, and the lack of women exploded into frenetic merry-making. A turbulent boisterousness seethed beneath the thin veneer of bourgeois respectability.

To a certain extent the Point served as a useful safety valve in the overwhelmingly male society, and for that reason Captain Deane tolerated the illegalities. Only reluctantly did he make arrests and then only to prevent lawlessness from spilling over into the remainder of the community.[24] Generally, then, as long as the denizens of the Point did not bother the general populace, the police sanctioned the existence of a segregated red-light district.

Seen from a different perspective, the Point heartlessly destroyed the dreams and hopes of many workers. The magnetic excitement of commercial immorality tempted many a miner to squander a month's wages in reckless abandon; a few hours at a crooked gambling table could retard the realization of a farm or the hope of bringing over a wife from Europe by months or years. The gay lights, merry music, and shrill laughter supplied shallow hospitality and quick relief from the dreary black workdays, but a drunken miner might be savagely assaulted and robbed of his cash.

Meanwhile, the river flats continued to be the haunting grounds for the riff-raff of Lethbridge. The red-light district had started there but moved up to the prairie with the arrival of the railway. Castaways of the industrialized community on top of the hill, a few miners, derelict tramps, rejected whores, and destitute families surviving in the decrepit shanties scattered among the trees were those who remained. The police virtually ignored the area except for futile efforts to stop native men pandering their squaws at bargain prices. The police, however, acted rather reluctantly because, as Deane put it rather condescendingly, "It is extremely inconvenient having a number of dirty squaws in the guard room.... They are much diseased and there have been several cases of venereal disease among the men lately."[25]

In a paradoxical yet meaningful way, the bottom lands embraced both extremes, exposing the two faces of Lethbridge society side by side. The imposing residence of Elliott Galt and the trim ranch-house of the Staffords contrasted sharply with the weather-beaten shacks of the outcasts.

Ethnic tensions also became a real part of life in the mining town. Probably in the fall of 1886 when he was reducing production costs, Sir Alexander Galt imported a large number of Hungarian miners from Pennsylvania because they were willing to work for less than the Nova Scotians.[26] These newcomers lived in a miniature ghetto of ramshackle shanties divorced from the main settlement. As long as both communities were small and separate they coexisted peacefully, but with the large influx of workers in 1890 the homes of both groups began to intermix and racial conflicts arose. The attitude of the English-speaking population toward this problem is expressed rather clearly by Captain Deane.

> There custom is to get into their houses a lot of beer for Saturday use. This they pour into tubs and sit around soaking their bread into the mixture. More or less noise is always made on these occasions and as long as they were in a settlement by themselves it did not very much matter whether they damaged one another's skulls or not but now they have neighbours within a little distance and they complain very much of the noise.[27]

Much of the disorderliness so prevalent in Lethbridge was blamed on the "foreign element," and to some extent justifiably so. One Sunday evening, for example, a merry wedding party among the Hungarians exploded into an unbridled ferocious affray and Captain Deane sent six men to help the town constable subdue the fracas. Eventually Deane dispatched his entire force, which after some difficulty restored order. Sixteen men were thrown into jail for the night and two more the next day.[28] Such large-scale brawls were uncommon, however, and usually the Hungarian quarters were no more restless than the Point.

The *Lethbridge News*, however, proclaimed that this incident was typical of Hungarian behaviour in a vehemently racist editorial condemning the foreigners. With undisguised contempt, the editor maliciously exaggerated the strange habits of the central Europeans:

For some time past we have had in our midst a large colony of Slavs and Hungarians. Although it has from the first been evident that they were not the proper class of men to assist in building up of a new country, so long as they conformed to our laws and behaved quietly and respectably we had no right to complain of them as immigrants. But during the last few months complaints have frequently been made by citizens having the misfortune to live in their neighborhood, of the great disturbance to them caused by the drunken orgies and unseemly conduct of the people of these races. Sunday, a day which is more especially regarded in the Christian community as a day of peace and quietness, being a holiday, appears to be the day which the Slavs and Hungarians in this place more especially mark by revelry and riotous conduct. But the discontent which has at last broken out in a blaze, fanned by the brutal conduct of these people last Sunday evening...has shown clearly that the existence of such a degrading class cannot be tolerated in a civilized community. If they cannot yield obedience to our laws and conform to our institutions the Hungarians and Slavs must go. As a race they are probably the most despicable that have yet found their way to Canada. Uncivilized and degraded in their habits, they might aptly be summed up in the words...: "Manners they have none, and their habits are beastly." Many of their customs are in the highest degree repulsive to civilized people. With them marriage with girls of tender age, who have not yet entered their teens, appears to be a common thing, and their mode of living is both filthy and unwholesome.[29]

While the police viewed the Hungarians with more understanding and less passion, their view was basically the same. Deane, who once characterized the Hungarians as "treacherous and cowardly," ordered a Hungarian constable to act as an undercover agent and gather evidence of illegal liquor traffic among the central Europeans, a tactic which produced some arrests. However, an undercover man was not sent among the English-speaking miners, nor were offenders from that group ever labelled by their ethnic origin when arrested.[30]

In sum, many Lethbridgeans thought that the central Europeans with their strange habits and foreign language did not belong in the neat picture of the nice respectable town they envisioned. They desired to build an idealized Ontario, or for that matter British, society, established by upright conscientious men full of enterprising zeal, who were determined to tame the wilderness and wrest from its bosom the rich natural resources. They believed in a myth: here in Lethbridge they had been given the chance to start a fresh, new, and better civilization freed from the mistakes of previous generations, and founded upon the principles of equality and democracy. Industry and progress were the watchwords of the new community: men would not inherit wealth but earn it with hard work. Mores were a fancied Victorian ethic, that is, a Christian society where the unchallenged authority of family, church, school, and police maintained law and order, sobriety, and morality. The ideal was a homogenized culture with one religion and one language.[31] The Slavonic people did not fit this mould, and the editor of the *News* and his compatriots, seeing their dream world crumble, blamed the destruction on the aliens. Afraid of the violence, intemperance, and moral degradation, which appeared to be the primary characteristic of the "foreign element," the newspaper writer viciously attacked the ethnic minority yet ignored the cancerous debauchery of the Point. Furthermore, the editor never condemned the individual incidents symptomatic of the larger ills of the community, for example, the intoxicated mounted police constables in the church parade or the alcoholic telegraph operator, who was often unable to transmit important messages.[32]

The town weekly, the *Lethbridge News*, was a product of Lethbridge's first heady months. The early rapid growth of the mining camp prompted the two publishers of the *Fort Macleod Gazette*, C. E. D. Wood and E. T. Saunders, to expand their operation to Lethbridge. Saunders, an ex-mounted policeman, took charge of the Lethbridge office and on 27 November 1885 he published the first edition of the *News*. Within months the paper moved from the rear of the Lethbridge hardware store to a plain, one-storey false-fronted building on Round Street. By November of the next year the rivalry between Fort Macleod and Lethbridge had broken up the partnership, and Saunders assumed full control over the *News*.[33]

While Saunders had a more parochial and less astute insight into western affairs than his former partner, he did create a reputable, lively weekly that mirrored the dreams and ambitions of the town's leading citizens at all times. Saunders enthusiastically supported every issue or event that could enhance the town's reputation or rate of growth. Items from the telegraph or other newspapers appeared in the *News* to keep Lethbridge in touch with the rest of the world, but the paper's main objective was to paint a picture of Lethbridge as a progressive town with unlimited prospects for expansion. While some of the editorials commented on regional or Canadian issues, the majority were hymns praising the inexhaustible supply of coal, the tremendous potential for industrialization, the benevolence of the Galts, the economic strength of the NWC&NCo, the congeniality of the citizens, or the balmy climate. He studiously neglected the largest segment of the community, the workers, and consciously overlooked the serious problems confronting the settlement such as labour strife or alienation of the immigrants. The result was an image of Lethbridge which, while it accurately reflected the views of the town's elite, was highly misleading.

Like the false-fronted building that housed the grimy newspaper workshop, Saunders created a romantic, idealistic conception of Lethbridge. He followed with keen interest the activities of the various clubs and lodges, gave a prominent spot to church news, and always featured the names of the leaders in these affairs. He chattered on endlessly about the splendid social institutions Lethbridge possessed, such as the drama club and the prestigious Lethbridge Scientific and Historical Society. At one time Saunders boasted that Lethbridge, unlike most frontier communities, had developed a respect for law and order because many of its citizens were ex-policemen whose families formed a stable core within a transitory society. He continued by noting that in 1881 there had been only seven "ladies" within a hundred-mile radius of Lethbridge, but that only eight years later there were several hundred, "and their influence is seen in brighter and better homes, a higher standard of morality, and the introduction of refinements of life. Ladies of superior intelligence, graduates of colleges, school teachers, music teachers are found as wives and mothers in the settlers' homes, superintending the domestic affairs and living contented and happy lives."[34] In this way Saunders pictured Lethbridge as an idyllic community perched on the banks of the Belly River. The robust citizens, breathing clear mountain air sweeping down from the majestic Rockies, were vigorously extracting fabulous wealth hidden beneath the lush prairies. The settlement, still small but dynamic, bubbled with economic activity, and with business booming, beautiful buildings sprouted out of the ground. The citizens of prosperous Lethbridge were happily engaged in building the industrial metropolis of the Northwest.

Glossing over the real character of Lethbridge society, environment, and climate became second nature to the *News* and many of its readers. When one critic complained, "there is little to be said in commendation of the Lethbridge climate. The prevailing feature is the rate at which the wind gambols over the prairies, dries up the soil with its hot breath and scorches the leaves of young trees, vegetables like frost," the editor immediately retorted that the winds "prevent an accumulation of dirt and rubbish, and after all when one gets accustomed to them are not very unpleasant."[35] On another occasion the weekly described the first Queen Victoria Jubilee Day celebrations in Lethbridge as a frolicking fun-filled sports day. According to the newspaper, most families participated and enjoyed track-and-field games, highlighted by a spirited tug-of-war match won by the citizens over the police. Exciting horse races filled the evening hours, while after dark dancing and fireworks capped a perfect day. In the opinion of the *News*, the day had seen a fine display of clean community fun and games.[36] Mrs. McKillop, wife of the Presbyterian pastor, arrived to join her husband that same day. Her comment was brief and to the point: "The day I arrived there was scarcely a sober man in the place."[37] While both witnesses might have visited different parts of town, the incident illustrated how the *News*, as a voice for the community leaders, viewed events from a particular perspective and emphasized only those social institutions it wished to foster.

Despite the editor's valiant attempts to portray the scene of a harmonious and contented community, at times a discordant note crept into his happy writings. Sometimes Saunders reluctantly admitted that life in a young and isolated settlement like Lethbridge was "very quiet." As usual, the editor understated the unfavourable, and "tedious" might have been a more apt description. Occasionally touring performers visited the town, and church groups or other clubs presented variety programmes, but by and large public entertainment was rare. Essentially the townsmen were forced to entertain themselves, a relatively easy task in the summer when outdoor activities and sports were possible. They might, for example, indulge in the aristocratic "fox hunt" using the lowly coyote as a substitute for the more noble creature.[38] In the colder seasons, however, indoor activities were needed and so the newspaperman recommended all sorts of cultural activities ranging from ice hockey to debating societies. In one editorial, Saunders provided a rare flash of insight into the real nature of the mining town:

> Life in a new country does not afford as many pleasures or methods of recreation as are to be found in older places and even those who are doing well here are apt to find life dull and monotonous. This feeling frequently changes to one of discontent with their position, and many good men, as the feeling grows stronger, which once engendered, it is almost certain to do, leave town in search of other and fresher pastures. It is true that the places of those who thus leave the town are promptly filled up, but it is not to our interest that the population should be a floating one and constantly changing. What our town requires is that those who are making their living amongst us should be permanent residents, and the interests of the Company also demand that their employees should remain steadily with them and not after a few years leave them and compel them to procure new men in their places.[39]

Most of the miners saw Lethbridge merely as a temporary residence. They came to the mines to earn enough money to begin life elsewhere, more than likely on a farm. Lethbridge fluctuated in size according to coal production, reaching its highest point in midwinter and its lowest in the summer. As a result, most of the citizens did not identify themselves with the community. Their aspirations were individualistic and materialistic and they did not include long-range community goals. Since the miners did not believe that expanding Lethbridge into a great metropolis would significantly improve their own material welfare, they did not share the exciting dream of growth and prosperity expressed by the *News*. They did not have a personal stake in the settlement and so they were not prepared to make a heavy investment of their time, talents, or money to improve cultural facilities. Some were content with gambling and drinking dens. For the rest there was little else. To them Lethbridge was a dull place where men did little but loaf around the stores and post office, or watch the trains come into the station.

The presence of so many transients and newcomers, particularly in a small town isolated on the vast unsettled prairies, often engendered feelings of melancholy loneliness, even severe depression. In its 1887 Christmas editorial the *News* inadvertently yet poignantly expressed this feeling when it urged the adults to fight homesickness and stop pining for the old country so that the children could experience the great happiness of the season.

In sum, life in Lethbridge had many unattractive features. The town had no street lighting, no water or sewer facilities, and no efficient fire protection. Although public institutions like churches and schools, banks, stores, and hotels improved year by year, most buildings tended to be crude and drab. The streets were filthy with garbage, ashes, and dung, dusty when dry and impassable quagmires when wet. Fresh fruits and vegetables were rare—oranges were available only at Christmas—and canned foods were the staple diet. Most people grew their own vegetables and baked their own bread simply because such commodities were not readily available in local stores. One urban pioneer vividly recalled many years later the day that Lethbridgeans lined up outside the butcher shop to buy "imported" sausages.[40] In sum, life in a pioneer town was nearly as primitive and difficult as that on the rural homestead.

The Lethbridge elite ignored these less than pleasant features. As expressed in their newspapers and memoirs, they preferred to stress a more favourable view of their society. For example, when Burton Deane fondly recalled, "there was in those days a camaraderie about life in the North-West which is entirely lacking now, and life was a great deal more worth living. . . . We constituted a little oasis in the desert, and were as happy a little community as one could find on the broad prairies,"[41] he certainly, perhaps unconsciously, repressed the realities of life in Lethbridge and definitely referred to only a small segment of its population. He and his fellows carried out their tireless campaign for more and better recreational facilities, public buildings, and community sports because they wanted to instil a civic pride that would spur the citizens of Lethbridge on to make their town a dynamic and amiable place to live. They wanted to give Lethbridge the appearance of a "civilized" central Canadian city because a community with a wide range of cultural institutions could better attract and retain settlers. A growing population, in their opinion, was essential to progress and expansion, the two prerequisites for economic prosperity.

The exuberant optimism with which Lethbridgeans viewed their community and activities had an economic basis and purpose. Their confidence rested on the abundance of fuel buried beneath the prairie. The enormous supply of coal, a surplus of precious energy, created the conviction that Lethbridge would grow unremittingly. Once again, the local newspaper expressed the views of the town leaders, if not those of the promoters of the resource, the Galts. Tottering dangerously on the fine line separating gross exaggeration from outright falsehood, the weekly boasted, "built upon a coal mine of practically limitless extent, whose output is and always must be in great demand as being the best steam coal in the Northwest, we have a sure foundation that ensures a steady growth and prosperity for our town."[42] Although several seasons had proven otherwise, the *News* crowed that neither season nor climate affected production, and unrealistically proclaimed that the railways would always continue to buy Galt coal. "So long as the boundless prairies of the Northwest are traversed by railways," the editor gloated, "there will always be a sure market for Lethbridge and our town will steadily prosper." As far as he was concerned, Lethbridge was bound to become an important industrial, agricultural, as well as commercial centre and certainly the first or perhaps the second-largest city in the Northwest. Thousands of people would be attracted by its plenteous resources, its excellent social facilities, and its reputation for law and order. "In no other place in the Northwest have all the requirements of

civilization and progress been acquired in so short a time," the
News concluded with a grand flourish, "and there is none that holds
out more brilliant prospects for the future." The enormous supply
of coal, the availability of the tools to extract it, and the apparent
financial stability of the company working the seam bred a smug
security and aggressive optimism among the promoters of Lethbridge.

The obsession with economic expansion blinded the town
leaders to the real problems facing the community. Once again the
Lethbridge News illustrated their attitudes. The paper, unlike the
clergy, attacked the matter of illegal trade in alcohol not on moral
or social grounds but entirely as a practical issue. The weekly
argued that prohibition was impossible to enforce because liquor
could easily be smuggled from Montana. More significantly, the
News estimated that ninety-five percent of the alcohol consumed in
southern Alberta was contraband, which was a disturbing fact
largely because such trade seriously drained the meagre financial
resources of the territory. The solution to the problem, therefore,
was liquor control by the territorial government with provisions
for local exemptions from the programme, education of the public
against abuse, and heavy fines for public drunkenness. When the
territorial government did authorize western breweries to manu-
facture low-alcohol beer, the *News* applauded the move mainly
because beer would certainly reduce the consumption of smuggled
whisky and thus keep territorial money at home.[43]

The self-assured confidence of Lethbridgeans led to vigorous
expansionism in which they ruthlessly subdued their nearest
neighbour, Fort Macleod. The editor of the *Fort Macleod Gazette*,
C. E. D. Wood, clearly recognized that the inflated boosterism that
filled the pages of the *News* week after week was not entirely hot
air. With great uneasiness he realized that the fledgling mining
town, blessed with rich natural resources and efficient transportation, would soon overshadow the old ranching and police centre of
Fort Macleod. Wood's self-centred concern for his community
fully matched the arrogant attitudes of some of the citizens of
Lethbridge and E. T. Saunders. A long and acrimonious argument
was inevitable. The editorial conflict is worth noting because it
reveals how the ideal of economic expansion and progress that

arose out of the technology of railways and resource exploitation created virulent rivalries among western towns for control of overlapping hinterlands.

As early as 1885 Wood noted with some alarm that many people were leaving "to swell the already large Fort Macleodite colony in the ambitious town of Lethbridge."[44] The greatest threat was Lethbridge's control over transportation. All of Fort Macleod's supplies, food, hardware, and mail came by way of NWC&NCo trains to Lethbridge to be trans-shipped by stage coaches and bull-trains. Since mud and snow often blocked the Lethbridge-Fort Macleod trail or swollen rivers swept away the ferries, perishable goods were often stacked for weeks along the route. Feeling particularly vulnerable to the vagaries of nature and the domination of Lethbridge merchants, the town desired its own rail connection, preferably with Calgary. Without a railway Fort Macleod would be sucked into the vortex of the Lethbridge commercial structure and its growth stifled. That cattle were already being shipped from the Macleod area by way of Lethbridge demonstrated to the *Gazette*'s editor the potential danger of competition between the neighbouring towns.

The clash came to a head in 1888. Early in the year, when Galt announced plans for a Calgary-Fort Benton railway, Wood applauded the promise of railway development but feared that the road might bypass Fort Macleod. He suggested that Galt spurn the desolate plains between Calgary and Lethbridge and build the line through the fertile foothills between Calgary and Fort Macleod with a short spur line to Lethbridge to serve the NWC&NCo colliery. When the *News* scornfully dismissed the idea as mere localism, the *Gazette* retorted angrily that its stand was based on solid economic facts. Wood was certain that settlers would prefer the foothills over the plains, making a railway through Fort Macleod the most profitable route.[45] Later in the year the *News* suggested that the proposal by Calgary lawyer James Lougheed for a second Calgary-Montana railway should be amalgamated with the Galt scheme. Tormented by the thought that such collusion could leave Macleod without any rail communication, Wood lashed out at the chauvinistic *News* in a full-page editorial. The Fort Macleod editor ridiculed his competitor's "childish claims" that Lethbridge was destined to become the great metropolis of southern Alberta. That honour he awarded to Calgary, which was then the largest distribution centre in the area. Surely, Calgary would build its railway through the rich coal, agriculture, and ranch lands of the foothills. Such a line, he hoped, would stop the alarming growth of Lethbridge and make Fort Macleod the distribution centre for the far south. "A line from Macleod would cut off Lethbridge and give Calgary the rich and prosperous foothills country, which with railway communication, will rapidly fill up with people."[46] In this way, Wood believed that Fort Macleod could escape the grasp of the ambitious Lethbridge entrepreneurs and progress instead along with Calgary.

The argument simmered through the winter to flare up again when Saunders once more published glowing predictions about the bright future of Lethbridge. The exasperated reply by the *Gazette* exposed Wood's stark desperation. Fully aware that Fort Macleod had lost the struggle for regional economic control, Wood's editorial clearly demonstrated how deeply western Canadian society had come to depend upon the technology of the railway, so recently introduced to the region:

> But Macleod is at present entirely without railway communication and requires it, and we consider it selfish, narrow minded and unjust to the whole country for the *News* to place any obstacle in the way of attaining this end. When it takes that stand we must and will resist it, and if to do so, unwelcome truths must be stated, we cannot help it. One would almost think that Lethbridge feared Macleod, and thought its own salvation depended wholly upon keeping us shut out from railway communication. Such feeling is not worthy of a community whose excellent natural prospects are so bright as those of Lethbridge.[47]

As rumours and plans of still more Montana railways were bandied about, the harsh polemics between the two newspapermen intensified. The Fort Macleod editor grew especially bitter because he more than ever before understood that the "salvation" of his town hinged on the location of the railways. In 1889 he went so far as to associate himself with a group of Calgary and Macleod businessmen in the Calgary, Alberta, and Montana Railway. At the same time, the North-Western Railway Company of Canada also secured a railway charter to Montana. In the spring of 1890 both these small companies sold their interests to the Calgary and Edmonton Railway Company.[48] Wood was delighted. With typical exaggeration he predicted that the proposed road would become a section of the great north-south axis route to the Gulf of Mexico.[49] When Galt announced plans for a railway from Lethbridge to the Crowsnest Pass by way of Fort Macleod, the *Gazette's* editor was ecstatic and rhapsodically intoned, "a duel by the locomotives ... will be the most inspiring music that Macleod has listened to for a long time."[50] His remarks typically embodied the aspirations of most western communities—the yearning for railways as the basis for expansion and development. The mere announcement of intent to build these railways was enough to snap Fort Macleod out of its lengthy period of economic stagnation. Twenty town lots were sold within a week. With two railways approaching Fort Macleod, substantial growth appeared inevitable.

It was not to be. Neither of the two railways were scheduled for several years, and even then the Calgary and Edmonton Railway terminated at Fort Macleod. Meanwhile both Calgary and Lethbridge continued to sap the strength of the small community. Calgary, with its excellent railway connections, became the ranching centre of southern Alberta, while Lethbridge took over much of the police work and became a major distribution centre for the area. Not only was it the principal supplier of fuel to the Canadian prairies, but it furnished groceries, furniture, machinery, mail, transportation, and other services for the southwestern region so that isolated settlements like Lees Creek (now Cardston), Pincher Creek, and Fort Macleod, as well as the scattered settlers and ranchers, began to regard Lethbridge as their marketing centre. At this point the metropolitan structure was extremely primitive but the aggressive merchants of Lethbridge had already taken advantage of the opportunities afforded by the facilities of the Galt companies to establish effective control over a still sparsely settled hinterland.

As with the large metropolitan link that Galt had forged between London and Lethbridge, the miniature structure created by the merchants of Lethbridge was not an impersonal organization but the product of human enterprise. By permitting Lethbridge to become a free town, Galt presented local entrepreneurs with the opportunity to utilize the company's resources, mainly the railway, to expand outwards and make the settlement a thriving commercial centre rather than merely an unprogressive mining camp. In other words, just as Sir Alexander had worked vigorously to extend the financial power of London to Lethbridge, so regional promoters, like Bentley and Higinbotham, strove to spread the influence of the town across the hinterland. Shop-keepers, company officials, and professionals hustled energetically to make their community prosperous and influential as the primary distribution centre for southern Alberta as well as the major industrial city of the Northwest. Theirs was a grandiose vision spawned in part by the abundant resources of coal and soil with which the area was blessed.

Since the achievement of this dream meant a concomitant increase in private wealth, it became firmly entrenched in the minds of local entrepreneurs, professionals, and executives. Members of the Lethbridge elite were public-spirited as no miner or railwayman could ever be because their personal fortunes depended upon the economic health of the town. These men wanted a progressive town, a community which could attract many other businessmen and thereby make it one of the leading cities in western Canada. Nowhere does this motivation reveal itself so clearly as in the drive for municipal incorporation.

Talk of incorporation was popular throughout 1888, but little was done. Instead, the community governed itself with makeshift measures. Whenever a need or problem arose, a few men nominated an *ad hoc* committee to collect funds by subscription and satisfy the want. At times these provisional arrangements worked, but usually they did not. One committee, for instance, successfully fenced the town square and transformed the ugly turn-about for bull-trains into an attractive sports field. Another time, however, a group collected funds to purchase a ladder and tarpaulin for fire-fighting but no one was placed in charge and the equipment was lost.[51] Lasting reform, it gradually became clear, required permanent government.

By the fall of 1889 several individuals realized that concerted action was necessary to bring about incorporation. On 16 September 1889 a small group of men met in a smoky back room of

Henderson's Lethbridge House and approved a motion to form a board of trade and civic committee. Two days later twenty-nine men signed their names to a declaration founding the board of trade and at the same time named a committee to draft a constitution. On 25 September elections were held and, to his great surprise, C. A. Magrath, who had kept himself in the background, was elected by acclamation as the first president. Magrath later reasoned that he had been chosen to prevent jealousy among the merchants, but his prominent position with the NWC&NCo was certainly an important factor. He implied this when he wrote that his election "turned out an excellent move, as it brought about a contact that grew into a harmonious and active co-operation between the citizens of Lethbridge and the Company for the development of the district which was of great moment to both."[52] Certainly the merchants were very conscious of the mutual interdependence of their businesses and the company: the town economy depended entirely upon the corporation while the mines and railways counted on the townsmen to feed, clothe, and house their labour force. As a result of this close relationship, company officials quite naturally played a prominent role in civic affairs, and C. A. Magrath, a high official, a close personal friend of Elliott Galt, and an inveterate booster of the town, was the logical choice to cement this crucial association.

As the title suggested, the primary aim of the Board of Trade and Civic Committee was the incorporation of Lethbridge, but at the same time it was also intended to promote reforms designed to enhance the status of the settlement. It launched a petition, for instance, for a court-house in Lethbridge because the police barracks were considered inadequate for this role. A few months later the committee asked for a local land registry office to eliminate long drawn-out transactions by mail with the Calgary office.[53] At another time the board planned to establish an inspector of nuisances, a move vetoed by Captain Burton Deane who felt that "such an expense was unnecessary" and, as he put it, "a reflection upon the Police."[54] Deane's statement indirectly pointed to the necessity of incorporation as the board had neither the authority nor the financial resources to govern Lethbridge.

To give businessmen the power to make reforms, the board of trade initiated and fostered the incorporation movement. As president, C. A. Magrath spent much of his time on this endeavour. On 17 April 1890 he guided a motion through the board meeting stating "that the executive committee...draft a scheme of incorporation to be submitted to the Board of Trade for approval and then to the ratepayers at a public meeting to be called."[55] At a subsequent meeting the board approved a motion defining the town boundaries, and in June the committee set the limit of the assessment rate at one-and-one-quarter cents per dollar, excluding school taxes.[56] To this point all the planning and execution of incorporation had been carried out by members of the board of trade; no one else had been consulted.

Apart from general apathy, the only real obstacle in the way of incorporation anticipated by the board was the matter of taxes, and so the advocates of the proposal had to convince the public that the marvellous improvements to follow local government were worth a tax levy. The editor of the *News*, himself a board member, expressed the sentiments of his compatriots by noting that incorporation was a necessary step in the evolution of the settlement because only a town council could introduce stability and organization to the amorphous litter of houses and people. A local government could build sidewalks, sorely needed when rain transformed the dusty streets into hopeless swamps; it could rid the town of putrid garbage and rotten carcasses strewn among the houses. The editor also pointed out that only a municipality could offer bonuses to attract the manufacturers and industrialists needed for the town's growth. The most important service it could provide, according to the newspaper, was water-lines, which would not only cut the cost of water but also provide fire protection and drastically reduce high insurance premiums.[57] The *News* argued that in all, the taxes, which had been set low, were justified because local control would make Lethbridge a more attractive place in which to live and work; incorporation was the essential step to ensure expansion to metropolitan stature.

The citizens were not the only ones to object to taxation. Elliott Galt made it quite clear that he would approve corporate status only if the assets of the NWC&NCo and the AR&CCo were exempted from any levies. Since no one dared to oppose the economic mainstay of the community, incorporation was impossible without Galt's consent. Accordingly, at a fourth meeting the board approved the principle of excluding the company's coal-shafts, workshops, engine houses, rolling stock, and track from taxation for a period of twenty years. The company remained liable for school taxes.[58] By granting this major tax concession, the planners removed the largest obstacle to incorporation and, by limiting the exemption to twenty years, the committee wisely avoided the folly of perpetual tax losses.

To this point Magrath's committee had written the entire incorporation scenario without any reference to the majority of the citizens of Lethbridge. To ascertain the feelings of this group, the committee decided to hold a referendum on 19 July 1890, a move strongly criticized by the *News*, which said that because the vote was not required by law it was a waste of time.[59] Although the voters approved the scheme, less than a third of those eligible cast their ballots. "From this we can only infer," the *News* fumed, "that we have amongst us a number of citizens who take such slight interest in the welfare of the town that they will not even take the trouble to attend the polls when such important questions ... are being agitated."[60] Unfortunately, the editor did not try to assess the reasons for this apathy nor did he ascertain the number of eligible voters. Had he done so he probably would have discovered that most of the railwaymen and miners were either unable to vote or did not think incorporation to be an important issue, and so were content to follow the aggressive leadership of the shopkeepers, professionals, and company officials.

Undaunted by the lack of popular enthusiasm, Magrath and the board of trade moved ahead. With the required census completed and a referendum held, the board sought authority from the territorial government to incorporate Lethbridge. The petition was granted late in August. On 29 December 1890 the residents were asked to approve the act of incorporation. The turnout, while better than before, was still only a handful as only 142 people approved and four rejected the measure. This time the *News* suggested that the vote was small because the workmen "feeling sure there would be no opposition did not take the trouble to go to the poll."[61] This explanation was reasonable when coupled with the fact that incorporation would make little difference to the workers personally. The apathy of labour contrasted sharply with the activity shown by the town's middle class, and clearly illus-

trated the growing gap between the two groups. The aspirations
of both segments regarding the future of Lethbridge as a community differed greatly; the workers did not share the merchants'
dream of major metropolitan status for the community.

The growing split between the aspirations of Lethbridge's
social leadership and the workers became evident in the first
municipal election. Two hundred miners petitioned William Stafford, the mine manager, to run for mayor, and they gathered at a
noisy Saturday afternoon meeting to nominate an entire worker's
slate. While Stafford, as a non-resident, was declared ineligible to
run, he did congratulate the workers for their display of enthusiasm and noted that such a meeting had never been possible before.
The attempt to elect a working man's council frightened the
business establishment, and their candidates vigorously asserted
that a labour ticket could only split the town. H. Bentley, who was
running for councillor, deplored the clash between "citizens and
workingmen" (a revealing distinction) because he felt that everyone was a worker interested in the good of Lethbridge.[62] Robbed
of a strong leader, the labour movement collapsed, never to
reappear. Since only a few of the company employees were both
property owners and British subjects, and hence allowed to vote,
on polling day five merchants and the company telegraph operator, who claimed to be a workers' candidate, were elected.[63] The
strong voice of the business community had been and would
continue to be heard in municipal government. The philosophy of
economic expansion was firmly entrenched.

Not surprisingly, the townsmen chose Charles Magrath to be
their first mayor. He was a logical choice. Friendly with Elliott
Galt, and a resident of Lethbridge since its birth, Magrath's
dedication to the town's growth was matched only by his loyalty to
the company. To him the good of the town, southern Alberta, and
the company were inseparable. He expressed this belief very
clearly in his inaugural address. The young mayor dauntlessly
proclaimed that Lethbridge would soon outstrip Winnipeg in size
because a large and progressive corporation was developing the
great staple product, coal. This abundant fuel, combined with the
projected Crowsnest Pass railway, he predicted, would attract
smelting and reduction industries, while nearby supplies of sand-
stone, clay, and water would lure other factories as well. Magrath's

speech stressed the friendly relations between town and company. "It is gratifying for us, gentlemen, to know and feel that the most cordial relations exist between the Town on the one hand and the Alberta Railway and Coal Company on the other and I am sure you will agree with me in saying that we fully appreciate the efforts of that Corporation, in their wish to further with us, the best interests of the Town, and more than that we trust this state of affairs may long continue."[64] Magrath furthermore declared that the aim of the first town council was to keep in step with the expansion of the company's activities. He argued that the progress of Lethbridge, initiated by the Galts, could be "accelerated or very much retarded through the measures passed by her first civic government." According to Magrath, the town, like the AR&CCo, required judicious and careful economic management to attract investors "to settle in our midst, and assist us building up what nature had intended to be a large and prosperous city."

Keeping in step with the interests of the company could lead to political pressure. In the general election of 1891 one of the issues was the high McKinley tariff recently imposed by the United States. Sir Alexander Galt, angered by the American move, advised the prime ministers of Canada and Britain to impose heavy duties on American goods while maintaining preferential tariffs within the empire. He promised to help the Conservatives in their election campaign: he contributed five thousand dollars to the party coffers and guaranteed the Lethbridge vote.[65] A few days before the election, C. A. Magrath chaired a public meeting in the company's largest boarding-house. One of the speakers was William Stafford, the mine manager. Although he firmly disavowed that any pressure would be used, his meaning was clear as he strongly recommended that the coal workers support the Conservatives, the party of the British connection and economic nationalism. They should follow the company's lead and support Donald Davis, the incumbent and a director of the AR&CCo. In the words of the sympathetic *Semi-Weekly News* (as the *Lethbridge News* was called for the first half of the 1890s), "the frequent outbursts of applause while he was speaking proved conclusively that the miners as a body have more respect for the honoured head of the colliery, who, although placed in authority over them, is in sympathy with them in every trouble, than they have for the claptrap arguments of political soreheads."[66]

Those claptrap arguments referred to the Liberals' unrestricted reciprocity platform, as the *News* carefully explained in a series of editorials, which must inevitably lead to the horror of annexation to the United States. Somehow all the editorials and political rhetoric skirted the fact that over half of AR&CCo coal was sold in the United States. Although Galt's policy appears to be contradictory at this point, it was in fact coldly logical. He sincerely believed that it was more profitable for Canada to cultivate close commercial ties with Great Britain than to risk economic annihilation by the United States. In the same breath he excused his association with Montana financiers as necessary to the survival of his coal-mine. Needless to say, the Lethbridge voters understood Galt's position; they followed William Stafford's advice and chose the Conservative option along with its strong British ties and anti-American feelings.

Keeping in step with the Galt companies also meant that the Lethbridge town councils were not as progressive and active as promised. The first council spent the public monies carefully and made only a cautious start on the two major public works—sidewalks and fire protection.[67] Magrath's prudence was continued by the second mayor, H. Bentley. While he began a tree-planting programme in the summer of 1893, he continued the slow pace of improvements, adding a few more sidewalks, replacing the faulty chemical fire extinguisher with a steam pump, and constructing three underground water tanks at strategic locations. The town council was very interested in the possibilities of irrigation and in 1892 sent to all representatives in Regina and Ottawa a resolution endorsing an irrigation project planned by the Galts, which it described as "the means of converting a waste prairie where one settler can not now be found into a rich and populous district."[68] A year later Bentley travelled to Ottawa to talk with officials about irrigation and other public works.[69] It was still a minimal effort as the town, hampered by lack of revenue, spent its money painfully.

The council's refusal to promote irrigation in a lavish manner was not due to a lack of interest. Lethbridge's men of business

Although Lethbridge resembled other western towns in many ways, the coal cars parked in front of the company-owned houses provided a unique feature at the turn of the century. (Glenbow Archives)

knew that the town economy was totally dependent upon the AR&CCo. "The town owes its origins and growth to the energy and enterprise of the 'Galt Company,' the interests of the town and the Company being bound up in each other," stated the *News*, "Whatever tends to the prosperity of the Company in the way of increased access to markets for coal output, will be to the mutual benefit of the town and its individual citizens."[70] However, sensing the danger in the paternalistic relationship between company and town, the *News* often warned that as long as Lethbridge remained a coal town it would never become wealthy. The weekly repeatedly urged its readership not to rest complacently in the company's shadow but actively promote the town, offer bonuses, town lots, and tax exemptions to industries, and above all launch a propaganda campaign in favour of irrigation.[71] Only a small minority of Lethbridgeans accepted the challenge, but they were not willing to increase taxes to implement the newspaper's programme. Nor did they dare to tax the AR&CCo. Instead they preferred to follow the direction set by the company.

Despite the strong expansionist sentiments promoted by the

News and shared by the business community, by 1893 Lethbridge was little more than a coal-mine and railway town where people threw garbage behind their houses and ashes on the streets. Even though leaders prophesied that within years Lethbridge would be the largest city on the prairies, cows, chickens, and pigs roamed on the roads at will. Despite the many predictions for a great industrial future, the town economy was still based entirely on the performance of the Galt companies. The presence of Sir Alexander Galt was felt throughout the town. Everyone in the territories spoke of "Galt Coal" and the "Galt Company," while in Lethbridge the Galt Hospital and Galt Park were two evident symbols of the influence and good will of Sir Alexander. Lethbridgeans claimed that Galt had pressured the federal government to locate a land office in their town and also that he had brought in a branch of the Union Bank of Canada, of which he was a director.[72] As long as his health permitted he had visited the community regularly and took an active interest in its affairs, ready to contribute to its charities. The economic symbiosis of town and company and the near veneration of the patriarchal Galt became crucial factors in the attitudes of Lethbridge citizens. The majority were content to let the company provide the necessary services and promote the economic development of the area, while a few leaders lustily cheered the Galts' efforts and heartily supported their attempts to expand the company's endeavours.

The first few years of Lethbridge's history showed clearly that a small group, consisting largely of businessmen, executives, and professionals, controlled community life. They were young men who wanted to establish their families and build their careers in this brand new town with a bright future. Naturally, they desired a pleasant place to live and so they strove to overcome the isolation of Lethbridge by organizing a variety of cultural activities and establishing the essential social institutions. Individuals like Bentley, Magrath, and Mewburn arranged cricket matches, amateur concerts, and evenings of quadrille; they founded schools, churches, and newspapers. Wishing to civilize the Northwest, they strove to suppress the wild and unruly nature of the mining town, to lift Lethbridge out of its crude pioneering stage, and recreate the idealized features of central Canadian society they had left behind. At the same time, however, these individuals made economic progress an integral part of the civilizing process. They also wanted Lethbridge to be a progressive town, a dynamic community that would supply the needs of the ever-growing numbers of settlers in the region. In this way they, like the founders of the mines, became agents of change. They wanted Lethbridge to become a great industrial and commercial metropolis that would come to dominate the entire western prairies. Incorporation had been but one step towards this ideal. In this, as in much of their activities, the promoters of Lethbridge seldom consulted the majority of the town population—the workers, whose aspirations hardly included building a city. Their obsession with expansion, which like that of Galt mixed selfishness with altruism, blinded these entrepreneurs to the existence of the miners and railwaymen other than as a labour force and as consumers. They consciously sought to minimize not only the seamy aspects of life in Lethbridge, but also the contributions of those whom they thought did not really understand the need to civilize the Northwest. Committed to the technology of coal-mining, railways, and city-building, they sought change for the sake of efficiency and profit. They shunned whatever and whoever stood in the way. Unfortunately, they failed to notice the looming burden created by the quest for efficiency.

Part 3

The burden of efficiency

We have in Alberta vast tracts of land situated
in a region the climate of which offers advantages for successful farming such as no other
section of the Dominion can offer. All that is
necessary to render this a magnificent agricultural country is water, and water can only be
spread over the lands by means of irrigation
canals. Let us have these canals and in a very few
years the local traffic will be sufficient to bring
all the railway companies required without there
being any necessity for bonussing them.

Lethbridge News, 8 June 1892

8

Land and water

For many years heavy snows have blanketed the craggy peaks and deep valleys of the Rocky Mountains, creating an enormous storehouse of precious moisture. Every spring, as the warm sun reappears, the frozen mass melts and water trickles down the sheer rock faces to join runnels and creeks that noisily tumble down the dark rills and canyons to spill into the many lakes that dot the valley floors. St. Mary Lake, a long and narrow basin in northern Montana, is one of the many natural reservoirs in the Rockies. Surrounded on three sides by the steep walls of several mountains, its eastern tip is open and through this gap the lake regularly releases cold water in quantities carefully measured by the seasons. Each spring overflow drains into the St. Mary River and seeks a tortuous escape through the foothills, rapidly dropping over boulders and rockfalls. Surprisingly soon, the stream reaches the open rolling plains, where its rapid waters have worn a wide and deep ravine into the soft substratum. The river, swollen by several tributaries, rapidly courses into Canada, the channel still narrow but the valley growing ever broader. By the time the swift water reaches Lethbridge, the valley is a mile wide and the banks, deeply scarred by coulees, tower up three hundred feet. A rich profusion of bushes and trees grow along the river, providing a cool haven for wildlife. The water level drops quickly as the summer approaches and the winter snow has melted; the flow dwindles to a languid slowness; most of the rough gravel floor lies exposed and little islands appear. Unless a sudden rainstorm causes a flash flood, the river does not resume its vigorous pace until the next spring runoff. Through the aeons the St. Mary has coursed through its natural cycles, its fluctuating tempo closely tied to the seasons; every year the river has flowed relentlessly and unhampered to the sea.

In contrast to the wooded river valley, the gently undulating prairies could be hot and dry. The fertile soil easily sustained the hardy, grey-yellow bunch grasses but the scarcity of rain and the searing winds discouraged all tall growth. For thousands of years the nutritious grasslands supported a vast animal population as well as small groups of men. It would not yield, however, to nineteenth-century agricultural techniques. While the Canadian government continued to praise the area's features, only a few foolhardy pioneers attempted to farm the land. Even officials of the several companies that owned large properties in the area had resigned themselves to the aridity of the region and conceded the land was suitable only for grazing.[1]

The Galts were among the few who recognized that this region could not support agricultural development. Unlike all other land grants given to railway builders, theirs did not stipulate that the land had to be "fairly fit for settlement," a provision deliberately omitted because the Galts intended to sell their land to ranchers rather than to farmers. The policy of granting subsidies in alternate sections, however, presented a serious obstacle to their plans because an isolated section was too small to sustain an efficient ranching operation. In October 1885, upon the completion of the Dunmore line, the NWC&NCo asked the government to grant the construction bounty in alternate townships rather than sections. In the case where a river bisected a township, the stream was to serve as the boundary. The company claimed that C. J. Brydges, the land commissioner for the Hudson's Bay Company, had agreed to take those sections reserved for his company in each township affected by the change elsewhere, provided he too could choose them in parcels of at least half a township. Lastly, the company suggested that school lands could be set aside somewhere else too. The government reacted favourably to the proposal and agreed to amend its land act to cover all colonization railways. Accordingly, the enabling legislation, passed without any significant opposition in June 1886, permitted railway companies to choose their grants in alternate townships provided the Hudson's Bay Company agreed to take sections elsewhere.[2] Once again the Galts had initiated a radical change in Canadian land policy, a new principle applied to several railway colonization companies, including the final portion of the CPR subsidy.

The Galts' clever manoeuvre, however, was blocked for a year by the Hudson's Bay land commissioner, C. J. Brydges. Perhaps he was still resentful that Sir Alexander had ejected him from the NWC&NCo board of directors, or perhaps he was genuinely concerned for the welfare of his company; in any case, he opposed the land swap. He claimed that the whole idea had been discussed only informally, that he was unaware of the legislation, and that he thought it ridiculous for the Hudson's Bay Company to give up valuable coal lands.[3] Officials of the department of the interior, who would administrate the land trade, reacted indignantly. They pointedly reminded Brydges that both he and Galt had written letters asking the federal government to approve the arrangement, that he knew about the coal-seams before he wrote his memorandum, and that the NWC&NCo would not get mineral rights anyway.[4] It took a year of correspondence between Elliott Galt, C. J. Brydges, senior Hudson's Bay officials, and federal bureaucrats to settle the issue. Brydges never approved of the scheme but he complied with the instructions from his superiors. In September 1887 he reluctantly met with Elliott Galt and concluded the details of the land exchange between the NWC&NCo and the Hudson's Bay Company.[5]

Although the way was cleared for the Galts to procure their properties in alternate townships, they still found it difficult to sell even to ranchers. The ranching boom in the United States attracted most of the foreign capital, while domestic investors preferred to take up the government's generous grazing leases. By 1889 they had sold less than an eighth of their grant. A number of individuals had bought small sections, while Sir R. W. Cameron, a director of the AR&CCo, purchased two parcels of ranching lands containing over five hundred thousand acres at $1.25 an acre. The Galts also sold ten thousand acres to Charles Ora Card, a Mormon settler from Utah.[6] The latter sale had a profound impact upon the Galt companies and the environment of Lethbridge.

Charles Ora Card, a very talented secular as well as religious leader, was born in 1839 in New York and moved with his parents to Logan, Utah, around 1856. The young Card became a successful farmer and entrepreneur, a gifted teacher and civic leader, as well as a high priest. In 1866 he was arrested for unlawful cohabitation with three wives but managed to escape to Canada where he selected lands near the junction of the St. Mary and Waterton rivers as a future colony for Mormon fugitives. After recruiting a number of families in Utah for the new settlement, Card returned to southern Alberta in the spring of 1887. The group elected to stay at Lee's Creek, which shortly became the town of Cardston, and within years established a prosperous settlement based upon a strong sense of religious community. Since the Mormons were accustomed to living in small hamlets and going out each day to work in the surrounding fields, Card petitioned the Canadian government for the right to buy an entire township.[7] The entry of the Mormons into western Canada, however, had aroused a vicious storm of protest, particularly from areas outside of southern Alberta, and the federal government, buffeted by bitter petitions against the supposedly polygamous Mormons, was afraid to grant special favours to the group. As a result, Card was instructed to settle his people according to the regular homestead regulations.[8]

Rebuffed by the government, Card next sought the aid of Charles Magrath, the land agent for the NWC&NCo. The two had become acquainted during Card's frequent trips to Lethbridge for supplies and land negotiations, and they had become close friends. Magrath worked out an arrangement whereby the NWC&NCo would choose as part of its land grant that township in which Cardston was located and subsequently sell the property to the Mormons. In this way, the federal government could not be accused of favouring the sect.[9] The cabinet was so sensitive to the Mormon issue that it refused to grant the NWC&NCo the required township, much to the disappointment of Card. Instead, the church purchased 9,690 acres from the company elsewhere at $1.25 an acre.[10]

Charles Card was the first to recognize the feasibility of utilizing the many rivers of southern Alberta to overcome the deficiency in rainfall. While a few individuals built several isolated ditches around Calgary and Fort Macleod, the Mormon leader provided the impetus to large-scale irrigation in southern Alberta. In Utah the Mormons had become leaders in the art of applying water to semi-arid soils and Card, who had extensive irrigation experience, immediately realized the possibilities in the Northwest. He impressed upon C. A. Magrath the potential wealth the territorial streams could create if the abundant waters were distributed onto the land. The two men approached Elliott Galt who enthusiastically endorsed the idea of large-scale irrigation as an alternative to ranching.[11] The three men formed an invincible partnership: Elliott Galt, carefully schooled in the craft of entrepreneurship and colonization by his father; C. A. Magrath, a meticulous surveyor and ardent land developer; and Charles Card, endowed with charismatic leadership and practical irrigation experience.

The responsibility of arranging the financial details for this enormous undertaking fell mostly on Elliott Galt. Although shy by nature, Galt had inherited his father's ability to conceptualize grand schemes and turn them into profit. Fully five years before the CPR came to southern Alberta he had recognized that the transcontinental and the settlers it promised to bring would become enormous consumers of coal; he had convinced his father to become the first to develop the rich coal-seams of the Northwest. His initial reaction to the wild boom of the CPR construction era had been reckless and irresponsible but the disastrous results of his land grab in Winnipeg and the adversities of the NWC&NCo had tempered him. By 1890 he was forty years old, still athletic, carrying his tall frame with quiet authoritative assurance. A close friend and business associate once noted that the son surpassed his father's financial genius.[12] This was probably so because Elliott Galt readily adjusted himself to newer, more complex business techniques, where crucial decisions were often made by a team of experts, and where company structures became increasingly intricate. With an open and constructive mind that was always ready to explore new solutions, and with a patient attention to detail, he was able to master these new ways of business and employ them to his advantage. Like his father had been before him, Elliott Galt was a man of his age, fully attuned to its demands.

Yet, Elliott Galt, like his father, was a paradox. In many ways

Although shy by nature, Elliott
Torrance Galt inherited his
father's determination.
(Glenbow Archives)

he had become a westerner. Having travelled across the prairies on
horseback, sleeping in the open, brushing off narrow escapes from
blizzards and grass fires, he knew the harshness of the West at
first hand. At the same time, he was the epitome of the gracious,
late Victorian gentleman, who often complained to his mother
about the difficulty of keeping servants in the Northwest. Socially
he was withdrawn. He never married, and had few friends.
Content to live in the rough isolation of Lethbridge, he had no
political ambitions and avoided public debates. His business, however, forced him to travel extensively and meet many different
people. In negotiations his quiet self-confidence commanded respect and his poised reserve never quite concealed an infectious
enthusiasm. Elliott Galt embraced grand projects with all the
gusto his father had always mustered. Beneath the facade of
reserve was an optimist with an unflagging faith in modern man's
ability to overcome the natural obstacles of the prairies. He knew
that eventually settlers would come to farm the western fertile
soil. He was confident that his own ventures would succeed.

Elliott Galt eagerly adopted the Card-Magrath irrigation

Charles A. Magrath, the Galts'
faithful lieutenant. (Glenbow
Archives)

scheme because his coal company was in serious financial difficulties. The closure of the Anaconda smelting works and the
strong competition from tariff-protected Montana coal-mines
seriously affected Lethbridge production. To strengthen his position and to liquidate some of his assets he and his father had
completed the reorganization of the NWC&NCo into the AR&CCo
and formed the Lethbridge Land Company to buy the mortgages
held by the new company. These tactics had done little to brighten
the firm's 1891 annual report, which announced a significant loss
in the operation of the collieries and railways to be recovered by a
cash transfer from the land reserves. The statement also asked the
bondholders to accept part of their interest payments in land.[13]
Clearly, then, the land assets were keeping the AR&CCo solvent
and were the means to extricate it from its financial problems.

Under increasing pressure to make the Lethbridge enterprises turn a profit, Elliott Galt negotiated an important agreement with the Mormons. The previous fall, he and Charles
Magrath had accompanied a group of Mormon church leaders on a
tour of Cardston and vicinity. The delegates were so impressed

with the progress made by the community and the tremendous opportunities available in southern Alberta that they authorized Card to purchase a large tract of land from the AR&CCo. In December 1891 Charles Card and John W. Taylor, the church president, signed a contract in which the Mormon church agreed to lease from the AR&CCo over 720,000 acres of land for two cents per acre annually for four years, after which it could buy the parcel at one dollar per acre. The church also pledged to build several villages on the properties, bring in settlers, and most importantly, have the incoming settlers provide the labour for the construction of the irrigation canals.[14] It was a gigantic project that, if successful, would strengthen the immediate financial position of the company and in the long run provide traffic for railways and consumers for coal.

The irrigation scheme, however, had to be aggressively pursued. Early in 1892 the CPR informed Galt that in October it would drastically reduce the quantity of coal it usually bought from his collieries. The warning was a serious blow to Galt and it spurred him on to quicker action. In March 1892 C. A. Magrath and C. O. Card completed an assessment of the rivers flowing through the Lethbridge region, and they concluded that the St. Mary was the most feasible source for the irrigation canal. Galt decided to go ahead and appointed Magrath as the irrigation canal co-ordinator.[15]

Charles A. Magrath was the ideal link between the technical experience of the Mormons and the financial expertise of Galt. A close friend of Elliott Galt, he shared the vision of reconstructing the wilderness into a productive society; a warm admirer of the industrious Mormons, he upheld their dreams of building a new community. So devoted was he to the AR&CCo and the task of developing the Lethbridge area that in 1891, when the AR&CCo was at a low ebb, he volunteered to reduce his own salary.[16] Furthermore, as a young and vigorous man, he was widely respected in Lethbridge and environs and, as the *News* put it, he was "closely identified with all the movements which wanted to advance and develop the town."[17] He declined an invitation to serve again as mayor only because Lethbridge had just elected him to be their first representative in the territorial assembly. To give a measure of continuity in municipal government, he agreed to sit as a councillor. Meanwhile, in the legislature he strongly advocated irrigation and drafted the territories' first coal-mining regulations. He wheedled enough money for an iron bridge across the St. Mary near Cardston and had the federal government string a telegraph-line from Lethbridge to Cardston. In every instance he sought the improvement and development of his constituency; his tenure as politician, which was but a component of his career in business, was a clear testimony to his energetic advocacy of economic growth.

Motivated by a strong desire to develop southern Alberta and to help his friend and his company, Magrath zealously pursued the task of bringing irrigation to western Canada. Early in 1892 he petitioned parliament to amend the AR&CCo charter, empowering it to construct an irrigation canal. He urged local editors to promote the company's cause in their newspapers and steered a resolution supporting its bid through the Lethbridge town council. Magrath felt compelled to hurry because he had learned that the Montana government was studying the possibility of diverting the St. Mary for an extensive irrigation project within the state. Should that plan become a reality, the river would be useless for any Canadian enterprise.[18]

Magrath's diligence was in vain, however, because Elliott Galt could not convince the London directors to back the project. Although the expense of labour was virtually eliminated, the task of taming nature still required the expensive technology of diverting part of a river, the construction of sluices, flumes, gates, and bridges. Few of the shareholders believed that they could recoup such a large investment when so much verdant land was still available on the western prairies. Only Burdett-Coutts supported Galt's plea but even he could not swing the board to favour the proposal. The British shareholders, who for over ten years had made heavy commitments to southern Alberta, refused to speculate on an unproven project that dwarfed the previous enterprises. No amount of enthusiasm on Galt's part could overcome the circumstances of the day. The expected throngs of immigrants still had not arrived in the Northwest and the prevailing economic depression closed the world's money markets to western Canada.

The opposition in London was a serious setback for Elliott Galt. It caused him great anxiety and his calm posture barely concealed his tense apprehension. The reverses suffered by the Lethbridge enterprises appeared endless and seemingly destined for disaster. Domestic consumers on the prairies were too few to support the expensive collieries. The Montana market was spoiled by too much competition. The CPR contract was sure to come to an end soon. The same problem that had troubled his father in the early 1880s came back to haunt him. The persistent flaw was the location of the mines. The resource may have been plentiful but it was too far removed from the market. How could he possibly survive the challenge of better coals extracted only minutes from the CPR main line? Perhaps one solution was the liquidation of the land holdings, but the Mormons refused to assume the financial burden of the irrigation project and even threatened to call off the entire arrangement. So, where else could he get the money? Could he scale down the project? Approach other investors? Arrange different terms? These were the questions that haunted him during the summer and fall of 1892.

Working more slowly this time, Elliott Galt began to piece together his strategy. During the early months of 1892 he success-fully negotiated the lease of the Dunmore-Lethbridge line to the CPR and won a large coal contract from that company.[19] At the same time he decided to press on with the irrigation plans. If the London men were afraid to expand the activities of the AR&CCo, then he would have to move on alone. Accordingly, during the winter he carried out extensive negotiations in Salt Lake City and London, which culminated in the formation of the Alberta Irriga-tion Company, formally incorporated in April 1893. The new company proposed to purchase 100,000 acres of land from the AR&CCo for $1.25 per acre and sign an option for another 150,000 acres to be taken up in July 1903. To prevent an uproar of anti-Mormon feelings, no churchmen were named to the board. Instead the act of incorporation listed Sir Alexander Galt, Elliott Galt, Charles Magrath, and several others as directors.[20] Despite the omission of the Mormon names, the new corporation repre-sented another step in the alliance between the Galts and the church, a partnership they hoped would alter the natural charac-ter of southern Alberta.

While Elliott Galt was busily negotiating the creation of the Alberta Irrigation Company and the CPR lease, C. A. Magrath was lobbying the federal government to subsidize the irrigation scheme. Without irrigation, Magrath argued, no farmer could colonize the area. Unfortunately, irrigation works were very costly, the AR&CCo's plan being especially expensive because for the first sixty miles the main canal had to traverse hilly territory requiring extensive flumes and side-hill work. Magrath argued that subsidies were even more urgent for irrigation than for railways because the canals and ditches had to be completed before any settler would consider buying the land. "The lands are value-less in their present condition," Magrath declared, but "...by assisting irrigation the balance of [these] lands will be so enhanced in value that one acre will bring as much as five and ten acres in other districts where irrigation is not absolutely required."[21] Even if the government decided not to assist individual corporations, Magrath concluded, it must at least conduct a survey of all territorial rivers and determine their suitability for irrigation.

This call for the systematic, government-assisted develop-ment of the region's water resources was supported by the ter-ritorial press, particularly the *Lethbridge News*, whose editor had close contact with C. A. Magrath. A staunch advocate of irriga-tion, over the years the *News* churned out a constant barrage of editorials insisting that the federal government, as the largest landowner in the territory, had a far greater interest than any private corporation in a plan that would increase land values; therefore, the Canadian government must bear the cost of sur-veys and water measurements, an expensive but necessary step to prevent a costly and inefficient conglomeration of haphazardly built irrigation ditches.[22] Once the study was completed, private industry could construct the canals and other necessary works. But here, too, the government should provide assistance, the *News* claimed, because irrigation ditches were as essential to settlement as railway tracks. "Railway after railway may be built through a section of the country until it is covered with a network of iron rails," the paper asserted, "but the country will never be a paying speculation until there is agricultural production."[23] Only irriga-tion could induce agricultural development in southern Alberta and therefore it deserved assistance. Just as the state had aided railways, so it should help finance irrigation projects. Once irriga-tion was shown to be profitable, capitalists would invest their

The first Galt irrigation canal was dug by Mormon settlers. (Glenbow Archives)

money and settlers would pour into the semi-arid region, adding to the general prosperity of Canada. The strident voice of the *News* was an important factor in shaping the growing public sentiment in western Canada for federal involvement in irrigation schemes.

Irrigation, however, was an issue much too local to interest federal politicians. Magrath's plea for a government subsidy to irrigation companies was rejected out of hand. The decision had actually been made a few years earlier when the matter of irrigation had been raised in the House of Commons and decisively repudiated. Although some western members had called for a government well-digging program, none of them had supported subsidized large-scale irrigation projects. In fact, R. Watson, a Manitoban, had angrily denounced the proponents of irrigation for circulating reports that sections of the prairies were arid, a tactic which would certainly alarm prospective settlers: "I think it not advisable to advertise that the North-West is a country where irrigation is necessary,"[24] he had lectured and so voiced the prevailing sentiment that it would be a silly mistake to spend large sums of money on irrigation when the West had so much unsettled land where rainfall was sufficient. Without the endorsement of the politicians, no administration was prepared to aid irrigation. Magrath's request never had a chance.

By 1893 the long-awaited rush of settlers had still not come to western Canada, and the Galt companies, as well as Lethbridge, suffered accordingly. The collieries, which were designed for a much larger market than supplied by Montana and the North West Territories, did not generate the great profits its shareholders had expected. Survival for the companies and even for the town of Lethbridge required still further expansion of the AR&CCo's activities. When local executives, aided by the town's councillors, sought delivery from their plight in irrigation, they found a willing ally in the Mormon church, which was seeking to preserve its life-style in the individual sections of the Galt properties. Elliott Galt, C. A. Magrath, and to a lesser extent C. O. Card, strove to bring irrigation to the region because they saw the expansive prairie lands largely in economic terms. The soil of southern Alberta had no value unless irrigated and sold. Ironically, their critics used this same economic measure to defeat the idea. Within the context of the general economic slump and the sluggish flow of settlers to the Canadian Northwest, few people outside the Lethbridge area saw any need for an experimental program of questionable necessity and doubtful investment potential. Economically, the concept was premature and the proponents of irrigation had to postpone their plans to eliminate the risk of drought for dry-land farmers. For some time yet the St. Mary would flow to the sea, uninterrupted and undisturbed.

Every farmer
his own rainmaker?

New Year's, 1894 held few bright prospects for Elliott Galt. He missed his father. Both in business and at play they had been very close. For the last fifteen years they had worked hard on the Lethbridge venture but they had always found time together for salmon fishing, deer hunting, or simply relaxing in the country-side. Now the younger Galt had to move on alone, searching out solutions without his father's shrewd advice. The problems were more pressing than ever. Coal and land sales were suffering from the slow growth of the prairie economy while irrigation still was not a popular issue. These matters had to be resolved soon, or the AR&CCo could go bankrupt.

Galt sought the answer to these issues in further expansion. Like so many of the large corporations emerging in North America in the last decades of the nineteenth century, the AR&CCo had to grow in order to live. In some ways, the company already displayed some of the characteristics of a big business.[1] The bulk of the company's two-million-dollar capitalization was no longer limited to family and friends but was distributed over a wide range of anonymous investors. Although still an investor himself, Galt's primary function was to safeguard this pool of capital. In his opinion the only policy was to make the company larger yet. Irrigation, he believed, was the key to the company's survival and so he began to devote more and more of his time to this illusive goal. Meanwhile, he increasingly delegated the day-to-day operations of the collieries and railways to experienced managers. The implementation of the irrigation project proved so complex that he only headed a team of experts.

Before Elliott Galt could devote all his energies to the irrigation project, several problems at the coal-mines diverted his attention. Early in January 1894 the Anaconda works in Montana closed again and Galt reacted to the loss in sales by dismissing all his 580 employees without any warning. Although he announced plans to hire 130 of his married coal workers at a seventeen-percent reduction in wages, the chosen men refused to return to work. The lock-out continued until the second week of March when about 150 miners, placated with some minor concessions, accepted Galt's terms and returned to work.[2] Galt had won his first labour dispute.

The victory was a hollow one for Galt. The strike cost him dearly in terms of lost revenue from coal sales and railway traffic. Even when idle, the collieries were expensive, and the railway had to operate despite reduced business. Galt could barely pay his fixed expenses and, to make matters worse, the strike ended just before the slack season began. Later in the summer the CPR informed Galt that the company was burning less fuel than it had contracted to buy from the AR&CCo under the 1893 agreement. The company's vice-president, Thomas Shaughnessy, informed Galt that a fuel contract with a railway was never to be "construed in a cast-iron fashion" and that he expected the AR&CCo to decrease shipments.[3] As an experienced man of business, Shaughnessy surely knew that Galt could not afford to cut production because he had to meet such fixed costs as loan payments. In fact, Galt could no longer satisfy his most immediate creditors and he asked Shaughnessy to guarantee a short-term load to ward off bankruptcy. Although Shaughnessy sternly lectured Galt that such a request was most unbusinesslike, he was too dependent upon Lethbridge coal to allow the AR&CCo to collapse. So he instructed the Bank of Montreal to lend the AR&CCo $33,000 to be repaid by the gross revenues of all coal sold to the CPR in excess of 3,000 tons per month.[4]

With the reduction in CPR consumption and the cutbacks in Montana, Galt continued to experience financial difficulties. By year-end the company had accumulated debts amounting to

£150,000, failed to meet dividend payments on shares, and could not pay the interest charges on a large first mortgage. Moreover, the Canada Life Assurance Company, which had financed the widening of the Dunmore-Lethbridge railway, seized control over the line in order to protect its investment. Once again the Lethbridge venture stood on the brink of ruin and Elliott Galt had to face the disgruntled shareholders in London. It seemed an impossible task because the outlook was so bleak and all that he could promise was a shaky CPR contract and stalled land negotiations. Fortunately, William Burdett-Coutts was still optimistic that the enterprises could succeed and he helped Galt persuade the directors to accept a complete rearrangement of the firm's capitalization, a scheme designed to make financial operations less expensive and render ultimate success more likely. It is a tribute to the enthusiastic salesmanship of Galt that he convinced the skeptical financiers to safeguard their investment by converting their relatively solid shares into more insecure stocks. After several stormy meetings, the directors agreed to reduce the ordinary share capital from $1,750,000 to $100,000, to decrease the interest rate on a preference dividend by one percent, to authorize a £125,000 prior lien debenture, and to convert the endangered first mortgage debenture and its overdue coupons into two new issues of debenture stock.[5]

The rearrangement of the financial structure nearly collapsed before it was formally concluded. Even during the winter months the CPR was not buying their full amount of coal and so the Bank of Montreal was hounding Galt for repayment of the CPR's guaranteed loan.[6] To make matters worse, the Western Federation of Miners, recently formed in Butte, threatened to call for a boycott of Galt coal in Montana unless Galt increased the rates for contract miners by seventy-five percent. Perhaps the labour union's demand was altruistic, but it would certainly ruin Galt's competitive position in Montana, causing a decrease in employment at the Lethbridge collieries, thereby increasing employment among the state's coal-miners. In any case, Galt rushed to Butte to dissuade the union, but it was to no avail. The union asked for the boycott.[7] If it should succeed and if the CPR's consumption remained sluggish, the AR&CCo would be unable to meet its creditors and bankruptcy was inevitable. Once again Galt sought out Shaughnessy and in April the two men agreed that the CPR would take delivery of 2,500 tons of coal per month for the next four months while the AR&CCo stored an equivalent amount to be used during the busy grain shipping season. The agreement was enough to save the AR&CCo's recapitalization, particularly because the American union's boycott had no effect upon coal sales in Montana.[8] The AR&CCo was saved for another year.

Even with the autumn grain shipments, the CPR hardly burned its regular allotments, let alone the stored coal. A pattern began to emerge. During the summer months, when traffic was slow, the CPR dropped behind in purchases but made up the shortfall during the busy autumn season.[9] Although the situation was far from ideal, particularly in regard to regular employment, Elliott Galt had forced the CPR to honour its contract and so saved the AR&CCo from collapse. In September 1895 he negotiated a large sale with the Great Northern but used the low price at which he sold the coal as an excuse to beat down demands for higher wages by the colliery drivers.[10]

By October 1896 the Lethbridge mines still were the largest producers of coal in the North West Territories. During the preceding twelve months they had extracted 120,000 tons of coal, fully twice as much as their nearest rival. Next in size was the McNeill colliery at Canmore, the exclusive supplier of fuel on the CPR Kamloops-Medicine Hat section. McNeill also suffered from the sluggish growth of CPR traffic and in 1895 readily accepted a suggestion by Shaughnessy that he build coke ovens and ship their product to the Trail smelters.[11] Canmore coke proved unsuitable and the experiment collapsed. The third largest enterprise was at Anthracite, which sold hard coal on the very competitive Winnipeg market. Its position improved somewhat when Pennsylvania producers increased their prices, but it still only sold a paltry 20,000 tons in 1896. Elsewhere, at Okotoks, Knee Hill, and Souris, individuals and small concerns dug coal out of river banks for local consumption but commercial production totalled less than a quarter of Galt's output. More promising was the Edmonton field where operators were beginning to use the Calgary and Edmonton railway to ship coal to Calgary.[12] For some time, however, the Galt collieries continued to dominate the domestic market.

Meanwhile much of Galt's effort was directed towards implementing the irrigation scheme. Success still seemed remote because so few people outside the Palliser Triangle saw any need for irrigation, while settlers within this semi-arid region hoped that the prevailing dry spell was but an aberration from a more moist climate. Without a ground swell of public support, the federal government was unlikely to grant federal assistance to irrigation projects; without subsidies, few investors were prepared to undertake such an expensive and risky venture.

The public official largely responsible for changing the government's attitude toward irrigation was William Pearce, officially the superintendent of mines but actually broadly in charge of western settlement. Pearce, stationed in Calgary, was an ardent advocate of western resource development who thought that the foremost problem in western Canada, the irregularity of rainfall, could best be remedied by irrigation.[13] As long ago as 1885 in his report to the department of the interior, he had urged the government to become actively involved in extensive irrigation projects, and subsequently in report after report he championed the cause. One of his chief concerns was that the lack of government regulation and support would lead to a chaos of small, disjointed irrigation projects, which would squander precious water. He also worried that Montana's irrigation plans might destroy the Galt proposal. Largely because of his interest in western settlement Pearce had met Charles Magrath and the two had become close friends. He also grew to admire the industrious Mormons, especially their leader C. Ora Card. Pearce, therefore, took a special interest in the St. Mary scheme and used all his powers of persuasion, including the threatened Montana diversion, to sway the federal government to support irrigation for southern Alberta.[14]

For a long time government officials were suspicious of Pearce's suggestions. The pace of western settlement was a great disappointment to them and so they feared that talk of irrigation could easily produce rumours that the Northwest contained only arid lands, scaring away prospective settlers. The deputy minister of the interior, A. M. Burgess, warned Pearce to "deal gently with the question of irrigation" as only a small section of the West could be treated. "At this stage of the history of the country," Burgess continued, "much harm would result from any public discussion which would seem to indicate that any considerable proportion of the land is unfit for cultivation except by the aid of irrigation."[15] Consequently, the government turned a deaf ear to all appeals made by local boards of trade or regional officials, particularly if such petitions included financial aid to irrigation. It was an attitude they could not maintain indefinitely. The prolonged drought lingering in southern Alberta during the 1880s and early 1890s created the nagging fear that perhaps dryness was the prevailing feature of the south. Western settlers, haunted by the spectre of failure, blamed the CPR and the Canadian government for leading them to this region and began to agitate for relief.

Persistent arguments by William Pearce, Charles Magrath, and the southern Alberta press suggested that at least the government could regulate the water resources of the territories in order to prevent wastage. Finally, the federal administration was spurred into action, albeit sluggish at best. In 1892 the minister of the interior summoned William Pearce to Ottawa to help draw a comprehensive water policy, and later in the year he commissioned J. S. Dennis, the chief inspector of surveys, to study various irrigation systems in the western United States in preparation for the required legislation. The government did not present a bill to the House of Commons until February 1893, and then withdrew it in favour of more pressing business, an action which greatly incensed the prairie press. The delay permitted a more carefully drafted bill as Pearce, who helped write the legislation, passed the measure around to various westerners like Magrath and Card for comments.[16] Parliament did not pass the North West Irrigation Act until 1894, when it vested all water rights in the crown and provided for the controlled use of the water resources of the Northwest.

Meanwhile Pearce and Magrath continued to mobilize western sentiment in favour of irrigation. They helped organize local associations such as the South West Irrigation League, launched in March 1894. At the founding convention of the league in Calgary the delegates sent a strongly worded resolution to the federal government asking for a comprehensive survey of the semi-arid portion of the prairies and a master irrigation plan for southern Alberta, statements that clearly bore the imprint of William Pearce and his staunch ally Charles Magrath. The league also marshalled a strong delegation that travelled to Ottawa on free CPR passes to meet with federal administrators, including the prime minister, Sir John Thompson. The group, led by Charles Magrath, once again underscored the need for a systematic approach to the use of western rivers for irrigation.[17]

By the fall of 1894 the federal government decided to determine which irrigation projects were feasible but to leave the actual implementation of the schemes to private developers. The following summer, C. J. Dennis, also an active advocate of irrigation, surveyed several rivers in southern Alberta "so that an intelligent control might be exercised in the application of the available water supply for the reclamation of unproductive areas."[18] Since the St. Mary project seemed most likely to go ahead soon, the party devoted most of its time to that river and it located a suitable intake as well as part of the route for the proposed canal. Even though they continued the surveys for several years and determined that irrigation was possible at a number of locations, the government refused to provide tangible financial assistance to any specific irrigation scheme.

Although the lack of funds had contributed to the failure of previous irrigation plans, the manner in which the AR&CCo held lands was also a factor. While alternate townships were convenient for ranching purposes, they proved unsuitable for irrigation because any canal had to traverse crown, school, and private as well as company lands, doubling construction costs and inflating land values at company expense. To make the project feasible, the AR&CCo had to have one solid block of land. Charles Magrath, aided at various times by Elliott Galt, spent four months in Ottawa during the early summer of 1895 gathering support for this major change in Canada's land policy. He was strongly supported by William Pearce who had recommended adoption of this principle as long ago as his 1885 annual report. After lengthy deliberations and considerable bickering, the minister of the interior, T. Mayne Daly, agreed that irregular and separated parcels of land would lead to small and wasteful irrigation projects; he concluded, therefore, that "to make irrigation practicable, and ... to utilize to the best advantage the supply of water ... the tracts to be irrigated must be defined with relation to the physical configuration of the country, and cannot be governed by the rectangular sectional system of survey."[19] Since the principle of land consolidation had been applied to settle the CPR subsidy, the minister of the interior argued that it could be extended to the AR&CCo as well. The issue was very sensitive to a cabinet beset by political difficulties and Prime Minister Bowell was afraid to make a politically unpopular decision. In the end, however, cabinet approved Daly's recommendation and permitted the AR&CCo to trade part of its land grant for a half-million-acre triangle of land southeast of the St. Mary River. The government clearly indicated that it was not prepared to grant financial assistance to any irrigation project as long as more humid lands remained elsewhere.[20] A few months later the government also renewed the Alberta Irrigation Company's charter authorizing it to build an irrigation canal to be completed within ten years.[21] All that remained for Elliott Galt was to seek the necessary capital to implement the irrigation scheme.

His search for financial backing was eased considerably by a complex series of events. The spectacular gold discoveries in South Africa were partially responsible for halting the decline in American wheat prices, which had risen steadily since 1893. At the same time, free land in the United States ran out, and settlers began to look to the Canadian Northwest. Agriculture was considered more profitable with the introduction of dry-farming techniques, well suited for wheat production. Rapid transportation of bulk wheat shipments overseas was made possible by the recently developed chain of grain elevators, railways, and large grain ships. Grain became one of Canada's great export commodities and her western lands began to attract farmers. Aided by the new era of optimism and economic buoyancy, the government revamped its immigration program and hundreds of thousands of American, British, and European immigrants came to Canada every year. As the trickle of settlers swelled to a flood, western Canadian development once again interested foreign financiers and finally made Alberta irrigation possible.

Several other more immediate factors, when added to the brightening economic outlook, made the irrigation project more feasible than before. In 1897 the Canadian government concluded an agreement with the CPR under which the railway company,

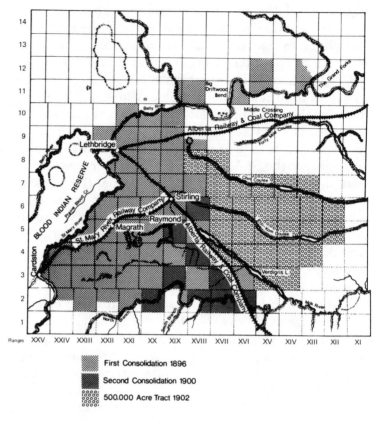

First Consolidation 1896

Second Consolidation 1900

500.000 Acre Tract 1902

Map II   Galt Consolidated Land Holdings

aided by government subsidies, undertook to build an extension through the Crowsnest Pass. The CPR was the administration's logical choice because in return for the subsidy, it wanted a reduction in some western freight rates. Neither the AR&CCo, which held the original charter, nor some of the other interested firms were able to make such a concession, and thus they did not win the government's favour.[22] The CPR began the survey of the Crowsnest route in April 1897 and later that summer commenced the grading of the road-bed. The commencement of construction work created a flurry of activity on the southwestern prairies. Hundreds of workers and contractors converged on the region. The new railway promised to end the economic stagnancy of the area because it would provide access to the rich coal-seams of the Crowsnest valley. The opening of coal-mines, in turn, would lead to the establishment of new towns, which in themselves would be a ready market for agricultural products. Consequently, the fertile lands held by the Galt companies, located so near this economic bustle, took on new value. Railway construction, as always, signalled the creation of new wealth, prosperity, and progress.

The CPR extension into the Crowsnest Pass also led to the tightening of its control over the AR&CCo. The transcontinental could not permit another company to control a vital part of its alternate route to British Columbia. Consequently, in September 1897 the CPR purchased the Dunmore-Lethbridge line for $976,950.[23] Considering that the road was of crucial importance to the CPR and that the AR&CCo had spent $900,000 to build and upgrade the railway (exclusive of interest charges), the deal was not overly generous. But Elliott Galt probably never expected to extract fabulous profits from a shrewd pair like Shaughnessy and Van Horne. To him it was sufficient that the arrangement relieved some of the financial pressure on the AR&CCo and at the same time cemented ties with the transcontinental. Galt could hardly afford to antagonize his most valued customer by remaining a rival in the field of transportation. In the past, his tenuous friendship with important CPR officials, particularly Thomas Shaughnessy, had given him a voice, however small, in the company's policies, but as the business grew larger every year, it became increasingly difficult for him to establish a personal relationship with CPR decision-makers. To survive in the shadow of the giant corporation, Galt decided to move circumspectly in the realms of railways and coal-mines while retaining as much freedom as possible in land sales and irrigation.

Perhaps the most important direct stimulus to Galt's irrigation project came from Clifford Sifton, who had become the minister of the interior shortly after the Liberals came to power in 1896. Sifton, a fervent advocate of progress and efficiency, viewed prairie colonization in business terms as a problem to be solved with proper marketing techniques. In his opinion, Canada's surplus lands had to be sold through aggressive advertising, and settlers required systematic processing like any other commodity.[24] Sifton was familiar with the southwestern prairies and had no qualms about adverse publicity emanating from the demands of irrigationists. In fact, he became an enthusiastic supporter of the concept, much to the surprise of Charles Magrath. In the summer of 1897, Magrath called on the new minister of the interior and during the initial pleasantries revealed that he was on leave from the AR&CCo because he planned to move from southern Alberta. He explained that there was little future for him in the region because its ranching economy required large investments but did not result in the rapid circulation of great amounts of money. Only irrigation could give the area a vigorous and dynamic economy. When Sifton retorted, "Why do you not irrigate it?" Magrath smiled benevolently and casually replied, "Where does the government come in on that task?"

"What do you want the government to do?" Sifton shot back. The question momentarily floored Magrath because he and Galt had long ago abandoned all hope of government subsidies. On the spur of the moment he asked Sifton to refund all the survey dues the AR&CCo had paid on its land grant. Without a moment's hesitation Sifton agreed and promised further help if the company fulfilled its obligations. Magrath later confessed that it was the "most amazing interview [he] had ever had with any man in... Public Life."[25]

The government grant was not large but it represented a definite commitment to irrigation and a tacit approval of the St. Mary scheme. It was also the signal Elliott Galt had waited for and he quickly dispatched Magrath to Utah to revive the old agreement with the Mormon church. Magrath shuttled back and forth between Salt Lake City and Lethbridge several times during September and on his last trip Elliott Galt accompanied him to sign a preliminary agreement. The Church of the Latter Day Saints promised to supply all the labour to dig the canals in return for payment of one-half in cash and one-half in land, the land with water rights being valued at three dollars per acre, to a total of $75,000 and 25,000 acres. The properties were to be divided into two large tracts twenty and thirty miles south of Lethbridge, each supporting a hamlet of about fifty families recruited by the Mormon church. Galt agreed to advance the settlers the cost of transporting the families to the new location.[26] Since the western Canadian promoters could "well imagine what a howl would go up

Parts of the irrigation works required expensive
structures such as the flume shown here. (Glenbow
Archives)

from some of the many narrow minded people in the East," they
decided to avoid the word "Mormons" when promoting the scheme
in favour of the euphemistic "Utah gentlemen" and "Utah
friends."[27]

Although the contract was not as large as the original 1891
accord, it was sufficient to mobilize the project. Magrath travelled
to Denver, Colorado, in November and hired the best known
irrigation expert in North America, G. G. Anderson, to supervise
the technical details of the undertaking. Meanwhile Galt approached Thomas Shaughnessy. Arguing that the irrigated lands
would attract a large body of settlers, resulting in a substantial
increase in CPR traffic, Galt asked the railway company to make a
contribution to the cost of the canal. Shaughnessy was impressed
with Galt's work, particularly because the Mormons, whom he
considered to be "the most efficient colonizing instruments on this
continent," were involved. Consequently, because of the settlement on irrigated lands, the CPR agreed to rebate the Alberta
Irrigation Company fifteen percent of the gross revenues earned
by the company on the Dunmore-Lethbridge line to a maximum
of $100,000 spread over ten years.[28]

Galt was ecstatic. The last six or seven years had been sheer agony, "walking through the valley of the shadow of death," he once confided to a close friend.[29] Sleepless nights and constant worry appeared to have been his lot in life as setback after setback pounded all his endeavours to near ruin. He had not dared to abandon the quest to convert the semi-arid ranching country into irrigated farm lands. For, as he once explained, "We had expended large sums and we were compelled to go ahead and protect what we had already invested."[30] Fortunately his deep-seated optimism had steadied him as he walked the edge of disaster; he had endured adversities even while failure appeared imminent. Finally things were falling into place. Christmas 1897 was an exhilarating time as he planned a trip shortly after the festive season to lay before the London directors the rejuvenated irrigation scheme. The negotiations might be difficult, even tricky. But, could he not reel off the exciting statistics proving increasing immigration, rising grain prices, expanding wheat production, and growing investments in western Canada? Could he not show them the agreement with the Mormon church, the CPR's $100,000 pledge, and the Canadian government's $50,000 rebate? The vote of confidence by each of these parties was no longer an idealistic pipe dream but a realistic, responsible investment. To be sure, the proposal, estimated to cost $600,000, might be too expensive for the Alberta Irrigation Company to handle, but it could begin the construction while he worked to organize a new company to buy up the required lands.

Despite Galt's enthusiasm, the directors of the Alberta Irrigation Company were skeptical of his scheme. They thought it was "experimental" and they dispatched a British engineer to Lethbridge to study the feasibility of the plan. When the consultant reported favourably in June 1898, the board cautiously endorsed the project. Galt was elated. "It is a great relief to me to have got everything in good shape, for as you know, I have worked hard to this end, and it would have been a great disappointment to me had I been obliged to drop the project, as it were, at the eleventh hour," he wrote his mother. "With the irrigation scheme operative, I shall have to spend a great deal more time in the Western country than of late years for I shall risk a great deal of money and I must give my whole energies towards making it succeed."[31] Later that summer he borrowed one of his father's old tricks and asked the minister of the interior to approve the rebate of the survey fees immediately rather than after the completion of one-third of the construction. Sifton had grown to admire the aggressive Galt and his grand expansionist schemes, but he was too much a business-man to grant the request.[32] Galt had to prove himself first.

On 26 August 1898, Charles Ora Card plowed the first furrow for the ditch. The plan called for the canal to be dug from the St. Mary at a point close to the international border, to angle northeastward, to pass near the present-day towns of Magrath and Stirling, and to terminate near Lethbridge. Such a long canal was necessary because the St. Mary ran nearly three hundred feet below the lands to be irrigated. So, to spare the cost of pumping stations, the company placed the water intake at an upstream site that lay above the lands to be watered. It was a gigantic under-taking as no steam shovels or dredges were used. During the fall and winter, thirty to forty teams excavated the heavy cuts and in the spring another two hundred teams joined them. They had to move well over a million cubic yards of dirt and use over a million board feet of lumber for the sluiceways, gates, and several build-ings. The work was difficult and sometimes the heavy rains that plagued the area that summer made the task nearly impossible. Ironically, wet weather prevented the completion of the project during the summer and at the end of 1899 about fifteen percent of the work remained to be done. Most of the crews had left the project for the foothills to cut wood for fencing and personal buildings.[33]

Charles Magrath headed the team of engineers, contractors, and teamsters who built the canal. It was a hectic time and, under pressure from Galt, he refused a nomination in 1898 for the territorial assembly. At dissolution he had been a minister without portfolio in Haultain's small cabinet, but politics took too much of his time. Since irrigation had been his ambition for the last eight years, the choice was easy and he energetically plunged into the tremendous task. He supervised the construction work, the trans-portation of the Mormon settlers and their equipment, and the founding of two villages, one of which was named after him and the other, Stirling, after a prominent Mormon. He arranged for the creation of school districts and used the buildings as reception centres. Meanwhile he launched an advertising campaign to attract more buyers for the land. During all this bustle Magrath found time to marry Mabel Galt, one of Elliott Galt's sisters.[34]

During 1899 Galt completed the financial arrangements for the undertaking. He founded the Canadian North-west Irrigation Company to purchase 73,374 acres from the AR&CCo and 26,626 acres of land from the Lethbridge Land Company at $1.25 per acre. The new company reserved the right to buy another 150,000 acres before July 1903. Capitalized at $400,000 in $100-shares, the firm's headquarters were in London. Elliott Galt was president and William Burdett-Coutts was vice-president. The Canadian North-west Irrigation Company's task was to sell the newly irrigated lands and to maintain the canal.[35]

In the spring of 1900 construction work resumed and by early summer it was finished. On 4 July 1900, G. G. Anderson wired Magrath: "Main Canal completed. I will turn water on in an hour and will report day by day."[36] Later in the month water flowed into Lethbridge and in September Governor-General Lord Minto officially opened the canal. Within a period of two years the workers had excavated 115 miles of canal, including the thirty-two-mile Lethbridge and twenty-two-mile Stirling branches.

With the completion of the canals the North-west Irrigation Company was ready to sell its lands to prospective settlers. It embarked upon an extensive advertising campaign in eastern Canada, the United States, and Europe. The company published several brochures, one of which labelled southern Alberta as the "Colorado of Canada" and included a testimonial from a prominent Mormon leader, Levi Harker, boasting of the fabulous yields possible on irrigated lands. The firm also advertised at a stockmen's convention in Salt Lake City, sent photographs to European exhibitions and, with the Lethbridge town council, subsidized an Ontario publicity tour by Charles McKillop, the local Presbyterian pastor. The federal government helped by preparing a special pamphlet, many copies of which were distributed at the Pan-American exhibition. The *Manitoba Free Press* and the Montreal *Herald* were only two of the many newspapers that featured stories on the irrigation project. All this promotional literature stressed the certainty of good crops with irrigation, for as one tract said, "The farmer is in fact his own rainmaker."[37]

Ironically, a rainmaker was not needed. Simultaneously with the construction of the irrigation works, the region experienced one of its wet spells. In 1898 and 1899 the countryside nearly drowned under torrential rains; floods turned creeks and coulees into raging rivers and badly eroded the freshly dug canals. One settler wrote:

On June 17th 1899 rain fell and soon became a deluge and for two weeks it rained without stopping. The canvas of our tent could no longer shed the water and it poured through [onto] the beds and all despite the tubs, pans and all else used to try and stay it.[38]

In 1902 three rainstorms swamped southern Alberta and washed out large portions of the canals, disabling the entire system. Prospective land buyers sarcastically remarked that the company should have built drainage rather than irrigation ditches.

Sales were extremely slow during these first few years and by the end of December 1901 the Canadian North-west Irrigation Company had signed only 145 water agreements, many of which were only with partial users.[39] Magrath, who was in charge of land sales, discovered that few settlers had enough money to buy the relatively expensive irrigated lands and water rights. Most of them preferred the cheaper and still abundant non-irrigated farmland. "Owing to the very large area of lands in this country not requiring irrigation and the exceedingly small settlements that we have I believe that irrigation projects in the West are from five to ten years in advance of their times," he confessed to Pearce and added significantly, "In our case there was no alternative; the coal Company had the lands and it became necessary to do something, as otherwise it looked as if the lands could never be utilized."[40] Even with the large investment in irrigation, the land had acquired no utility, no real economic value to Magrath and the company. Not until the more usual dry weather returned, and more and more colonists scrambled for the rapidly shrinking acres of un- cultivated prairies, did the Lethbridge area offer a profitable alternative to dry land farms, and so bring the returns for which Magrath and his associates had toiled.

During this period of sluggish land sales Elliott Galt continued to stimulate the region's economy with still more investments. In much of this work he received valuable assistance from Clifford Sifton. Sharing Galt's driving ambition for change and expansion, the minister of the interior applauded the promoter's innovative efforts in southern Alberta. The two men instinctively understood each other and they became close associates in the business of developing western Canada. They held numerous meetings and Sifton, who was by this time an enthusiastic convert to irrigation, handsomely supported Galt's companies with government funds and lands. He permitted the AR&CCo to consolidate another 360,000 acres of land so that most of its holdings were in one solid unit of land south of Lethbridge. He also forgave the company the survey dues on an additional 320,000 acres, bringing the total reimbursement to $80,000. Third, the minister sanctioned the surrender of over 22,000 acres that Galt considered too far removed from the consolidated holdings. Although the AR&CCo had paid only ten cents per acre for this land, the government redeemed it at three dollars per acre. In return for all these favours, the Canadian North-west Irrigation Company enlarged the main canal to allow for an increased flow of water and promised to expand the whole system to several thousand more acres.[41] Galt's companies, with their proven record of performance, were the beneficiaries of the heady boom mentality that sprang out of the explosive population growth hitting the prairies at the turn of the century. Although people and capital suddenly flowed in abundance to this new land of opportunity, government officials still felt obliged to encourage further investments with generous concessions.

The government's munificence, incited by the reckless spirit of unprecedented economic growth, also favoured Galt's railway expansion. In 1900 he incorporated the St. Mary's River Railway Company to build a railway from the AR&CCo line at Stirling to the intake of the canal, and with a branch line to Cardston. During the summer the new company completed the first thirty miles and received a federal bonus of $2,500 per mile.[42] The next year Galt asked the government to grant a further bonus on the remaining thirty-two miles for a bridge across the St. Mary and for the widening of the AR&CCo line from Lethbridge to the international border. In a letter seeking support from Sifton, Galt extolled the virtues of his companies. "We are filling up our District in the North West with desirable settlers & any assistance afforded to us by the Government means more rapid development & acts as [a] stimulus to other [companies] holding large areas of land to follow in our steps instead of letting their lands remain vacant & useless."[43] The cabinet refused the petition and so Galt did not extend the St. Mary railway that year. During the next year Galt wooed the support of Wilfrid Laurier, Clifford Sifton, and A. G. Blair, the minister of railways. In 1903 the government reconsidered and agreed to bonus the remainder of the railway at the usual rate.[44] Galt completed the work that year.

Galt also sought to improve the economic climate in southern Alberta by upgrading the obsolete Montana railway to standard gauge. In December 1900 at the AR&CCo annual meeting he sought approval for this improvement but was disappointed by the reluctance of his fellow directors to invest more money in southern Alberta railways. "My people here recognize things [have] greatly improved but worry and harrass me with stupid difficulties in the way of carrying through change of gauge," he complained to Magrath. "They move slowly and the delay causes me more annoyance than anything else."[45] Never one to be rebuffed by demurring financiers, Galt crossed the ocean in January to meet with J. J. Hill in St. Paul, Minnesota, and propose to him that the Great Northern purchase the Lethbridge-Great Falls railway. Hill was not interested but because he did want the Great Falls-Shelby portion he agreed to buy the American part of the road for £150,000 if Galt widened the Canadian section. With the agreement in hand Galt crossed the rough wintery Atlantic once again to obtain the directors' consent. They supported the project largely because half of the revenues derived from the sale covered the expense of standardizing the Canadian line while the other half could pay off some prior lien debenture stock.[46]

Galt also had a hand in another large project for the region. He encouraged Jesse Knight, a wealthy Mormon, to build a sugar refinery at Raymond. Working through Clifford Sifton, Galt obtained a tariff exemption on all the American machinery for the factory. Knight bought 60,000 acres of land and secured an option for an additional 200,000 acres near Raymond. Late in the summer of 1901 he used eighty teams in a row to break the land in preparation for the following year's seeding of sugar-beets. The sugar factory commenced production in 1903 and operated sporadically until 1917 when it closed due to heavy national competition and the lack of sugar-beets.[47]

Also in the summer of 1901, C. A. Magrath eagerly accepted an offer by Professor William H. Fairfield, superintendent of the experimental station of the College of Agriculture at Laramie, Wyoming, to establish a model farm at Lethbridge. Under an agreement worked out at a meeting in Salt Lake City, the company provided land, buildings, seed, equipment, and one labourer, while Fairfield and his brother Harry furnished the remaining labour and supervisory staff. The brothers promised to commence repayment of all these expenses after three years of operation. It was a happy arrangement. Fairfield experimented with a variety of grains, grasses, fruits, and shelter-belt trees. He spoke to organizations about his findings and advised settlers on irrigation techniques. The most notable contribution was his discovery that southern Alberta lacked the nitrogen-fixing bacteria essential to healthy alfalfa growth. To solve this problem he imported some soil from a Wyoming alfalfa field and scattered it about his farm. After this treatment alfalfa grew abundantly and local farmers could obtain infected soil from the model farm. Despite the experimental nature of the farm and Fairfield's advisory duties, the two brothers made the concern a self-sufficient, even profitable endeavour, which was of immeasurable value to the local settlers.[48]

By 1902 Elliott Galt was certain that the irrigation experiment was going to be successful and, with the increasing flow of immigrants into western Canada, he believed he could sell more irrigated lands. He asked the government to subsidize an even more ambitious irrigation plan than the St. Mary project. The cabinet, by this time liberated from any fears about adverse publicity, was eager to help the irrigationists and in December 1902, authorized the fourth land subsidy to the Galt interests. Under this agreement the government sold the Canadian Northwest Irrigation Company half a million acres of land, directly south of Lethbridge, adjoining the consolidated land grant, for three dollars per acre. The federal government gave the company a credit of $300,000 for irrigation works already completed and promised a further credit of $700,000 on account of the cost of constructing new facilities. The remaining $500,000 was to be paid in ten equal instalments at five-percent interest, but the first payment was not due until 1 December 1907. Any lands unsold after fifteen years were to revert to the Crown.[49] The settlement was most generous, particularly because it repaid the company half the cost of constructing the original canal and, through a literal interpretation of the contract, company officials managed to win several lucrative bonuses that were outside the spirit of the agreement.

Galt's company spent $250,000 on a canal to divert water from the Milk River to the southern portion of the newly acquired properties but it soon abandoned the project when Montana revived its plans to dam the St. Mary and divert water through the Milk River to arid lands in Montana. Without a clear-cut treaty regulating the use of these two international rivers, Galt refused to spend more money on the Milk River scheme. Undaunted, however, he used the remainder of the credits on improving and expanding the existing St. Mary system. By 1906 the company had extended the canal nine miles northward from Lethbridge and a shorter distance eastward. That summer three large crews with teams and steam dredges enlarged the main canal to twice its former capacity.[50] Meanwhile company officials simply sent the government statements of the monies spent and the bureaucrats honoured them. The deputy minister of the interior explained that there was "nothing in the agreement requiring the company to build canals to serve any described tract nor to irrigate any portion of the tract sold."[51] As a result of this strict interpretation of the contract the company was able to buy half a million acres of land cheaply and sell off portions at the government maximum ceiling of five dollars an acre without irrigating any of it. The credits were used to improve the existing irrigation system that served the lands received earlier as railway subsidies.

The sudden turn in fortunes of the Lethbridge enterprises enabled Elliott Galt to engineer his most brilliant financial feat yet. After an extremely difficult round of negotiations early in 1904 he brought about the merger of all his companies under one corporation. The new firm, called the Alberta Railway and Irrigation Company (AR&ICo), was incorporated in Canada in June and came to life on 1 October 1904. All the stockholders of the Canadian North-west Irrigation Company, the Alberta Railway and Coal Company, the Lethbridge Land Company, and the St. Mary's River Railway Company were generously rewarded for their patient trust in Galt's vision. They were compensated by various combinations of cash settlements and the conversion of old securities into new shares on very liberal terms. The new corporation was capitalized at $7,750,000: $3,250,000 in shares, $1,250,000 in a four-percent prior lien debenture, and $3,250,000 in five-percent debenture stock. In the end the new board of directors contained only those whole-heartedly committed to the Lethbridge ventures. Included were Elliott Galt's closest allies in London, W. Burdett-Coutts and Colonel K. R. B. Wodehouse; Montreal financiers W. M. Ramsay and E. S. Clouston; and his younger brother, John Galt of Winnipeg. Elliott Galt was chosen president of the AR&ICo, while C. A. Magrath became the land commissioner and assistant to the president. For his royal salary of $6,300 per year he was expected to manage land sales and water distribution, stimulate colonization and industrial development, and maintain and expand the canal system.[52]

The creation of the AR&ICo as a big business attracted the attention of Augustus M. Nanton, the Winnipeg-based partner in the prestigious Toronto financial firm of Osler, Hammond, and Nanton. One of western Canada's most prominent financiers, Nanton had settled in Winnipeg in 1884 as an employee of the company to find new investment opportunities for some Scottish clients. With shrewd prudence, rare in those reckless days, the hard-working Nanton built a prosperous portfolio in railways, insurance, mortgages, and real estate. So notable was his success that in 1890, at the age of thirty, his employer made him a full partner. With the mushrooming western Canadian economy, Nanton's career blossomed. He was involved in railways in southern Alberta, including the CPR, and he assumed directorships in a great variety of companies. In 1900 he became an agent of the AR&CCo and so learned to know the business well. At the end of 1904 his firm began to buy up AR&ICo shares and in June 1905 Nanton took the position of managing director.[53] For the first time in its corporate history, Lethbridge enjoyed the backing of Toronto capital.

Nanton took on the task of managing the AR&ICo at a most favourable time. The only trouble spot in the company's domain was the mining enterprise at Lethbridge. Although the phenomenal influx of settlers onto the prairies and the frantic expansion of railways across the Northwest generated a prodigious appetite for fuel, the Lethbridge mines did not grow accordingly. In fact their output dropped slightly from 168,000 tons in 1898 to 154,000 tons in 1902, rose quite steeply to 230,000 tons in 1903 and to 270,000 tons in 1904, but then fell again to 223,000 tons in 1905.[54] Even though the position of the colliery by 1905 was much better than in the early 1890s, it failed to keep pace with the unprecedented growth of the prairie population.

In 1900 P. L. Naismith, the mine manager, still blamed this poor performance on the limitations of the regional market. He explained that the territorial coal industry had been "a struggling one for years" because of "the sparsely settled conditions of the country and the absence of manufacturers."[55] While Naismith's comments explained the quandary of the industry as a whole, it hardly accounted for the special problem facing the Galt mines. The reason for their unspectacular growth during a time of unprecedented economic expansion was that too many promoters were scrambling to take advantage of the rapid rise in fuel consumption. The CPR extension through the Crowsnest Pass, for example, opened the rich coal-seams there to several large mines. In 1902 when none of these were yet sufficiently developed to harm the Lethbridge collieries, a government mine inspector predicted, "There is no doubt this mine must suffer from the large developments in the Blairmore District as the coal from that point is a much superior Steam Coal, the Lethbridge Mine having mainly to depend now on Domestic sales which are much larger in the winter months."[56] Within the next three years four more companies opened mines on the Alberta side of the pass while further north another joined the McNeill company in the Kicking Horse Pass. Whereas in 1901 the Galt mines produced fully one-half of all the coal in the Alberta district, five years later it had slipped to one-third. The future was obvious: the AR&ICo was going to lose the relatively stable railway market and become more and more dependent upon the wildly fluctuating demands of domestic consumers.

The AR&ICo never fully adjusted to the tremendous wild swings of home fuel consumption. The highly seasonal market, which peaked in the winter and slumped badly in the spring, crippled the efficiency of the colliery because costly machinery stood idle in the off season while the scarcity of labour prevented their full use at the busy time. The large investment in a highly mechanized mine demanded a stable year-round market creating a steady income to offset its high fixed costs. By the end of 1905 the Galt collieries were wringing the maximum benefit from the most advanced mining technology of the time, but it was not enough. They were the largest and most efficient producers of domestic coal in western Canada but they barely recovered their expenses. The problem was exacerbated by the dozens of new operators who every year optimistically but foolishly started new mines. The plethora of small, wasteful, and underfinanced mining endeavours, which sprang up each autumn everywhere in the province in the hope of quick returns, in fact competed each other to death and simultaneously robbed the larger efficient producers of profits.

The AR&ICo could sustain the low returns on its coal-mines because it enjoyed revenues from railways, irrigation canals, and land sales. In June 1905, when A. M. Nanton assumed the managing directorship, Galt released the company's first annual report covering the previous nine months. For the first time in many years he announced a dividend on the company's stock. The profits that year were still small, he explained, because the land was being sold on credit; consequently, a hefty $100,000 profit on paper had dwindled to a $5,000 return in cash. Nevertheless, he predicted a possible $300,000 cash surplus for the coming year consisting of about $250,000 from the railway and coal operations, $36,000 from interest on mortgages, $10,000 from water rentals, and $10,000 from land sales. Although the income from railways and coal-mines loomed large in Galt's tally, promising potential revenue was from land sales. The company still owned nearly a million acres of underdeveloped farmlands with an estimated value of over ten million dollars. The company already held $760,000 in mortgages, a figure that rose with every acre sold and earned interest in ever-increasing amounts. Finally, the land was sold to settlers who used the railways and burned coal. As Galt declared, with the collieries and railways finally paying their own way, the land was a handsome bonus.[57]

The creation of the AR&ICo and the appointment of A. M. Nanton climaxed Galt's career. His health was failing and he lost interest in the Lethbridge enterprises. "I hope I shall be given a new lease on life by being relieved of a large portion of my responsibilities which, owing to my health, were becoming more than I could carry," he confessed to Magrath, "Now if large sums of money require to be raised or if bad times come, I shall not have to carry the burden alone."[58] For the last twelve years he had carried on his shoulders the worry of a faltering enterprise hovering near bankruptcy. He could not allow himself to fail, however. The very abhorrence of defeat spurred him on. Failure, he confided to his close friend Burdett-Coutts, would have been a personal financial disaster to him, his mother, and his sisters. Nor could he bear the thought of disappointing his friends in England who had backed him for so many years.[59] Once committed to the project, he had to carry it to completion; once the goal was attained, he lost interest.

Elliott Galt had devoted almost twenty-five years of his life to the Lethbridge enterprises. They had been difficult years as he discovered that the exploitation of the natural resources of western Canada was not the easy job it appeared to be when he first visited Sheran's coal-mine in 1879. Single-minded perseverance had been required to endure the countless trips by train across the continent, or across the stormy Atlantic in uncomfortable ships. How many nights had he spent in lonely hotel rooms? How often had he faced irate shareholders? Once made, the original investment could be saved only by pushing for continual growth. As he once explained to a Winnipeg reporter,[60] it was a course which led him from a coal-mine to steamboats, railways, and irrigation. Although he had guided its direction, the process of growth had nevertheless been necessary and inevitable.

Elliott Galt was more steadfast and introverted than his father. Sir Alexander's resourceful mind had flitted from project to project and his schemes were always part of a grand design for the nation or even the empire. To be sure, profit had been the senior Galt's aim but that, too, was viewed within the broad context of Canada's welfare. His son's quest for material gain was confined almost entirely to the companies. Elliott Galt's primary concern was to manage the firms as efficiently as possible and that had demanded all his attention. There was no time for public affairs, no interest in political office. He exacted from his senior administrators the same devotion to the business. In 1903, for instance, when Prime Minister Laurier and Clifford Sifton asked Galt if Magrath could become a Liberal candidate, he emphatically refused.[61] The affairs of the companies came first, and he and his assistants had to expend all their energies on its extensive operations.

Ironically, under Galt's intensive leadership, the companies grew so large that they came to overshadow their president. To the popular mind of the time (and even more to that of today) it was the AR&ICo that brought irrigation to southern Alberta. To some extent Elliott Galt stood in the shadow of his more famous father so that when people spoke of Galt coal they thought only of Sir Alexander and not of his son. More importantly, however, the AR&ICo acquired an identity of its own. It was never Elliott Galt's company.

The public admired the AR&ICo. For many years the Canadian Northwest had been a cul-de-sac overlooked by millions of immigrants flocking to the undeveloped countries of the world. The Canadian government had spent millions of dollars on subsidies to railways and colonization companies, law enforcement and administration, and advertising and transportation bonuses, but the expected flood of settlers had not come. Throughout this period the Galt companies had actively promoted southern Alberta and carried out their obligations. They had always been in the vanguard of settlement, guaranteeing a reliable fuel supply to future colonists and prospective railways, providing winter jobs for pioneer farmers, constructing railways and an irrigation canal even before the settlers arrived. Newspapers and magazines eulogized the ventures because the companies had transformed a wilderness into a productive countryside. The *Free Press* enthusiastically claimed, "The well-being and progress of the district and the enlarged prosperity of the town are due to the faith of [Galt and Magrath] in the country and to their enterprise in the conversion of the prairie waste into a land of well tilled farms, capable of the highest production and with the characteristic comfortable homes belonging to a thriving agricultural community."[62] The prevailing belief of the day taught that Canada's prosperity could best be achieved if one farmer and his family settled on every half-section of land, built his house and barns, cultivated the soil, and planted his crops. The plan envisioned many towns and distribution centres, with industries and packing plants, dairies, and flour mills all connected by a growing network of railways. The AR&ICo completed the infrastructure for this objective just at the start of the greatest flow ever of immigrants to Canada. And so it earned national acclaim. The *Free Press* summed it up nicely: "In view of the far-reaching and magnificent results of the undertaking of the irrigation company in adding to our country's wealth and productivity, the work of the concern loses all aspects of a small municipal enterprise and rises to the dignity of a vast national undertaking."[63]

The *Free Press* unwittingly touched on perhaps the most significant change that the Galts and many other promoters had brought to the prairies. In 1879, when Elliott Galt first arrived on the banks of the Belly River, the lands he saw belonged in practice to whomever was using it at the time. It had no commercial worth. That changed the moment the Canadian government granted land to a company or sold it to a settler. Then the land became real estate which had to be developed, a commodity subject to the economic norms of supply and demand, profit and utility. For decades land remained in over-abundance and the Galt holdings were little more than a burden, useful only as collateral for other projects. "In our case," Galt recalled, "we had to spend large sums of money to give our land value."[64] In the new civilization, which he had helped bring to the Northwest, the yardstick that measured the performance of a company was also applied to the land. The soil had to earn a profit, be it for the large company or the individual settler.

Coal town
in wheat country

During the 1890s the economic base of Lethbridge was still coal. In the intense darkness of the deep underground, interrupted only by tiny jabs of light from their lamps, the miners chipped away at the black fuel, while behind them timbermen erected sets to support the heavy burden of rock and soil bearing down upon the low passageways. Elsewhere drivers and their horses distributed empty coal cars, gathered the full ones, and pulled them through the narrow coal-encrusted tunnels to the shaft. Here labourers hurriedly loaded and unloaded the cages, which lifted the one-ton coal cars onto the tramway and tipped their loads onto the sorting screens and into waiting railway cars, while other men hauled away the unwanted shale and other refuse to the dump. The blackened surface structures of the collieries, standing on the edge of the benchlands, were the centre of the mines. They were vibrantly alive with hissing steam engines, whining gears, revolving drums, shrieking cables, thundering coal cars, and clanging screens. Everywhere the black dust rained and settled in deep layers on tracks, tipples, horses, and men. Day after day the trickles of coal, collected from the many underground rooms, surged along the tracks and welled up the shaft. This flow was the life-blood of Lethbridge and the black surface complex was its heart. When it ceased to pump coal, Lethbridge stagnated.

The stream of coal was seldom constant, however. It ebbed and advanced along with the seasons of summer and winter. This cycle of seasonal production created employment uncertainty and with this came many migrant workers and a disproportionate number of unmarried men. In the town of Lethbridge itself, the mixture of married and single men and women was fairly normal, but in the area north of the tracks, which fell outside the municipal boundaries, the number of single men was high (*See* Table I). In this settlement, variously known as the north ward or Stafford-ville, nearly two-thirds of the population were men while three-quarters of the males were single. Not only do the figures confirm the predominance of men in coal-mining society but they reveal that the railway was a visible boundary between the incorporated town of Lethbridge and the informal settlement of coal workers.

Table I   Population and Conjugal Condition, 1901[1]

	Population			Conjugal Condition	
	Town	North Ward		Town	North Ward
male	834 (57)*	546 (63)	single male	582 (40)	401 (46)
female	628 (43)	318 (37)	single female	384 (26)	191 (22)
total	1,462	864	married male	252 (17)	145 (17)
			married female	244 (17)	127 (15)

*figures in parentheses denote percentages of total population

Although some miners retained their residence in Lethbridge, the majority preferred to live in the shanties and small houses near the mine shafts. Since the shopping and recreational facilities re-mained in Lethbridge, the town was becoming more and more a service centre for the mines and the surrounding area, and a domicile for the merchants, professionals, as well as government and company officials. An 1896 poll listed only thirty-three miners in Lethbridge, but thirty-seven businessmen, six professionals, and eight executives.[2]

The fluctuating production of the collieries affected the rail-way workers as well. These men had much in common with the coal workers. They came from a wide variety of cultural and social backgrounds and were highly mobile. Their occupation was just as stratified and ranged from the respected engineer and station employees through the shopmen and train crews to the lowly section men. Their variable hours of work led to alternating extremes of excessive or scanty pay and a casual attitude toward spending. Since the railroaders travelled often and worked irregular shifts, they had little contact with the townsmen. Only a few of them established homes in Lethbridge; most lived either in hotels or boarding-houses in town or in shacks in the north ward. Yet, their very mobility and isolation from the town residents strengthened their occupational identity. Like the mineworkers, the railway employees regarded their work a man's job of which they were immensely proud.[3]

The masculine solidarity of the collieries and railways naturally carried over into community and family life. Some of the single coal workers lived in company or private boarding-houses near the mine entrances north or just south of the railway yards. Others preferred to stay in shacks and shanties scattered along the river valley and tablelands. Most of the married miners lived in small, often company-owned houses set near the mine shafts. In these homes the men were the bread-winners and masters. They expected their wives to remain quietly in the background serving them and their children. In the closely knit neighbourhoods, recreation and social activities catered to the men and stressed the manly virtues of strength and virility. Usually this simply meant week-ends of heavy drinking, often interrupted by full-fledged brawls. Sometimes these fights degenerated into vicious battles where knives or guns were brandished freely with consequent injuries, even death. Convictions in these serious affrays were rare because the workers, particularly the Europeans, protected each other from police interference so that investigations seldom proved anything conclusive.[4] The violence was rarely a symptom of deep-seated hatred, however, but rather the mark of an overly masculine society, a group of lonely men who, working and living together in a dangerous tough environment, enjoyed feats of brawn and admired physical courage and power. The braggadocio and jovial camaraderie created by the male-oriented underground workings and railways also survived on the surface and in the town.[5]

The nature of the work, the migratory population, and the settlement's isolation had produced a boisterous, lusty society. One of the more conspicuous manifestations of the town's mas-

Coal-mining companies usually built houses for their
employees according to one standard plan. (Glenbow
Archives)

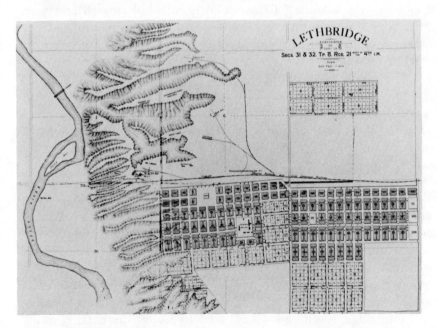

Map III   Lethbridge Town Plan, 1890
Map drawn by C.A. Magrath for the AR&CCo's land department. Of particular interest is the location of the north ward, in the top right quadrant of
the map. Note how Lethbridge's streets are aligned with the main rail line
rather than the more usual township grid. (Glenbow Archives)

culinity was the Point, the prominently displayed red-light district perched on one of the promontories just south of the mine shafts. Gambling was widespread, conducted in a relatively professional manner in the saloons or hotel back rooms, more informally at prize-fights or horse-races, and most commonly in the miners' shanties. The police kept a casual eye on these activities and only occasionally ran a particularly obnoxious character out of town.[6]

The police were in a difficult position, especially in regard to liquor law violations. In 1892, when the federal government withdrew from the field of alcohol control, the territorial assembly instituted a system of licences with restrictions in hours of operation to hotels and wholesalers. The system was wide open for abuse. The territorial inspectorate was understaffed, and in out-of-the-way Lethbridge, virtually non-existent. Several retail stores began to sell liquor illegally, and hotels became noisy saloons with little regard for closing hours. The mounted police were loathe to act because the matter was outside their jurisdiction and they were reluctant to assume the highly unpopular task of closing the saloons.[7] Consequently, alcohol flowed freely in Lethbridge, notably on week-ends when many mine and railway workers seemed bent on spending their entire pay in one boozy whirl of revelling.

The police also ignored the thriving emporium of vice still located at the Point. Instead of rigid enforcement, Captain Burton Deane preferred a policy of supervision over a compact, segregated red-light district, out in the open where he could exercise a measure of control. Occasionally he affirmed his authority by making an arrest and securing a conviction. In one instance, when a well-known citizen appealed his sentence for frequenting, Deane asked permission to represent the state at a higher court: "I am very much interested in the eventual decision," he explained, "because there are a few persons in town, pimps, etc., who are at the bottom of most of the rows that take place and I am bent on making them understand that when they get a Police hint to behave themselves or leave town they must comply forthwith."[8]

The position of the NWMP was in fact very difficult because the Lethbridge town council refused to accept financial responsibility for law enforcement. Although by law the mounted police had no authority in municipalities, the council believed that the

NWMP, which was stationed nearby, should assume this duty free of charge. In 1891 the town council, headed by C. A. Magrath, refused to supply a house for the police constable unoffically assigned to the town. Deane withdrew his man and Magrath in turn hired a licence inspector primarily to collect taxes and licence fees and incidentally to keep law and order. The inspector, who had no constabulary powers, was unable to enforce the law and thus the town council backed down. When it agreed to pay half the rent of a house in the business district, the police assigned a man to town patrol.[9] Clearly, the council, which was willing to make some physical improvements in the town, was not interested in paying for the social burdens of the young industrial society.

Not all Lethbridgeans approved of this policy. Early in 1891 one concerned citizen lamented that Lethbridge was the only town in western Canada where prostitutes were allowed to have open public dances. "Surely there are enough law-abiding people in Lethbridge to compel the harlots and other dissolute persons with which this town is infested, to make themselves a little less conspicuous,"[10] the protestor demanded. But nothing was done until 1894 when the Methodist and Presbyterian pastors called a public meeting to discuss the "flagrant violations of law relating to liquor-selling, gambling, and public morals."[11] Since public entertainment was never abundant in Lethbridge, a large crowd turned out and with great amusement heard Reverend Charles McKillop, the Presbyterian preacher, angrily instruct the council to rid itself of these evils, particularly the "soiled doves." The "soiled doves," however, had sent a lawyer to the assembly and he eloquently and forcefully pleaded that Lethbridge's anti-prostitution bylaws were *ultra vires*, that is, beyond the power of the town. The federal government, the solicitor pointed out, was the rightful guardian of public morals, and so he advised anyone wishing to close the Point to swear out a complaint before a justice of the peace who could prosecute under dominion statutes.[12] Everyone but the clergy saw the wisdom of this advice and the citizenry decided to leave the matter with the police.

The two ministers, and to a lesser extent the congregations they served, viewed the process of establishing a new civilization in the West from a broader perspective than either the town councillors or the mounted police. Concerned with the spiritual welfare of the community, the goals of the pastors were not limited to the material advancement of the town or the most efficient means of law enforcement. Consequently, they urged municipal officials to pass tough morality bylaws and demanded that the police strictly enforce them. The town council, which by and large represented the business establishment, refused while the police, who preferred the town's apathy over the preachers' zeal, resented ministerial interference in their field of expertise. "If [the pastors] would turn their attention to the juvenile depravity and promiscuous fornication that is going on under their own eyes and in their own congregations," wrote Burton Deane, himself an Anglican, "they would be kept so busy that they would have no time to think of the professional ladies, who at all events are orderly, clean, and on the whole not bad looking."13

The tacit but uneasy alliance between police and council was briefly broken in 1895. Early that year a man committed suicide after finding his wife in the arms of their lodger, a Joseph Donaldson. When the unrepentant boarder turned up as the chief mourner at the deceased's funeral, Lethbridge reacted angrily. That night a small group of men hauled Donaldson out of bed, tarred a few feathers on his head, and locked him up in Henderson's hotel. The next morning a large crowd derisively escorted the embarrassed lover to the station and put him on the outbound train. Captain Deane took a dim view of the proceedings, especially when he discovered that the town constable had been among the vigilantes. Before Deane could lay charges, the policeman absconded to the United States with some forty dollars in town revenues. When the parsimonious municipal council tried to collect the stolen money from the NWMP, Deane angrily told the town to look after its own problems, including the maintenance of law and order.14 Consequently, for the next two years Lethbridge employed a full-time inspector to maintain the law and collect taxes and fees. When the inspector resigned in 1897, the town's administrators hired Corporal Thomas Lewis, an active NWMP officer, to be stationed in town at a bonus of twenty-five dollars a month above his regular salary.

Meanwhile, the forces of morality redoubled their efforts to rid the town of the red-light district. In the summer of 1898 their efforts bore fruit. Lethbridge passed another morality bylaw that ordered fines for the keeping of bawdy-houses, houses of ill-fame, and disorderly houses, and threatened to arrest anyone who was not a bona fide resident found in such a place.[15] Even though the regulations were vague in describing bona fide residency, the mounted police were unhappy and Inspector A. R. Cuthbert, acting for Deane, clearly defined police policy regarding prostitution. "I informed the Town Council for obvious reasons, that should houses of ill-fame be removed from the municipality, they would not be allowed to exist in the District and outside the Municipality," he wrote his supervisors. "It is needless to add that the best course is to leave them within the Municipality where they can be under a certain amount of control without more than the usual Police supervision."[16] At a hastily-called special meeting, a chastened Mayor Bentley and his councillors reconsidered their actions and left the matter to the discretion of the NWMP.

The zealous guardians of morality, led by Charles McKillop, did not accept defeat easily. Late in 1899 the Presbyterian minister attacked the town officials on another front. He accused them of failing to provide means of law enforcement. The basis of the problem, according to McKillop, was that Corporal Lewis had the impossible task of serving two masters, the town and the NWMP. When challenged, McKillop reluctantly admitted that he had seen few drunks on the street lately, but nevertheless, he hastily retorted, "hotels have been open after hours . . . Chinamen worked on Sundays and certain shops were open after hours and on Sundays."[17] Hoping to shock his insouciant listeners, the embattled minister dropped a bombshell: "The law is very clear on this subject, yet, the official who is paid by the town to see that the law is enforced, says that he is under orders from Captain Deane of the North-West Mounted Police and some members of this Council to overlook it."

Captain Deane, who never retreated from a fight, eagerly raised defences against McKillop. In a long letter to the council he explained that the territorial government refused to contest the appeals of those convicted of liquor offences. Deane's letter concluded, "I had thus done everything in my power to uphold the liquor law, and as I had not received the reasonable support the case demanded, I made up my mind that I would try no more liquor cases and instructed Cpl. Lewis that as there was a Licence

Inspector in Town, paid by the North West Government, for the express and sole purpose of enforcing the liquor ordinance, it was not necessary for him to take steps in the matter at all and I ordered him to leave the enforcing of the liquor ordinances to the duly appointed official."[18]

Ironically, the incident created so much publicity that the NWMP headquarters ordered Deane to withdraw Lewis from town duty, effective 1 January 1900. The corporal's extra-paid position was clearly against police regulations and so Deane had no choice but to obey the order without protest. The town unsuccessfully tried to retain a full-time constable and later that year, when the hubbub over Lewis's case had died down, town council rehired him, this time at only ten dollars per month above his regular salary.

Captain Deane expressed his satisfaction with the turn of events. In his report to headquarters he pointed to a basic problem in Lethbridge. While most western towns were reluctant to spend money on law enforcement, Lethbridge was even more parsimonious because of the presence of the mounted police division. "The trouble," he suggested, "is that although the Police have no municipal responsibility, yet people look to us, and with a body of men in the barracks it is difficult to convince the public that they should have their own paid officials."[19] Deane was not complaining. He preferred to police Lethbridge himself and so ensure a common expert policy for town and country. "Personally, I think the matter is better in our hands," he explained. "Some crank or well meaning enthusiast will at times talk about things which he does not understand but the responsible people of the Town are satisfied that they get better service from us than from anyone else."

Therefore, Deane's policy of loose supervision rather than rigid repression triumphed again. From his cosy town office, Corporal Lewis looked placidly down the street to several brightly lit noisy saloons and brothels, his hands never far from the telephone so should affairs get unmanageable he could call the barracks for reinforcements. Lethbridge's reputation for illicit entertainment and loose law enforcement endured. The saloons remained open after regulation time, a certain level of gambling continued, and the red-light district, properly segregated of course,

endured. Single settlers, farm labourers, and especially cowboys
from miles around flocked to the town on week-ends to join the
miners and railroaders in unrestrained escape from monotonous
loneliness and strenuous or dangerous jobs. There was money to
be spent and Lethbridge businessmen eagerly welcomed the weekly influx of farm and ranch hands. Some people jocularly claimed
that the cowboys, who preferred an evening of singing and
dancing with their alcohol and sex, raised the level of Lethbridge's
bordellos several cuts above the average whore-house on the
prairies. Others, of more serious nature, pointed to the decrepit
shacks of the rejected prostitutes huddled in the river valley, the
recurring brawls of drunken miners, and the cruel robberies of
besotted workers by crooked gamblers and thieves. Although
McKillop's attempt to cure the ills of an urbanizing society with
repressive laws was perhaps impolitic and certainly outdated,
Deane's approach, however expedient and wise, showed an inability to deal with the festering side-effect of an immature,
isolated, and partially industrialized society.

By 1902, fully twelve years after incorporation, Lethbridge
took the first step toward a regular independent police force
when it hired Thomas Lewis at sixty dollars a month as the first
full-time town constable. The appointment did not end the law
enforcement burlesque because the town also named the engineer
as a special constable to help Lewis in times of need. Within days,
Lethbridgeans regaled themselves with the tale of the bungling
clumsy engineer who, preening his new authority, had demanded
the gratuitous services of a Japanese prostitute. When the girl
refused to accommodate the grossly overweight engineer, he
threatened to arrest her unless bought off with fifty dollars. The
harlot paid but, recognizing a dangerous precedent when she saw
one, complained to a prominent citizen who in turn informed the
town council. That body summarily dismissed the special constable and appointed a second full-time constable, also at sixty
dollars a month.[20] Unfortunately, the councillors failed to rank the
men and so it was only a matter of time before the two were
embroiled in jealous arguments. Council tried to solve the matter
by assigning one man to day and the other to night shifts but that
failed, and so in 1905 it fired them both and hired two others. A
year later in response to the municipality's rapid growth, Leth-

bridge hired a third constable and laid the basis for a more systematic and serious approach to law enforcement.[21]

The establishment of municipal police did not change the basic attitude of most Lethbridgeans toward the Point, a stance which occasioned sporadic but futile protests throughout the years. In 1903 reformers once again pressed town council to enforce its own ordinances. Always mindful of economics, the councillors affirmed that the presence of whore-houses so near the business district "was the cause of serious deterioration in the value of other properties and a source of danger as recent fires have testified."[22] They instructed Constable Lewis to enforce the town bylaws rigidly starting on 1 September. The appeal to property rather than moral values had little effect, however. A bevy of prostitutes successfully petitioned council to move the deadline one month later to permit them to make other arrangements. Only one madam complied with the law. She built a sumptuous house at the southern approach to Lethbridge near Henderson Lake, a convenient location for out-of-town visitors.[23] The other prostitutes trusted that her gesture was enough to appease the councillors. Their assumption proved correct and nothing was done. The passage of yet another morality bylaw in 1904 was a pointless move. The madams were property owners and taxpayers; commercial pleasure was a lucrative enterprise even (if only indirectly) for the conventional businessman. Therefore, without the whole-hearted support of the citizenry even the most zealous reformer could not eradicate the red-light district, the bordellos, and the drinking and gambling dens.

By 1906, therefore, when Lethbridge became a city, it continued to show the strain of commercialization and industrialization. It remained a rough town. Even juvenile delinquency reared its head. In one of several editorials the *Lethbridge Herald* complained, "They wander about the streets, when they should be sound asleep. They talk back to their elders and swear at their companions bearing all the evidence of lack of training in obedience and morality."[24]

The red-light district and the excessive violation of liquor and gambling laws were not the only problems the mining town faced. Racism was also prevalent. The techniques of coal-mining required a large, cheap, and migrant labour force.[25] Newly arrived immigrants, anxious to find employment, fulfilled this need. Lethbridge housed large numbers of central and south Europeans, including Hungarians, Slovaks, and Italians, as well as a few Croats and Poles, all popularly labelled as Slavs. Most of the Europeans were transients who chose mining as a temporary expedient to earn enough money to buy a farm at home or in Canada. They were a hard-working group obsessed with accumulating as much money as they could and as quickly as possible.[26] But their cliquish behaviour, their strange customs, and their impenetrable language isolated them from their Anglo-Saxon co-workers. The latter increasingly viewed the continental Europeans with suspicion and distrust, particularly because they suspected that the "foreigner" drove down wages by willingly accepting minimal pay. In 1899 one Lethbridge labour leader warned that Canada's liberal immigration policy would destroy the union movement by introducing "hordes of half-civilized people who can live on . . . a crust and an onion."[27]

Many Lethbridgeans even blamed the town's rowdiness on the large numbers of continental Europeans in their midst. This belief was based upon tales of disorderly week-end parties and noisy weddings among the newcomers, and seemed to be confirmed by the practice of the local newspaper and police, who used ethnic labels to identify non-Anglo-Saxon trouble-makers. The assumption was false, however. The Donaldson tar-and-feather incident clearly showed that those of British descent were very much involved in town disturbances. The hotels and saloons, for instance, were owned and operated exclusively by Canadians and Britons. A survey of the population demonstrates that most of the continental Europeans lived outside the Lethbridge corporate limits north of the railway tracks. Undoubtedly some of them visited the town business and entertainment establishments, but the number of continental immigrants actually living in Lethbridge was too small for them to be a major factor in the crude and tough nature of the town.

The 1901 census provides a rough indication of Lethbridge's ethnic mixture. Unfortunately, the figures are not precise because the census employed the term "ethnic origin" to identify the country of birth other than Canada or the next male ancestor no matter how many generations removed. According to this definition, no one could be a native of Canada. The 1901 census claimed that fifty-six Lethbridgeans were of French origin but, as the 1911 census makes clear, most of them were Quebeçois. Nevertheless, the figures are useful and show that of Lethbridge's 1,462 inhabitants, four-fifths were of British descent. If those of French parentage are excluded, only sixteen percent of the town's citizens were of continental European, Asian, or other extraction (*See* Table II). Of the entire population only seven percent were of Austro-Hungarian ancestry.

Table II   Place of Origin, 1901[28]

Origin	Town	North Ward
British	1163 (80)*	409 (47)
European	198 (14)	399 (46)
French	56 (4)	49 (6)
Indian	7	—
Metis	4	—
Chinese	29(2)	1
Other	5	6
Total	1462	864

*figures in parentheses denote percentages of total

The 1911 census is more precise because it furnishes the place of birth as well as ethnic origin. It reported that in 1911 forty-one percent of Lethbridgeans were born in Canada while thirty-six percent were born elsewhere in the British empire. Significantly, thirteen percent were born in the United States and only eight percent in continental Europe. Put in absolute figures, 3,263 people had been born in Canada (1,460 in Ontario alone); 2,858 persons had been born in the British Isles (only 34 came from the mining regions of Wales); and 1,823 were foreign-born (1,043 Americans, 664 Europeans, and 112 Asians). However the numbers are arranged, the conclusions are the same. Lethbridge was firmly rooted in the Anglo-Saxon stream of history; those alien to Canada's cultural heritage were a small minority.

Immediately north of the railway yards the situation was radically different. In 1901 those of continental, excluding French, descent made up nearly half of the population. Those of Austro-

Hungarian origin alone constituted more than one-third of the settlement. The population mix also included a few Germans, Scandinavians, Russians, Italians, and Swiss. Unlike Lethbridge, which had a relatively large Chinese community, Lethbridge North had only one Asiatic. In sum, these statistics (as those on conjugal relations) suggest that the less affluent continental immigrants preferred to live north of the tracks, in the small houses and shacks clustered around the mine shafts. The north ward, unlike the town, established strong links with central European traditions. The physical as well as cultural division of the small settlement by the railway tracks was clearly recognized by all.

Even though most of the central Europeans lived outside the corporate limits of Lethbridge, the townsfolk still disliked them. In 1891, for example, the Lethbridge *Semi-Weekly News* expressed its antipathy when it commented on the violent labour disputes in the American coalfields. The paper chastized the mine owners for bringing in Hungarian strike-breakers, not so much because the editor admired the labour movement but because "the introduction of this foreign element—ignorant, vicious, and imbued with socialistic and communistic ideas—cannot fail to have an evil effect on the labour market of America."[29] Later, in 1897, when Lethbridge coal workers struck against Galt, the *News* blamed the dispute on the "foreign element." The charge contained some truth because the immigrants, who held the lowest-paid jobs, were the most vocal of the malcontents in this particular strike. Working and living in a mining town, the *News* staff must have known that without the support of the other workers, particularly the contract miners, no European loader could hope to cripple a colliery. The prejudice of the editor's analysis surfaced when he declared, "It is to be hoped that the present trouble will be the means of clearing out the Hungarian and Slav element from the mines. As citizens they have never been valuable or desirable as a class."[30] He continued with his main complaint. The Europeans spent their money only on bare essentials "on which the merchant as a rule makes very little profit," he charged, and added that because they mailed most of their savings home, "their employment is [of] little or no benefit to the town." In other words, in the materialistic view of the *News*, the presence of the immigrant labourers was not profitable: they did not contribute to the economic growth of Lethbridge.

The racist remarks of the *News* did not go unchallenged. Father Van Tighem, the Roman Catholic priest who had worked among the Europeans since 1884, dismissed the slurs as based on sheer ignorance. He angrily denounced the charge that the Hungarians instigated the strike and vigorously defended his parishioners as a "moral, peaceful, clean and hard working class of people." Admitting that they were not educated, he nevertheless affirmed that they were honest and paid their bills.[31] Unfortunately, Van Tighem's voice represented the outcast minority, and racism remained strong in Lethbridge, rising to a crescendo in the 1910s when it was directed particularly against the Chinese.

Religion also divided the two communities on either side of the track. In 1901 nearly one-third of all Lethbridgeans considered themselves Presbyterians (*See* Table III). Fewer in numbers were the Anglicans at twenty-one percent, the Roman Catholics at nineteen percent, and the Methodists at twelve percent of the population. The remaining fifteen percent were distributed among the Baptists, Mormons, Lutherans, the "Greek Church," the Salvation Army, and various sects. The mixture was entirely different in Lethbridge North. Not unexpectedly, the largest single group—fully thirty-nine percent—belonged to the Roman Catholic faith. Next were the Presbyterians and Anglicans, who made up sixteen and twelve percent of the population respectively. And, as in Lethbridge, the Methodists were the fewest in number of those who had erected churches in the town. The north ward

Table III   Religions, 1901[32]

Religion	Town	North Ward
Presbyterian	479 (33)*	137 (16)
Anglican	313 (21)	107 (12)
Roman Catholic	279 (19)	333 (39)
Other	213 (15)	37 (4)
Methodist	171 (12)	85 (10)
Unspecified	7	165 (19)
Total	1462	864

*figures in parentheses denote percentages of total

had only a few representatives from other denominations such as the Baptists, Lutherans, and unspecified sects.

The surprising feature of the religious composition of the settlement north of Lethbridge is that fully nineteen percent of the inhabitants specified no religion at all, the highest such statistic for any subdistrict census in Alberta. In the town of Lethbridge, for instance, less than one-half of one percent claimed to have no specific religious ties. Undoubtedly, the figures for Lethbridge are a measure of its transitory population, of the presence of a large group of people who wandered from place to place and who had lost all contact with traditional social institutions. These individuals were not necessarily of central European extraction. The large numbers of Roman Catholics indicates the contrary. In fact, if all the nationals of traditionally Protestant countries are added together, they outnumber the stated religious affiliation in the Protestant churches. Moreover, convention, custom, or simply subconscious social pressure probably compelled many to claim a religious association when in fact they never attended religious services. Many of the coal workers, particularly among those of Anglo-Saxon extraction, had rejected any formal association with the institutional church.

Throughout the turn-of-the-century period the churches that had been founded at the birth of Lethbridge remained small, that is, they failed to keep pace with the floating yet growing population. Both Knox Presbyterian and St. Augustine Anglican churches built extensions and became self-supporting in 1891, but their existence was extremely precarious. Although these churches enjoyed the membership of the town's leading businessmen, company officials, and professionals, they both experienced serious financial difficulties. In 1893 Knox's board of managers decided "that owing to the stringency of finances and the removal of many members and adherents, the congregation could not afford a summer replacement for its vacationing minister."[33] A year later St. Augustine's vestry resolved "that until the financial circumstances of the Parish are placed on a more satisfactory footing" it would not consider offertories for outside causes.[34] The Anglican congregation seriously considered closing their church, but with the bishop's help and by skimping on their minister's salary, they managed to survive. As late as 1901, when their pastor resigned, the vestry planned to sell the rectory and seek an unmarried successor. Just across the street, the managers of the Knox church were agonizing over "the changes which take place in the Congregation, and especially one situated like ours, where the population is much more migratory than in older, settled places."[35] They resolved to launch an intensive campaign to rescue their congregation from financial disaster.

To a certain extent Knox's managers were correct in blaming their church's poor performance on Lethbridge's transient population, which was primarily concerned with secular goals and fostered little need for spiritual values. On the other hand, they nor the parishioners of St. Augustine made much of an effort to reach these migratory workers. In 1891 Bishop Pinkham, in town for a confirmation service, sternly exhorted his charges to become active in the community at large.[36] Such a claim of inactivity could not be laid against Reverend Charles McKillop, the fiery preacher of Knox Church. In 1891 his congregation presented him with a Christmas gift for the "manly and fearless stand you have always taken in denouncing the many evils to be found in western towns."[37] Yet, McKillop's ministry was largely aimed at eradicating the most blatant and obvious sins, prostitution, gambling, and drinking, which were actually only visible symptoms of the deep-seated ills of an industrializing society. McKillop's faithful ally, J. D. Higinbotham, took a more incisive approach by establishing a Sunday school for the town children. It was the only evangelistic outreach of the main line churches. They did not concentrate their energies to bring the gospel to the mine workers, particularly those living north of the tracks. Nor did they help solve the bewildering problems of the new, highly mobile, technologized society.

At various times a small group of Baptists met in one of the company buildings in the north ward. The Salvation Army was also active there and in 1906 the Methodists began a once-a-month worship service for the Hungarians.[38] But the only churchman consistently active among the coal workers was Father Van Tighem. Ever since his first visit to Coal Banks in 1884 he had been deeply concerned with the spiritual welfare of the miners. He was able to converse with them in English, French, German, or even Flemish. He could hear confessions in Hungarian and Italian. His was a lonely task, however, for—unlike McKillop, whose sermons were sometimes published verbatim by the Presbyterian editor of the *News*—Van Tighem did not enjoy the friendship and admiration of Lethbridge's social leaders, who were almost exclusively Protestant and belittled his work among the "foreign element." Nevertheless, Van Tighem continued his endeavours, particularly to establish a distinctive Roman Catholic education for the children of his parish. In 1891 he built a convent for the Sisters of the Faithful Companions and a school in which they could teach. Throughout his long stay in Lethbridge the children and the school were his first loves and he fought hard to secure for them a fair share of the district's school taxes.

Father Van Tighem's separate school was disliked by Lethbridge's non-Catholic majority, a position nicely enunciated by the *Lethbridge News*. Utilizing some Canadian crime statistics, a lengthy editorial contended that uniform public schools were the essential instruments in setting basic moral and civil standards. In other words, the character of the new civilization western Canadians were building rested on the school system. An efficient method of education was particularly important in the Northwest, where hundreds of continental Europeans were absorbed annually. "Many of [these immigrants]," the *News* warned, "bring with them hatred of Government, hatred of liberty, and hatred of humanity."[39] Only a good, uniform school system could uproot these undesirable animosities, so the editorial argued, and in the usual purple prose concluded that "the public schools are the incandescent light that will illuminate the houses of the land." Then, by grossly distorting the numbers, the weekly echoed the contemporary Protestant view that Roman Catholics were more prone to crime than any other religious group. With equally wild mental contortions, the *News* asserted that religious instruction was no help in crime prevention. In the eyes of the editor, therefore, Roman Catholic schools served no useful purpose. Although the position of the *News* was not unusual for a western Canadian newspaper, it was expressed more strongly and pointedly.[40] Van Tighem's school in Lethbridge was doubly suspect because it catered not only to Roman Catholics but also to the children of the Slavonic coal workers, therefore retarding even more the homogenization of Canada's population.

Since they considered the public school to be of prime importance, the people of Lethbridge were prepared to spend money on it. In January 1891 the school-board closed the old wooden school and opened a brand new two-storey brick edifice with six classrooms. The Gothic structure, centred on four town lots, was typically ornate with stone facings and window sills, an imposing double-door entrance, and a tower replete with belfry. Despite this major expenditure, the board built a small schoolhouse that same year in the north ward. Although the modesty of the north school contrasted starkly with the splendour of the town school, its existence nevertheless testified to the school-board's fear that the danger of crossing a busy railway yard would discourage the coal workers' children from attending school at all.

In the next few years the student body grew slowly so that by 1898 the average attendance at both schools was less than 170 pupils. With the rapid influx of immigrants during the next decade, the school population more than doubled and in January 1906, Lethbridge opened the Westminster school, another two-storey brick building.[41] Obviously, the community felt that the cost of instilling the many newcomers with Canadian values was money well spent.

Shortly after the establishment of the Westminster school, the mayor expressed his preference for a more "thoroughly commercial course" that would be more practical for those not going to college than a "smattering" of French and German.[42] Fifteen years earlier, after the *News* had staunchly defended the patriotic value of education, it also trumpeted its practical advantage: "Not only will beneficial benefits result to the town ... but there will be strong inducements to persons in the east to settle in ... [this] vicinity."[43] Utility or profit were core criteria even in social institutions. The modern school buildings were part of the image of Lethbridge as a business-minded, progressive town, attractive to ambitious settlers.

The drive to civilize the West, then, did not include a sympathetic concern for the social burdens that accompanied this process. In fact, during the early 1890s, Lethbridgeans were even reluctant to spend money on physical improvements or economic stimulators. The optimistic boosterism, which had marked the

early years of Lethbridge, had a decidedly hollow ring. The townsmen had been unable to translate the ambitious vision of a great
industrial metropolis into concrete action. During the first five or
six years after Lethbridge was incorporated, the economic depression certainly contributed to the lack of results. So did ab-
sentee landownership. In 1891 nearly half of the town's assessed
properties were owned by company shareholders, the largest
proprietor being Sir Alexander Galt. As late as 1897 the English
investors still possessed empty town lots assessed at more than
sixty thousand dollars.[44] Such extensive outside interests, when
coupled with a highly migrant population, meant that only a few
people cared to become involved in civic affairs. Throughout the
early 1890s it became increasingly difficult to find men willing to
accept public office or to fill a quorum at a council meeting. The
town administration prided itself on keeping taxes at a minimum
and spending as little as possible. Basic improvements like sidewalks came only slowly, causing one irate citizen to exclaim, "It is
something new to see Town Councils making the means of access
to saloons and houses of illfame easy, whilst they condemn so
large a number of resident property holders to struggle through a
sea of mud that is to be found in wet weather."[45] In 1891 private
citizens, not the town administration, introduced street lights and
a telephone network. Even such an elementary service as the
hospital was built by Sir Alexander and donated to the town.
Everyone agreed that Lethbridge must diversify its economy to
escape the dominance of the Galt companies, but no one took any
positive action.

　　With the marked improvement in the economy after the mid-
1890s, Lethbridge came alive. By the end of 1897 all the empty
buildings that had plagued the town for years were filled to
capacity. Building activity increased so rapidly that the *News*
proudly complained of a shortage of skilled craftsmen. The Bank
of Montreal expressed its confidence in Lethbridge's future by
opening a branch office. As the surrounding countryside filled
with eager settlers, Lethbridge grew steadily, a phenomenon
heartily applauded by the town's second weekly, founded in 1905.
Matching its competitor's preoccupation with materialistic expansion, the newly established *Herald* noted, "The settlement of the
lands in the vicinity, which is taking place steadily with a good class

of people from the United States, Eastern Canada and England, will bring grist to the cash boxes of our stores and compel them to enlarge and employ more hands."[46]

The swelling amounts of grist in the cash boxes of the merchants during this turn-of-the-century period had a profound psychological impact upon the Lethbridge business establishment, an effect shared by colleagues across the nation. The phenomenal growth of western settlement and the rapid expansion of the Canadian economy sparked yet another era of exuberant national optimism. It refueled the exhilarating spirit of economic process. The Lethbridge municipal council, spurred on by the merchants it represented, joined the wild scramble for a share in the West's booming prosperity. Like their counterparts throughout the West, they abandoned their cautious fiscal policies and recklessly borrowed funds for lavish public works and bonuses to attract industries.

In the late 1890s irrigation and railways were still the prime objectives of Lethbridge's expansionary urge because both endeavours promised to lessen the town's dependence upon the coalmines. Harry Bentley, the town mayor, spent several months in Ottawa during the summer of 1897 successfully lobbying the government to induce the CPR to construct the Crowsnest Pass route at Lethbridge.[47] A year later the town council reacted quickly to a board of trade petition for a substantial bonus to the AR&ICo to extend the canal into Lethbridge itself. Both Elliott Galt and Charles Magrath met with town officials and worked out the details, which were presented to the public for approval during the next summer. While it was by far the largest single expenditure to date for the community, the voters overwhelmingly agreed that council issue a $30,000-debenture to be held by the AR&ICo for delivering water to 20,000 acres of land in and around Lethbridge.[48] The citizens obviously believed that the cost was merely a safe investment in future prosperity.

The *Lethbridge News* expressed this sentiment in several editorials that urged readers to support the bonus bylaws. It emphasized the wealth that irrigation was certain to bring to Lethbridge and make it "the commercial and industrial centre of southern Alberta."[49] Irrigation, so the *News* wrote at another time, would

transform the entire character of the region; it would civilize the
West:

> Where in the past roamed a few herds of cattle over the
> boundless expanse of prairie, will be found the homes of
> thousands of prosperous settlers, with well-tilled and fenced
> fields, stacks bulging with the fatness of the harvest, cattle
> lowing in the pastures.... From a shadeless town in the midst
> of a shapeless and comparatively barren prairie, we shall now
> have at our doors the only necessity wanting for transform-
> ing it into a place of beauty and a haven of rest such as only
> the presence of trees and the rustle of foliage can afford.[50]

Irrigation would bring settlers to the town's hinterland as well as
flour mills, creameries, cheese factories, implement dealers, and
warehouses to the municipality; it would improve the community
water supply and sanitation, make Lethbridge a beautiful, populous city, and ensure that the community received its just portion
of the phenomenal population growth of western Canada.

As the pace of western development accelerated, so did
Lethbridge's frantic rush to participate in the general affluence.
Not only did it publish thousands of promotional pamphlets and
hold out bonuses to attract industries, but it greatly increased its
physical services to the community in order to maintain a progressive town image. With boundless optimism Lethbridge expanded
its civil administration, planted hundreds of trees, replaced wood-
en with concrete sidewalks, improved street lighting, and embarked upon the first stage of an expensive water and sewer
system, costing over $200,000 and completed in 1905. At the same
time it granted the CPR and AR&ICo a twenty-year tax exemption on all railway properties as well as free water in exchange for
making Lethbridge a divisional point complete with a large station.[51] With all this activity the town's budget doubled within an
eight-year period stretching from 1897 to 1904. The municipal
debt soared from a cautious, manageable $10,000 in 1899 to a
heedless, costly $164,000 only four years later.[52] The reckless
spending, encouraged by the boom mentality of the business
establishment, made the community a more attractive place in

which to live, but it also led to financial difficulties that were not resolved until the establishment of a managerial system of government in 1928.

Most of the council's expenditures were for material items: miles of sidewalks, sewers, road maintenance, and firefighting equipment. The same attitude that contributed to lack of control over the red-light district and the emphasis on the practical benefits of education set municipal priorities. The town spent nothing on recreational facilities. A yearly but minimal grant to the company hospital was set aside, but council tried to avoid responsibility for epidemics, and cautiously approached a bid to acquire a Carnegie-funded library. Like many of its western counterparts Lethbridge bid furiously against other towns to attract a brewery or a flour mill but was very frugal whenever a destitute family appealed for help. Railway tickets to Montana were the favourite form of welfare. Determined to surpass Calgary and Edmonton in size, the town council measured spending in accordance with the norms of growth. Standards were entirely commercial and everyone laboured energetically for all things that were profitable.[53]

The responsibility for the welfare of the community, particularly recreation, rested with the private citizen. For the sports-minded member of the English-speaking establishment, this was no problem. Opportunities were plentiful. With almost clocklike precision, Lethbridge witnessed the rise and fall of baseball, soccer, rugby, lawn tennis, and cricket clubs. The town square, which after a succession of abortive beautification schemes was still a flat grass field, served as a convenient playing ground. Cycle enthusiasts formed the Chinook Cycle Club, which for years promoted casual riding, races, and rallies. In 1891 a turf association began a program of annual horse races, a delight for the betters and horse lovers. When winter drove people indoors, the churches had social groups for men, women, and children. Several lodges, debating societies, and music clubs provided another form of diversion. So did public dances and card games. Political meetings, too, were a popular pastime. Touring theatrical groups and musicians were rare and second-rate, and so the townsfolk organized their own variety programmes with local talent. As the town grew larger, the inhabitants older, and society less intimate, all these forms of public amusement became less frequent and were replaced by private house parties and invited gatherings.

The organizers, executives, and honorary presidents of these various activities were, like the town council and board of trade, drawn from the same circle of businessmen, professionals, and managers. Apart from the colliery band, few workers ever participated in the round of social activities. Even the sports clubs remained exclusive. The community leaders sought a more sophisticated entertainment than the coal or rail worker who, after a hard day of physical work, was content to relax at home, sit in a nearby saloon, shoot a game of pool, or simply lean against his favourite wall and tease girls. As late as 1906 the *Lethbridge Herald* scolded the young men for loafing downtown on Saturday nights, crowding the sidewalks so that ladies could not pass without being jostled about, ruining their skirts in the streams of tobacco juice.[54]

By 1906, when Lethbridge was legally incorporated into a city, it was taking on more and more of the trappings of a modern urban centre. Patriotic citizens proudly pointed to the motley array of business establishments that stalwartly lined the town square. Skipping quickly over the modest wooden buildings remaining from pioneer days, a host would draw attention to the large three-storey brick buildings such as the functional Bentley block or the new Hudson's Bay store with modern showcase windows. The streets might still be gravel but the sidewalks were solid cement. Should a visitor remark that the spindly trees bordering the square in unimaginative ruler-straight lines looked unimpressive, even impoverished, any loyal Lethbridgean would hastily retort that by the time these trees were fully mature, Lethbridge would be a thriving industrial metropolis. Surely the stately homes of druggist Higinbotham, lawyer Conybeare, and merchant Bentley proved that successful men had confidence in the city's future? Pleased with Lethbridge's past progress, citizens smugly remarked that their city possessed all the accoutrements of modern civilization. Most of the houses sprawled across the prairies behind the business district were linked into the water and sewer system, connected to the telephone network, and hooked into the electrical plant. Why, some people marvelled, the municipal council was seriously considering the purchase of electric streetcars to whisk people about the city! Never mind the "knock-

This 1906 view of the barren Galt square, framed by a
single line of small trees and surrounded by an impressive
array of buildings, is mute testimony to the young
town's priorities. (Glenbow Archives)

ers" who scoffed that the combined population of Lethbridge and
Staffordville totalled less than three thousand souls, too few to
support such an expensive means of transportation. The low
figures could be explained away quite easily by citing the large
exodus of miners during the prolonged strike at the Galt mines.
And, with the flow of immigrants still unabated, Lethbridge's
takeoff to metropolitan status was just around the corner.

Yet, unfortunately, it was sometimes difficult to shake off the
vestiges of the unglamorous past. That summer the *Herald* complained about the many cows and calves tramping through the
streets in the mornings before being taken to pasture by the town
herder. The animals were ruining the newly-planted trees but,
more importantly, surely the people must see "the absolute fool-
ishness of Lethbridge pretending to be a city when it has roaming
about its streets a herd of cattle—a mark of village life?"[55]

The remarks were appropriate because, as a result of irrigation, Lethbridge was experiencing the effects of the settlement of
its hinterland. A casual stroll through the business district would
reveal this change in the community's economic orientation. Per-

The bustle of Lethbridge's Round Street intersecting
Redpath, seen here in 1906, attests to the city's role as
supplier to southern Alberta. (Glenbow Archives)

haps the largest establishment was Bentley Co. Ltd., one of the
first in Lethbridge, a prosperous wholesale and retail firm in all
manner of dry goods, groceries, and hardware, with one large
store and two warehouses in the city and branches in the Crowsnest Pass. Another firm, thriving on the flourishing agricultural
hinterland was that of George Rogers, a large wholesale lumber
business with outlets in Raymond, Magrath, Stirling, and Taber.
An obvious sign of the agricultural revolution sweeping through
southern Alberta was that Rogers was named an agent for the
farm implement company of Massey Harris. Yet a third establishment was the Winnipeg-based firm of A. Macdonald & Co.,
with two general goods shops in Lethbridge that served the city
but also specialized in the ranch trade. In sum, a variety of stores,
banks, dealers, artisans, and teamsters made up the elements of a
service station for the growing agricultural hinterland.

By 1906 Lethbridge was becoming a strange two-headed
creature. One pamphlet aptly called it a coal city in wheat country.
The wealth of coal beneath its streets was still vital to its economic
health. Although the miners had their own co-operative stores,

the merchants of Lethbridge still provided many commodities and services to the coal workers and the collieries. Staffordville was really but an appendage of the city and therefore Lethbridge experienced all the effects of industrialization. The mines brought an ebullient, lusty population, basically masculine in character, largely foreign in origin. Some of the workers sought their amusement in the commercial places of the city, the brothels, saloons, pool halls, and gambling rooms. These establishments, however, also served men from the surrounding farms and ranches. So did the city's wholesalers and retailers. Lethbridge, therefore, was also becoming a product of the rapidly growing agricultural population. In a rare reversal of stages, the experience of an old agrarian tradition was overwhelming the portents of a new industrial state.

The dichotomy in the economic basis of Lethbridge seemingly worsened the split between labour and the establishment. The merchants, the professionals, and to a lesser extent, the executives did not have any mining experience at all and thus could not understand the coal workers. More specifically, they·could not trust the men and women from continental Europe with their strange habits, impenetrable language, and alien tradition. Although both groups were concerned with material profit, most of Lethbridge's leaders saw this personal gain also in terms of the prosperity of the larger community. Their dream of bringing civilization to the West may have been more parochial than Galt's but it was theirs nevertheless. On the contrary, few miners shared this vision of economic progress wrapped in the trappings of late Victorian culture. These were the fundamental differences, which precluded any collaboration in defining community objectives or any harmony in social action. That basic cleavage was unwittingly expressed by a *Herald* editorial written late in 1905 in praise of the many American settlers who were flooding into southern Alberta at the time. In one long run-on sentence, the article summed up the fears, prejudices, and ambitions of Lethbridge's leading citizens:

> Thus shall our vast tracts of God's bountifulness—of which we have enough and to spare for all—be peopled by an intelligent, progressive race of our kind, who will readily be developed into permanent, patriotic citizens, who will adhere

to our flag—that which protects our homes and their rights—
and whose posterity will be educated in our schools, become
part of our commonwealth and eventually assume their
logical positions as important factors in our commercial and
political life—in fact become by natural evolution a part and
parcel of and inseparable from our proud standards of Cana-
dianism.[56]

The *Herald*'s editorial, which announced the demise of the industrial metropolis dream and the probability of its agriculturally-
based replacement, also implied, paradoxically, that while the
workers were instruments of achieving the town's economic
objectives, they were not to be a part of its cultural goals.

In a superficial sense, therefore, Lethbridge was compart-
mentalized into two sections, symbolically split by the railway.
The establishment cloistered itself from the workers to the north
and, to a lesser extent, from the dens of pleasure to the west.
Peaceful coexistence was possible as long as these communities did
not spill over into each other. A more penetrating examination,
however, reveals that Lethbridge was in fact not simply severed
into two social classes but segmented into many complex groups.
The miners and railroaders, for instance, were not a homogeneous
class unto themselves but were ranked by occupational and ethnic
prejudices. The contract miner belittled the loader. The Hungarian disliked the Slovak and the Englishman disdained them both.
Among the townsfolk, financial income created distinct social
groups as rich merchants snubbed the lowly teamsters. The
Anglican twitted the Methodist for his moralistic fervour while
they both scorned the Catholic. Some miners built homes in
Lethbridge, intending to stay and establish their families there,
while some businessmen saw the town only as a launching pad to
greater wealth elsewhere. How many prominent citizens were
seen furtively leaving the Point or how many miners never went
there? In sum, Lethbridge was a conglomeration of little groups
whose boundaries were sometimes clearly defined but at other
times blurred. In one aspect they might overlap and in another be
strictly polarized. Some co-operated with each other while some
were often at odds. The coal-mines that Galt built on the banks of
the Belly River created an intricately fragmented kaleidoscopic
society.

11

Anatomy of a strike

Underground, the coal-mine is completely foreign to the human senses. From the instant the hoisting cage drops the miner dizzily into the coal blackness of the shaft, he is surrounded by a hostile, alien environment. At first the darkness is overpowering. Unlike the person walking on the surface at night with a lantern, the worker below ground has no peripheral vision. He can see only that to which he points with the light mounted on his helmet, and he loses all perception of dimensional space. Even more striking is the silence of the mine. The miles of underground passages, the heavy stale air, and the blotterlike walls of coal absorb all sounds and eliminate all echoes. Most miners work in the farthest reaches of the colliery. They can hear only the dampened scrapings of their shovels, the dull thuds of the coal they load. While waiting for a filled car to be exchanged for an empty one, an individual can be utterly alone, and in the overwhelming dark silence he begins to hear the voices of the mine: the soft murmur of escaping gas, the faint gurgle of freed water, and the muffled creaking of burdened timbers. It is in this moment of solitude, when the darkness confines sight and the dusty air clogs the nostrils, that the stillness is most oppressive. It marks the greatest difference from the living noises and colours on the earth's surface.

The nineteenth-century coal-mine, therefore, was an alien environment, and the very technique of underground mining created an industrial worker very unlike his counterpart in the factory. As in most North American collieries, the Galt mines used the pillar and room system, in which, to use the metaphor of a city, the rooms were the streets and the pillars the blocks. These pillars, huge in girth, supported the roof and were never removed until that particular section of the mine could be abandoned and the roof permitted to collapse. By 1900 the extensive underground works at Lethbridge were structured around two main entries or tunnels, which ran like spines side by side, thirty feet apart for two miles in a north-south direction. On both sides of these passageways and parallel to them were entries each four hundred feet apart. In the case of Lethbridge, the miners dug still other tunnels or rooms every thirty-four feet at right angles to these entries for a distance of about two hundred feet when they broke through into the room coming from the adjacent entry. The rooms were twenty feet wide and measured as high as the coal-seam, a neck-bending five and one-half feet.[1] Because only one miner and his helper worked in each room, they were completely isolated from the other men and the only contact they had with the rest of the mine was the rails and pneumatic hoses.

In the Galt collieries the job of undercutting the coal, formerly the most arduous and dangerous work, was no longer done manually. Instead of worming his way beneath the coal-seam, pick in hand, the miner used a compressed air machine to cut a strip out of the lowest part of the seam, four and one-half feet deep, twelve inches high at the front, and three inches at the rear. Next he used a long hand-driven auger to bore several holes into the coal-face, which he filled with black powder and tamped down with wet mud. After a thorough inspection by a supervisor, the fuse was lit and the coal blasted from the seam. Even at the moment of explosion, the leaden, lifeless atmosphere of the mine muffled the sounds of the charge and the falling coal to a dull thump. Once the dust had settled to tolerable levels, the workers moved back into the room to scoop the crumbled coal into a waiting coal car. Loading coal was back-breaking and tedious, a task largely left to low-paid labourers.

The miner's pay was based entirely on the amount of coal shipped to the surface. Consequently skill and speed were important factors in his earnings. So too were the quality of the coal, the thickness of the seam, the character of the roof. For this reason the

Within twenty years of discovering coal on the unsettled prairies, the Galts had built this modern coal-mining complex. Shown here is Shaft 3 in 1906. (Galt Museum)

miner almost considered the room to be his personal possession, the place to be worked at his own speed and according to his own methods. Moreover, because the motivation was internal, he needed little supervision. In fact, the boss's primary duty was the enforcement of safety rules, and he seldom visited an experienced, trusted miner more than once a day. In a way, then, the coal-miner resembled the pre-industrial cottage worker, toiling alone in his room at his own speed. The technique of mining and the method of payment created a worker independent and free as no factory employee could ever be.

The method of transporting coal through the sprawling network of underground roads also influenced the character of mining. Shaft 3 at Lethbridge stood at the centre between the two entries. An endless rope, driven by an engine at the top of the shaft, moved continuously through the two tunnels and dragged the coal cars from the shaft to the various cut-offs. At these points drivers released the cars from the rope and, with the help of horses, hauled them to the rooms. After exchanging the empties for loaded cars, the drivers, who like the loaders were on a day wage and were called company men, returned to the other main entry and clamped the cars onto the return rope to be towed to the shaft and hoisted to the surface.[2] Not only was this system fraught with danger, it was also slow and cumbersome. All too much of a miner's time was spent waiting for empty wagons, a frustrating experience even if it gave him time for rest, lunch, or if so inclined, a visit with a friend.

The passageways were also used for ventilation. Fans forced outside air into the mine and circulated it through every entry and room by means of an elaborate system of stops, baffles, and doors. For a number of years the Galt mines suffered from inadequate ventilation but in 1899 the company instilled a powerful new fan, which forced enough air into the colliery to supply oxygen for men and horses.[3] It was scarcely enough, however, to clean out the stale smoke and powdered coal. Consequently, black dust settled everywhere, on machinery, tools, clothing; it penetrated into every nook and cranny, including the lungs. The coalmine was dirty and dank, its environment noxious to man.

Danger, too, lurked everywhere. Although Lethbridge seldom encountered explosive or suffocating gases and its strata were relatively level and stable, the relentless pressure of three hundred feet of rock often loosened chunks of slate from the ceilings large enough to crush a man's skull. The heavy coal cars careering through the narrow passageways could trap an unwary walker; a sudden break in the coal-face might loosen a cascade of ore and bury an unsuspecting worker. Unfortunately, many of the men were maimed or killed through pure carelessness and a blatant disregard for safety. A track improperly spiked, a prop poorly placed, a shot badly tamped were all potential killers and levied their unnecessary toll. At Canmore one miner pried open his locked safety lamp to light a friend's pipe and blew up a highly gaseous mine, killing eight men.[4] In 1898 an inspector urged the AR&CCo to draft a complete set of safety rules "for the guidance of your employees"[5] because he was disturbed by drivers who stopped the heavy coal cars by jumping in front of them, a common but highly dangerous practice that had already caused several serious injuries. The inspector reckoned that the company would encounter considerable resentment from the hidebound, undisciplined miners if a safety code was enforced. A year later, when he found the mine's ventilation system inadequate, he laid some of the blame on the miners' union. "I must admit that the management is under some disadvantage through having allowed the Miners' Union to gain too much of the managing power of the mine indirectly, so much so that it does seem that to urge pointedly any particular step would almost be an injustice."[6] The constant pressure of danger and the independent character of the coal workers, created by the special techniques of mining, bred a nonchalant, even contemptuous disregard for all hazards.

Despite the perilous conditions, the coal-mines in the Northwest operated for eight years without any government regulations. Neither the territorial nor federal governments showed any concern for mining safety. Of course, the small number of collieries partially explains the lack of interest. When legislation did come it was management—which certainly had a financial if not humanitarian interest in accident prevention—and not the workers or the bureaucrats who inspired it. In 1893 Charles Magrath, then a member of the Northwest Assembly and still a senior employee of the AR&CCo, introduced a bill to regulate the coal-mining industry. Based on similar acts in Great Britain and British Columbia, the ordinance addressed itself primarily to safety. It required the company to keep a daily record of all employees in the mine and to submit reports on all accidents and statistics on production. It also defined minimum ventilation requirements and explicitly spelled out blasting procedures. Before any shot could be detonated, a qualified person, known as a fire boss, had to inspect the charge. The legislation also specified that all excavations and machines be properly fenced. It compelled a complete examination of gaseous mines before every shift and permitted miners to appoint a committee to tour the colliery at their expense at any time and report all infractions of safety regulations to government officials.[7] Magrath's ordinance may have gone somewhat beyond the wishes of his employers but as the representative of a mining constituency he could hardly have made it less restrictive than the models he copied. In any case, the legislation placed all the mines under a minimal but uniform code, a desirable goal in any competitive industry.

The territorial government amended the mining ordinance from time to time. In 1897, after extensive consultations with mine owners and managers, it ordered that all pit- and fire-bosses be properly qualified and certified. The legislation caused a critical shortage of overseers, partly because only the AR&CCo provided a training program and partly because a very good contract miner could earn substantially more than a salaried supervisor.[8]

In 1899, L. G. DeVeber, the member from Lethbridge, piloted an ordinance through the territorial assembly forbidding any miner to spend more than eight hours underground in any one day. The legislation, clearly designed for the coal workers' benefit, had been drafted without extensive consultation with industry officials and it was greeted with little enthusiasm. The contract miner, whose pay was based on tonnage extracted, resented being restricted in the number of hours he could work. Even the unskilled workers, who worked the mines during the winter season to supplement their income, grumbled at the reduction in hours. The most vociferous objections, however, came from management. In a lengthy letter to the minister of public works, the manager of the Galt mines, P. L. Naismith, complained that he could not satisfy the great demand for coal in the wintertime with an eight-hour shift, nor could he find enough men for a second crew. If local men could do the job in ten hours, he demanded, what was the point of hiring extras only to fire them in March? "So long as conditions exist, as at present, in this country, where there is not enough labour to fill the requirements and demands for coal to any extent only exist during four of the winter months," he wrote, "I humbly submit that the enforcement of this law imposes a grievous burden on the capitalist who has for years been endeavouring to build up an industry in a new country."[9] With the modern ventilation equipment and mining machinery employed at Lethbridge, Naismith could see no harm in permitting coal workers to stay in the mine as long as they wished, particularly during the wintertime, which was their opportunity to earn a substantial amount of money by working long hours. Although he was not explicit, Naismith suggested that the reduction in working hours pared company profits by decreasing the output but not the cost of operating a highly mechanized colliery. The government, although convinced that no man should spend more than eight hours a day in a harmful, dusty environment, buckled under the resistance and only a year later repealed the law.[10]

When Alberta became a province in 1905, she assumed responsibility for regulating the coal-mines within her jurisdiction. At the first session of the provincial assembly in May 1906, the members passed the Coal Mines Act,[11] a measure much superior to the territorial ordinance. The new legislation set out in considerable detail many safety regulations regarding gas, water, explosives, safety lamps, and signals and established procedures for official inquiries into serious accidents. The act also demanded that all managers, pit- and fire-bosses be properly trained, and then tested and certified by a board of examiners. Companies were required to submit yearly reports on ventilation, keep up-to-date blueprints of the mine, and if they employed more than twenty men, furnish a dressing-room where men could dry their wet work clothes and change into street wear. Females and boys under twelve were not permitted to work in the mines at all, while boys between twelve and sixteen had to be able to write, read, and do simple arithmetic before being allowed to work underground. The new law also legalized the contract system and permitted miners to appoint, at their own expense, a "checkweigher" to audit the accuracy of the company's tally of coal extracted by the miners. With some insight into the miners' life-style, the legislation specified that no wages be paid "at or within any public house, beer shop or place for the sale of any spirituous or fermented liquor, or other house of entertainment." While the act was relatively comprehensive for its time, it made no effort to revive the eight-hour day for Alberta's coal-miners.

Perhaps the most significant way in which the state intervened in the industry was through the establishment of an inspectorate. In 1894, the territorial administration had appointed William Stafford, formerly the mine manager at Lethbridge, to this new post. Stafford's assignment was merely part-time. He was asked to inspect only the three largest mines, those at Anthracite, Canmore, and Lethbridge, and was paid a small fee and expenses for each visit. Supervision became more systematic when Stafford resigned in 1897 and Dan Evans, a manager from Edmonton, replaced him. Evans toured all the operating mines in the province and reported that most collieries were very primitive and highly dangerous, and that few operators or workers abided by the ordinance. The newly appointed inspector noted that the Galt collieries were well managed and he observed only a few minor infractions.[12] Evans's position was still part-time, however, and the inspectorate remained a haphazard proposition until the rapid growth of the industry in the next decade necessitated a more systematic enforcement of the mining regulations. In 1901 Frank B. Smith, a well-qualified engineer, was appointed the territories' first full-time inspector. The industry expanded so rapidly within the next few years, however, that still greater control was needed. By 1906 Alberta had sixty-one mines, which employed over three thousand men. That year the provincial Coal Mines Act greatly expanded the duties and powers of the inspector of mines. The government also appointed a second inspector.[13] Although the two men still had to cover a tremendously large field and encountered many hostilities, particularly among the small mine owners, they were determined to bring Alberta's crude and rough mining industry under government safety regulations.

In addition to the high rate of accidents, the coal workers also faced frequent periods of unemployment. The coal market was highly seasonal. Coal sales, for example, reached their peak in the cold winter month of February, and then dipped sharply into their usual summer lull.[14] With the opening of several steam coal-mines in the mountain passes, the Galt collieries became more and more dependent upon domestic consumption, where demand was even more uncertain than among railway users. Moreover, Galt coal deteriorated when exposed to air, and thus the company was unable to stabilize its output by stockpiling for extended periods. Storing coal was also expensive, and so production and employment followed the oscillations of the market-place. At the beginning of any year, the AR&CCo employed well over four hundred workers six days per week; but with the coming of spring the company first reduced the work week and then began the annual procedure of dismissing employees. By May the company might have slashed its work-force to two hundred men working no more than three days a week. In mid-summer the firm reversed the process, first by increasing the days of operation and next by rehiring the men so that by December the mine ran at full capacity with the maximum number of workers.

Only a few of those discharged remained in town to live on their winter's earnings and odd jobs. Most of the workers left

Lethbridge, some of them never to return. Fortunately, the slack season of the mines coincided with the busy period of the farms and so many coal workers either supplemented their income with agricultural labour or operated their own farms. They would return to Lethbridge in the fall to secure a cash income. At that time, the totally migrant worker would also come. The pool of permanent employees at the Galt collieries was, therefore, relatively small. Only a small percentage of the Lethbridge work-force made a long-term commitment to the company or the community.

In sum, the techniques of coal-mining bred a unique strain of industrial worker, characterized by an individuality fully savoured by the coal workers. The relative freedom from discipline and supervision saved the miners from the deadly monotony of the assembly line, a feeling shared by the drivers and other company men. Even though the job was temporary, even if the work was dismally dirty, highly dangerous, and totally unnatural, the mineworker was proud of his occupation. It was a man's work. The heavy equipment, the stubborn coal-face, the powerful explosives, and even the constant danger challenged his virility. No matter how black and inanimate the depths, the miner and his helper felt themselves to be an integral part of the mine and its masculine society. They took pride in the colliery's expansion, in a well-squared room, a neat blast, a record production. Perhaps the near-veneration of the work was a compensation for the many unpleasant aspects of coal-mining, the black dust that clogged nostrils, the low ceilings that cramped muscles, the constant darkness that impaired vision. It certainly unified the labour force. The brawny hazardous toil spawned an esprit de corps not unlike an army in combat. Beneath the surface tensions and confusion of tongue, race, and culture surged a vibrant loyalty to the mine and its population. In their battle against the tremendous forces of nature, coal-miners, like soldiers, developed a strong sense of camaraderie, which in time of crisis interlocked into mutual support. Be it a mine explosion or an underground fire, the masculine solidarity of the colliery overcame all the personal animosities prevalent in any community, and produced the vital features of supportive brotherhood.[15]

Despite the obvious signs of comradeship, so prominently displayed during times of emergency, the colliery's work-force had a distinct social hierarchy. At the top were the supervisors and managers, including fire- and pit-bosses. Next came the contract miners, the engineers, craftsmen, and even drivers. At the bottom were the loaders, the timbermen, and slate pickers. Almost without exception, English-speaking workers captured the highly paid jobs from contract miner to fire-boss, while the continental European immigrants filled the onerous, poorly paid tasks. Elitism and bigotry flourished even among the mineworkers, a harsh reality that came to the fore especially during labour disputes.

Early in 1894, for example, after the Anaconda works in Montana closed, Elliott Galt dismissed all his 518 employees without warning and announced plans to rehire only 130 married miners who had "an interest" in Lethbridge and were willing to sign a contract for a seventeen-percent wage cut. About 150 of the more transient workers left town immediately while the remainder dug in for a protracted siege. The stalemate continued until the end of February when Galt posted the names of 145 men he was willing to rehire at the reduced wage. Since it was the height of the coal season, the miners were confident that they could defeat Galt and no one broke the group's solidarity.[16]

As the conflict progressed, tempers grew increasingly ugly. The local NWMP commander, Captain Burton Deane, had the memory of the bloody coal workers' riots in Latimer, Pennsylvania, of 1892 still fresh in his mind, and took steps to defuse an explosive situation. Not only did he place a permanent guard around the mines but he also assumed the role of mediator. On the afternoon of 7 March 1894 he attended a meeting of the miners and, by disclosing a few minor concessions he had obtained from Galt, gained their confidence. The next day Deane took a committee of workers to talk with the mine superintendent. After a lengthy heated discussion, the superintendent agreed to lower the price of explosives from six to four dollars a keg (the AR&CCo charged a very high price for powder to prevent the pulverization of coal through over-use), reduced the price of wedges and pick-handles, promised to pay slightly more for impure "bone" coal, and increased the rate of pay for married contract miners to one dollar per ton. Lastly, he consented to pay the miners twice instead of once a month and not to overhire during busy periods.

Deane's hopes for a quick resolution to the conflict were

dashed abruptly. At a strikers' meeting held that evening to discuss the new terms, a vocal minority ridiculed the company's offer and broke up the gathering. In retaliation, the AR&CCo threatened to evict all recalcitrants from the company's cottages. The eviction notice broke the coal workers' solidarity. On 10 March, even as a large crowd of strikers milled about the mine offices hoping to intimidate the waverers, a small but influential group of miners picked up their tools and returned to work. Every day more men went back. What remained was a core of about 150 Hungarians angrily determined to break the company's wage policy. They were bitter, and although their numbers dwindled, violent confrontations increased. In one particularly nasty fight, some brawlers brandished knives and even a pistol.

Although the strike was effectively over, the threat of re-newed violence, a rash of petty thefts, and the prospects of heavy welfare rolls aroused the Lethbridge business establishment. A joint meeting of the board of trade and town council decided to ask Galt to give all the locked-out workers free passes to Montana. Galt concurred and even volunteered reduced rates as far as Texas. The strikers refused the offer and also scorned Captain Deane's suggestion that they work as labourers on the CPR main line at $1.25 per day. When the men grumbled that the pay was too low, Deane complained to his superior. "I am endeavouring to instill in the thick Scandinavian skull [Deane's terminology was confused], the principle that 'half a loaf is better than no bread'."[17] All hope of victory, however, withered with the approach of the slack summer season, and finally the frustrated remnant capitu-lated. The cowed men asked Deane for help, and he in turn virtually coerced Galt to reinstate the free passes. On 2 April 1894 thirty-two men, some with wives and children, boarded the south-bound train. Elliott Galt had won his first labour dispute.

Galt's victory was in no small measure due to the lack of solidarity among the coal workers. This basic weakness surfaced again in 1897. Early in the year, some newly arrived Englishmen, well versed in labour union activity, protested the temporary closure of Shaft 1 without any warning to the dismissed employ-ees. Somewhat later they denounced the installation of larger coal-screens, which decreased the earnings of the contract miners. Without the support of all the workers, the agitators were unable to gain satisfaction and the ill will lingered.[18] Later in the summer, when railway construction in the Crowsnest Pass boosted wages in southern Alberta, the company men asked for a pay raise. When the AR&CCo refused, the workers turned in their tools and effectively closed the mine. Many of the men left for the Crowsnest Pass, but to their consternation the CPR refused to hire any strikers, and to add insult to injury, the AR&CCo charged three of the leaders with a breach of the master-servant ordinance. The company failed to register a conviction but the incident further embittered the men. They resolved to wait until the company resumed negotiations.[19]

Facing a deadlock between the company and its employees, and with violence a real possibility, Captain Burton Deane intervened once again. He arranged several meetings between management and the strikers, mediated at these sessions, and explained the negotiations to the men at large. After several sessions company officials conceded a few minor points. They agreed to pay contract miners extra for working in water, to pay them for company work on cross-cuts, entries, and rooms, and for tracklaying. They promised to replace broken beams if caused by roof pressure and pledged to provide more cars and distribute them more equally. Ironically, the real beneficiaries of the terms were the contract miners and they wanted to accept the AR&CCo offer. The lower paid company men, who had called for the strike, won only a pledge for a six-day work week for the next six months, and they refused to return to work. Captain Deane would not have it. Supported by the contract miners, he badgered the loaders, drivers, and other company men to return to work. Deane's own position had changed since the last strike since he no longer spoke directly with Galt but met only with the superintendents. He was also decidedly less sympathetic towards the strikers. "The men should consider themselves liberally dealt with," he wrote, and predicted that the lingering discontent might resurface in the form of a labour union. "The fact is that the miners want to control the situation, restrict the output if they think necessary, and in other ways to hold the management in the palms of their hands, so that they can compel compliance with their demands however ridiculous."[20] Deane, like many of his middle-class compatriots, was worried that the workers were becoming too powerful, and he took deep satisfaction when the workers returned to their jobs at the end of August without signing a formal agreement. The *Lethbridge News* warmly praised Deane's disinterested help and Superintendent Barclay's flexible position.[21]

The bitter defeats in the strikes of 1894 and 1897 taught the Lethbridge miners that by themselves they could not withstand the overwhelming power of the company. The two disputes revealed that the business and professional community were by their very nature partial to the company and its management. Even Captain Burton Deane of the NWMP had worked not so much for the welfare of the miners as for the general maintenance of law and order. Although state intervention through legislation and inspection ameliorated the working conditions for Alberta's coal-miners, the prevailing economic and political strength of their employers blocked attempts at greater economic security. Like their bosses, the workers sought to maximize their profits. But, in their struggle against a constantly expanding and increasingly impersonal corporation, they needed tighter internal organization and better external leadership. For that, they would have to go outside their isolated community and seek allies in the American labour unions.

The labour movement in the United States had arisen out of the rapid industrialization of the late nineteenth century, a process which alienated the worker from customary control over his job or trade. Technology and machines overruled the regular pulsations of nature and the rhythms of human life; it compelled the worker to divorce his familiar culture and marry a new strict routine. It also destroyed the old master-servant relationship and the personal contacts that had humanized the work place. The contract miner could still take pride in his skills, but as the growing corporations, buffeted by ferocious competition, sought relief in the installation of more machinery and the creation of more efficient and larger organizations, his status suffered. The various labour-saving, cost-cutting techniques were adopted not for the benefit of the employees, but to soften the quirks of the economy. In fact, the worker became but a tool in the production process, to be used as cheaply as possible. There was little concern for his aspirations or his living conditions. In the isolated mining camps of the Appalachians, for instance, conditions were abysmal; there the workers were often exploited migrants ruled in tyrannical fashion by baron-like managers who conveniently ignored the more humane features of feudalism. Under these circumstances, violent revolt was inevitable. In 1892, the shooting of fifty-five Slavonic workers by Pennsylvania sheriffs was but one sorry episode in the long-running tragedy of the American coal-miners. Bewildered by the strange new society, dominated by gigantic corporations in league with insensitive governments, resentful of being rammed into an alien regularized routine, and angry at the economic suppression, industrial workers across America sought protection and stability in organized labour and a host of other voluntary associations.[22]

Lethbridge's first dalliance with labour unionism was with the Western Federation of Miners, an organization formed primarily for hard-rock miners. The federation had been founded in Butte, Montana, in 1893, a product of the cyclonic transformation of a highly individualistic mining frontier into a complex corporate economy. The copper capital of the United States, Butte had mushroomed in the early 1890s from a primitive mining camp into a full-blown industrial city. It housed 30,000 people and boasted an impressive array of schools, hospitals, waterworks, and electricity. As in many other large urban centres, an elegant façade of ostentatious homes eclipsed the dreary ghettos of the workers, crowded with tenements, saloons, and gambling dens. The swift change from frontier status to industrial city had brought little prosperity and contentment to the labourer, and when the full fury of the depression in the early 1890s hit the mining industry, the bewildered Butte workers joined their fellows from the surrounding region to establish the Western Federation of Miners.[23]

Although the environment at Lethbridge was more benign than in the dismal American mining camps, workers there still sought security in unionization. The lot of the Lethbridge coal-miner was better not only because he was paid more, but more importantly, because his employer lived in town. Elliott Galt may have frequented a social milieu entirely foreign to his labourers, but he did meet them occasionally and he could never use his managers to screen himself entirely from their predicament. Yet, as an employer, Elliott Galt was part of the turn-of-the-century business world, which had divorced its religious convictions from the market-place. The total secularization of business, when coupled with the obsession for efficiency and profits, made money the primary standard of measurement. Although vestiges of paternalism lingered in isolated cases, more and more capitalists viewed the labourer in abstract economic terms—not as a fellow man or co-worker, but as a commodity like coal, a tool like the steam-engine. Aggravating this attitude was the current dogma that society should unfold in a natural unrestricted way. The only restraints to curb the entrepreneur were limitations imposed by the market and competitors. Unfortunately, the ethic of the market-place dictated ruthless action. Whenever the CPR, for example, squeezed the profits of the AR&CCo, Elliott Galt arbitrarily fired his workers or slashed their wages. By the same token, neither Sir Alexander nor his son Elliott paid any attention to the squalor on the river flats, the debauchery on the Point, or the racism in the collieries and the town. Like most businessmen of the time, the Galts were well trained to manage economic affairs with a keen eye for profit, but they were blind to social distress and unequipped to bring about reform.

To protect themselves from the onslaught of the increasingly materialistic world, and to gain for themselves a larger share of the wealth produced by their travail, the workers turned to organized labour. Most of Lethbridge's coal workers had experienced labour unions elsewhere. Several of the central Europeans in Lethbridge were refugees from the malicious battles of 1892 and 1893 in the Pennsylvania coalfields. There were also men from Britain where the labour movement was well advanced. The Lethbridge workers, in fact, could draw upon a collective experience accumulated from the earliest days of mining in America and Europe.

Early in October 1897, a delegate from the Sand Coulee, Montana, Miners' Union visited Lethbridge, signed up sixty members, and formed the Lethbridge Miners' Union, automatically an affiliate of the Western Federation of Miners.[24] The Lethbridge local was not very strong. Although it sponsored a highly successful co-operative store, it never served as a forceful bargaining agent simply because Elliott Galt refused to recognize it as the official representative of his employees. Like so many businessmen of the time, he firmly believed that he and the shareholders were the sole owners of the collieries. Ultimately, only they had the right to set company policy. Although willing to discuss any grievances with his workers, Galt wanted to deal with them directly and not through a union. As a consequence, his company never signed an agreement with the Lethbridge Miners' Union.

The abortive strike of 1899 is a good illustration not only of Galt's intransigence, but also of the union's aspirations and inherent weakness. In compliance with a territorial ordinance, the AR&CCo had shortened workdays from ten to eight hours. While day workers' wages were raised to compensate for the loss in hours, the company refused to increase rates for the contract miners. Late in October 1899 the union presented the AR&CCo with an ultimatum—either new contract rates would be negotiated or the miners would quit work on 11 November. Company officials refused to bargain with the union and instead threatened to close the mine. Faced with a lock-out, the miners backed down. They no longer enjoyed the support of all their members, particularly the Hungarians and Slavs, who as company workers had already received a pay increase.[25] Apart from the divided membership, a public statement by the union implied that the wage increase, while desirable, was not crucial. The declaration claimed that the highly dangerous and skilled nature of mining entitled the coal workers to more than the average wage and even some luxuries. "The prosperous times which are overwhelming the country," the notice declared, "as a whole are very desirable and we would like our share."[26] The Union badly miscalculated the timing of the ultimatum. Although October through November was the time that the mines geared up for the peak winter season, it was also the period when agricultural workers flooded into Lethbridge looking for winter jobs. The last thing these men wanted was a strike, especially if their pay was not unreasonably low. They could never hope to recover the lost wages in a single season. It was a serious error in judgement—one that Alberta miners would not repeat. The union backed down and on 24 November 1899 it sent the following laconic, yet caustic, letter to a Winnipeg labour paper:

The miners and their representatives after a conference with the company and calmly discussing the situation, resolved to continue at work. The company granted a few slight concessions and work at the mines will proceed as usual. The silk dresses and diamonds which some of us were so rash as to promise our wives and sweethearts will have to be abandoned until the coming of the new time.[27]

It was a brave face to hide a stinging defeat. The contract miners had tried to force Galt to his knees without the whole-hearted support of the other coal workers. Theirs was a serious blunder that not only cost the workers a raise in pay but emasculated their union for the next six years. To Lethbridgeans, 1899 became known as the year Elliott Galt broke the miners' union.

The set-back was only temporary. For the time being, the coal workers' deep sense of individual freedom was stronger than their concern for mutual responsibility. The seasonal production cycle, the contract system, the migratory workers, and the complex ethnic mosaic were all factors that prevented a cohesive association. Yet, camaraderie spawned in the alien, dangerous, masculine underground eventually overrode the diversities. As the twentieth century unfolded and brought an unprecedented economic boom to western Canada, Lethbridge's mineworkers once again turned to the labour union as the tool to capture a larger share of the new wealth.

The first decade of the twentieth century witnessed the fulfilment of Canada's fifty-year-old dream of western settlement. As the great stream of immigrants flooded the plains and the harried railways expanded their prairie empires, the demand for coal exploded. Alberta's treasure trove of coal suddenly took on new and urgent importance. Every year dozens of companies launched new mining ventures to exploit the fabulous resource and satisfy the growing market. Although most of the enterprises were shoe-string operations, others, particularly those in the mountain passes and foothills, were well-planned and heavily capitalized concerns. Within a relatively short span of time the simple frontier economy of southern Alberta was remoulded into a complex industrial system based on sophisticated mining technology and dedicated to the quest for profit.

The sudden prosperity did not come without a price. The mushrooming western Canadian economy carried with it social upheaval and stress. Each year thousands of strangers had to be absorbed into a young and unformed community, a traumatic experience that revolutionized western society. The church, for example, was bewildered by the rapidity of the change and found herself unable to cope with the deluge of young and single men caught up in the spirit of a secular and materialistic age. For the newcomer, too, the times were unsettling. Each cherished the hope that on the pristine frontier one became rich quickly and with little effort. Reality, however, was harsher than the dream, and nowhere was this more evident than in the coal-mining towns of British Columbia and Alberta. Only the fortunate few, those already well connected financially or lucky enough to meet a unique opportunity, grew wealthy or assumed social prominence. Most of the others met disillusionment and frustration. The mine-workers found themselves mere cogs in an industrial technological process, living in isolated, one-industry towns, toiling for impersonal companies devoted to profit rather than the welfare of the employees. As the collieries grew larger, the labourer no longer even met his boss and the chasm between him and the management grew even wider. The plight of the European immigrant was still worse. Not only did he endure the drudgery of a menial task in a harsh and hostile work place but he also suffered the segregation of an outsider in an unfamiliar cultural environment. With family life disrupted, the church impotent, conventional customs in jeopardy, and paternalistic labour relations destroyed, confrontation was imminent.[28]

Meanwhile, the Western Federation of Miners had virtually lost favour in the coalfields of Alberta. The federation had become too radical for the mine operators as well as the Canadian government. The bitter Rossland strike of 1901, in which the government backed the employers, effectively broke the back of the union in Canada. The coal workers themselves also spurned the federation for its obsession with socialist ideology and abstract idealism. They preferred the more moderate and businesslike United Mine Workers of America (UMWA), which had a pragmatic concern for raising wages and improving working conditions. By the summer of 1903 an organizational drive was well underway and in September the new union, after a short strike, secured its first contract with the Crows Nest Pass Coal Company. On 9 November 1903, District 18 of the UMWA was organized to cover the coalfields of Alberta and British Columbia's Crowsnest Pass. The initial membership stood at 3,293 miners. F. H. Sherman was elected the district's first president.[29]

Frank H. Sherman was both a theorist and an activist. Born and raised in Wales, he learned the miner's trade before emigrating to Canada. In Wales, too, he had been actively associated with the labour movement and its leaders; he had acquired a rich and broad experience in labour relations. Although a dedicated unionist, Sherman was a Socialist who believed that trade unions were elitist, of benefit only to the few, and in the long run ineffective. The union, Sherman argued tirelessly, could not change the economic order. "The day of the union is passed," he once wrote, "a union is now only useful to grapple with the petty tyranny of the bosses."[30] Lasting reform could come only if workers, united behind a labour party, democratically gained control of the government and abolished the wage system in favour of a co-operative commonwealth. So Sherman, as a leader in the Socialist Party of Canada, struggled for long-range ideological goals. In the meantime, he served as district president of the UMWA in order to fight for immediate concessions.[31] As a unionist, he preferred to settle differences through negotiations, but was quick to call a strike when thwarted. In 1905, when a temporary economic slow-down brought intensified competition, a fall in coal prices, and 500 unemployed miners, Sherman still led his Crowsnest members out on strike. In this instance he learned the value of the European immigrants to the union and he asked headquarters to send over multi-lingual organizers.[32] Yet, in spite of this important insight, Sherman could not comprehend the foreign mind, and in the 1906 strike at Lethbridge he lost control over the Hungarians.

The UMWA moved into Lethbridge in January 1906. From the union's point of view, the Galt collieries were too large to remain unorganized and employ cheap non-union labour. The UMWA organizers spent several months in Lethbridge. Their task was especially difficult because most men feared that the AR&ICo would lock out the union. This was not the case and management let it be known that while it would not bargain with any unionists, neither would it fire any.[33] Once this became known, the organizers had better luck. By mid-February they had signed up more than 360 members and on 21 February they founded the Lethbridge local of District 18 of the UMWA.[34]

The new local did not tarry long before flexing its muscles. On the last day of February, at a stormy meeting held in Staffordville, the miners resolved to strike if the AR&ICo did not recognize their organization. An undercover policeman who was present at the meeting noted, "The Hungarian and Slav elements at the meeting last night were very rowdy and were in favour of a strike right away, but were somewhat stayed by the English speaking community."[35] Although a majority may have favoured strike action, the demands were moderate. The miners asked for union recognition, the right to strike, deduction of union dues from their wages, a checkweighman, and a pit committee to supervise safety and settle grievances. Three of the detailed requests included an eight-hour day for underground workers, a ten-hour day for surface men, as well as more equitable distribution of cars. In regard to wages, the contract miners called for a minimum rate of three dollars per day when confronted by abnormal conditions or when working for the company. They also demanded that the weight of coal they extracted be calculated before being screened.[36] These and other items were relatively modest and represented the desire of a new union to establish a regular, basic working agreement with its employer. Recognition was by far the most important demand and the outstanding cause of the dispute.

The newly formed local faced a different opponent than the miners' union had tackled in 1899. The relatively small coal company had grown into the multi-million-dollar AR&ICo with several diverse interests, all of which, except its coal-mines, were earning good profits. Also in 1899, Elliott Galt, as company president, had been actively involved in the strike but by 1906 he left all executive decisions to A. M. Nanton, the managing director. Nanton, who lived in Winnipeg and occasionally visited Lethbridge in the company's private railcar, directed the AR&ICo operations through a general manager, P. L. Naismith. He had explicitly instructed Naismith not to negotiate with the UMWA and so the union faced the frustration of not being able to speak directly to anyone with authority.

In accordance with his instructions, Naismith refused to

recognize the local union executive as the representative of his employees and threatened to fire all union members if they continued to press their demands. With the workers equally persistent, a strike was but a matter of time. On 7 March 1906 Frank Sherman, accompanied by a number of district board members, arrived in Lethbridge but Naismith refused to see him. Later, at a public meeting, Sherman declared that the union was prepared to retract some of its monetary demands if the AR&ICo proved it could not afford the proposals. He refused to relent on the union recognition issue and announced the immediate start of the strike, a precipitant action that needlessly provided the company with a genuine grievance. Sherman assured the strikers that they would receive financial support from the American headquarters and promised Lethbridgeans that the strike would be orderly "unless the men are driven to [violence] by acts of injustice and then it is hard to say what the mixed nationalities will do."[37] On 9 March 1906 the largest mine in the province, employing 524 men, came to a halt.

Despite Sherman's assurances, P. L. Naismith still worried about violence. He immediately asked for extra police to protect the small work-force needed to run the water pumps and ventilators and care for the horses in the mine. He feared that the strikers might intimidate the non-union men, shut the mine completely, and cause a flood. Like so many of his contemporaries, Naismith mistrusted the central Euopeans. "A large majority of our men are foreign" he wrote the commissioner of the Royal North West Mounted Police, "and with a little urging on the part of their leaders, are capable of doing anything."[38] He also warned the local police commander to prepare for a major riot on 17 March when 500 miners could be expected to go on a drunken rampage after receiving their last pay.[39]

The police responded readily to Naismith's appeal for help. Since their primary function was to maintain law and order and protect private property, they moved quickly to guard the collieries and quell an anticipated riot. Implicit in their prompt response, however, was the general attitude. Ever since the Canadian government had acquired the Northwest, the aim had been to settle the plains as soon as possible. To that end it had endeavoured to dispel the notion that the frontier was necessarily wild and disorderly. The mounted police were established only a few years after the take-over to make this a reality.[40] Industrial violence, like lawlessness, could not be tolerated because it would damage Canada's image abroad. Moreover, government officials believed that prospective settlers would also be discouraged if fuel supplies on the cold prairies were periodically jeopardized by strikes. Deep concern about public opinion drew the police into the dispute, and soon they became active participants in the conflict.

As the miners' pay-day approached, the police began to prepare for a major confrontation with the strikers. The commander of the Lethbridge division, J. O. Wilson, had no previous experience with labour disputes, was unsure of himself, and therefore prone to over-react. Although he professed to be neutral in the conflict, socially and culturally he sympathized with management and he often conferred with A. B. Hardie, the mine superintendent, and P. L. Naismith. He eagerly sought their advice because "they do not appear to be men easily stampeded and . . . they are both men of experience."[41] Like Naismith, he could not understand the Hungarians. "As most foreigners," he wired his supervisors, "impossible to say what they will do under influence of liquor."[42] Nervous about rumours of threats against non-union members and their families, he worried that the miners might use the explosives stored in their homes. In fact, on 8 March a small bomb had blown up just outside the house of a worker opposed to the UMWA. What would he do, Wilson fretted, if a major riot broke out? How could he possibly read the riot act to a mob that could not understand English? These and more questions troubled his mind. Mostly, however, he feared that he might have to order his men to fire their guns. To Wilson, the only answer was a strong show of force by the police; he urgently wired for reinforcements.[43]

The response from headquarters in Regina was immediate and thorough. Commissioner Perry assured Naismith that the police would do all they could to protect the company's properties and employees.[44] He instructed Wilson to close all bars and saloons and to keep a fire-hose ready at the mine to repel invaders. He dispatched two inspectors and twenty-one constables to Lethbridge, and held another twenty-one men in reserve. He also instructed Wilson to be extremely patient yet firm, resolute but not provocative. The strikers must be told that while the police would take no sides they would "protect [the] Company's property from injury and any men who desire to work."[45] In the context of the private enterprise philosophy of the day, with its over-emphasis on the rights of the employer, Perry's policies were sure to be applauded by the general public. Yet they clearly placed the worker at a serious disadvantage.

The weakness of the miners soon became apparent. Three police officers, thirty-one constables, and eleven company-paid but deputized watchmen guarded the mine and the twenty-five men retained to keep the mine operative. All, except a few labourers, boarded at company expense in railway cars parked near the mine shafts. A few mounted policemen continuously patrolled the streets of Staffordville.[46] A few of the workers preferred to live at home and the police escorted them back and forth. The strikers wanted to stop this traffic and thereby cripple, even ruin, the mines. On 14 March about fifty men, some blowing horns and pounding tin cans, began to follow and berate a small police-escorted party.[47] For both police and workers it was a harrowing experience, and as the numbers of protestors grew daily, it invited trouble. Two days later Superintendent Wilson ordered a Sergeant Raven to break up the demonstrations. Raven gathered a party of six mounted police to escort three mine workers home. A noisy crowd of more than 150 strikers pursued the small group, making a racous din with horns, mouth organs, and tin cans. Two men carried a large banner sporting the inscription "Cure for Scabs." Sergeant Raven commanded the crowd to cease but the noise merely increased. He then grabbed one of the men as if to arrest him. The mob pressed on and several arms reached out to rescue the hapless prisoner. The six policemen panicked and drew their revolvers. Suddenly an uneasy hush fell over the crowd. For a few seconds tension mounted. Then Sergeant Raven, who had regained his composure, seized the initiative and quietly explained that police orders had to be obeyed. To his immense relief the people listened and their leaders promised to go home and not follow the workers again.[48]

The incident, which could easily have turned to tragedy, created an uneasy peace. Later in the day, a small, home-made bomb exploded harmlessly in an open field, but its deliberate innocuousness gravely warned of potential destruction. Ironically, too, the last pay-day proved to be the quietest in Lethbridge's history. Although some mineworkers had laid in their own supply of liquor and beer, no public drinking places were open and extra police patrolled Staffordville throughout the night. No incidents occurred. Although Superintendent Wilson still fretted about the prevalence of explosives and hand-guns in town, he felt secure enough to send some of the extra police back to their home posts.[49]

By protecting company property and those men refusing to strike, the police tipped the balance in favour of the AR&ICo. By the third week of March the small work-force had grown to thirty men, all of them living in the company's railcars, some of them with their families. Superintendent Wilson noted, "had it not been for the Force here there would not have been a man at work, as the men are afraid to work, without protection and the probabilities are there would have been trouble."[50] Naismith echoed Wilson's sentiments and expressed them in a congratulatory letter to the RNWMP comptroller. He also pointed to a very significant effect of the police role upon the strike. "At present everyday the property is worked the strikers are losing ground."[51]

The docility of the strikers ended the last day of March when they launched a last-ditch effort to check the trickle of men returning to work. That day a group of strikers forced a party of police, who were escorting a blacksmith to the mine, to draw their guns. Three days later a crowd of about one hundred men and women threw stones at three workers visiting a house in Staffordville. The police rescued the three men, and arrested two strikers on the spot and six others several days later. On 4 April the strikers tested the strength and nerves of the police to the limit. Ten officers were required to break up a fight at the colliery gates between the police and company guards on the one hand and several strikers and their wives on the other. Later that evening an explosion demolished a house abandoned by a returned worker. A short while later a second explosion blew the windows out of yet another empty house in Staffordville. Still later that night a third empty house was set afire and had to be extinguished by a bucket brigade. Although there were no more outbursts that night, no one rested peacefully. There was an uneasy feeling that the coal-miners of the Galt collieries were in revolt.[52]

The violence ended as abruptly as it had exploded. The arrival of a special contingent of fourteen policemen imposed an uneasy calm on the city and village. Although Superintendent Wilson warned the new men not to use their firearms except as clubs or in the most extreme danger, he did insist on a tough stand. "Your duty is to protect property from damage and at the same time to afford protection to persons wishing to work," he instructed his men and, demonstrating new-found confidence in his ability to handle the strikers, he arrogantly declared, "these workmen should be able to walk through the streets without being molested in any manner."[53] To guarantee this freedom of movement, the RNWMP commander detailed six mounted police to patrol Staffordville in the evenings and two shifts of two men each at other times.

The riot and subsequent explosions turned public indifference to the strike into opposition. This was particularly noticeable in the *Lethbridge Herald*, which broke editorial silence immediately after these incidents. The paper complimented the strikers' conduct up to this point but caustically added, "they cannot expect to gain any sympathy or encouragement from law-abiding citizens if they attempt to persecute and mob men working in the mines."[54] The weekly conceded the workers the right to strike. "This is a free country, and a man should be allowed to work if he wants to. If he wants to strike he has a perfect right to do so." But, the *Herald* quickly added, "Lethbridge does not want to be the scene of riots that will give it an unenviable reputation, especially at the present time when hundreds of people are seeking homes here."

Apart from some sporadic but harmless explosions, excessive drinking, and the inevitable brawls, the violence ceased. By the end of April, with no sign of settlement in sight, more and more of the single strikers abandoned Lethbridge for the United States, leaving behind a core of married homeowners. At the same time, the trickle of men returning to work grew daily and on 28 May 1906, a skeleton crew of about eighty men resumed production. For the first time in months the AR&ICo whistle triumphantly summoned the men to work. It also lured still others back to work. One group even came back from the United States but, when a number of brawny picketers ominously offered to pay their return fares, they took the first train back again. Nevertheless, the piercing whistle at the mine mockingly reminded the strikers that they had lost another crucial battle, and that from now on they were fighting a rearguard action. By mid-July more than 160 men were at work.[55]

As the strike drifted into the hot summer months, the police began to question their role in the affair. The relative calm and the prolonged duration of the conflict caused boredom and discontent among the police guards. They were also becoming uncomfortably aware that their actions were a major factor in the ability of the AR&ICo to resume operations. Yet, Superintendent Wilson hesitated to withdraw his men. For a while his irrational fear of the Europeans restrained him. "If it were not for the foreign element, I would have no hesitation in recommending the reduction of strength but, as you are aware," he wrote his superior, "these people have been ruled by force for generations, and in consequence, it now requires a show of force to keep them in order."[56] Yet, as the constables grew more restless, Wilson had to act and early in July he informed the AR&ICo managers that he intended to dismiss the police guard.

Wilson's declaration drew an immediate and angry response from company officials. Naismith complained directly to Commissioner Perry and argued that, in view of the many bombings, a withdrawal of the police could be interpreted as a licence to destroy property.[57] In response, the comptroller of the RNWMP, Fred White, asked Elliott Galt if there was any hope of settlement. The protection of the mine, he wrote, with obvious exasperation, "is most distasteful to our men," causing desertions and an unusual frequency of discipline problems. White reluctantly conceded that the company was entitled to help from the police, but he quickly added that his men were not recruited or trained for prolonged guard duty amid hostile and jeering strikers.[58] Galt, who knew White personally, lightly replied that he had no opinion on the strike because he left all such matters entirely to the discretion of the managing director, A. M. Nanton.[59] Having received no satisfactory response from Galt, the police determined to press ahead. After a stormy interview with Naismith, Superintendent Wilson was convinced that the strike would drag out for some time yet and he informed Naismith that some of the constables would be withdrawn from the site.[60] This prompted yet another angry letter. "Although matters are now quiet at the mine," Nanton wrote, "I am satisfied that this is due to the presence of the Police and if they are withdrawn before the strike is settled that there will be both riot and bloodshed, as there is a large and ignorant foreign element."[61]

The spectre of a riot by the strange and unpredictable Hungarians deterred the police from dismissing the entire guard and so they merely reduced their numbers. Two events in early August seemed to vindicate their caution. In the first a patrolling policeman tried to arrest an intoxicated Hungarian miner. The drunk's frantic howling attracted a crowd that quickly came to the rescue and pushed him into a nearby house. Accompanied by a colleague, the officer entered the house only to be confronted by a small angry mob replete with screaming, spitting women. Eight policemen were needed to quell the miniature riot and make the arrests.[62] Five days later, on the night of 13 August, a vicious explosion rocked the home of a Jack Scott, a mechanic working at the Shaft 3 mine. The blast tore out a veranda, all the front windows, and a door. More seriously, however, Scott's wife was in the house and, although not injured, she was badly shaken. Since the house was occupied and within the city limits, the Lethbridge police and AR&ICo detectives launched an intensive investigation and within days arrested an Hungarian miner.[63]

The explosion came very shortly after the company had openly acknowledged its anti-union stand. Earlier, in mid-July, the business community, emulating a previous attempt by the Lethbridge clergy, had arranged a meeting between strikers and management. A committee of two businessmen and eight strikers visited Nanton and proposed a conciliation board comprised of two workers and two officials. Nanton adamantly rejected the idea, refused to talk to union officials, and warned the strikers that the company would resume full operations soon and lock out all recalcitrants.[64] Several weeks later Naismith reinforced Nanton's unyielding stance in a statement published by the *Herald*. The mine manager offered jobs to all the old men who were not members of the union and lamented that the UMWA stood between him and his employees. He dismissed the conciliation board idea because "never having had an opportunity of discussing with our employees any grievance they may have, we have nothing to arbitrate."[65] Five days later the bomb burst in Scott's house, the first explosion in an occupied house within the city limits.

The repercussions of the bombing reverberated throughout Lethbridge. Public opinion in the city moved still further away from the strikers. The *Lethbridge Herald* decried the violence and vigorously defended the rights of any person to work whenever he pleased.[66] F. H. Sherman, on the other hand, hired two lawyers to defend the bombing suspect and at a Labour Day rally charged that two AR&ICo detectives had instigated the whole affair in order to inflame public opinion against the strike.[67] His accusation upset city councillors, who challenged the union president to produce evidence to enable the police to prosecute. When Sherman did not supply proof, the *Herald* called his allegations a fabrication and once again pointed out that violence was economically detrimental to Lethbridge because it hurt the city's image. "Lethbridge, as a city, is injured in the eyes of the outside public, by the reports of explosions here."[68] The weekly voiced the growing sentiment in the city and in much of the West that Sherman had lost control over the strikers and that the recurring violence might discourage prospective settlers.

The explosion was the last outburst, however. The mine, although severely crippled, was operating. The strikers had resigned themselves to a lengthy siege. Under these circumstances the mounted police withdrew all their men except one constable.[69] The stalement was firmly set; only a third party could break the deadlock.

The deadlock, however, had to be broken. In 1906 the Galt collieries, as one of the largest producers of domestic coal, was a vital part of the prairie fuel supply, particularly in Saskatchewan. The previous year all western coal-mines, virtually idle during the summer but operating at peak capacity during the winter months, had barely managed to satisfy the demand. Neither the production nor distribution facilities could cope with the sudden critical demands during the cold winter season. The summer of 1906 had produced an unusually large crop and an extraordinary growth in population. Both events created an unprecedented increase in fuel consumption as well as crowded railways unable to carry coal. Moreover, strikes at Fernie and Taber, although short-lived, aggravated the dearth of coal. In addition, when coal dealers thought to await the settlement of all strikes before ordering coal, a fuel famine loomed as a real possibility. By September consumer complacency was rudely shattered as people suddenly realized they could not order their coal on short notice as in the past.[70] The fuel crisis was reality.

With the advent of cold winter winds, the public became increasingly fearful. The extreme cold of early November was interpreted as a harbinger of a severe winter. Newspapers across the prairies began to demand government intervention in the dispute. In the first week of November a survey conducted by the Saskatchewan government revealed that the province faced a very critical shortage of fuel. The provincial commissioner of agriculture immediately hurried to Lethbridge to study the situation but soon discovered that no solution appeared likely. He urged immediate action to prevent a coal famine, which would bring hardship to settlers and discourage future immigrants. "The problem must be solved in the very near future, if the progress of the country is not to be impaired," he stated. "If the people who have thoughts of locating in Canada learn that it is impossible to get fuel to meet the strenuous winters in Saskatchewan, immigration will get a black eye."[71] A week later, Premier Walter Scott of Saskatchewan left for Ottawa to urge the federal government into action. In a public statement he insisted that the strike had to be settled quickly because Saskatchewan's fuel bins were empty and her people could not afford to buy the more expensive American coal.[72]

In response to Walter Scott's desperate appeal, the federal minister of labour, Rodolphe Lemieux, asked his deputy minister, William Lyon Mackenzie King, to travel west and conciliate in the coal-miners' strikes. The young bureaucrat, described by the *Lethbridge Herald* as "one of the most advanced and best informed students of labour problems in the world,"[73] was confident he could end the dispute. In a manner typical of the progressive-reformist minds of the era, King assumed that an "expert" like himself could dispassionately study a dispute and make impartial recommendations.[74] At the same time he knew that public opinion could be used to force key concessions from the combatants and so he became a master of the judiciously released news item or the timely threat to publish an unfavourable report. The Alberta problem did cause King some concern, however, because in 1905 he had angered the UMWA by his role in the Nanaimo strike. Frank Sherman made it very clear that he would not meet with King, and under the federal conciliation act of 1900 no arbitrator could intervene unless both parties approved.

To override Sherman's objections, King decided to travel to Minneapolis and explain his position to John Mitchell, president of the UMWA. Before leaving, he asked Premier Scott to state in writing that unless the strike was ended soon his government would send men to work the Lethbridge mines under police protection. King planned to use this letter as a club to impress upon Mitchell that provincial intervention would seriously weaken the union's cause in Canada. He also intended, if the UMWA proved stubborn, to place the responsibility of the fuel scarcity upon the union. In this way, he wanted Mitchell to realize "in what peril his organization might be placed, if they were to maintain an unreasonable stand."[75] Next he composed a letter to Frank Sherman over the minister's signature, which clearly implied that a refusal to accept his services as a conciliator would mean that the district president would assume personal responsibility for the pending coal shortage. Lastly, King drafted a letter to A. M. Nanton "requesting the Company in the name of the Government in view of the serious situation to do all in his power towards effecting a settlement."[76] Although Mackenzie King professed expert impartiality, his letters revealed social and professional deference to management and a stern approach to labour.

With the preliminaries out of the way, King left for Lethbridge. He made two important stops en route. On 19 November he secretly met John Mitchell between sessions of a labour convention in Minneapolis. By pointing to the possibility of a government-operated mine, King extracted from Mitchell the union's approval of his mediation effort and a promise that, as long as the AR&ICo did not discriminate against union members, the UMWA would permit non-members to work in the mines. With this important concession in hand, King next visited A. M. Nanton in Winnipeg. He told Nanton about his confidential interview with Mitchell and expressed his belief that on the basis of "the true liberty of the individual" a man must be free to join or not to join a union. He argued that while the union should not compel anyone to become a member, neither should the company forbid such an association. King also told the managing director that in his view the AR&ICo had to pay employees wages comparable to those paid at other mines in the area. Unlike Mitchell, Nanton was unimpressed by King's arguments and he refused to make any concessions.

Although the AR&ICo's position was very strong, Nanton, as did King, knew that the company was vulnerable to public opinion. November was proving to be one of the coldest months on record and, as the icy winds piled snow drift upon snow drift, the public demanded an end to the strike. Earlier in October the AR&ICo had tried to assuage the fears of a coal famine by publishing an open circular to all its dealers. The letter stated that, although no orders could be accepted yet, "as soon as the great demand for harvest labour is over, the Company expects that there will be many labourers anxious for a full winter's work, and if such is the case, the output of the mines will be materially increased, and the Company will be able to fill its orders."[77] In his mid-November interview with King, however, Nanton had to admit that he believed intimidation by the strikers had scared away his usual winter labour force. Without a full complement of experienced coal workers, the mine could not operate at full capacity and the fuel shortage would worsen. Here was the chink in the AR&ICo armour.

From Winnipeg, Mackenzie King journeyed to Lethbridge. Immediately upon his arrival he met with union officials, next with P. L. Naismith, the mine manager, and then toured the colliery. From the interviews and his visit to the mine, King concluded that intimidation was no longer a factor in the strike and that the AR&ICo needed at least a year to train the green work-force operating the mine.

For the next week, Mackenzie King shuttled back and forth between Naismith and the union executive, the latter fortified by F. H. Sherman and an international board member. Using all the techniques of the conciliator—sympathy or indifference, flattery or insults—King sometimes pleaded, often threatened his way to small concessions, which he then used to draw out yet another step toward an agreement. His only goal was the resumption of efficient coal-mining operations and to that end he was determined to impose upon both parties what he thought was a reasonable settlement. Without apology, King demanded that the strikers make the largest sacrifice. Theirs was the easiest to obtain because he could deal with them directly. The union negotiators, weakened by the duration of the strike and their own ambiguous goals, were unable to withstand King's changing moods, patronizing condescension, and petulant anger. On the other side, distance protected company management from King's tactics. Naismith was but a mouthpiece for A. M. Nanton, who was at the bedside of his ailing mother in Ottawa. Every little change in the company's position required the managing director's consent by telegraph. To King's great annoyance, he could not confront the company's decision-maker directly. He could, however, impress upon each party in private that they alone would be held responsible for Saskatchewan's fuel famine. This was his most powerful weapon and he used it effectively.

Late Monday evening, 26 November 1906, the union men capitulated. Sherman and the international board member visited King in his hotel room and concurred with the deputy minister that, in view of the public sentiment building up in the West, there was little to be gained by holding out any longer. The two men accepted King's compromise provided that UMWA President Mitchell consented. To save time and prevent any misunderstandings, Sherman and King decided to head a delegation to union headquarters in Indianapolis and explain the terms to Mitchell directly. Although he feared public criticism of a Canadian government official seeking the consent of a foreigner to end a domestic dispute, King decided that he could use the trip to Indianapolis as a tactical advantage, for as he confided in his memoirs, "I have the men now in a position that it can be positively shown that unless this strike is settled it is because one man in the United States has it in his power to allow people to freeze to death through a large part of the Dominion."[78]

Even though King did not have the consent of A. M. Nanton, he left for Indianapolis. He trusted that personal pressure by the minister of labour, Rodolphe Lemieux, and the prime minister, Wilfrid Laurier, would swing around the businessman. King's view proved correct and both politicians impressed upon Nanton his responsibility toward the freezing farmers of Saskatchewan. With Nanton's compliance, confirmed in a telegram on Wednesday night, the strike was virtually over. On Saturday morning, 1 December 1906, after he had arrived in Indianapolis, King showed Sherman the official acceptance by Naismith of the agreement. Sherman immediately wired his men to return to work. On 3 December the Lethbridge miners returned to work for the first time in nine months.[79]

What had the men gained from their nine-month strike? They realized a ten-percent pay increase and the company's agreement to pay the checkweighman from their wages. All other deductions were limited to those specified in the final settlement, including rent, doctors' and hospital fees, coal, oil, powder, and other supplies, sick benefits, and the library fund. Most important perhaps, the agreement included an elaborate grievance procedure that created a formal means of communication with management, and therefore signified a limited recognition of workers' rights.[80] In sum, the mineworkers at Lethbridge benefitted materially from the intervention of Mackenzie King. He secured a better settlement than they could have acquired on their own. Compared to their colleagues in North America, even those in Nova Scotia and Vancouver Island, the employees of the AR&ICo were well paid and had some say over their working conditions. On the other hand, however, the coal-miners were deeply disappointed because they did not win union recognition or the allied issues of the "closed shop" and the "check-off." Because these ideas were considered to be absolutely crucial to the health and strength of the labour union, they became deeply coveted ambitions that sparked industrial strife for the next two decades.[81]

The officials of District 18 learned some valuable lessons from their experience in Lethbridge. The 1906 strike confirmed a pattern to be copied in nearly all subsequent disputes. Henceforth work stoppages were called in the spring when production slumped, the mass of migrant workers returned to the fields, and hours of work were reduced. By autumn the return of the agricultural worker, the resumption of peak earning hours, and the public concern for winter fuel supply all contributed to the finalization of an agreement. The leaders also realized that in a very competitive industry where the resource of coal and supply of casual labour was abundant, a union could not afford to hold only one company to ransom at a time. In keeping with the trend toward large coal-mining companies and the growing solidarity among mine operators and public officials, District 18 of the UMWA began a move to bargain collectively for all the locals under its jurisdiction and only sign an agreement to cover as many of the operators as possible. This approach meant that the strike burden was no longer borne only by the workers and the companies but that, in case of a fuel shortage, also by the public. Since fuel famines were detrimental to Canada's Northwest civilization policy, this strategy invited government intervention. In the following years the federal government often played an influential role in settling the disputes in western Canada's coal industry.

The tenacious ferocity of the strikers impressed company officials. They might still detest the union movement and try to thwart it at every turn, but they could no longer ignore it as they had before. Elliott Galt, for example, had always considered the union to be a dangerous nuisance, robbing him of his power to control the firm that he and his father had built. He sincerely believed that he was just and humane, and was deeply hurt whenever anyone suggested the contrary. He persistently maintained that he had never heard a valid complaint that he had not remedied; therefore, he could not comprehend why his workers had to be represented by a labour organization.[82] In 1899, when he was still directly in charge of the company, he easily emasculated a weak local torn by dissension. Six years later the coal-miners' union had come of age, and Galt's managers had to make concessions to break a stalemate. They could no longer arbitrarily impose their will on their employees.

To consolidate their waning strength, the managers of the AR&ICo decided to combine forces with other coal producers faced with similar labour problems. On 22 October 1906 the administrators of the largest collieries in the region met at Canmore and founded the Western Coal Operators' Association "for the purpose of offensive and defensive protection of the coal interests of the Crow's Nest Pass and Alberta Coal Mines."[83] Indicative of their purpose and style was a short notation in the minutes of their second meeting. The managers agreed that the

Pinkerton detective, hired "to secure information for the general benefit of the association," was not productive enough, and so they instructed him to infiltrate the UMWA.[84]

The Lethbridge strike also aroused intense public interest. Although the dispute had only a marginal effect upon the coal shortage, those people afflicted by the crisis reacted hysterically. Whipped up by the emotional response to newspapers and politicians, they questioned how the fuel supply, so critical for survival on the cold and harsh prairies, could be guaranteed. The *Lethbridge Herald*, following the lead of several western papers, recommended the most drastic solution of all. Still concerned with the West's image abroad, it argued that at least some mines should be owned and operated entirely by the government. "If corporations and the unions are going to be engaged in warfare whenever they feel like it, then it is the duty of the government to guarantee protection to the people by establishing government mines so that the people who are in the west will be assured that life in the winter months will always be worth living."[85] A more moderate but no less angry response came from the opposition in the House of Commons. Here R. S. Lake, the Conservative member for Qu'Appelle, whose district was severely hit by the fuel famine, demanded to know why the government failed to act in the crisis:

> If suffering should unfortunately take place, the people will not be satisfied with a mere formal expression of regret on the part of the government that they did not possess power to deal with the question beyond the power which is vested in the Department of Labour. The people will want to know that there is some authority which realizes its responsibility in this matter and is prepared to discharge that responsibility and so do it that the people of that country have an opportunity to obtain a sufficient supply of fuel to see them through the rigorous winter which may occur, and that at no too ruinous price.[86]

On 10 December 1906 the Conservatives launched a wide-ranging debate on the coal question in western Canada. John Herron, the member from Alberta whose constituency embraced Lethbridge and the Crowsnest Pass, called for strict regulations of all coal lands not yet alienated to private companies. He hoped that this measure would stimulate greater production and a better return to the federal government. In support of Herron's motion, several Conservatives advocated a variety of remedies to ease the chronic fuel shortages, including higher royalties, compulsory arbitration, provincial control of resources, and even government ownership of the coal-mines. The discussion soon sank into pure partisanship when one speaker charged that the prairie consumers were dominated by a coal monopoly controlled by influential Liberals. In other words, the opposition complained that the valuable coal resources of the West were being manipulated by a few friends of the government at the expense of western Canadians. It appeared as if the Conservatives had memorized the Liberal speeches of the 1880s and 1890s.

As could be expected, the Liberals vigorously defended the government's policy. The minister of the interior, Frank Oliver, pointedly chided the opposition for thinking that royalties or stricter regulations might increase production. Neatly side-stepping the issue of the recurring strikes, Oliver asserted that the coal reserves were enormous but there was insufficient capital to develop them. Skilled labour was scarce as was the means of distribution. Among the several defenders of the government was J. G. Turriff, the member for East Assiniboia, whose constituency suffered badly from the coal shortage. He displayed some insight into the recurring problem when he suggested that farmers traditionally waited until after the harvest to buy their fuel but by then the freight cars were full with grain rather than coal. The fuel scarcity, he correctly pointed out, was a dilemma of too great a demand in too short a time. In essence, all Liberal speakers agreed that western Canada's coal problem could best be solved by encouraging still greater investments in coal-mines and railways. No one seemed to notice that this was precisely the Conservative policy of the late nineteenth century, a programme the Liberals had damned on many occasions.

The government's stance was a belligerent, political front shielding its inability to solve a very contentious issue. A reliable supply of cheap energy was imperative to growth-oriented policies of railway-building and western settlement. Also, western municipal and provincial governments were pressing the federal government to intervene in lengthy labour disputes that obstructed regional development.[87] The problem was that this era, so preoccupied with economic goals, still idolized the entrepreneur as the dynamic force in an expanding economy. Since his actions were considered to be in the end always good for society, the businessman had to be free to make crucial innovative decisions that underlaid economic vitality. The public distrusted the labour union because it wanted to dictate its own wages and working conditions. By doing so it threatened to usurp the capitalist's decision-making power, disrupt the expert management of the firm, and cripple the growth and prosperity of the nation.[88] Yet bureaucrats and politicians alike acknowledged that the labour movement could no longer be suppressed, and so they searched for a policy that would least hamper the individual independence of the businessman while still offering a measure of bargaining power to the unions.

The politicians dumped the problem on the laps of the bureaucrats and to their relief the deputy minister of labour, W. L. M. King, provided an answer. The solution had come to him on his last night in Lethbridge. He had concluded "that a little bit of tact and a disposition to understand aright the position of the other by each of the parties might have averted the whole [Lethbridge] trouble."[89] He decided to write a book explaining the effect of open communication and public opinion upon strikes. More directly, he resolved to ask parliament to extend the provisions of the Railway Labour Disputes Act of 1903 to the coal-mines. Such legislation was necessary, King believed, because "coal is in this country one of the foremost necessaries, on which not only a great part of the manufacturing and transportation industries but also ... much of the happiness and life itself depends."[90] Although King shied away from compulsory arbitration, his ideas formed the basis of the Industrial Disputes Investigation Act passed by parliament in 1907. The new act forbade any strikes or lock-outs in coal-mines or public utilities until a tripartite board had investigated the dispute and recommended a settlement, trusting on public opinion to enforce the award.

The attempt by government to ford the chasm between management and labour with legislation failed. The new act may have defused a few disputes but for many years strikes erupted in the western coalfields on schedule nearly every second year. The act was simply not designed to deal with the complexity or the heart of the unrest at the mines. Legislators failed to understand that the mining camps collected representatives from across Europe and North America, men who carried in their cultural baggage encounters with the broad sweep of radicalism on two continents. Marooned in these isolated one-industry towns was a restless, cosmopolitan labour force of young immigrants uprooted from their native soil, working in a hostile environment, and surrounded by an alien society. The short history of Lethbridge demonstrates that under such conditions the coal workers had little to invest in their communities and had virtually no interest in better working conditions or recreational facilities. Some of their leaders, like F. H. Sherman, fostered idealistic hopes for a better, reordered society, but the majority had no vision for the community in which they lived. Civilizing the West was not their dream. Their primary interest was to leave the mines as soon as possible, preferably with money in their pockets. So, with control of the company vested somewhere in the vague outside world, with the product of their labour disappearing on the outbound trains, there was little incentive in their work apart from monetary gain. The labour union became the vehicle to maximize the workers' profits, protect members from management, and seek security against wage cuts, unemployment, and irregular hours. The union was not created to build bridges of understanding with management, but designed to further the individualistic concern for material goods. Like their employers, the unionists believed in the predominance of economics in society and so strove for maximum gain. The union became a weapon to grab a bigger share of corporate wealth and an instrument of class warfare. So, when the companies' shareholders hired expert technicians to operate their firms at the lowest possible cost and the largest possible profit, management and labour were on a collision course. Even if government could bring peace to the work place, certainly legislation based on public opinion, which also embraced the ideals of the market-place, could not.

Lethbridge, so hopefully founded in a pristine environment, was but a microcosm of the continent. Although the setting was small, its history nevertheless illustrates how economics had come to dominate Canadian society. Ever since the marriage of business and technology early in the nineteenth century, economic activity had accelerated in the western world and its principles had undermined men's ideals to such an extent that money became the primary measure, especially in industrial relations. The managers of large companies increasingly estimated the worth of their labourers in terms of the state of the market, in terms of the profits to the shareholders. They lost their respect for the worker and no longer considered him as a fellow member of the business community. When the labourer became only a part of the machinery of business, the unity of the work place was shattered and its comprehensive purpose lost. Once management concentrated on achieving the largest possible dividend, labour had to fight for maximum wages, and the best available working conditions. In Alberta's coal-mining industry there was no sharing of interests, no community of ideals. As Mackenzie King forcefully reminded both sides, coal had to be mined not just for corporate earnings, not just for the wage packet, but also for the welfare of the nation. In the end, the Galt enterprises provided fuel to make prairie settlement possible, furnished irrigated lands for settlers, and created jobs for workers. In bringing civilization to the West, the Galts considerably improved the standard of living for many, but also introduced a shattered fellowship between workers and employers.

Epilogue

The 1906 strike was very costly for the AR&ICo in terms of coal production, which fell to 90,000 tons from 220,000 tons the year before. In 1907 the output rose to 260,000 tons and the company was preparing plans for a new mine to be built two miles north of Shaft 3. The proposed colliery would have two four-hundred-foot shafts, labelled Shaft 5 and Shaft 6, 225 feet apart. Crews began to excavate Shaft 5 early in 1908 and reached the coal-seam in December. Late that same summer work was begun on Shaft 6, the main hoisting shaft, and was completed the following year. By 1912 the entries of Shaft 6 were so extensive that the mine-workers needed an hour to get from the surface to the coal-face. By that year the AR&ICo hoisted coal only from Shaft 3 and Shaft 6, the former producing about 500 tons, the latter about 800 tons per day.[1] With these two collieries in operation, the AR&ICo was among Alberta's largest and most efficient mines. It no longer dominated the market, however. Although western Canada's population during these years expanded at a phenomenal rate, the proportion of coal-mines grew even more rapidly.

Expansion was also the order of the day for the AR&ICo irrigation department. Between 1902 and 1911 the Galt interests spent more than a million dollars on new construction work and at

This irrigation duct took water right into Lethbridge,
visible in the background. (Glenbow Archives)

the end of this period the network and laterals totalled 290 miles,
irrigating about 47,000 acres for 750 farmers.[2] By 1911 the system
had reached maturity and the AR&ICo never again spent that
much money in a single decade.

The impact of irrigation on the region was enormous. Irrigation transformed the expansive, open grasslands into cultivated,
fenced farms and homesteads. As early as 1906 John Stewart, the
federal commissioner of irrigation, on tour of the AR&ICo irrigation works, noted that there was much seeding and planting
activity all along the canals. "I might add," he wrote, "I travelled
through this section of country some twelve years ago when there
were no settlers between Lethbridge and Cardston—now it is not
only settled but towns grown up when there was nothing at that
time but a few scattered cattle on the prairie, and it seems to be
that this irrigation scheme is the cause of all the improvement that
has taken place in that time."[3]

Early in 1912 the CPR, which was also actively engaged in
irrigation elsewhere in southern Alberta, bought the majority of
AR&ICo shares and its department of natural resources assumed

control over the smaller company's administration. Although the two firms retained separate corporate identities, P. L. Naismith, the AR&ICo general manager, also became the head of the CPR's natural resources department.[4] A. M. Nanton, the AR&ICo managing director, whose firm of Ostler, Hammond, and Nanton had extensive interests in the CPR, was named a director of the railway company in 1914, two years after the take-over.[5] The transaction spelled the end of an era in southern Alberta because after thirty years of activities, the Galts were no longer in control of the economic development of the area. This economic power fell to the CPR.

The change in management also included the AR&ICo holdings of a 500,000-acre tract of land,[6] a questionable part of the transaction because the companies violated the spirit of the contract and in so doing earned substantial profits. At the termination of the agreement the AR&ICo had paid about $487,000, including interest, for almost 465,000 acres of land which it could sell for a maximum price of five dollars per acre. The entire tract could therefore conceivably generate nearly two million dollars in profit. Since construction costs from 1902 to 1917 totalled 1.5 million dollars, the profit from these land sales easily covered capital expenditures. Although maintenance costs throughout this period exceeded revenues, the AR&ICo was also selling railway land grants. While there are no records available to determine exactly the extent of the profits, it is evident that this 500,000-acre tract of land substantially added to the AR&ICo land sales profits. The CPR was eager to acquire this property with so much lucrative potential.

The 500,000-acre tract earned more money than even Elliott Galt had envisioned. The original agreement stipulated that all the lands in the parcel not sold by 1917 had to revert to the Crown. To side-step this legal obligation, the AR&ICo craftily sold all the land to one buyer, its parent company, the CPR. While E. F. Drake, the federal superintendent of irrigation, questioned the ethics of the transaction, he did concede "So far as I am aware, there is no way in which the Government can prevent a so-called sale of these lands by the Alberta Railway and Irrigation Company, but the direct transfer from the original company to the controlling company strikes me as being rather crude."[7] Deputy Minister of

Justice E. L. Newcombe agreed and also pointed out that once the land was sold, the CPR was no longer bound by the maximum selling price of five dollars set by the government but that it could be raised to as high as the market could bear.[8] The CPR justified its position by assuring the department of justice that it was merely the largest stockholder in the AR&ICo and that the two firms had separate corporate identities.[9] Since the CPR was legally correct, Newcombe decided that the department of the interior could not stop the sale of the AR&ICo lands to the CPR.[10]

James B. Hedges, in his discussion of this transaction, comments that the companies violated the spirit of the agreement, but, because they carried out the settlement obligations, they "did a valuable work."[11] His assessment echoes that of the Liberal government, which wanted virtually two farmers for every section of prairie land and was prepared to subsidize the heavy cost of irrigation just as it was generously assisting two transcontinental railways at the same time. In this respect Prime Minister Laurier differed little from his predecessors. Consequently, the public paid an extravagant price to convert a region perfectly suited for ranching purposes into agricultural lands primarily to satisfy the government's desire for settlement and the AR&ICo's quest for profits.

The expansion of the coal-mines and irrigation canals and the transformation of the region to an agricultural economy did not stimulate the growth of Lethbridge as much as some city boosters desired. Despite their valiant efforts, the city did not attract the industries it so desperately wanted. While Sick's Brewery, the Lethbridge Iron Works, and Ellison's Milling and Elevator Company settled in Lethbridge, the city lagged behind the spectacular expansion of Calgary and Edmonton. The introduction of hard spring wheat to the region sparked a land rush in 1910 that stimulated the city's construction industry, but by 1916 the gap had not closed appreciably.[12] Obviously, Lethbridge, with its small geographic hinterland away from the CPR main line, had to be content with a minor commercial role in southern Alberta. Since it did not have the high quality coal required by heavy industries, it did not become the large metropolis so proudly predicted by its leaders. In fact, Lethbridge became a relatively small and pleasant marketing and distribution centre for southwestern Alberta communities like Cardston, Stirling, Magrath, and Taber. The greatest contribution irrigation made to Lethbridge was that, by attracting settlers to the area, it provided the city with a greater measure of economic independence. Consequently, Lethbridge was able to survive the decline of the coal industry in the late 1950s.

The different dreams and aspirations that had subdivided the mining camps into several diverse segments continued to fragment the city. Merchants remained aloof from labourers, while Protestants kept their distance from Catholics. As long as the collieries were in operation, Lethbridge slighted Staffordville, even after the village was amalgamated with the city. So too, the Anglo-Saxons snubbed the central and southern Europeans. Time and a succession of children educated in the same schools tended to blur the sharpness of the divisions, but the partitions survived nevertheless. This was strikingly illustrated in the programme of Lethbridge's golden jubilee celebrations in 1935. Part of the festivities included a pageant celebrating the early history of the city. Particularly notable was that the names of the actors depicting such figures as explorers, mounted policemen, and citizens were almost exclusively Anglo-Saxon, while those representing the miners were nearly all central European.[13]

Divergent aspirations also continued to mar industrial relations, not only between management and labour but also among the workers themselves. Alberta's Coal Mining Industry Commission of 1919 discovered that at the Galt mines many drivers and loaders worked well beyond the legal limit of eight hours per day and that low-paid seasonal work made economic survival difficult for those unable to leave Lethbridge for the summer.[14] Discontent was rife and strikes remained prominent features of the Lethbridge labour scene. In labour disputes, the Galt mines were no longer in the forefront but, as they became integrated into the province-wide union organization, they surrendered their former leadership to those in more populous areas such as Crowsnest Pass and Drumheller. Still, some of the problems in the early years of Lethbridge's experience lingered on in western Canada. The district executive was never able to mould the coal workers into a cohesive whole, and in the turbulent years after the First World War, District 18 nearly disintegrated under the onslaught of radicalism. The brief flirtation with socialism, embodied within the One Big Union, served only to weaken unionism in Alberta and, ironically, to strengthen the employers.[15] The chaos of the period also reaffirmed a tradition rooted in the early years, the interference of government authorities in the labour troubles at the mines, an intervention not discouraged by moderate union leaders.

After the merger of all the Galt companies into the AR&ICo in 1904, the two principals in the founding of Lethbridge and its early development, Elliott Galt and Charles Magrath, gradually disassociated themselves from the city. Magrath resigned from his post with the AR&ICo in 1906, shortly after A. M. Nanton was appointed managing director. Very active in public life, he sat as a member of parliament for Medicine Hat from 1908 to 1911, became Canada's fuel controller during the First World War, and served as the chairman of the Canadian section of the International Joint Commission from 1914 to 1936. He died in 1942. His mentor and close friend, Elliott Galt, suffering from chronic illness, retired in 1908. He died in New York in 1928.

Although contemporary Lethbridge will continue to revere Sir Alexander Galt as its founder, it should also ascribe a prominent role to Elliott Galt and his close aide Charles Magrath. For twenty years these two friends lived in the Northwest and strove to mould what they thought to be rough, unproductive prairies into cultivated, fertile fields. Born and raised in central Canada, they were the vanguard of Canadian culture, working to transpose its values and traditions to the West. Behind them came the merchants, professionals, and managers from Ontario, the miners from Nova Scotia, Britain, the United States, and continental Europe. By bringing British development capital to western Canada, they exposed southern Alberta to the broad range of western civilization, including technology. The author of Lethbridge's golden jubilee pageant caught the sense of this act when he wrote the introduction to episode number four—the arrival of the railway:

As the lights slowly come up, the Indians are discovered sitting quietly and for a moment we hear the music indicative of the passing glory of the Red Man. Suddenly in the midst of this tranquility arrive the railroad workers. First the surveyor with his helper, who proceed to motion the Indians off the stage. Civilization is moving westward and the railroad has arrived.[16]

Appendices

Appendix I

List of persons holding shares

North Western Coal and Navigation Company, Limited
on the Seventh Day of September 1882
and on the Sixteenth Day of February 1891

Name	Residence	Number of Shares 1882	Number of Shares 1891
Aclaud, Alfred Dyke	London	—	500
Awdry, Charles	London	3	100
Awdry, Herbert	London	—	10
Baker, Walter Reginald	Winnipeg	5	—
Balsillie, John	Winnipeg	10	—
Bischoff, Thos. W.	London	1	20
Blake, The Hon. Samuel Hume	Toronto	—	100
Blanchard, Sedley	Winnipeg	20	—
Bompas, George Cox	London	10	100
Bourke, The Hon. Edward B.	London	—	200
Brown, Alfred	London	—	200
Brown, Fanny, Mrs.	London	—	200
Brunton, Spencer	London	—	300
Brydges, Charles John	Winnipeg	20	—
Brydges, Fred K. Henderson	Winnipeg	20	—
Burdett-Coutts, William	Picadilly	50	1,350
Cameron, Sir Roderick William	New York	—	260
Carman, Thomas Horsefield	Winnipeg	10	—
Chaplin, Ernest	London	—	300

Name	Residence	Number of Shares 1882	Number of Shares 1891
Colmer, Jos. G.	London	1	17
Crabb, Edward	London	20	1,500
Crabb, Lucy, Miss	London	—	200
Crown, Verschoyle	London (Ont.)	—	10
Currie, Bertram Wodehouse	London	—	500
Cutbill, Arthur	London	—	100
Cutbill, Beatrice Mary	Kent	—	10
Cutbill, Edward	London	—	20
Cutbill, Frederick Thomas	London	—	110
Cutbill, Martha Jane	Kent	—	30
Cutbill, Reginald	London	1	10
Cutbill, Walter John	London	3	160
Eden, Arthur Francis	Winnipeg	5	—
Ellis, John Cough Williams	Northampton	5	440
Fellows, James Israel	London	—	23
Fenwick, Charles Harry	Huntingdon	—	60
Fenwick, Ernest Guy	Huntingdon	—	90
Fenwick, Georgina May	Huntingdon	—	30
Fenwick, Newton Noel	London	—	60
Fenwick, Richard Louis	London	—	60
Ford, William	London	15	500
Frewin, Alfred	London	—	60
Gale, H.	London	—	37
Galt, Alexander Tilloch, Sir	London	50	770
Galt, Elliott Torrance	Winnipeg	20	—
Galt, George Frederick	Winnipeg	5	—
Goldsmed, Sir Julian	London	—	200

Name	Residence	Number of Shares 1882	Number of Shares 1891
Guild, Samuel Eliot	Boston	—	50
Guinness, Sir Edward Cecil	London	—	1,000
Hughes, Arthur Saunders	London	1	—
Kingsford, Wm. Lethbridge	London	—	300
Kirby, Charles Harrison	London	—	300
Lethbridge, William	London	60	560
McGreery, Thomas	Quebec	10	—
Middleton, Elizabeth Kennedy	New Brunswick	—	50
Mulock, William Redford	Winnipeg	5	—
Ogden, Jr., Isaac G.	Winnipeg	5	—
Patterson, Jacob Lunard	London	—	420
Pattison, Wm. Henry Lucard	London	—	20
Ramsay, William Miller	Montreal	15	80
Redpath, Peter	London	—	500
Rigby, John	London	10	200
Ross, Arthur Wellington	Winnipeg	20	—
Ross, James Gibb	Quebec	30	250
Round, Edmund	Temple	10	450
Sitken, Alex Muirhand	London	—	200
Smith, The Hon. Donald A.	Montreal	—	200
Smith, William Henry	London	50	740
Whitburn, Chas. Joseph Sofer	London	—	300
Willingdon, Baron	London	—	390
Wolverton, Estate of Baron	—	—	400
Wood, William	London	—	60
Total Ordinary Shares		490	14,450

Source: Great Britain Public Record Office, PRO Box Reference No. 2974, Annual List of Members and Summary of Capital and Shares, NWC&NCo, 7 September 1882; 16 February 1891.

Note: In 1891 William Lethbridge, William Burdett-Coutts, and Sir Alexander Tilloch Galt each also held three deferred or founders' shares.

Appendix II

A matter of profits and losses

It is impossible to calculate with any accuracy the profits enjoyed by either the various Galt companies or those of their individual investors. At present, no complete run of annual reports or company books is available. No complete financial assessment can be made without this basic data.

A rough indication, however, of the welfare of the several companies can be gleaned from a variety of other statistics. Tables IV to VII illustrate some aspects of the companies' operations such as the amount of coal produced and freight and passengers carried. They also give some idea as to the size of investments, capital expenditures, and floating debts. Lastly, the tables account for most of the corporations' revenues be they from coal operations, railway concerns, or land sales.

The figures must be used cautiously. Coal revenue statistics, for example, are based on the average price of coal as declared by the company to government officials. Moreover, there is no record of company income for water rentals between 1900 and 1906. Consequently, the revenue figures are neither complete nor entirely reliable.

The records of company expenditures are even more fragmentary. There are no accounts of company expenditures on maintenance and labour costs for the collieries. In fact, capital expenditures on the coal-mines are no longer included in the companies' declarations after 1898. There are no figures to cover the repairs of the AR&ICo canals and laterals. Finally, there are no indications of how much the principal investors actually paid into the ventures and how much they took out. In other words, because of a lack of sufficient data, a clear reconstruction of the companies' balance sheets is impossible.

An assessment of profits and losses, therefore, depends largely on the remarks made by the principal investors in their private correspondence. From the letters, it can be concluded that during the last decades of the nineteenth century, the collieries were a losing proposition, the railways earned their keep, and the hope of lucrative land sales maintained investor confidence. By 1906, however, the rapid colonization of the West stimulated the company's real estate business, which in turn improved the performance of the whole enterprise. Appendix III presents a contemporary analysis of the AR&ICo position in 1906.

Table IV
Coal Production Statistics, 1884–1906

		Quantities (1000s of tons)	
Year	Galt Mines	Region	Galt Share of the Region (%)
1884	3	3	100
1885	21	21	100
1886	31	43	72
1887	59	75	79
1888	109	115	95
1889	83	97	86
1890	128	129	99
1891	165	174	95
1892	131	184	71
1893	160	238	67
1894	116	200	58
1895	114	186	61
1896	123	226	54
1897	120	267	45
1898	168	350	48
1899	191	440	43
1900	171	578	30
1901	171	810	21
1902	154	914	17
1903	230	1,274	18
1904	283	1,529	19
1905	241	1,871	13
1906	94	2,075	5
Total	3,066	11,799	26

Values
(1000s of dollars)

Galt Mines	Region	Galt Share of the Region (%)
11	11	100
74	74	100
108	108	100
208	208	100
163	183	89
123	180	68
195	198	98
413	447	92
328	473	69
400	611	65
278	505	55
227	408	56
308	619	50
300	668	45
421	845	50
479	1,023	39
428	1,235	35
428	1,772	24
346	1,956	18
542	2,709	20
677	2,843	24
575	3,785	15
248	4,328	6
7,280	25,189	29

Sources: PAC, Mineral Resources Branch Records (RG 87) vol. 5, no. 35, part 1; vol. 9, no. 49, part 1; Canada, Dominion Bureau of Statistics, *Canadian Mineral Statistics, 1886–1956* (Ottawa, 1956), p. 101.

Notes: The term "region" refers to the coal-mines in Saskatchewan, Alberta, and the Crowsnest Pass area of British Columbia. The dollar values given are no more than estimates based on average prices paid at the minehead as reported by the company managers.

Table V
Freight and Passengers Carried by the Galt Railways

Year	Passengers	Total Freight (1000s of Tons)
1886	1,304	21
1887	1,598	41
1888	1,608	95
1889	1,868	93
1890	1,854	92
1891	2,476	185
1892	3,043	135
1893	3,394	118
1894	2,442	74
1895	1,098	31
1896	1,112	43
1897	1,016	44
1898	2,416	40
1899	2,145	59
1900	2,944	54
1901	4,203	70
1902	6,774	60
1903	9,434	61
1904	14,304	79
1905	15,183	107
1906	18,709	106
Total	98,925	1,608

Coal (1000s of Tons)	% of Coal to Total Freight	% of Coal Shipped from Total Production
17	83	55
36	89	61
92	97	84
86	92	103
82	89	63
167	90	101
130	96	99
114	96	71
72	98	62
29	93	25
41	96	33
44	100	37
38	94	23
57	96	30
30	55	18
26	36	15
33	55	21
34	56	15
27	35	10
27	26	11
27	26	29
1,208	75	39

Sources: PAC, Canadian Transport Commission Records (RG 46), vols. 853, 854, 859, and 995.

Notes: From November 1893, when the CPR commenced its lease of the Lethbridge–Dunmore line, to the end of 1894 there seems to have been some confusion as to which company should be credited with the various statistics. From 1895 on, however, the figures clearly indicate freight and passengers carried on the Lethbridge and Montana line only.

Table VI
Galt Railways Statistics

Date	Paid-Up Capital To Date	Floating Debt	Capital Expenditures
1886	1,338,041	—	790,821
1887	1,353,225	—	202,845
1888	1,406,953	—	56,818
1889	1,738,500	—	83,756
1890	1,738,500	—	—
1891	4,691,046	261,929	3,863,489
1892	4,691,046	194,496	—
1893	4,691,046	182,965	—
1894	5,480,092	207,944	553,329
1895	5,480,092	233,888	—
1896	1,100,000	618,172	1,319,693
1897	5,353,333	619,252	802
1898	6,453,333	64,091	—
1899	6,453,333	88,966	—
1900	6,453,333	70,148	612,404
1901	6,453,333	43,482	—
1902	6,453,333	45,831	—
1903	6,453,333	80,043	301,205
1904	6,521,324	85,387	313,185
1905	7,750,000	617,047	2,714,858
1906	7,746,000	718,028	147,712
Total	7,746,000	718,028	8,951,464

Operating Expenses Railways	Gross Revenues Railways	Net Earnings Railways	Gross Revenue Real Estate
60,757	106,284	45,527	26,875
99,127	126,727	27,600	3,137
106,328	230,198	123,870	280
116,150	177,848	61,698	81,312
132,198	181,522	49,324	4,801
242,693	290,115	47,422	11,996
178,936	209,948	31,012	—
139,700	175,994	36,294	973,253
77,650	127,348	49,698	—
48,010	54,396	6,386	—
85,991	99,461	13,470	—
84,784	101,562	16,778	—
77,421	130,249	52,828	—
85,596	147,669	62,073	—
92,244	153,080	60,836	—
106,744	157,059	50,315	62,500
101,484	140,036	38,552	66,904
100,538	204,889	104,351	86,247
101,480	129,823	28,343	156,357
123,093	156,433	33,340	164,139
125,817	159,652	33,835	939,538
2,286,741	3,260,293	973,552	2,577,818

Sources: PAC, Canadian Transport Commission (RG 46), vols. 853, 854, 859, 955; GAI, L. P. Burns, "The Alberta Railway and Irrigation Company, 1893-1946," History of Irrigation in Western Canada, History of Agriculture (A Glenbow Foundation Research Project, Typewritten).

Notes: Paid-up capital to date includes investments in the collieries, irrigation, as well as the railways. The large floating debts of 1905 and 1906 include the $500,000 owing to the federal government on account of the 500,000-acre land purchase. Capital expenditures include the estimated costs of the irrigation project. The sum in 1900 includes all investment up to and including that year. After 1900 the company no longer included colliery investments in railway statistics. The total capital expenditure figure, therefore, is low.

Table VII
Galt Railways
Subsidies and Revenues from Subsidies

Subsidies	Cost
1885—420,480 acres for 109.5 miles, Lethbridge-Dunmore	$42,048
1889—280,320 acres for 109.5 miles, Lethbridge-Dunmore	28,032
—413,568 acres for 64.62 miles, Lethbridge-Montana	41,357
1897—remission of survey dues	-48,000
1899—$30,000 bonus, Lethbridge	
—$100,000 bonus, CPR	
1900—remission of survey dues	-32,000
—surrender of 22,000 acres at $3.00 per acre	-66,000
—$75,000 bonus for 30 miles, St. Mary railway	
1902—500,000 acres at $1.00 per acre	500,000
1903—$80,000 bonus for 32 miles, St. Mary railway	
Total—1,592,368 acres	$465,437
—$285,000 cash	

Date	Acres of Land Sold	Land Revenues	Average Revenue Per Acre
1886	21,500	$26,875	$1.25
1887	1,087	3,137	2.88
1888	80	280	3.50
1889	63,971	81,312	1.27
1890	724	4,800	6.63
1891	8,283	11,996	1.44
1892	—	—	—
1893	738,407	973,333	1.32
1894	—	—	—
1895	—	—	—
1896	—	—	—
1897	—	—	—
1898	—	—	—
1899	—	—	—
1900	—	—	—
1901	50,000	62,500	1.25
1902	45,141	66,904	1.48
1903	67,385	86,247	1.27
1904	72,985	156,357	2.14
1905	13,190	164,139	12.44
1906	171,035	939,538	5.49
	1,298,969	$2,644,322	$2.06

Source: PAC, Canadian Transport Commission (RG 46), vols. 853, 854, 857, and 995.

Appendix III

Alberta Railway & Irrigation Company, Prospectus 1905

In the current year the market values of the securities of this Canadian enterprise have appreciably advanced, and at the present time the Five per Cent. Debenture stock, redeemable at par at any time at the option of the Company on three months' notice, is quoted at 98; while the Four per Cent. Prior Lien Debenture stock, also redeemable at part at any time at the Company's option on three months' notice, is quoted at 99; and the Capital stock, upon which no dividend has yet been paid, is at 94½. From an examination of the Company's affairs, we are convinced that the advance in values is justified, and that stockholders would be well advised not to be tempted to part with their holdings at present prices. The railway property consists of two lines of railway, one extending from Lethbridge, District of Alberta, to Coutts at the International boundary, a distance of about 65 miles, and the other is the St. Mary's branch, of 54 miles in length. The Company possesses 943,995 acres of unsold land, and owns mortgages upon sold land amounting to $758,624. Of the land unsold 170,000 acres are irrigable and 773,995 acres are non-irrigable, and are termed winter wheat lands. Also the Company owns a number of town lots in the towns of Lethbridge and of Raymond. The land is situated on a large plateau at the eastern base of the Rocky Mountains, 48 miles north of the boundary of the State of Montana and 250 miles north-east from Spokane, Washington. The climate is genial, and the district is known as "sunny Southern

Alberta." Further, the Company possesses 10,640 acres of coal lands containing bituminous coal of good quality admirably suited to household purposes. And beyond its railway, its land, and its coal mines, the Company owns a valuable canal system embracing over 150 miles of canals and laterals, by means of which it supplies farmers settling upon its lands with the water they need for irrigation purposes. It is somewhat difficult to measure the total value of the Company's property; but there can be no doubt that the value of its assets is greatly in excess of its capital. In the past year the Company has sold non-irrigable land at $4½ and $5 per acre, and irrigable lands at from $12 to $30 per acre, the average coming out at $9.25c. per acre. Were we to value the non-irrigable land as worth about $5 per acre, and the irrigable land at $12 per acre, its 170,000 acres of irrigable land would be worth $2,040,000 and its 774,000 acres of non-irrigable land $3,870,000, a total of $5,910,000. But beyond this the Company possesses mortgages for $758,000, making a total value of $6,668,000. On the other hand, its capital consists of $1,246,000 of Four per Cent. Debenture stock, $3,250,000 of Five per Cent. Debenture stock, and $3,250,000 of Common stock, beyond which it owes to the Dominion Government $500,000, making a total liability on capital account of $8,246,000, or only $1,600,000 in excess of the sum representing the value of its lands when they are sold at the prices mentioned. Of course, were anything to occur to cause the value of land in Canada to fall, this calculation would have to be revised. Certainly, at present, the indications point rather to a further advance in the value of Canadian land than to depreciation. As far as the value of land is governed by the flow of immigration and the import of capital there is likely to be no decline. The Mother Country, indeed we may say Europe, is as much impressed with the value of land in the north-west of Canada as the farmers of America and of Eastern Canada, and incoming settlers are likely to find no difficulty in borrowing the money they need for stocking their farms and for the purchase of agricultural machinery. It must be recognised that the land will be only gradually sold, and that the profit realised from land sales will be spread over a long period of years. To obtain the present value of the sums likely to be received in payment of the land sold, allowance has to be made for accruing interest on capital until the purchase money is received.

As far as this Company is concerned, however, it appears probable that its profits from land sales will be in the nature of a bonus, and that it will be able to pay interest and dividends upon its capital from the earnings of its railway, its coal mines and its canal. We should explain that the present Company was formed by the amalgamation of the Alberta Railway and Coal Company, the Canadian North-West Irrigation Company, the St. Mary's River Railway Company, and the Lethbridge Land Company, which took effect on October 1, 1904. The first report of the amalgamated Company recently issued is for the nine months ended June 30 last. In this period its net revenue was $193,471, and after meeting the London expenses and directors' fees, there is a surplus of $21,000 available for dividend upon the Common stock. Gauged by the profits for the four months to the end of October the Company is now earning a revenue of about $300,000 per annum, equal to the full interest upon the Four per Cent. and Five per Cent. Debentures, and to a surplus of about $72,000 for the Common stock, equal to a distribution of about 2½ per cent. These profits include very little income derived from the sale of land. In the nine months to the end of June the net profit from the sale of land was $100,426; but, inasmuch as this money will be received in instalments only $5,358 was reckoned as profit for the year, being the proper proportion of the actual cash received for lands free from the trust, the balance of $95,067 being placed to reserve to be dealt with as the outstanding instalments are received. This net income of $300,000 consists of about $10,000 from water rentals, $36,000 from interest on mortgages, $250,000 from the railway and coal properties, and only about $10,000 from profit on land sales.

The inflow of immigrants into the district will add to the Company's income in five ways: (1) It will add to its profits from the sale of land; (2) it will add to its income from the sales of water for irrigation purposes; (3) it will add to the interest it will receive from money left as mortgage upon the land sold; (4) it will increase the quantity of freight and number of passengers passing over its railway; and (5) it will appreciably add to its sales of coal. Thus, so long as immigrants continue to flow into the country, and are attracted to the Company's lands, the growth in the Company's revenue will be cumulative.

Some idea can be formed of the rate of development from the fact that in the past year the cultivated area tributary to the Company's railways has increased from about 30,000 acres to 70,000 acres, and that the area has produced in the present season about 1,000,000 bushels of wheat, as well as considerable quantities of oats and barley. Further, the district is well adapted to the cultivation of beets, and a factory known as the Knight Sugar Beet Factory will this year treat 35,000 tons of sugar beets, the product of which will be about 3,500 tons of refined sugar. Thus it will be evident that the inflow of population into Canada is bringing, and is likely to continue to bring, increasing prosperity to the Company. The interesting speech made by Mr. Elliott T. Galt, the Chairman of the Company, at the meeting held this week, will be found among our meeting reports on page 826.

Source: *The Statist*, 4 November 1905.

Appendix IV

Schedule of wages, 1906 settlement

All coal to be paid for on screened basis, one ton being considered 2000 pounds.

	Cents per Ton
Pick mining rate for pillar and stump work	66
Pick mined rooms to be paid at the rate of	82
Machine runners (rooms)	13
Machine scrapers (rooms)	09
Machine loaders (rooms)	50
Machine runners (narrow work)	19
Machine scrapers (narrow work)	14
Machine loaders (narrow work)	77

Underground day work

	Cents per Hour
Brattice men	30
Timbermen	30
Drivers	30
Track layers	30
Miners on company's work	30
Couplers (men)	30
Couplers (boys)	15 to 25, according to age
Switch boys	11 to 25, according to age
Grippers	30

Pipe fitters helper 30
Pumpmen 32
Cagers 30
Car pushers 30
Stablemen .... $65.00 per month
Pick carriers .... 11 to 25, according to age
Clutchmen 30

Outside labour

Cents
per Hour

Top cagers 24
Dumpers 24
Car trimmers 24
Greasers (boys) .... 10 to 17, according to age
Screen engine tender 24
Box car loader engineer 30
Slate pickers (boys) .... 10 to 17, according to age
Tally boys 12½
Timbermen 24
Blacksmith... 35
Blacksmith helper 24
Leading carpenter 35
Carpenter helper 24
Car repairers 28
Machinists.. 30 to 35
Machinists' helpers 24
Hoisting engineers 35
Haulage engineer 30
Leading firemen (man holding certificate) 30
Firemen helpers and ash wheelers 24
Other outside labourers 20

All other conditions and prices to remain on the same basis as they were previous to March last.

Source: *Labour Gazette*, December 1906, p. 660.

Notes

Preface

1. *The Globe* (Toronto), 15 July 1862.

2. Charles Tupper, *A Letter to the Earl of Carnarvan by Charles Tupper in Reply to a Pamphlet Entitled 'Confederation'* (n.p., 19 October 1866), p. 42.

3. *The Gazette* (Montreal), 26 March 1880.

Chapter 1

1. Robert Webb, Alexander Johnston, and J. Dewey Soper, "The Prairie World," in *Alberta: A Natural History*, ed. by W. G. Hardy (Edmonton: M. G. Hurtig, 1967), pp. 93-116.

2. John Warkentin, "Steppe, Desert, and Empire," in *Prairie Perspectives 2*, ed. by Anthony W. Rasporich and Henry C. Klassen (Toronto: Holt, Rinehart and Winston of Canada, 1973), pp. 102-36.

3. G. S. Dunbar, "Isotherms and Politics: Perception of the Northwest in the 1850's," in *Prairie Perspectives* 2, pp. 80-101.

4. Richmond W. Longley, "Climate and Weather Patterns," in *Alberta: A Natural History*, pp. 55-56.

5. J. G. Nelson, *Man's Impact on the Western Canadian Landscape*, Carleton Library No. 90 (Toronto: McClelland and Stewart, 1976), pp. 44-68; idem, *The Last Refuge* (Montreal: Harvest House, 1973).

6. Gerald Berry, *The Whoop-Up Trail: Early Days in Alberta-Montana* (Edmonton: Applied Arts Products Ltd., 1953), pp. 39-40; and Paul F. Sharp, *Whoop-Up Country: The Canadian American-West, 1865-1885* (Minneapolis: University of Minnesota Press, 1955).

7. R. C. Macleod, *The North-West Mounted Police and Law Enforcement, 1873-1905* (Toronto: University of Toronto Press, 1976), pp. 22-37; and George F. G. Stanley, *The Birth of Western Canada: A History of the Riel Rebellions* (Toronto: University of Toronto Press, 1961), pp. 194-242.

8. Public Archives of Canada (hereafter cited as PAC), Galt Letters, vol. 8 supplemental, Galt to Lady Galt, 4 September 1882.

Chapter 2

1. *The Globe* (Toronto), 6 July 1858.

2. Jennie W. Aberdein, *John Galt* (London: Oxford University Press, 1936); Ian A. Gordon, *John Galt: The Life of a Writer* (Toronto: University of Toronto Press, 1972); Clarence Karr, *The Canada Land Company Early Years: An Experiment in Colonization, 1823-1843* (Toronto: Ontario Historical Society, 1974).

3. The only scholarly treatment of Galt is the very sympathetic account by Oscar Douglas Skelton, *Life and Times of Sir Alexander Tilloch Galt*, Carleton Library No. 26 (Toronto: McClelland and Stewart, 1966). This edition was edited and given an introduction by Guy MacLean.

4. Helen I. Cowan, *British Emigration to British North America: The First Hundred Years* (Toronto: University of Toronto Press, 1961), pp. 135-37.

5. Norman Macdonald, *Canada, 1763-1841: Immigration and Settlement, The Administration of the Imperial Land Regulations* (London: Macmillan, 1939), pp. 286-99.

6. Skelton, *Life and Times of Sir Alexander Tilloch Galt*, pp. 14-15.

7. A. T. Galt, *A Letter to the Chairman and Deputy Chairman of the North American Colonial Association* (London: J. Unwin, 1847), p. 7.

8. Gerald J. J. Tulchinsky, *The River Barons: Montreal Businessmen and the Growth of Industry and Transportation, 1837-53* (Toronto: University of Toronto Press, 1977), pp. 127-68; 236-38.

9. G. R. Stevens, *Canadian National Railways*, vol. 1, *Sixty Years of Trial and Error, 1836-1896* (Toronto: Clarke, Irwin, 1959), p. 57; Tulchinsky, *The River Barons*, pp. 134-40, 152-64.

10. Galt to Gillespie, April 1849, cited by Skelton, *Life and Times of Sir Alexander Tilloch Galt*, p. 65.

11. George Parkin Grant, *Technology and Empire: Perspectives on North America* (Toronto: House of Anansi, 1969); H. van Riessen, *The Society of the Future* (Philadelphia: The Presbyterian and Reformed Publishing Co., 1957.)

12. Luwik Kos-Rabcewicz-Zubkowski and William Edward Greening, *Sir Casimir Stanislaus Gzowski* (Toronto: Burns and MacEachern, 1959).

13. It is still impossible to estimate how much money Galt earned in the transactions with the Grand Trunk. The Toronto *Globe*, 5 February 1861, reported that Galt earned $10,312 acting for the Atlantic and St. Lawrence and another

$186,030 in the transfer of the St. Lawrence and Atlantic stock to the Grand Trunk. To that must be added the profits earned on the various construction companies and rail rolling mill. G. R. Stevens, *Canadian National*, p. 245 simply says that "In their [Grand Trunk] deals with Alexander Tilloch Galt that colonial land salesman had fleeced them at every turn." *See also* A. W. Currie, *The Grand Trunk Railway of Canada* (Toronto: University of Toronto Press, 1957), pp. 14, 116, 171; Edward Chase Kirkland, *Men, Cities and Transportation: A Study in New England History, 1820-1900* (New York: Russell & Russell, 1948), pp. 208-12, 478.

14. Evelyn Cartier Springett, *For My Children's Children* (Montreal: Unity Press, 1937), pp. 18-19.

15. *See* for example *The Globe* (Toronto), 6 July 1858.

16. *The Globe* (Toronto), 8 July 1858; Canada Legislative Assembly Journals, 1858, p. 815.

17. *The Globe* (Toronto), 9 August 1859.

18. G. P. de T. Glazebrook, *A History of Transportation in Canada*, vol. 2, Carleton Library No. 12 (Toronto: McClelland and Stewart, 1964), p. 39.

19. Leonard Bertram Irwin, *Pacific Railways and Nationalism in the Canadian Northwest, 1845-1873* (New York: Greenwood Press, 1968), pp. 30-31.

20. W. L. Morton, *The Critical Years: The Union of British North America, 1857-1873* (Toronto: McClelland and Stewart, 1965), pp. 60-64.

21. G. E. Cartier, J. J. Ross, and M. East [A. T. Galt] to Sir Edward Bulwer Lytton, 25 October 1858; idem, 25 October 1858 (private and confidential), cited by G. P. Browne, *Documents on the Confederation of British North America*, Carleton Library No. 40 (Toronto: McClelland and Stewart, 1969), pp. 15-19.

22. Galt to Lytton, 22 November 1858, cited by Skelton, *The Life and Times of Sir Alexander Tilloch Galt*, pp. 103-4.

23. *The Globe* (Toronto), 16 November 1859.

24. A. T. Galt, *Canada: 1849 to 1859* (Quebec: Canada Gazette Office, 1860), pp. 28-29.

25. W. T. Easterbrook and H. G. Aitken, *Canadian Economic History* (Toronto: Macmillan of Canada, 1956) pp. 370-77; also, D. F. Barnett, "The Galt Tariff: Incidental or Effective Protection?" *The Canadian Journal of Economics*, 9 (August 1976), pp. 389-407 concludes that "the evidence suggests . . . that the main purpose [of the tariff] was to protect, with increased revenue being incidental."

26. D. G. Creighton, *Road to Confederation: The Emergence of Canada, 1863-1867* (Toronto: Macmillan of Canada, 1964), pp. 114-15, 167-69, 236.

27. Galt gave what is perhaps the clearest exposition of the constitutional and economic implications of Confederation in a three-hour speech to his constituents at Sherbrooke on 23 November 1864. The address was published by Galt

as *Speech on the Proposed Union of the British North American Provinces* (Montreal: H. Longmoore & Co., 1864).

28. Canada, Legislative Assembly, *Parliamentary Debates on the Subject of the Confederation of the British North American Provinces*, (Ottawa: King's Printer, 1865; reprint ed., 1951), p. 64.

29. Galt to Amy Galt, 4 May 1865, cited by Skelton, *The Life and Times of Sir Alexander Tilloch Galt*, pp. 164-65.

30. J. M. S. Careless, *Brown of the Globe*, vol. 2, *Statesman of Confederation* (Toronto: Macmillan of Canada, 1959), pp. 203, 212-17.

31. PAC, Galt Papers, vol. 3, Galt to Amy Galt, 2 July 1867.

32. Ibid., 3 November 1867.

33. Ibid., 1 November 1867.

34. Cited by Skelton, *The Life and Times of Sir Alexander Tilloch Galt*, p. 208.

35. Ibid., p. 207.

36. Elaine Allan Mitchell, "Edward Watkin and the Buying Out of the Hudson's Bay Company," *Canadian Historical Review* 34 (September 1953), p. 227.

37. PAC, Galt Papers, vol. 3, Galt to Amy Galt, 14 January 1867.

38. Ibid., Brydges to Galt, 18 July 1869. Since Skelton incorrectly links the Brydges proposal to the Gzowski-Macpherson invitation, he fails to explain Galt's lack of interest in the Toronto-based bid for the Pacific contract.

39. Brian J. Young, "Railway Politics in Montreal, 1867-1878," Canadian Historical Association *Historical Papers 1972*, pp. 89-108.

40. Brydges to Macdonald, 19 April 1870, cited by Irwin, *Pacific Railways*, p. 156.

41. Brydges to Macdonald, 25 January 1870; Macdonald to Brydges, 28 January 1870, cited by Joseph Pope, *Correspondence of Sir John Macdonald*, (Toronto: Oxford University Press, 1921) pp. 123-25.

42. Cited by Glazebrook, *History of Transportation*, vol. 2, pp. 49-54.

43. Delores Greenberg, "A Study of Capital Alliances: The St. Paul and Pacific," *Canadian Historical Review* 57 (March 1976), pp. 28-29; Irwin, *Pacific Railways*, p. 169.

44. PAC, Galt Papers, vol. 3, King to Galt, 21 February 1871.

45. Ibid., Galt to Amy Galt, 25 May 1865.

46. Ibid., 14 January 1867.

47. Canada, House of Commons, Debates, 21 February 1870.

48. Galt refused to accept the leadership of an independence movement since he believed such a movement would lead to annexation to the U.S. *See* Skelton, *The Life and Times of Sir Alexander Tilloch Galt*, pp. 217-26.

49. Macdonald to Brydges, 28 January 1870, cited in Pope, *Correspondence of Macdonald*, p. 125.

50. PAC, Galt Papers, vol. 8, Galt to Ferrier, 3 September 1875.

51. Macdonald to Rose, 23 February 1870, cited in Pope, *Correspondence of Macdonald*, p. 128.

52. PAC, Galt Papers, vol. 8, Galt to Ferrier, 3 September 1875.

Chapter 3

1. Canada, House of Commons, Debates, 15 April 1880.

2. The idea of "financial imperialism" is discussed by John Bartlet Brebner, *North Atlantic Triangle: The Interplay of Canada, the United States and Great Britain*, Carleton Library No. 30 (Toronto: McClelland and Stewart, 1966), pp. 179-80. The nationalistic views of Galt and Macdonald are examined by David M. L. Farr, *The Colonial Office and Canada, 1867-1887* (Toronto: University of Toronto Press, 1955), pp. 17-19; Donald Creighton, *John A. Macdonald*, vol. 2, *The Old Chieftain* (Toronto: Macmillan of Canada, 1955), p. 277; and Skelton, *The Life and Times of Sir Alexander Tilloch Galt*, pp. 247-48.

3. Wesley Barry Turner, "Colonial Self-Government and the Colonial Agency: Changing Concepts of Permanent Canadian Representation in London, 1848 to 1880" (Ph.D. diss., Duke University, 1970), p. 256.

4. PAC, Macdonald Papers, vol. 216, Galt to Macdonald, 30 October 1879; also 18 October 1879.

5. *The Gazette* (Montreal), 26 March 1880.

6. The differences between Galt's speech and his official instructions have caused some disagreements among historians. *See* G. P. de T. Glazebrook, *A History of Canadian External Relations*, vol. 1: *The Formative Years to 1914*, Carleton Library No. 27 (Toronto: McClelland and Stewart, 1964), pp. 132-35; David M. L. Farr, *The Colonial Office and Canada, 1867-1887*, pp. 265-67; and Turner, "Colonial Self-Government," pp. 261-62.

7. Great Britain, Public Record Office (hereafter cited as PRO), CO42, vol. 761, general instructions. A copy of the draft instructions are in PAC, Galt Papers, vol. 8.

8. PAC, Galt Papers, vol. 4, Galt to Macdonald, 12 June 1880. Two sons, Elliott and John, remained in Canada. Galt's disposition was probably not improved when he was told to be careful with public expenditures because the Liberal opposition was watching him carefully. Ibid., Macpherson to Galt, 2 May 1880.

9. PAC, Macdonald Papers, vol. 217, Galt to Macdonald, 26 May 1880.

10. PAC, Galt Papers, vol. 4, Macdonald to Galt, 26 May 1880.

11. Strangely, the very politically conscious Galt seemed to forget a fundamental political rule when he asked permission to publish a number of foreign language pamphlets in London. He received a sharp rebuke from Macdonald's secretary, Pope, who wanted them printed in Canada for patronage purposes: "Now all those things are precisely those we cannot do without." Ibid., Pope to Galt, 22 December 1880.

12. PAC, Macdonald Papers, vol. 217, Galt to Macdonald, 7 June 1880.

13. PAC, Galt Papers, vol. 4, Galt to Macdonald, 12 June 1880.

14. PRO, CO42, vol. 763, memo by Bramston, 9 November 1880; and W. A. Carrothers, *Emigration From the British Isles* (London: Frank Cass & Co. Ltd., 1965), pp. 230–31.

15. PAC, Macdonald Papers, vol. 217, Galt to Macdonald, 16 December 1880.

16. Ibid., vol. 267, Stephen to Macdonald, 7 April 1881.

17. Ibid., vol. 259.248, Rose to Macdonald, 24 March 1881.

18. PRO, CO42, Vol. 763, memo by Bramston, 9 November 1880.

19. PAC, Macdonald Papers, vol. 267, Stephen to Macdonald, 5 May 1881.

20. Creighton, *Old Chieftain*, pp. 313–16.

21. PAC, Macdonald Papers, vol. 218, Galt to Macdonald, 4 January 1881.

22. Ibid., vol. 217, Galt to Macdonald, 20 and 27 May 1880; Galt Papers, vol. 4, Macdonald to Galt, 8 December 1880.

23. PAC, Macdonald Papers, vol. 267, Stephen to Macdonald, 8 May 1881.

24. PAC, Galt Papers, vol. 4, Dennis to Galt, 16 February 1881.

25. Ibid., Macdonald to Galt, 25 June 1880.

26. Canada, Order-in-Council, 23 December 1881; André N. Lalonde, "Settlement in the North-West Territories by Colonization Companies, 1881–1891" (Ph.D. diss., Laval University, 1969).

27. PAC, Galt Papers, vol. 4, Dennis to Galt, 17 March 1881.

28. Ibid., vol. 4, Brassey to Galt, 23 June 1881.

29. PAC, Galt Papers, vol. 4, Galt to Macdonald, 5 May 1881. In one instance Galt, J. G. Ross, and John Torrance invested heavily in a California silver mine that demanded increasingly larger expenditures with very little returns. PAC, Galt Papers, vol. 8 supplemental, Mulsten to Galt, 17 February and 9 July 1881.

30. PAC, Galt Papers, vol. 4, Macdonald to Galt, 27 February 1881.

31. Ibid., Galt to Macdonald, 13 March 1881. In order to cut expenses Galt moved the immigration office into his home. *See* Ibid., Instructions, 20 May 1880.

32. PAC, Macdonald Papers, vol. 267, Stephen to Macdonald, 7 April 1881.

33. Ibid., vol. 219, Galt to Macdonald, 13 February 1882.

34. Ibid., 11 February 1882. In fact, as an agricultural venture, the Moosomin experiment failed; most of the Jewish immigrants quickly moved to Winnipeg.

35. Ibid., 7 February 1882.

36. Macdonald to Galt, 26 February 1882, cited in Pope, *Correspondence of Macdonald*, p. 286.

37. PAC, Macdonald Papers, vol. 219, Galt to Macdonald, 11 February 1882.

38. Ibid., 27 April 1882.

39. Ibid., 27 April 1882 (confidential); *see also* Creighton, *Old Chieftain*, pp. 333-34.

40. PAC, Macdonald Papers, vol. 219, Galt to Macdonald, 27 April 1882.

41. While Tupper actually labelled the area a garden spot in the 1870s, he reaffirmed his belief in the summer of 1882. Ibid., vol. 267, Tupper to Macdonald, 16 October 1882. *See also* Alex Staveley Hill, *From Home to Home, Autumn Wanderings in the North-West, in the Year 1881, 1882, 1883, 1884* (New York: O. Judd Co., 1895), pp. 153-57.

42. Henry Youle Hind, *Manitoba and the North-West Frauds* (Windsor, N.S.: By the author, 1883), p. 13.

43. Heather Gilbert, *Awakening Continent: The Life of Lord Mount Stephen*, vol. 1, *1829-91* (Aberdeen: Aberdeen University Press, 1965), pp. 84-85, 110-23; Pierre Berton, *The Great Railway*, vol. 2, *The Last Spike, 1881-1885* (Toronto: McClelland and Stewart, 1971), pp. 34-38; and Creighton, *Old Chieftain*, p. 330.

44. Gilbert, *Awakening Continent*, pp. 95-97.

45. PAC, Macdonald Papers, vol. 267, Stephen to Macdonald, 11 January 1882.

46. Ibid., 13 January 1882.

47. Gilbert, *Awakening Continent*, p. 118.

48. PAC, Department of the Interior Records, vol. 53, Galt to Burgess, 7 October 1882.

49. PAC, Macdonald Papers, vol. 267, Stephen to Macdonald, 28 October 1882.

50. Ibid., 27 and 28 December 1882.

51. Ibid., vol. 220, Galt to Macdonald, 9 January 1883.

52. Rose to Macdonald, 4 January 1883, cited in Pope, *Correspondence of Macdonald*, pp. 294-95. Rose continued to say in his letter, "I think Stephen is wrong in attributing to Galt intentional or malevolent misrepresentations about the N.W. He may have been indiscreet in expressing his opinion; and he is, no doubt, in a cross and unpleasant frame of mind, but I do not believe that the *purpose* of making mischief is one that he can be justly charged with."

53. Alexander T. Galt, *The Relations of the Colonies to the Empire, Present and Future* (London: McCorquodale & Co., 1883), p. 29.

54. Macdonald to Galt, 21 February 1883, cited in Pope, *Correspondence of Macdonald*, pp. 298-99.

55. PAC, Macdonald Papers, vol. 220, Galt to Macdonald, 8 March 1883; *see also* 16 January 1883.

56. Farr, *The Colonial Office*, pp. 19, 288-89, 297.

57. PAC, Galt Papers, vol. 8, Galt to Lady Galt, 18 January 1883.

58. PAC, Macdonald Papers, vol. 220, Galt to Macdonald, 26 April 1883 and Galt to Derby, undated memorandum.

59. Hudson's Bay Company Archives, Public Archives of Manitoba (Hereafter cited as HBCA, PAM), D44/2. Memorandum for a joint land agreement between the Canadian Pacific Railway, Hudson's Bay Company, and Canada North West Land Company, 2d proof, 10 March 1883.

60. PAC, Macdonald Papers, vol. 220, Galt to Macdonald, 26 April 1883.

61. Ibid.

62. Ibid., 16 February 1883.

63. Ibid., 28 June 1883; Creighton, *Old Chieftain*, pp. 348-50.

64. PAC, Galt Papers, vol. 8, Galt to Lady Galt, incomplete date, December 1882.

65. Turner, "Colonial Self-Government," pp. 290-300; Farr, *The Colonial Office*, pp. 227-28, 238-41, 268; Skelton, *The Life and Times of Sir Alexander Tilloch Galt*, pp. 269-71.

66. PAC, Galt Papers, vol. 8, Macdonald to Galt, 7 January 1882.

Chapter 4

1. George M. Grant, *Ocean to Ocean: Sandford Fleming's Expedition through Canada in 1872* (Edmonton: M. G. Hurtig, 1967; org. ed., 1873), p. 205.

2. Alfred R. C. Selwyn, "Observations in the Northwest Territory on a Journey Across the Plains, From Fort Garry to Rocky Mountain House," Geological Survey of Canada *Report of Progress 1873-1874* (Montreal: Dawson Brothers, 1874), p. 50. Other reports include R. W. Ellis, "Report on Boring Operations in the North West Territory, Summer of 1875," Geological Survey of Canada *Report of Progress 1875-1876* (Montreal: Dawson Brothers, 1877) pp. 288-89; R. C. Dawson, "Report on the Exploration from Fort Simpson on the Pacific Coast to Edmonton on the Saskatchewan Embracing a Portion of the Northern Part of

British Columbia and the Peace River Country, 1879," Geological Survey of Canada, *Report of Progress 1879-1880* (Montreal: Dawson Brothers, 1881), pp. 134B-35B.

3. Berry, *Whoop-Up Trail*, pp. 39-40.

4. Warkentin, "Steppe, Desert and Empire," p. 124.

5. Jean Stafford-Kelly, "Early Days of Lethbridge from 1882," *Lethbridge Herald*, 11 July 1935.

6. Sharp, *Whoop-Up Country*, p. 224.

7. The exact reasons for the change of route are not clear. For a discussion of the problem *see* F. G. Roe, "An Unsolved Problem in Canadian History," Canadian Historial Association *Annual Report 1936*, pp. 65-77; Glazebrook, *History of Transportation*, vol. 2, p. 275; and Berton, *The Last Spike*, pp. 12-19.

8. George M. Dawson, "Preliminary Note on the Geology of the Bow and Belly River Districts, North West Territory, with Special Reference to the Coal Deposits," Geological Survey of Canada *Report of Progress 1880-1881* (Montreal: Dawson Brothers, 1882), p. 6-10.

9. George M. Dawson, "Report on the Region in the Vicinity of the Bow and Belly Rivers, North West Territories," Geological Survey of Canada *Report of Progress 1882-1884* (Montreal: Dawson Brothers, 1884), p. 5C.

10. Canada, Department of the Interior, *Annual Report 1883* (Ottawa: King's Printer, 1884), p. 8.

11. Donald G. Paterson, *British Direct Investment in Canada 1890-1914: Estimates and Determinants* (Toronto: University of Toronto Press, 1976).

Chapter 5

1. PAC, Galt Papers, vol. 8 supplemental, Galt to Lady Galt, 4 March 1882.

2. W. H. Smith & Son Archives, Hambledon Papers, W. H. Smith Diary, 1872. *See also* Viscount Chilston, *W. H. Smith* (Toronto: Routledge & K. Paul, 1965).

3. PAC, Magrath Papers, vol. 4, file 31.

4. *Dictionary of National Biography, Supplement, 1901-1911*, (London: Oxford University Press, 1951), pp. 259-66.

5. Berton, *The Last Spike*, pp. 27-29, 59, 75-79; J. K. Johnson, ed., *The Canadian Dictionary of Parliament, 1867-1967* (Ottawa: Public Archives of Canada, 1968), p. 506. Ross's Portage, Westbourne, and North-Western Railway subsequently became the Manitoba and North West Railway.

6. PRO, Articles of Association of the North Western Coal and Navigation Company, Limited, document 2, 25 April 1882, provides a list of shareholders. Biographical details of the Canadian investors are found in Johnson, *Directory of Parliament*, p. 508; Henry James Morgan, *The Canadian Men and Women of the Time: A Handbook of Canadian Biography of Living Characters* (Toronto: W. Briggs, 1912), p. 926.

7. PRO, Articles of Association of the North Western Coal and Navigation Company, Limited, document 2, 25 April 1882.

8. Dawson, "Report on Bow and Belly Rivers," p. 5C. Dawson's estimates are contained in pages 127C–29C. By 1915, estimates of coal reserves were still very optimistic; Alberta supposedly contained 1,072,627,400,000 tons of coal. These figures were reduced considerably by later reports. *See*, for example, Canada, *Report of Royal Commission on Coal, August 1960* (Ottawa: Queen's Printer, 1960).

9. The director of the Geological Survey wrote, "In any case, the evidence of the past season's work tends still further to confirm the opinion that the coal fields of the North-West may be regarded as practically inexhaustible." Canada, Department of the Interior, *Annual Report 1882*, part II, p. 4.

10. Ibid., *Annual Report 1881*, p. ix.

11. Canada, House of Commons, Debates, 14 March 1881.

12. Canada, Order-in-Council, 17 December 1881.

13. Canada, House of Commons, Debates, 27 March 1882.

14. Ibid.

15. Canada, Order-in-Council, 30 June 1882.

16. Ibid.

17. PAC, Macdonald Papers, vol. 219, Galt to Macdonald, 11 February 1882.

18. Canada, Order-in-Council, 21 December 1882.

19. Stafford-Kelly, "Early Days in Lethbridge," p. 83.

20. PAC, Department of the Interior Records, vol. 53, Galt to the Minister of the Interior, 26 June 1882.

21. PAC, Macdonald Papers, vol. 219, Galt to Macdonald, 7 February 1882.

22. PAC, Galt Papers, vol. 8 supplemental, Galt to Lady Galt, 4 September 1882.

23. PAC, Department of the Interior Records, vol. 53, Galt to Burgess, 7 October 1882.

24. Canada, Department of the Interior, *Annual Report 1882*, p. 136; *Fort Macleod Gazette*, 14 September, 4 and 14 December 1882.

25. *Lethbridge News*, 9 January 1891.

26. PAC, Galt Letterbook, Galt to Elliott Galt, 7 April 1883; Galt to Lethbridge, 26 June 1883.

27. Ibid., Galt to Cutbill, 25 June 1883.

28. C. A. Magrath, *The Galts, Father and Son: Pioneers in the Development of Southern Alberta* (Lethbridge: Lethbridge Herald, 1936).

29. PAC, Galt Papers, vol. 8, Galt to Elliott Galt, 19 April 1872.

30. PAC, Macdonald Papers, vol. 216, Galt to Macdonald, 5 April 1879.

31. PAC, Galt Papers, vol. 8, Elliott Galt to Galt, 22 July 1880.

32. Earle G. Drake, *Regina: The Queen City* (Toronto: McClelland and Stewart, 1955), p. 11.

33. PAC, Campbell Papers, Elliott Galt to Campbell, 3, 23, and 25 January 1882; 6, 7, and 22 February 1882; 10 and 22 March 1882.

34. Glenbow-Alberta Institute (hereafter cited as GAI), Dewdney Papers, file 57, Elliott Galt to Dewdney, 21 February 1883.

35. *Fort Macleod Gazette*, 24 January and 14 March 1883.

36. Ibid., 24 March and 14 and 24 April 1883.

37. PAC, Macdonald Papers, vol. 220, Galt to Macdonald, 6 July 1883. Elliott Galt, always conscious of profits, loaded the empty hull with coal for the Regina police post.

38. Alexander Johnston, compiler, *Boats and Barges on the Belly River* (Lethbridge: Lethbridge Branch, Historical Society of Alberta, 1966) and PAC, Magrath Papers, vol. 7, file 30, Memorandum re: the construction and operation of fleet of steamers and barges operated by the North Western Coal and Navigation Company on the Saskatchewan River, out of Lethbridge, signed by Macbeth, no date. Both sources claim that the Galts acted out of ignorance of the water levels of the Belly River by putting steamers on it, rather than out of short-term expediency.

39. Stafford-Kelly, "Early Lethbridge," pp. 83, 85.

40. *Fort Macleod Gazette*, 14 August 1883.

41. PAC, Macdonald Papers, vol. 220, Galt to Macdonald, 28 June 1883.

42. Reports on the various collieries are found in *Fort Macleod Gazette*, 24 January, 24 April, and 1 October 1883. *See also* Dawson, "Report on Bow and Belly Rivers," p. 770.

43. Canada, Order-in-Council, 19 October 1883.

44. PAC, Macdonald Papers, vol. 220, Galt to Macdonald, 6 and 16 July, 16 August 1883.

45. Ibid., 30 August 1883.

46. PAC, Van Horne Letterbooks, book 1, Van Horne to the CPR board of directors, 2 March 1883.

47. PAC, Macdonald Papers, vol. 267, Stephen to Macdonald, 13 August 1883.

48. PAC, Galt Letterbook, Galt to Lethbridge, 11 and 22 September 1883; Van Horne Letterbooks, book 3, Van Horne to Galt, 25 and 26 October 1883.

49. Canada, Order-in-Council, 19 October 1883.

50. James B. Hedges, *The Federal Railway Land Subsidy Policy of Canada* (Cambridge: Harvard University Press, 1934), pp. 70-76.

51. Canada, Order-in-Council, 19 October 1883. Since Hedges overlooked the Order-in-Council of 4 June 1883, which raised the price of railway lands to $1.50 per acre, he failed to recognize the generosity of the government. Ibid., pp. 86-87, Chester Martin makes the same error. *See* idem., *"Dominion Lands" Policy*, Lewis H. Thomas, ed., Carleton Library No. 69 (Toronto: McClelland and Stewart, 1973), p. 55.

52. PAC, Galt Letterbook, Galt to Lethbridge, 12 October 1883.

53. Ibid., 11 September 1883; *see also* Canada, Order-in-Council, 19 October 1883.

54. PAC, Macdonald Papers, vol. 220, Galt to Macdonald, 7 January 1884.

55. PAC, Galt Letterbook, Galt to Dove, 2 April 1884.

56. PAC, Magrath Papers, vol. 7, file 30, copy of a contract, North Western Coal and Navigation Company and the Canadian Pacific Railway Company, 26 October 1883.

57. Canada, *Statutes of Canada*, 47 Victoria, chapter 86, 19 April 1884.

58. David H. Breen, "The Canadian West and the Ranching Frontier, 1875-1922" (Ph.D. diss., University of Alberta, 1973), p. 67. Arthur Springett, Sir Alexander Galt's son-in-law, became the ranch manager.

59. Canada, *Statutes of Canada*, 47 Victoria, chapter 74, 19 April 1884.

60. Canada, House of Commons, Debates, 1 February 1884.

61. Cited in Johnston, *Boats and Barges*, pp. 23-24.

62. HBCA, PAM, A12/24, Brydges to Armit, 6 April 1885, ff. 161-63.

63. PAC, Galt Papers, vol. 8, Galt to Lady Galt, 5 August 1884. Galt's financial difficulties can be amply documented. On his difficulties with Montreal real estate, *see* PAC, Galt Letterbook, Galt to Montchieff, 5 February 1883; Galt to Buchanan, 24 February and 2 March 1883. The author uncovered only one instance where Galt's actions are clearly questionable. He instructed his financial agents, Glyn, Mills, Currie, and Co., to make a temporary transfer of thirty

NWC&NCo shares, adding, "I request however that you will not register this transfer as it would disqualify me as a Director [presumably of the NWC&NCo]." Ibid., 7 April 1883.

64. PAC, Macdonald Papers, vol. 220, Galt to Macdonald, 21 July 1884.

65. Ibid., 25 July 1884.

66. Ibid., 10 July 1884.

67. Canada, Order-in-Council, 27 September 1884.

68. W. H. Smith & Son Archives, 307/41, Smith to Ford, 10 September 1884.

69. PAC, Galt Papers, vol. 8 supplemental, Galt to Lady Galt, 11 and 13 September 1884.

70. PAC, Department of the Interior Records, vol. 15, Tupper to Macdonald, 4 September 1884.

71. Canada, Order-in-Council, 27 September 1884.

72. PAC, Galt Papers, vol. 8 supplemental, Galt to Lady Galt, 16 and 18 October 1884.

73. Ibid., 24 October 1884.

74. Hedges, *Railway Land Policy*, pp. 79–109.

75. Cited in ibid., pp. 79–80.

76. The Winnipeg and Hudson Bay Railway and Steamboat Company was the first firm, other than the CPR, to receive a free land grant, but because of its size and purpose cannot be included with the small railway colonization companies.

77. PAC, Galt Letterbook, Galt to Lethbridge, 21 November 1884.

78. Canada, Order-in-Council, 17 January 1885.

79. Canada, House of Commons, Debates, 27 March and 10 and 11 June 1885.

80. PAC, Galt Letterbook, Galt to Van Horne, 24 November 1885.

81. *Fort Macleod Gazette*, 2 January, 7 and 28 February 1885.

82. PAC, Galt Letterbook, Galt to Burdett-Coutts, 16 June 1885; Galt to Lethbridge, 26 June 1885; Galt to Elliott Galt, 8 July 1885; *Fort Macleod Gazette*, 2 January, 28 March, 16 May 1885.

83. *Fort Macleod Gazette*, 16 January, 25 April, 9 and 23 May 1885.

84. PAC, Galt Letterbook, Galt to Cutbill, 28 August 1885. Galt argued that no railway could run without a telegraph and so he persuaded the directors that it was cheaper to lease the line and charge the government for its messages than to pay for each company message.

85. PAC, Macdonald Papers, vol. 220, Galt to Macdonald, 27 April 1885. *See* Lalonde, "Colonization Companies," pp. 176–99 for an account of the devastating effects of the Riel Rebellion on the various colonization companies.

86. PAC, Macdonald Papers, vol. 220, Galt to Macdonald, incomplete date, March 1885.

87. Ibid., 27 April 1885.

88. Galt to Macdonald, 28 March 1885, cited in Desmond Morton and Reginald H. Roy, eds., *Telegrams of the North-West Campaign 1885* (Toronto: The Champlain Society, 1972), p. 17.

89. Galt to Caron, 31 March 1885; ibid., p. 52. Galt also asked that Caron remember that his son Jack Galt was in the wholesale business in Winnipeg and could be supplier to the armed forces.

90. Galt to Caron, 6, 7, and 15 April 1885; ibid., pp. 117, 132, 180–81.

91. Ibid., p. liv.

92. Peel, "The Coal Fleet," in Johnston, *Boats and Barges*, pp. 10–13. Only the *Minnow*, sold by the NWC&NCo, was ever used again. The company stripped the boilers and engines of both the other steamers for use in the collieries but allowed the lumber to be salvaged by the miners for shacks.

93. PAC, Galt Letterbook, Galt to Cutbill, 15 and 16 May 1885; Galt to Elliott Galt, 8 July 1885.

94. Ibid., Galt to Lethbridge, 10 August 1885.

95. Galt to Caron, 14 April 1885; Middleton to Caron, 15 April 1885, cited in Morton, *North-West Campaign*, pp. 177, 180.

96. *Fort Macleod Gazette*, 2, 9, 23, and 30 May, 13 and 23 June, 28 July, and 11 August 1885.

97. Ibid., 6 October 1885.

98. The Dunmore-Lethbridge railway was estimated to cost $550,000 less $50,000 transportation costs, which the CPR was taking in coal. Using an exchange rate of $4.86 per pound sterling, Galt calculated the cost to be £102,880, to be raised by two sales of debenture bonds, one (sold in March 1885) for £53,625 and the second (still being sold in August) for £49,255. Since both issues were sold at 75% of par value, their actual combined worth was £119,298. By early August, Glyn & Co. had sold or taken itself a total of £62,300 worth of debentures. *See* PAC, Galt Letterbook, Memo Financial Position of Contract, 8 August 1885.

Chapter 6

1. *Lethbridge News*, 4 December 1885.

2. Ibid., 31 December 1885; 5 February and 5 April 1886.

3. PAC, Galt Letterbook, Galt to Cutbill, 28 August 1885.

4. Ibid., Memorandum, 17 November 1885.

5. Ibid., Galt to Elliott Galt, 24 November 1885; Memorandum, 26 November 1885.

6. PAC, Van Horne Letterbooks, Van Horne to Elliott Galt, 20 November 1885; *Lethbridge News*, 12 February 1886.

7. PAC, Galt Letterbook, Galt to Lethbridge, 29 March 1886; Canada, Department of the Interior, *Annual Report 1886*, p. 22.

8. Galt Museum, GM 973.5158-GM 973.5161, Galt to Stafford, 23 February 1886.

9. *Fort Macleod Gazette*, 16 March 1886.

10. PAC, Galt Letterbook, Galt to Lethbridge, 29 March 1886.

11. Ibid., Galt to Cutbill, 27 April 1886.

12. *Fort Macleod Gazette*, 14 December 1886.

13. PAC, Galt Papers, vol. 8 supplemental, E. T. Galt to Lady Galt, 2 February 1887; *Lethbridge News*, 12 January, 20 and 22 March 1887.

14. *Lethbridge News*, 2 April and 6 July 1887; *Fort Macleod Gazette*, 21 June and 12 July 1887.

15. *Fort Macleod Gazette*, 12 July 1887.

16. Ibid., 8, 15, and 22 February 1887.

17. *Lethbridge News*, 5 February 1886.

18. Ibid., 26 October 1887.

19. Magrath, *The Galts*, p. 37.

20. *Fort Macleod Gazette*, 29 February 1888.

21. PAC, Macdonald Papers, vol. 220, Galt to Macpherson, 21 May 1885; Galt Letterbook, Galt to Conrad, 17 October 1885.

22. PAC, Galt Letterbook, Galt to Barclay, 22 December 1885.

23. Henry James Morgan, *The Canadian Men and Women of the Times: A Hand-Book of Canadian Biography* (Toronto: W. Briggs, 1898), pp. 144-45, 842-45; the names of the directors are listed in Canada, *Statutes of Canada*, 52 Victoria, Chapter 50, 20 March 1889.

24. James McClelland Hamilton, *From Wilderness to Statehood: A History of Montana, 1805–1900* (Portland: Binfords & Morts, 1957); Michael P. Malone and Richard B. Roeder, eds., *The Montana Past: An Anthology* (Missoula: University of Montana Press, 1969); Rodman Wilson Paul, *Mining Frontiers of the Far West, 1848–1880* (New York: Holt, Rinehart and Winston, 1963); and Sharp, *Whoop-Up Country*.

25. Albro Martin, *James J. Hill and the Opening of the Northwest* (New York: Oxford University Press, 1976), pp. 339–40.

26. Ibid., p. 340.

27. Canada, House of Commons, Debates, 12 March and 17 May 1886; *Lethbridge News*, 15 January, 5 and 19 February, and 26 March 1886; *Fort Macleod Gazette*, 9 November 1886. Besides the Medicine Hat, Dunmore, and Fort Benton Railway, Galt also sought a charter for the Alberta Railway Company to go from Lethbridge via the coal-rich Crowsnest Pass to Butte, Montana.

28. Canada, House of Commons, Debates, 4 May 1886.

29. Ibid.

30. Galt wrote, "I regard therefore the control of our railway is the key of our position and that it is more to our interests to allow a larger return from the railway than the colliery—whatever tariff we adopt for ourselves we must by law extend to the public generally—and if, we should put the cost of transporting coal to its simple expense we should have to do the same for other mines, who could then compete with us." Thus he suggested to take less profit on the colliery and more on the railway "to keep others out." PAC, Galt Letterbook, Galt to Cutbill, 22 July 1885.

31. Canada, *Statutes of Canada*, 49 Victoria, chapter 86, 2 June 1886.

32. Ibid., chapter 87, 2 June 1886.

33. Canada, Department of the Interior, *Annual Report 1886*, p. 23.

34. *Prospectus of the Canadian Anthracite Coal Company: Collieries at Banff Station, Canadian Pacific Railway, District of Alberta* (Ottawa, 1885); Canada, Department of the Interior, *Annual Report 1886*, p. 23; *Fort Macleod Gazette*, 12 October 1886.

35. PAC, Macdonald Papers, vol. 429, Stewart to Macdonald, 2 September 1886.

36. PAC, Macdonald Papers, vol. 270, Stephen to Macdonald, 4 September 1886.

37. PAC, Shaughnessy Letterbooks, vol. 10, Shaughnessy to Whyte, 10 February 1887.

38. Ibid., Shaughnessy to Whyte, 25 April 1887; Shaughnessy to Elliott Galt, 11 May 1887.

39. Canada, Department of the Interior, *Annual Report 1889* p. xvi.

40. *Fort Macleod Gazette*, 29 February 1888.

41. Canada, House of Commons, Debates, 10 May and 2 June 1887.

42. *Fort Macleod Gazette*, 8 February, 3 and 17 May, 14 June, 8 November and 20 December 1887.

43. *Lethbridge News*, 29 December 1887.

44. Ibid., 5 January and 7 December 1887.

45. W. L. Morton, *Manitoba: A History* (Toronto: University of Toronto Press, 1970) pp. 211-16, 234-40.

46. Canada, House of Commons, Debates, 27 March 1888. Since no records of the AR&CCo have come to light, one can no more but surmise that Galt dissolved the original company as soon as it completed the Dunmore railway and that he re-incorporated the company for the Montana project.

47. *Lethbridge News*, 16 May 1888.

48. Canada, House of Commons, Debates, 19 May 1888.

49. Ibid.

50. PAC, Department of the Interior Records, vol. 291, file 62709-3, Galt to Macdonald, 23 May 1888.

51. Ibid., Macdonald to Galt, 26 May 1888.

52. Canada, Order-in-Council, 31 May 1888.

53. Canada, House of Commons, Debates, 22 February 1889. The House debated Galt's bill on 20 and 22 February and 1 May. For the sake of clarity, the author has presented the issue as a single debate. *See* note 97 and *Lethbridge News*, 6 March 1889 for the actual prices of coal. From these sources it is safe to conclude that Watson's charges were exaggerated.

54. Ibid., 1 May 1889.

55. Ibid., 22 February 1889.

56. Ibid., 1 May 1889. Shanly also spoke on 20 February 1889.

57. Ibid., 20 February 1889.

58. Ibid., 1 May 1889.

59. Canada, Department of the Interior, *Annual Report 1887*, part I, p. 15; *Annual Report 1888*, part I, p. 12.

60. *Ford Macleod Gazette*, 29 March and 24 October 1887.

61. Canada, Department of the Interior, *Annual Report 1887*, part I, p. 15.

62. Ibid., *Annual Report 1888*, part I, p. 12; *Annual Report 1889*, part I, p. 25.

63. PAC, Shaughnessy Letterbooks, vol. 10, Shaughnessy to Elliott Galt, 29 December 1887.

64. PAC, Macdonald Papers, vol. 220, Galt to Macdonald, 13 March 1889.

65. PAC, Department of the Interior Records, vol. 561, file 172441-1, Elliott Galt to Dewdney, 11 May 1889; Dewdney to Elliott Galt, 15 May 1889.

66. PAC, Galt Papers, vol. 8 supplemental, Galt to Lady Galt, 1 June 1889. William Ford was W. H. Smith's lawyer and also a close and life-long friend.

67. *Lethbridge News*, 2 October 1889; *Fort Macleod Gazette*, 3 October 1889.

68. Martin, *J. J. Hill*, pp. 340–47.

69. *Lethbridge News*, 2 October 1889.

70. PAC, Department of the Interior Records, vol. 561, file 172441-1, Galt to Dewdney, 9 October 1889.

71. PAC, Macdonald Papers, vol. 220, Macdonald to Galt, 17 October 1889.

72. E. H. Wilson, "Lethbridge and the A.R.&I.," *Lethbridge Herald*, 11 December 1947.

73. PAC, Macdonald Papers, vol. 220, Galt to Macdonald, 27 November 1889; PAC, Van Horne Letterbooks, no. 32, Van Horne to Galt, 11 December 1889. Van Horne privately expressed his doubts about the feasibility of a narrow gauge railway to Galt only.

74. PAC, Macdonald Papers, vol. 220, Galt to Macdonald, 18 November, 14 and 18 December 1889; Macdonald to Galt, 22, 25, and 28 November 1889.

75. Canada, Department of the Interior, *Annual Report 1889*, part I, p. 25.

76. *Lethbridge News*, 30 January, 5 February, and 18 June 1890.

77. Ibid., 19 February, 23 April 1890. On 4 March 1890, the company directors passed a by-law for new rates. Freight rates ranged from a high of 15 cents per 100 pounds for 10 miles to 57 cents per 100 pounds for the full 110 miles. Coal transportation cost $2.45 per ton for the entire trip plus 5 cents per 100 pounds for transfer of all goods. Passenger fares stood at 5 cents per mile and 2.5 cents per mile for the return trip. Children under five rode free and those from five to twelve at half price.

78. Canada, *Statutes of Canada*, 53 Victoria, chapter 85, 26 March 1890.

79. Ibid., chapter 3, 26 March 1890.

80. Canada, Order-in-Council, 11 March 1890. Canada, *Statutes of Canada*, 53 Victoria, chapter 89, 26 March 1890. The company did intend to convert to standard gauge eventually as Elliott Galt continued the policy of widening the road beds with excess coal and shale from the colliery and ordered the section men to replace worn narrow gauge ties with standard ones. *Lethbridge News*, 5 March 1890.

81. Canada, *Statutes of Canada*, 53 Victoria, chapter 89, 26 March 1890.

82. *Fort Macleod Gazette*, 31 October 1889.

83. William James Cousins, "A History of the Crow's Nest Pass" (M.A. thesis, University of Alberta, 1952), p. 42; *Fort Macleod Gazette*, 9 January 1890.

84. *Fort Macleod Gazette*, 7, 21, and 28 November and 13 March 1889.

85. PAC, Van Horne Letterbooks, no. 33, Van Horne to Galt, 10 February 1890.

86. PAC, Macdonald Papers, vol. 220, Galt to Macdonald, 2 November 1889.

87. PAC, Van Horne Letterbooks, no. 33, Van Horne to Galt, 10 February 1890.

88. *Fort Macleod Gazette*, 15 May 1890.

89. *Lethbridge News*, 18 June 1890.

90. Ibid., 18 June and 2 July 1890.

91. PAC, Macdonald Papers, vol. 190, Bowell to Macdonald, 28 August 1890. For reports on construction progress *see* the almost weekly articles in the *Lethbridge News* and *Fort Macleod Gazette*.

92. PAC, Macdonald Papers, vol. 220, Galt to Macdonald, 18 September 1890.

93. PAC, RCMP Records, RG 18, A-1, vol. 39, no. 137, Lethbridge monthly report for October 1890.

94. Ibid.; *Lethbridge News*, 24 October 1890. Galt's luck held true to the end because only a month later the Barings, who had underwritten very large loans in Argentina, faced bankruptcy when the wild era of expansion in Latin America suddenly stopped and evaporated Argentina's credit. Interestingly enough, one of Galt's chief backers, W. H. Smith, risked his personal fortune to bail the Barings out of trouble. Moreover, the Bank of England was forced to buy gold from abroad to ward off financial disaster. The Baring crisis virtually ended overseas investments for over a decade and had Galt not finished his railway when he did, the project would have been delayed for some time. Chilston, *W. H. Smith*, pp. 332-33; H. S. Ferns, *Britain and Argentina in the Nineteenth Century* (Oxford: Clarendon Press, 1960), pp. 436-84.

95. Canada, Department of the Interior, *Annual Report 1890*, p. xvii; *Semi-Weekly News* (Lethbridge), 6 January 1981.

96. *Semi-Weekly News* (Lethbridge), 17 February 1891.

97. In 1890 Galt sold about 12,000 tons of coal in Winnipeg at $6.75 per ton while the Pennsylvania firms disposed of 18,000 tons at $8.00 per ton. Canada, Department of the Interior, *Annual Report 1890*, p. xvii; *see also Annual Report 1891*, part I, pp. 6-9.

98. *Semi-Weekly News* (Lethbridge), 7 September and 23 November 1891.

99. Canada, *Statutes of Canada*, 54-55 Victoria, chapter 77, 31 July 1891.

100. *Burdett's Official Intelligence for 1896* (London, 1896).

101. The report was reprinted in the *Lethbridge News*, 27 January 1892.

102. Magrath, *The Galts*, p. 59.

103. Canada, Department of the Interior, *Annual Report 1892*, part I, p. 20; *Annual Report 1893*, part I, p. 20.

104. PAC, Shaughnessy Letterbooks, vol. 36, Shaughnessy to Whyte, 7 April 1893; *see also* vol. 27, Shaughnessy to Whyte, 1 May 1891; vol. 30, Shaughnessy to Whyte, 14 April 1892.

105. *Lethbridge News*, 25 May 1892.

106. Harold A. Innis, *A History of the Canadian Pacific Railway* (Toronto: University of Toronto Press, 1971), p. 139.

107. PAC, Shaughnessy Letterbooks, vol. 35, Shaughnessy to Galt, 27 February 1893.

108. Ibid., Memorandum for the lease and purchase of the Dunmore-Lethbridge Railway to the Canadian Pacific Railway; *see also* Shaughnessy to Whyte, 4 July 1893.

109. PAC, RCMP Records, RG 18, A-1, vol. 74, no. 73, Lethbridge monthly report, 30 November 1893.

110. PAC, Galt Papers, vol. 8, Burgess to Galt, 28 June 1893.

111. Springett, *Children's Children*, p. 20.

112. Cited in Skelton, *The Life and Times of Sir Alexander Tilloch Galt*, p. 279.

113. *Globe* (Toronto), 20 September 1893.

114. *Gazette* (Montreal), 20 September 1893.

Chapter 7

1. *Fort Macleod Gazette*, 14 November 1884.

2. Ibid., 6 October 1885.

3. Ibid., 27 October 1885.

4. GAI, Higinbotham Papers, vol. 6, file 71.

5. John D. Higinbotham, *When the West Was Young: Historical Reminiscences of the Early Canadian West* (Toronto: Ryerson Press, 1933), p. 113.

6. Magrath, *The Galts*, p. 34; *see also* GAI, Higinbotham Papers, vol. 7, file 101.

7. Magrath, *The Galts*, pp. 26–34.

8. For examples of police activity *see Lethbridge News*, 23 February, 17 August, and 29 December 1887.

9. R. Burton Deane, *Mounted Police Life in Canada: A Record of Thirty-One Years' Service* (London: Cassell, 1916), p. 48.

10. S. Evangeline Warren, *Seventy South Alberta Years* (Ilfracombe, Devon: Arthur H. Stockwell Ltd., 1960), pp. 7-14.

11. *Lethbridge News*, 19 February 1886.

12. GAI, Higinbotham Papers, vol. 7, file 70 and 73, and Notebook A, p. 57; Canada, Department of the Interior, *Annual Report 1886*, part IV, pp. 17-33, *Annual Report 1887*, part V, pp. 21-38, and *Annual Report 1888*, part IV, pp. 54-65.

13. Higinbotham, *When the West Was Young*, p. 118.

14. Frank Van Tighem, "Father Leonard Van Tighem, O.M.I.," *Alberta Historical Review* 12 (Winter 1964), pp. 18-19; *see also* GAI, Edna-Kells-Pioneer Interviews, "Interview with Clyde W. Gilmour," p. 52.

15. GAI, Higinbotham Papers, vol. 7, file 73; *Lethbridge News*, 6 April 1887.

16. Van Tighem, "Father Van Tighem," p. 19.

17. Cited by Higinbotham, *When the West Was Young*, pp. 158-59.

18. *Fort Macleod Gazette*, 6 and 13 April 1886.

19. PAC, RCMP Records, RG 18, A-1, vol. 21, no. 373, Lethbridge monthly report, July 1888.

20. Ibid., vol. 39, no. 137, Lethbridge weekly report, 24 November 1890.

21. Ibid., Lethbridge monthly report, 31 October 1890.

22. *Lethbridge News*, 3 December 1890.

23. James H. Gray, *Red Lights on the Prairies* (Toronto: Macmillan, 1971), p. 162, paints a very colourful picture of the frontier prostitute and the single settler; while his lighthearted approach underscores the utility of the brothel in the male-dominant West, it ignores the seamy aspects of prostitution.

24. At one time, two women attacked an ex-constable and made such a racket that the police arrested the "notorious and objectionable prostitute named Madge Blake" (PAC, RCMP Records, RG 18, A-1, vol. 30, no. 130, Lethbridge weekly report, 21 September 1889). At another time the police jailed a harlot "who describes herself as 'a blue blooded lady of Spain' but is the worst of the lot" (ibid., vol. 39, no. 137, Lethbridge monthly report, 1 January 1890). On yet another occasion the police rounded up a number of saloon keepers, four of whom were ex-policemen (ibid).

25. Ibid., vol. 30, no. 130, Lethbridge weekly report, 21 November 1889.

26. No documentation is available on this point. The author was told by a grandson of William Stafford that he had read a letter from Sir Alexander to Stafford instructing the mine manager to hire Hungarians in favour of Nova Scotians because the former were willing to work for lower wages.

27. PAC, RCMP Records, RG 18, A-1, vol. 21, no. 373, Lethbridge monthly report, 1 July 1888.

28. Ibid.

29. *Lethbridge News*, 28 June 1888.

30. PAC, RCMP Records, RG 18, A-1, vol. 21, no. 373, Lethbridge monthly report, 1 July 1888.

31. P. F. W. Rutherford, "The Western Press and Regionalism, 1870-1896," *Canadian Historical Review* 52 (September 1971), pp. 287–305, shows how this myth was commonly expressed in most western newspapers, but he does not link it to anti-racial feelings.

32. PAC, RCMP Records, RG 18, A-1, vol. 39, no. 137, Lethbridge monthly report, 30 April 1890.

33. Edward Hagell, "The Lethbridge News, 1885," *The Story of the Press*, vol. 1, no. 4, part 1 (Battleford, Saskatchewan: Canadian North-West Historical Society Publications, 1928), pp. 78–80; GAI, Higinbotham Papers, file 70, Notebook A, p. 60; *Fort Macleod Gazette*, 30 November 1886.

34. *Lethbridge News*, 24 April 1889.

35. Ibid., 3 December 1890.

36. Ibid., 22 June 1887.

37. Cited in the *Lethbridge Herald*, 11 July 1935, p. 11.

38. *Fort Macleod Gazette*, 5 December 1889.

39. *Lethbridge News*, 9 April 1890.

40. *Lethbridge Herald*, 11 July 1935, p. 99.

41. Deane, *Mounted Police Life*, p. 44.

42. *Lethbridge News*, 5 July 1888.

43. Ibid., 21 and 28 September, 30 November 1887, and 22 March 1888.

44. *Fort Macleod Gazette*, 15 December 1885.

45. Ibid., 4 and 18 April 1888.

46. Ibid., 15 November 1888.

47. Ibid., 21 February 1889.

48. Canada, *Statutes of Canada*, 53 Victoria, chapter 84, 24 April 1890.

49. *Fort Macleod Gazette*, 8 May 1890.

50. Ibid., 15 May 1890.

51. *Lethbridge News*, 3 May 1888 and 30 January 1889.

52. Magrath, *The Galts*, p. 40.

53. *Lethbridge News*, 5 February and 29 October 1890.

54. PAC, RCMP Records, RG 18, A-1, vol. 30, no. 130, Lethbridge monthly report, 30 September 1889.

55. PAC, Magrath Papers, vol. 4, file 27, extracts from the minutes of the board of trade, 17 April 1890.

56. Ibid., 31 May and 3 June 1890.

57. *Lethbridge News*, 9 July 1890.

58. PAC, Magrath Papers, vol. 30, file 27, extracts from the minutes of the board of trade, 20 June 1890.

59. *Lethbridge News*, 9 July 1890.

60. Ibid., 23 July 1890.

61. *Semi-Weekly News* (Lethbridge), 6 January 1891.

62. Ibid., 27 January 1891.

63. Ibid., 3 and 6 February 1891. Since this study is limited to Galt's role in western Canada, it cannot examine in detail the sociological and political structures of Lethbridge. It must be stated at this point, however, that this particular municipal election does not support the thesis of a conspirational elitist control over local politics. All that can be said at this point is that a few businessmen, professionals, and company officials had the time and interest to work for the economic expansion of Lethbridge and the town council was one of the tools used to obtain this end. *See* Nelson W. Polsby, "Power in Middletown: Fact and Value in Community Research," *The Canadian Journal of Economics and Political Science* 26 (November 1960), pp. 592-603, for an excellent modification of the strict Marxist interpretation of community politics.

64. City of Lethbridge, City Clerk's Office, file 1891, Inaugural Address.

65. PAC, Galt Papers, vol. 4, Galt to Gladstone, 26 February 1891; Chamberlain to Galt, 10 March 1891; and Macdonald Papers, vol. 220, 7 February 1891.

66. *Semi-Weekly News* (Lethbridge), 3 March 1891.

67. *See* for example the discussion on the first debenture, which was finally reduced from the proposed $15,000 to $10,000 for the purchase of a fire extinguisher and sidewalks. City of Lethbridge, City Clerk's Office, Minute Books, 3 June 1891. The citizens displayed their enthusiasm for civic government by a massive turnout of thirty-six voters; only two turned down the proposal.

68. Ibid., 30 March 1892.

69. Ibid., 24 June 1896. In addition to the financial stringency, Bentley faced the problem of the rapid turnover of councillors. His first council contained three and his second five new members. The lack of continuity reflected the scant interest in local politics and it hampered the body's effectiveness.

70. *Semi-Weekly News* (Lethbridge), 23 January 1891.

71. *Lethbridge News*, 23 March 1892.

72. PAC, Galt Letterbook, Galt to Cutbill, 3 July 1885.

Chapter 8

1. HBCA, PAM, A 12/26, Brydges to Armit, 19 September 1887, f. 232.

2. Canada, Order-in-Council, 19 October 1885; PAC, Department of the Interior Records, vol. 291, file 62709-2, Burgess to Wilson, 25 February 1886; Canada, *Statutes of Canada*, 49 Victoria, chapter 12, 2 June 1886.

3. HBCA, PAM, A 12/25, Brydges to Burgess, 14 December 1886, ff. 208-11.

4. Ibid., Burgess to Brydges, 28 December 1886, ff. 4-6.

5. Ibid., A 12/26, Robinson to Brydges, 20 June 1887, f. 24; Brydges to Donald Smith, 12 April 1888, f. 34; Aldous to Brydges, 8 October 1887, f. 295; Galt to Brydges, 14 and 28 September 1887, ff. 260, 261; GAI, NWC&NCo Papers, box 1, file 1, Burgess to Galt, 4 December 1886; Douglas to Magrath, 4 April 1887; Ibid., file 2, Land Patents, 16 May 1887.

6. By November 1890 the AR&CCo had acquired rights to 839,216 acres at 10 cents per acre for a total of $83,921.60, in addition to $39,120 worth of coal lands for a total expenditure of $123,041.60. It had sold 103,090.54 acres for $133,356.98 as well as several hundred acres of coal lands and surface rights for $5,666.25. Revenues exceeded expenditures by $15,881.63, a cheery prospect for the remaining 740,000 acres. GAI, NWC&NCo Papers, file 9, Statement of Railway Land Grants and Coal Lands, 12 November 1890; file 3, undated report on land sales to 31 December 1889.

7. A. James Hudson, *Charles Ora Card, Pioneer and Colonizer* (Cardston: Alberta: By the author, 1963).

8. University of Alberta Archives (hereafter cited as UAA), Pearce Papers, box 42, 14-b-11, no. 2275, Ferguson to Magrath, 3 June 1889; Pearce to Magrath, 20 November 1888.

9. Ibid., Magrath to Pearce, 15 November 1888.

10. Ibid., Card to Pearce, 6 August 1889.

11. Magrath, *The Galts*, p. 41.

12. Ibid., p. 11.

13. *See* pp. 153-54 of this text.

14. GAI, Jacobsen Project, file 234, Charles Ora Card, p. 9.

15. PAC, Magrath Papers, vol. 10, file 51, Magrath to Pearce, 17 March 1892.

16. Magrath, *The Galts*, p. 37.

17. *Semi-Weekly News* (Lethbridge), 20 January 1891.

18. PAC, Magrath Papers, vol. 10, file 51, Magrath to Pearce, 17 March 1892; Magrath to Ferguson, 26 March 1892.

19. *See* p. 157 of this text.

20. *Burdett's Official Intelligence for 1903*, p. 1051, Canada *Statutes of Canada*, 56 Victoria, chapter 69, 1 April 1893.

21. PAC, Magrath Papers, vol. 10, file 51, Magrath to Daly, 4 February 1893. The substance of this draft letter was reiterated on 6 and 29 March 1893.

22. *See* for example the *Lethbridge News*, 20 November 1889.

23. Ibid., 8 June 1892.

24. Canada, House of Commons, Debates, 14 April 1890.

Chapter 9

1. Glenn Porter, *The Rise of Big Business, 1860-1910* (New York: Thomas Y. Crowell Company, 1973) pp. 8-9, lists some of the characteristics of big business.

2. For a more detailed discussion of this strike *see* Chapter 11.

3. PAC, Shaughnessy Letterbooks, vol. 40, Shaughnessy to Whyte, 14 August 1894.

4. Ibid., Shaughnessy to Galt, 31 August 1894; Shaughnessy to Ogden, 31 August 1894.

5. Canada, *Statutes of Canada*, 59 Victoria, chapter 45, 28 June 1895; *The Stock Exchange Official Intelligence for 1902* (London, 1902), p. 285.

6. PAC, Shaughnessy Letterbooks, vol. 41, Shaughnessy to Whyte, 25 January 1895.

7. PAC, RCMP Records, RG 18, A-1, vol. 104, file 131, Lethbridge monthly report, 31 January 1895.

8. Ibid., 28 February 1895; PAC, Shaughnessy Letterbooks, Vol. 41, Shaughnessy to Whyte, 18 April 1895.

9. PAC, Shaughnessy Letterbooks, vol. 49, Shaughnessy to Whyte, 20 October 1896.

10. PAC, RCMP Records, RG 18, A-1, vol. 104, file 131, Lethbridge monthly report, 30 September 1895.

11. PAC, Shaughnessy Letterbooks, vol. 43, Shaughnessy to McNeill, 29 July 1895; see also vol. 52, Shaughnessy to Whyte, 7 May 1897.

12. Canada, Department of the Interior, Annual Report 1894, part I, p. 23; Annual Report 1895, part I, p. 18; Annual Report 1896, part I, pp. 25-31.

13. E. Alyn Mitchner, "William Pearce and Federal Government Activity in Western Canada, 1882-1904" (Ph.D. diss., University of Alberta, 1970).

14. N.F. Dreisziger, "The Canadian-American Irrigation Frontier Revisited: The International Origins of Irrigation in Southern Alberta," Canadian Historical Association, Historical Papers 1975, pp. 211-30, makes the point that the government's attitude toward irrigation changed because it wanted to establish a prior claim to the St. Mary River. This may have been the position of William Pearce, who would marshall any argument he could to promote irrigation, but Pearce was thoughtful enough to find an alternate water source for Galt's scheme. In fact, Dreisziger's point cannot be sustained and he himself admits that the justice department believed the creation of a "prior claim" or "vested rights" on the Canadian side could accomplish no more than to "add strength" to Ottawa's arguments in any negotiations with Washington (p. 218). The voluminous Pearce correspondence (UAA, Pearce Papers, 9/2/13/1) clearly describes the irrigation project as a commercial enterprise rather than a diplomatic manoeuvre. See Pereira to Pearce, 11 December 1894, "... it is thought if the Americans wish to carry out the scheme ... they cannot be prevented from doing so, even if this Government or a Company in the meantime utilized the waters of the St. Mary's River for irrigation purposes."

15. UAA, Pearce Papers, box 8, no. 3-35, Burgess to Pearce, 21 January 1891.

16. Ibid., box 71, no. 22-83, Pearce to Magrath, 23 November 1893.

17. PAC, Magrath Papers, vol. 10, file 51, Notes on the earlier efforts to bring about irrigation in southern Alberta; see also Mitchener, "Pearce and Western Canada," pp. 239-40.

18. Canada, Department of the Interior, Annual Report 1895, part III, p. 35. The minister of the interior wrote, "These surveys [of the Bow and St. Mary rivers] were made for the purpose of proving definitely that the waters of these streams could be used for the irrigation of the areas in question."

19. Canada, Order-in-Council, 18 January 1896, bears the attached memorandum by Daly, misdated 16 November 1885 instead of 1895.

20. Ibid.; for Magrath's role in the consolidation see PAC, Magrath Papers, vol.

10, Memorandum on John W. Taylor; for the political problem *see* GAI, NWC&NCo papers, file 10, for correspondence among Galt, Daly, Ferguson, and Magrath, particularly Lougheed to Magrath, 9 January 1896.

21. Canada, *Statutes of Canada*, 59 Victoria, chapter 44, 23 April 1896.

22. W. Kaye Lamb, *History of the Canadian Pacific Railway* (New York: Macmillan, 1977), pp. 207-13; T. D. Regehr, *The Canadian Northern Railway: Pioneer Road of the Northern Prairies, 1895-1918* (Toronto: Macmillan, 1976), pp. 62-65.

23. Canadian Pacific Railway Company, *Annual Report 1897* (Montreal: Macmillan, 1898), p. 6.

24. D. J. Hall, "Clifford Sifton: Immigration and Settlement Policy, 1896-1905," in *The Settlement of the West*, ed. by H. Palmer (Calgary: Comprint Publishing Company, 1977), pp. 60-85.

25. PAC, Magrath Papers, vol. 10, file 51, Memorandum: The beginning of irrigation in a large way in southern Alberta, incomplete date, April 1942; Canada, Order-in-Council, 6 January 1898.

26. GAI, NWC&NCo Papers, Galt to Sifton, 15 December 1897; PAC, Magrath Papers, Magrath to Sifton, vol. 10, file 51, 8 November 1897; Order-in-Council, 6 January 1898.

27. PAC, Pearce Papers, box 71, no. 22-83, Magrath to Pearce, 13 December 1897.

28. PAC, Shaughnessy Letterbooks, vol. 56, Shaughnessy to Galt, 5 January 1898.

29. PAC, Galt Papers, vol. 8, Galt to Burdett-Coutts, 4 April 1905.

30. Ibid., transcribed interview of Galt in Sifton's office, 16 May 1904.

31. Ibid., Galt to Lady Galt, 19 June 1898. In a letter to Clifford Sifton (GAI, NWC&NCo papers, box 2, file 22, incomplete date, September 1898), Elliott Galt outlined the source of the irrigation company's capital: W. Burdett-Coutts, $25,000; United States Debenture Corporation, $25,000; Industrial and General Trust, $20,000; Baring Brothers & Company, $18,500; William Lethbridge, $17,000; The Right Honourable Lord Ireagh, $15,000; Trustees, Executors & Securities Insurance Cooperation, $15,000; F. Shaw Kennedy, $5,000; Hon. T. C. Farrar, $5,000; Colonel K. R. B. Wodehouse, $42,500; International Investment Trust, $2,000; E. T. Galt and Canadian friends, $50,000.

32. PAC, Sifton Paper, vol. 228, Sifton to Galt, 15 October 1898.

33. GAI, Sam G. Porter and Charles Raley, "A Brief History of the Development of Irrigation in the Lethbridge District" (typewritten manuscript, Lethbridge Public Library, 1925), p. 18; Melvin S. Tagg," A History of the Church of Latter Day Saints in Canada, 1830-1963" (Ph.D. diss., Brigham Young University, 1963), p. 179; UAA, Pearce Papers, box 19, file 9-7, Pearce to Secretary,

Department of the Interior, 10 December 1898; box 71, file 22-83, Magrath to Pearce, 4 July 1899 and 10 February 1900.

34. Magrath, *The Galts*, p. 52; UAA, Pearce Papers, box 71, no. 22-83, Magrath to Pearce, 4 July 1889; PAC, Magrath Papers, vol. 4, file 9, untitled memorandum on political career, incomplete date, January 1935.

35. *The Stock Exchange Official Intelligence for 1903* (London 1903), p. 1051.

36. GAI, Charles Raley, "A Scrapbook Compiled in the Office of the Alberta Railway and Irrigation Company, 1896-1956," Anderson to Magrath, 4 July 1900.

37. GAI, Canadian North-west Irrigation Company, *Irrigated Lands in Southern Alberta* (Winnipeg: Storel Co., 1900); *The Colorado of Canada, Irrigated Lands, Southern Alberta* (n.p., 1900); L. P. Burns, "The Alberta Railway and Irrigation Company, 1893-1946," in "History of Irrigation in Western Canada, History of Agriculture" (typewritten manuscript, a Glenbow Foundation Research Project); C. Raley, "AR&I Scrapbook," contains clippings from several newspapers in which Charles McKillop inserted articles on Lethbridge.

38. GAI, Anna Brandley Ostlund, "Theodore Brandley" (typewritten manuscript, 1960).

39. GAI, Burns, "Alberta Railway and Irrigation Co.," 28 December 1901.

40. UAA, Pearce Papers, box 19, file 9-7, Magrath to Pearce, 20 September 1900.

41. GAI, Burns, "Alberta Railway and Irrigation Co.," Memorials, Canadian North-west Irrigation Company, 15 March 1900 and 9 September 1902; Canada, Orders-in-Council, 17 and 25 August 1900 and 20 April 1905; GAI, NWC&NCo papers, file 11, Galt to Sifton, 27 June 1900.

42. Canada, House of Commons, Debates, 12 July 1900.

43. PAC, Sifton Papers, vol. 99, Galt to Sifton, 13 May 1901; Galt to Blair, 27 February 1901.

44. Canada, House of Commons, Debates, 20 October 1903.

45. PAC, Magrath Papers, vol. 7, Galt to Magrath, 15 December 1900.

46. Ibid., Galt to Magrath, 19 February and 18 March 1901; vol. 4, file 13, Galt to Magrath, 4 March 1927; *The Stock Exchange Official Intelligence for 1902* (London, 1902), p. 285.

47. GAI, Porter and Raley, "Development of Irrigation," p. 26.

48. GAI, W. L. Jacobson, "Biographical Sketch of William Harmon Fairfield (1874-1961)" in "History of Irrigation in Western Canada, History of Agriculture" (typewritten manuscript, a Glenbow Foundation Research Project, 1959-1960), pp. 1-8; Agriculture Canada Research Station Archives, Lethbridge, Alberta, Alex Johnson, "Early Agriculture and the Dominion Experimental

Station, Lethbridge" (unpublished paper presented to the Historical Society of Alberta, 1973), pp. 4-6.

49. Canada, Order-in-Council, 12 December 1902.

50. GAI, Burns, Alberta Railway & Irrigation Co., Stewart to Department of the Interior, 3 May 1906; for a summary of the expenditures made by the irrigation company *see* GAI, Documents relating to the Alberta Railway and Irrigation Company, 1902-1919, Copy of Data from the Files of the Department of Land and Mines, Keys to AR&ICo, 7 March 1908.

51. GAI, Documents relating to the Alberta Railway and Irrigation Company, Drake to Campbell, 14 April 1910.

52. *The Stock Exchange Official Intelligence for 1906* (London, 1906), p. 276; Canada, Statutes of Canada, 4 Edward, chapter 43, 6 June 1904; PAC, Magrath Papers, vol. 10, file 51, Galt to Magrath, 1 October 1904.

53. PAC, Magrath Papers, vol. 10, file 51, Galt to Magrath, 10 December 1904 and 30 June 1905; R. G. Macbeth, *Sir Augustus Nanton: A Biography* (Toronto: The Macmillan Company of Canada, 1931).

54. Alberta, Mines Division Records, file 13003, annual returns, 1898, 1902-1905.

55. Ibid., Naismith to Dennis, 6 April 1900.

56. Ibid., Smith to Dennis, 10 July 1902.

57. *The Statist* (London), 4 November 1905; *The Stock Exchange Official Intelligence for 1906* (London, 1906), p. 276.

58. PAC, Magrath Papers, vol. 7, Galt to Magrath, 13 July 1905.

59. PAC, Galt Papers, vol. 8, Galt to Burdett-Coutts, 4 April 1905.

60. *Manitoba Free Press*, 9 September 1904.

61. PAC, Sifton Papers, vol. 142, telegram, Galt to Sifton, 22 July 1903.

62. *Manitoba Free Press*, 21 November 1903. The reference to Galt and Magrath by name in no way detracts from the point made in the previous paragraph concerning the de-personalization of the company. This statement was made in 1903 when the AR&ICo had not yet come into existence and irrigation was controlled by the relatively small North-west Irrigation Company.

63. Idem.

64. Ibid., 9 September 1904.

Chapter 10

1. Canada, *Census of Canada 1901*, pp. 132–33. The census must be used cautiously. If it was taken during a production slump, it missed many of the transients who were largely male and single.

2. Galt Museum, Lethbridge Tax Rolls, 1896.

3. For an excellent analysis of the railroaders *see* Jean Burnett, *Next-Year Country: A Study of Rural Social Organization in Alberta* (Toronto: University of Toronto Press, 1951). pp. 97–99.

4. PAC, RCMP Records, RG 18, A-1, vol. 49, no. 192, Lethbridge monthly report, 28 February 1891.

5. Ibid., vol. 104, no. 131, Lethbridge monthly report, 31 December 1895; vol. 143, no. 19, Lethbridge monthly report, 31 August 1898; *Lethbridge Herald*, 18 December 1905.

6. *Lethbridge Herald*, 18 December 1905.

7. PAC, RCMP Records, RG 18, A-1, vol. 91, No. 148, Lethbridge monthly report, 30 November 1894; vol. 126, no. 5, Lethbridge monthly report, 31 October 1897; *Lethbridge News*, 6 and 13 January 1892.

8. PAC, RCMP Records, RG 18, A-1, vol. 74, no. 73, Lethbridge monthly report, 31 October 1893.

9. PAC, RCMP Records, RG 18, A-1, vol. 49, no. 192, 8 May and 19 and 30 September 1891.

10. *Semi-Weekly News* (Lethbridge), 9 January 1891.

11. Lethbridge, Town Council Minutes, 21 May 1894.

12. J. H. Carpenter, *The Badge and the Blotter: A History of the Lethbridge Police* (Lethbridge: Whoop-Up Country Chapter, Historical Society of Alberta, 1975), pp. 11–13.

13. PAC, RCMP Records, RG 18, A-1, vol. 91, no. 148, Lethbridge monthly report, 31 July 1894.

14. Ibid., vol. 104, no. 131, Lethbridge monthly report, 28 February and 30 June 1895; Carpenter, *The Badge and the Blotter*, pp. 14–15.

15. Lethbridge, Town Council Minutes, 6 May 1898.

16. PAC, RCMP Records, RG 18, A-1, vol. 143, no. 17, Lethbridge monthly report, 30 September 1898.

17. Cited in Carpenter, *The Badge and the Blotter*, p. 17.

18. Ibid., pp. 17–18.

19. PAC, RCMP Records, RG 18, A-1, vol. 183, no. 202, Lethbridge monthly report, 31 August 1900.

20. Carpenter, *The Badge and the Blotter*, pp. 22–23.

21. *Lethbridge News*, 6 August 1903; Lethbridge, Town Council Minutes, 3 August 1903.

22. Gray, *Red Lights on the Prairies*, pp. 165–66.

23. Carpenter, *The Badge and the Blotter*, pp. 25–27.

24. *Lethbridge Herald*, 15 November 1905.

25. For a full discussion of the social divisions within the colliery, *see* Chapter 11.

26. Victor R. Greene, *The Slavic Community on Strike: Immigrant Labor in Pennsylvania Anthracite* (Notre Dame, Indiana: University of Notre Dame Press, 1968).

27. *The Voice* (Winnipeg), 24 March 1899.

28. Canada, *Census of Canada 1901*, pp. 394–95.

29. *Semi-Weekly News* (Lethbridge), 8 May 1891.

30. *Lethbridge News*, 10 August 1897.

31. Ibid., 18 August 1897.

32. Canada, *Census of Canada 1901*, pp. 270–71.

33. Knox Presbyterian Church, Board of Managers Minutes, 12 August 1893.

34. St. Augustine Anglican Church, Vestry Minutes, 22 August 1894.

35. Knox Presbyterian Church, Board of Managers Minutes, 17 August 1901.

36. *Semi-Weekly News* (Lethbridge), 13 January 1891.

37. Ibid.

38. *Lethbridge Herald*, 17 January 1906.

39. *Semi-Weekly News* (Lethbridge), 27 March 1891.

40. For a good overview of western Canadian attitudes towards their schools *see* Manoly R. Lupul, *The Roman Catholic Church and the North-West Question: A Study in Church-State Relations in Western Canada 1875–1905* (Toronto: University of Toronto Press, 1974).

41. *Semi-Weekly News* (Lethbridge), 24 December 1890, 6 January and 18 November 1891; *Lethbridge News*, 8 January 1896; *Lethbridge Herald*, 3 January 1906.

42. *Lethbridge Herald*, 12 July 1906.

43. *Semi-Weekly News* (Lethbridge), 27 March 1891.

44. Galt Museum, Lethbridge Tax Rolls, 1891 and 1897.

45. Semi-Weekly News (Lethbridge), 15 May 1891.

46. *Lethbridge Herald*, 27 December 1905.

47. Lethbridge, City Clerk's Office, Railway File, 1897.

48. Lethbridge, Town Council Minutes, 12 December 1898 and 27 January 1899; Bylaws 107 and 108.

49. *Lethbridge News*, 1 December 1898.

50. Ibid., 9 August 1900.

51. Lethbridge, Town Council Minute Book, Bylaw 203. For other expensive decisions *see* 21 January and 18 March 1901; 21 September 1903; and 15 January 1906.

52. Ibid., Statements of receipts and expenditures for the years 1897, 1899, and 1904.

53. The impressions in this paragraph were gleaned from the minutes of the town council (1891-1906), the *Lethbridge News* (1891-1905), and the *Lethbridge Herald* (1905-1906). The minute books relate the bare-boned decisions while the newspapers provide the underlying thoughts behind these judgements. In their general attitudes, the Lethbridge council was remarkably similar to that of Calgary. *See* M. L. Foran, "The Calgary Town Council, 1884-1895: A Study of Local Government in a Frontier Environment" (M.A. thesis, University of Calgary, 1970).

54. *Lethbridge Herald*, 21 June 1906.

55. Ibid., 26 July 1906.

56. Ibid., 15 November 1905.

Chapter 11

1. North-West Territories, Department of Public Works, *Annual Report 1901* (Edmonton, 1902), pp. 14-15.

2. Alberta, Mines Division Records, file 13003, Heathcote to Stocks, 28 January 1908.

3. Ibid., Inspector's report, 8 June 1899 and 15 April 1901; North-West Territories, Department of Public Works, *Annual Report 1900* (Edmonton, 1901), p. 16.

4. North-West Territories, Department of Public Works, *Annual Report 1900*, p. 11.

5. Alberta, Mines Division Records, file 13003, Dennis to Hardie, incomplete date, November 1898.

6. Ibid., Inspector's Report, 8 June 1899.

7. North-West Territories, Ordinances of the North-West Territories, No. 5 of 1893, 16 September 1893.

8. North-West Territories, Department of Public Works, *Annual Report 1898*, p. 87; *Annual Report 1900*, p. 17.

9. Alberta, Mines Division Records, file 13003, Naismith to Dennis, 6 April 1900; North-West Territories, Department of Public Works, *Annual Report 1899*, p. 14.

10. *Lethbridge Herald*, DeVeber to the editor, 7 February 1907.

11. Alberta, *Statutes of Alberta 1906*, chapter 25.

12. North-West Territories, Department of Public Works, *Annual Report 1898*, p. 87; Alberta, Mines Division Records, file 13003, Inspector's report, 9 February 1898.

13. Alberta, Department of Public Works, *Annual Report 1906*.

14. Alberta, Mines Division Records, file 13003, Naismith to Dennis, 6 April 1900. After 1910 the Alberta government kept track of the production of each mine in the province, the number of men employed and the days of operation for every month of the year, a record which clearly outlines the cyclical nature of coal output during the years.

15. The literature on coal-mining is unanimous on this adulation of the job and spirit of camaraderie. *See* Norman Dennis, Fernando Henriques, and Clifford Slaughter, *Coal is Our Life: An Analysis of a Yorkshire Mining Community* (London: Eyre & Spottiswoode, 1956); Carter Goodrich, *The Miner's Freedom: A Study of the Working Life in a Changing Industry* (New York: Arno Press, 1977, org. ed., 1925); Joseph Husband, *A Year in a Coal Mine* (New York: Arno Press, 1977, org. ed., 1911); Mike Ross, "Mike Ross Talks About the Life Style of the Coal Miner," *United Mine Workers Journal*, July 1970; pp. 12-15.

16. PAC, RCMP Records, RG 18, A-1, vol. 91, no. 148, Lethbridge monthly report, 31 March 1894.

17. Ibid., 31 March 1894. *See also* 30 April 1894.

18. Ibid., vol. 126, file 5, Lethbridge monthly reports, 28 February and 31 March 1897.

19. Ibid., 21 [31?] August 1897; *Lethbridge News*, 10, 18, and 25 August 1897.

20. PAC, RCMP Records, vol. 126, file 5, Lethbridge monthly report, 21 [31?] August 1897.

21. *Lethbridge News*, 25 August 1897.

22. Herbert G. Gutman, "Work, Culture, and Society in Industrializing America, 1915-1919," *American Historical Review* 78 (June 1973), pp. 531-88; Melvyn Dubofsky, *Industrialism and the American Worker, 1865-1920* (New York: Crowell, 1975).

23. A penetrating analysis of western American radicalism is provided by Melvyn Dubofsky, "The Origins of Western Working Class Radicalism, 1890-1905," *Labour History* 7 (Spring 1966), pp. 131-55; also valuable is John Laslett, *Labor and*

the Left: A Study of Socialist and Radical Influences in the American Labor Movement, 1881–1924 (New York: Basic Books, 1970).

24. *Lethbridge News*, 25 August 1897.

25. PAC, RCMP Records, RG 18, A-1, vol. 166, no. 195, Lethbridge special report, 1 November 1899, Lethbridge monthly report, 30 November 1899; vol. 161, file 86, MacLeod monthly report, 30 November 1899; *Lethbridge News*, 26 October and 2 November 1899.

26. *Lethbridge News*, 2 November 1899.

27. *The Voice* (Winnipeg), 24 November 1899.

28. *See* A. R. McCormack, *Reformers, Rebels, and Revolutionaries: The Western Canadian Radical Movement, 1899–1919* (Toronto: University of Toronto Press, 1977) pp. 6-14; and Rowand Tappan Berthoff, *An Unsettled People: Social Order and Disorder in American Society* (New York: Harper & Row, 1971).

29. C.J. McMillan, "Trade Unionism in District 18, 1900–1925: A Case Study" (M.B.A. thesis, University of Alberta, 1969) pp. 41–49; McCormack, *Reformers, Rebels, and Revolutionaries*, pp. 44, 51.

30. *Western Clarion*, 21 March 1908, cited by McCormack, *Reformers, Rebels, and Revolutionaries*, p. 55.

31. McCormack, *Reformers, Rebels, and Revolutionaries*, pp. 53–55.

32. McMillan, "Trade Unionism in District 18," p. 72.

33. *Lethbridge Herald*, 3 January and 21 February 1906.

34. *United Mine Workers Journal*, 9 August 1906.

35. PAC, RCMP Records, RG 18, A-1, vol. 316, file 238, Goodwin, under the signature of Wilson to the commissioner, 1 March 1906. Unfortunately the only known records of the strike are contained in the RCMP Records and the *Lethbridge Herald*. Since neither source was sympathetic to the strikers the author approached them with caution and tried as much as possible to see the events also from the perspective of the workers.

36. *Lethbridge Herald*, 1 March 1906.

37. Ibid., 15 March 1906; also 8 March 1906.

38. PAC, RCMP Records, RG 18, A-1, vol. 316, file 238, Naismith to Perry, 12 March 1906.

39. Ibid., Wilson to Commissioner, 14 March 1906.

40. R.C. Macleod, "Canadianizing the West: The North-West Mounted Police as Agents of the National Policy, 1873–1905," in *Essays on Western History*, ed. by Lewis H. Thomas (Edmonton: University of Alberta Press, 1976), pp. 101–12.

41. PAC, RCMP Records, RG 18, A-1, vol. 316, file 238, Wilson to Commissioner, 15 March 1906.

42. Ibid., Wilson to Perry, 14 March 1906.

43. Ibid., Wilson to Commissioner, 14 March 1906; *see also* Wilson to Perry, 12 March 1906.

44. Ibid., Perry to Naismith, 14 March 1906.

45. Ibid., Perry to Wilson, 15 March 1906.

46. Ibid., Wilson to Commissioner, 15 March 1906.

47. Ibid., 14 March 1906.

48. Ibid., Raven to Wilson, 17 March 1906.

49. Ibid., Wilson to Commissioner, 17 and 19 March 1906.

50. Ibid., 19 March 1906.

51. Ibid., Naismith to White, 23 March 1906.

52. Ibid., Wilson to Commissioner, 1 April 1906; sworn affidavits by officers involved; Wilson to Commissioner, 3 and 4 April 1906; affidavits, Raven under Wilson's signature to Commissioner, 5 April 1906; *Lethbridge Herald*, 5 April 1906.

53. PAC, RCMP Records, RG 18, A-1, vol. 316, file 238, Wilson to Camies, 8 April 1906.

54. *Lethbridge Herald*, 5 April 1906.

55. PAC, RCMP Records, RG 18, A-1, vol. 315, file 202, Lethbridge monthly report, 31 July 1906.

56. Ibid., vol. 316, file 238, 2 May 1906.

57. Ibid., Naismith to Perry, 18 July 1906.

58. Ibid., White to Galt, 19 July 1906.

59. Ibid., Galt to White, 20 July 1906.

60. Ibid., Wilson to Commissioner, 24 July 1906.

61. Ibid., Nanton to White, 30 July 1906.

62. Ibid., Wilson to Commissioner, 8 August 1906.

63. Ibid., 13 and 14 August 1906; *Lethbridge Herald*, 6 September 1906.

64. *Lethbridge Herald*, 26 July 1906.

65. Ibid., 9 August 1906.

66. Ibid., 16 August 1906.

67. Ibid., 30 August and 6 September 1906.

68. Ibid., 20 September 1906.

69. PAC, RCMP Records, RG 18, A-1, vol. 315, file 202, Lethbridge monthly report for September 1906.

70. Saskatchewan, Department of Agriculture, *Annual Report 1906*, pp. 64–84; *Annual Report 1907*, pp. 68–78.

71. *Lethbridge Herald*, 8 November 1906. The immigration argument was a good tactic to use on federal officials who were themselves monitoring the fuel situation closely. *See* PAC, Immigration Branch Records, vol. 416, "Fuel Famine in the North West, 1906–08," cited in William Baker, "The Mediator and the Miners: Mackenzie King and the 1906 Lethbridge Strike," unpublished paper.

72. *Lethbridge Herald*, 15 November 1906.

73. Ibid., 22 November 1906.

74. Robert H. Babcock, *Gompers in Canada: A Study in American Continentalism Before the First World War* (Toronto: University of Toronto Press, 1974), p. 202.

75. PAC, King Papers, vol. 13, confidential memorandum re: Lethbridge strike, 14 November 1906. The only known record of the settlement of the strike is King's memorandum thus making interpretation of the strike's settlement difficult. A detailed reconstruction of King's role in the 1906 Lethbridge strike is contained in Baker, "The Mediator and the Miners" cited in note 71. The author is indebted to Professor Baker for several observations made in this chapter.

76. PAC, King Papers, vol. 13, confidential memorandum re: Lethbridge strike, 16 November 1906.

77. *Lethbridge Herald*, 11 October 1906.

78. PAC, King Papers, vol. 13, confidential memorandum re: Lethbridge strike, 26 November 1906.

79. In addition to King's memorandum cited above *see* Canada, House of Commons, Debates, 29 and 30 November 1906.

80. *See* Appendix III for copy of the agreement.

81. *See* McMillan, "Trade Unionism in District 18"; Emil Bjarnason, "Collective Bargaining in the Coal Mining Industry of Canada, 1825–1938" (M.A. thesis, Queen's University, 1965).

82. *Lethbridge Herald*, 20 December 1906, reprinted interview with E. T. Galt from the *Globe* (Toronto).

83. GAI, Western Coal Operators' Association Papers, Minutes, 22 October 1906.

84. Ibid., 15 December 1906.

85. *Lethbridge Herald*, 29 November 1906.

86. Canada, House of Commons, Debates, 26 November 1906.

87. Stuart Marshall Jamieson, *Times of Trouble: Labour Unrest and Industrial Conflict in Canada, 1900–1966* (Ottawa: Information Canada, 1971), p. 10.

88. McCormack, *Reformers, Rebels, and Revolutionaries*, pp. 5-16; John William Michael Bliss, "A Living Profit: Studies in the Social History of Canadian Business, 1883-1911" (Ph.D. diss., University of Toronto, 1972), pp. 268-71.

89. *Labour Gazette*, December 1906, p. 661.

90. Ibid., p. 662.

Epilogue

1. Alberta, Mines Division Records, file 13003, annual returns and inspector reports, 1906-1912.

2. GAI, Burns, "AR&I Collection," Statement of Expenditures, undated.

3. Ibid., Stewart to the Department of the Interior, 3 May 1906.

4. Ibid., Peters to Pereira, 13 April 1912.

5. R. C. Macbeth, *Sir Augustus Nanton*, pp. 79-81.

6. The acquisition of this land is discussed above, pp. 230-31. A detailed history of this property is presented in GAI, AR&ICo Documents.

7. Ibid., Drake to Cory, 22 May 1917.

8. Ibid., Newcombe to Beatty, 7 July 1917.

9. Ibid., Beatty to Newcombe, 13 July 1917.

10. Ibid., Newcombe to the Department of the Interior, 27 November 1917; Cote to Cory, 4 December 1917.

11. Hedges, *Land Policy*, p. 122.

12. Calgary's population mushroomed from 4,398 people in 1901 to 43,704 in 1911, a phenomenal 894 percent growth rate, while Lethbridge expanded from 2,072 to 8,050, a mere 289 percent rise in comparison. In 1916 Calgary had a population of 63,305 while Lethbridge had only 11,097 inhabitants. Canada, *Census of Canada, 1911*, vol. 1, p. 535; Canada, *Census of Canada, 1916*, vol. 1, pp. 397-99. In 1971, Lethbridge's population was 41,217.

13. GAI, Lethbridge, "Official Programme, Golden Jubilee, City of Lethbridge, Alberta, July 22nd, 23rd and 24th, 1885-1935" (CB .L647A).

14. David Jay Bercuson, ed., *Alberta's Coal Industry 1919* (Calgary: Historical Society of Alberta, 1978), pp. 205-16.

15. David Jay Bercuson, *Fools and Wise Men: The Rise and Fall of the One Big Union* (Toronto: McGraw-Hill Ryerson, 1978).

16. GAI, Lethbridge, "Official Programme, 1935," p. 5.

Bibliography

Primary sources

A Note About the Primary Sources Consulted

Three of the more important sources consulted for this study of the Galts are at the Public Archives of Canada. The most essential of these is the large collection of *Galt Papers* consisting of eight volumes of letters addressed to Sir Alexander Galt, speeches and pamphlets written by him, and various other items. Fortunately the papers also contain letters Sir Alexander wrote to his wife, Amy, in which he expressed some of the ideas that motivated his actions. The *Galt Papers* are supplemented by two letterbooks, the one covering the period just before confederation, the other the mid-1880s. The second letterbook was more valuable for this study because it dealt with the financing, construction, and early operation of the Dunmore-Lethbridge railway. The third major source was the *Macdonald Papers*, which contain several volumes of letters from Galt to Sir John A. Macdonald. Their correspondence was very frequent and extremely detailed, first when Galt was high commissioner in London and again when he was involved in his western enterprises.

The Public Archives also has preserved several other collections relevant to an examination of the Galts and western Canada. The *RCMP Records* are particularly valuable because Lethbridge enjoyed the presence of Captain Burton Deane whose monthly reports went far beyond the customary horse-and-saddle-count to include all sorts of observations on social, political, and economic life in Lethbridge. Both the *Van Horne* and *Shaughnessy Letterbooks* provided an interesting commentary on the relationship between the CPR and the various Galt companies. The *Magrath Papers*, although incomplete and heavily edited by C. A. Magrath, furnished much factual information, particularly about the irrigation projects. This data is corroborated and expanded by the extensive files on the Galt companies in the *Department of the Interior Records*.

Several other collections at the Public Archives of Canada, while not directly relevant, nevertheless yielded important information. The *King Papers*, for example, told the story of the 1906 strike, while the *Sifton Papers* showed how the minister of the interior assisted the Galt irrigation projects. The *Campbell Papers* furnished a few details about Elliott Galt's real estate dealings and the *Immigration Branch Records* revealed that department's concern about the effects of the 1906 strike. The *Mineral Resources Branch Records* and the *Canadian Transport Commission Records* provided detailed statistics on the coal-mining and railway operations.

The story of irrigation in southern Alberta could not have been written without the extensive collections held by the Glenbow-Alberta Institute in Calgary. The *North Western Coal and Navigation Company Papers* and the *Documents Relating to the Alberta Railway and Irrigation Company, 1902–1919* contain much of the official correspondence between these companies and the federal government. This correspondence is amplified by Charles Raley, *A Scrapbook Compiled in the Office of the Alberta Railway and Irrigation Company, 1896–1956*; by L. P. Burns, "The Alberta Railway and Irrigation Company, 1893–1946," in "History of Irrigation in Western Canada, History of Agriculture" (a Glenbow Foundation research project consisting primarily of official documents); and the *Jacobsen Project*. Edited memoirs, interviews, and personal papers of pioneers like Anna Brandley Ostlund's "Theodore Brandley"; the *Edna Kells Pioneer Interviews*; and the *Higinbotham Papers* provided interesting comments on the social history of the region. The *Western Canada Coal Operator's Association Records* were useful only for the post-1906 period, while the *Dewdney Papers* yielded some details of Elliott Galt's career with the Indian department. Lastly, the programme of Lethbridge's golden jubilee celebrations makes a rewarding comment on social distinctions in Lethbridge.

Several other archives were visited for this study. The Hudson's Bay Company Archives at the Public Archives of Manitoba has, in the *London Correspondence Inward From the Commissioners*, the very valuable commentaries of C. J. Brydges on railways, land sales, coal-mining, and the prairie economy in general. The Public Record Office in London has the very important Colonial Office papers relevant to Galt's high commissionership as well as the incorporation documents and two lists of shareholders of the NWC&NCo. The W. H. Smith Company Archives at Wembley, England, contain the *Hambleden Papers*, which provide some useful personal background on W. H. Smith and William Lethbridge, but say virtually nothing about their investments in Canada. In Lethbridge, the Galt Museum has several letters from Galt to Stafford as well as the very useful city tax assessment rolls. The Lethbridge city clerk's office still possesses early files, which contain not only the minutes of the town and city councils but also correspondence on such topics as irrigation and railways. The vestry minutes of St. Augustine's Anglican Church and the board of managers minutes of Knox Presbyterian Church can be combed for details on the history of these two congregations. Indispensable for the study of irrigation are the *Pearce Papers* held by the University of Alberta Archives. Lastly, the files of the Mines Division of the Government of Alberta contain several bulky files on the Galt collieries including all the inspectors' reports, production and sales figures, as well as mine plans.

Some insight into the thoughts of Sir Alexander Galt can be gleaned from his many writings and speeches. Some of those published include *A Letter to the Chairman and the Deputy Chairman of the North American Colonial Association* (London: J. Unwin, 1847); *Canada: 1849 to 1859* (Quebec: Canada Gazette Office, 1860); *Speech on the Proposed Union of the British American Provinces* (Montreal: H. Longmoore & Co., 1864); *Civil Liberty in Lower Canada* (Montreal: D. Bently & Co., 1876); *Church and State* (n.p.: Dawson Brothers, 1876); and *The Relations of the Colonies to the Empire, Present and Future* (London: McCorquodale & Co., 1883). The reminiscences of Galt's daughter, Evelyn Cartier Springett, *For My Children's Children* (Montreal: Unity Press, 1937) contain interesting details on Sir Alexander's personality.

Apparently, Elliott Galt did not leave as extensive a documentary heritage as his father. In any case, researchers have not yet uncovered any significant collection of his papers. There are letters from, to, and about Galt in the *Galt Papers*, *Sifton Papers*, and *Magrath Papers*, but these compose only a vague outline of Galt's personality. Only marginally more useful are the recollections of

C. A. Magrath, *The Galts, Father and Son: Pioneers in the Development of Southern Alberta* (Lethbridge: Lethbridge Herald, 1936).

Contemporary newspapers, periodicals, and magazines are indispensable sources for a study of western Canadian society. The descriptions in this work on life in Lethbridge are based largely on accounts in the local press, including the *News*, the *Semi-Weekly News*, and the *Herald*, amplified by references from the *Fort Macleod Gazette*. The *Nor'-Wester*, the Manitoba *Free Press*, the Montreal *Gazette*, and the Toronto *Globe* provided perceptions about economic development of western Canada. The Winnipeg *Voice*, the *United Mine Workers Journal*, and the department of labour's *Labour Gazette* were useful guides to labour attitudes.

Government documents, too, proved to be valuable sources of information. In some cases as in the annual reports of the federal department of the interior, the territorial department of public works, and the Alberta department of public works, the entire run relevant to the period was examined and consequently yielded statistical and historical data as well as statements of government policy. Government publications such as House of Commons Debates, *Statutes of Canada*, Orders-in-Council, and *Census of Canada* proved useful when consulted on specific items.

Other primary sources

Printed Government Documents

Alberta. *Royal Commission on the Coal Mining Industry in the Province of Alberta, 1907.*

Canada, Dominion Bureau of Statistics. *Canadian Mineral Statistics, 1886–1956.* Ottawa, 1956.

Canada, Legislative Assembly. *Journals*, 1858.

Canada, Legislative Assembly. *Parliamentary Debates on the Subject of the Confederation of the British North American Provinces*. Org. ed., 1865. Ottawa: King's Printer, 1951.

Canada, *Royal Commission on Coal, August 1960*.

Dawson, George M. "Preliminary Note on the Geology of the Bow and Belly River Districts, North West Territory, with a Special Reference to the Coal Deposits." Geological Survey of Canada. *Report of Progress, 1880–1881*. Ottawa: Dawson Brothers, 1882.

Dawson, George M. "Report on the Region in the Vicinity of the Bow and Belly Rivers, North West Territories." Geological Survey of Canada. *Report of Progress, 1882–1884*. Ottawa: Dawson Brothers, 1884.

Dawson, R.C. "Report on the Exploration from Fort Simpson on the Pacific Coast to Edmonton on the Saskatchewan Embracing a Portion of the Northern Part of British Columbia and the Peace River Country, 1879." Geological Survey of Canada. *Report of Progress, 1879–1880*. Montreal: Dawson Brothers, 1881.

Ellis, R.W. "Report on the Boring Operations in the North West Territory, Summer of 1875." Geological Survey of Canada. *Report of Progress, 1875–1876*. Montreal: Dawson Brothers, 1881.

Saskatchewan, Department of Agriculture. *Annual Report 1906, Annual Report 1907*.

Selwyn, Alfred R.C. "Observations in the North West Territory on a Journey Across the Plains from Fort Garry to Rocky Mountain House, Returning by the Saskatchewan River & Lake Winnipeg." Geological Survey of Canada. *Report of Progress, 1873–1874*. Montreal: Dawson Brothers, 1874.

Miscellaneous Printed Primary Sources

Browne, G.P., ed. *Documents on the Confederation of British North America*. Carleton Library, No. 40. Toronto: McClelland and Stewart, 1969.

Burdett's Official Intelligence. Yearly reports on the London Stock Exchange.

Canadian Anthracite Coal Company. *Prospectus of the Canadian Anthracite Coal Company: Collieries at Banff Station, Canadian Pacific Railway, District of Alberta*. Ottawa: Maclean, Roger & Co., 1885, GAI.

Canadian North-west Irrigation Company. *Irrigated Lands in Southern Alberta*. Winnipeg: Storel Co., 1900, GAI.

Canadian North-west Irrigation Company. *The Colorado of Canada, Irrigated Lands, Southern Alberta*. 1900, GAI.

Canadian Pacific Railway Company. *Annual Report, 1897*. Montreal: 1898.

Deane, Burton R. *Mounted Police Life in Canada: A Record of Thirty-One Years' Service*. London/Toronto: Cassell, 1916.

Grant, George M. *Ocean to Ocean: Sandford Fleming's Expedition Through Canada in 1872*. Org. ed., 1873. Edmonton: M.G. Hurtig, 1967.

Higinbotham, John D. *When the West Was Young: Historical Reminiscences of the Early Canadian West*. Toronto: The Ryerson Press, 1933.

Hill, Alex Staveley. *From Home to Home, Autumn Wanderings in the North-West in the Years 1881, 1882, 1883, 1884*. New York: O. Judd Co., 1885.

Hind, Henry Youle. *Narrative of the Canadian Red River Exploring Expedition of 1857 and of the Assinniboine and Saskatchewan Exploring Expedition of 1858*. Org. ed., 1860. Edmonton: M.G. Hurtig, 1971.

Hind, Henry Youle. *Manitoba and the North-West Frauds*. Windsor, N.S.: By the Author, 1883.

Johnson, J.K., ed. *The Canadian Directory of Parliament, 1867–1967*. Ottawa: Public Archives of Canada, 1968.

Johnson, J.K. and Stelmack, Carole B., eds. *The Letters of Sir John A. Macdonald: 1858–1861*. Vol. II. Ottawa: Public Archives of Canada, 1969.

Macoun, John. *Manitoba and the Great North-west.* Guelph: The World Publishing Company, 1882.

McCormick, Annie, ed. *Job Reed's Letters: Life in Lethbridge: 1886–1906.* Lethbridge: Whoop-Up Country Chapter, Historical Society of Alberta, 1978.

Morton, Desmond and Roy, Reginald, eds. *Telegrams of the North-West Campaign, 1885.* Toronto: The Champlain Society, 1972.

Ormsby, W. G. "Letters to Galt Concerning the Maritime Provinces and Confederation." *Canadian Historical Review* 34 (March 1953): 166–69.

Pope, Joseph. *Correspondence of Sir John Macdonald: Selections from the Correspondence of the Right Honourable Sir John Alexander Macdonald, G. C. B., First Prime Minister of the Dominion of Canada.* Toronto: Oxford University Press, 1921.

Stafford-Kelly, Jean. "Early Days of Lethbridge from 1882," *Lethbridge Herald,* 11 July 1935.

Stock Exchange Official Intelligence. Annual reports on the London Stock Exchange.

Tupper, Charles. *A Letter to the Earl of Carnarvon by Charles Tupper in Reply to a Pamphlet Entitled "Confederation."* n.p., 19 October 1866. PAC.

Warren, S. Evangeline. *Seventy South Alberta Years.* Ilfracombe, Devon: Arthur H. Stockwell Ltd., 1960.

Secondary Sources

Books

Aberdein, Jennie W. *John Galt.* London: Oxford University Press, 1936.

Babcock, Robert H. *Gompers in Canada: A Study in American Continentalism Before the First World War.* Toronto: University of Toronto Press, 1974.

Bercuson, David J. *Fools and Wise Men: The Rise and Fall of the One Big Union.* Toronto: McGraw-Hill Ryerson, 1978.

Bercuson, David Jay, ed. *Alberta's Coal Industry, 1919.* Historical Society of Alberta, Vol. 2. Calgary: Historical Society of Alberta, 1978.

Berry, Gerald. *The Whoop-Up Trail: Early Days in Alberta-Montana.* Edmonton: Applied Arts Products Ltd., 1953.

Berthoff, Rowland. *An Unsettled People: Social Order and Disorder in American History.* New York: Harper & Row, 1971.

Berton, Pierre. *The Last Spike,* Vol. 2: *The Great Railway, 1881–1885.* Toronto: McClelland and Stewart, 1971.

Bliss, Michael, *A Living Profit: Studies in the Social History of Canadian Business, 1883–1911.* Toronto: McClelland and Stewart, 1974.

Brebner, John Bartlett. *North Atlantic Triangle.* Carleton Library, No. 30. Toronto: McClelland and Stewart, 1966.

Burnett, Jean. *Next-Year Country: A Study of Rural Social Organization in Alberta.* reprint. Toronto: University of Toronto Press, 1978.

Careless, J. M. S. *Brown of the Globe,* Vol. 2: *Statesman of Confederation.* Toronto: Macmillan of Canada, 1959.

Carpenter, J. H. *The Badge and the Blotter: A History of the Lethbridge Police.* Lethbridge: Whoop-Up Country Chapter, Historical Society of Alberta, 1976.

Carrothers, W. A. *Emigration From the British Isles.* London: Frank Cass & Co. Ltd., 1965.

Chilston, Viscount. *W. H. Smith.* London: Routledge & K. Paul, 1965.

Cowan, Helen I. *British Emigration to British North America: The First Hundred Years.* Toronto: University of Toronto Press, 1961.

Creighton, Donald. *John A. Macdonald*, Vol. 2: *The Old Chieftain.* Toronto: The Macmillan Company of Canada, 1955.

Creighton, Donald. *The Road to Confederation: The Emergence of Canada, 1863–1867.* Toronto: The Macmillan Company of Canada, 1964.

Currie, A. W. *The Grand Trunk Railway of Canada.* Toronto: University of Toronto Press, 1957.

Dennis, Norman; Henriques, Fernando; and Slaughter, Clifford. *Coal is Our Life: An Analysis of a Yorkshire Mining Community.* London: Eyre Spottiswoode, 1956.

Dictionary of National Biography. London: Oxford University Press, 1950.

Dictionary of National Biography, Supplement, 1901–1911. London: Oxford University Press, 1951.

Drake, Earl G. *Regina: The Queen City.* Toronto: McClelland and Stewart, 1955.

Dubofsky, Melvyn. *Industrialism and the American Worker, 1865–1920.* New York: Crowell, 1975.

Easterbrook, W. T. and Aitken, H. G. *Canadian Economic History.* Toronto: Macmillan of Canada, 1956.

Farr, David M. L. *The Colonial Office and Canada, 1867–1887.* Toronto: University of Toronto Press, 1955.

Ferns, H. S. *Britain and Argentina in the Nineteenth Century.* Oxford: Clarendon Press, 1960.

Gilbert, Heather. *Awakening Continent: The Life of Lord Mount Stephen*, Vol. 1: *1829–91.* Aberdeen University Press, 1965.

Glazebrook, G. P. de T. *A History of Transportation in Canada.* 2 vols. Carleton Library, No. 12. Toronto: McClelland and Stewart, 1964.

Glazebrook, G. P. de T. *A History of Canadian External Relations*, Vol. 1: *The Formative Years to 1914.* Carleton Library, No. 27. rev. ed. Toronto: McClelland and Stewart, 1966.

Goodrich, Carter. *The Miner's Freedom: A Study of the Working Life in a Changing Industry.* Org. ed., 1925. New York: Arno Press, 1977.

Gordon, Ian A. *John Galt: The Life of a Writer.* Toronto: University of Toronto Press, 1972.

Grant, George. *Technology and Empire: Perspectives on North America.* Toronto: House of Anansi, 1969.

Gray, James H. *Red Lights on the Prairies.* Toronto: Macmillan, 1971.

Greene, Victor R. *The Slavic Community on Strike: Immigrant Labor in Pennsylvania Anthracite.* Notre Dame, Indiana: University of Notre Dame Press, 1968.

Hamilton, James McClellan. *From Wilderness to Statehood: A History of Montana, 1805–1900.* Portland, Oregon: Binfords & Mort, 1957.

Hedges, James B. *The Federal Railway Land Subsidy Policy of Canada.* Cambridge: Harvard University Press, 1934.

Hudson, A. James. *Charles Ora Card, Pioneer and Colonizer.* Cardston, Alberta: By the Author, 1963.

Husband, Joseph. *A Year in a Coal Mine.* Org. ed., 1911. New York: Arno Press, 1977.

Illich, Ivan. *Tools for Conviviality.* New York: Harper & Row, 1973.

Innis, Harold A. *A History of the Canadian Pacific Railway.* Foreword by Peter George. Toronto: University of Toronto Press, 1971.

Innis, Harold A. *Empire and Communications.* Toronto: University of Toronto Press, 1972.

Irwin, Leonard Bertram. *Pacific Railways and Nationalism in the Canadian-American Northwest, 1845-1873.* New York: Greenwood Press, 1968.

Jamieson, Stuart Marshall. *Times of Trouble: Labour Unrest and Industrial Conflict in Canada, 1900-1966.* Task force on Labour Relations in Canada, Study No. 22. Ottawa: Information Canada, 1971.

Johnston, Alexander, compiler. *Boats and Barges on the Belly.* Lethbridge: Lethbridge Branch, Historical Society of Alberta, 1966.

Karr, Clarence. *The Canada Land Company Early Years: An Experiment in Colonization, 1823-1843.* Toronto: Ontario Historical Society, 1974.

Kirkland, Edward Chase. *Men, Cities and Transportation: A Study in New England History, 1820-1900.* New York: Russell & Russell, 1948.

Kos-Rabewicz-Zubkowski, Ludwik and Greening, William Edward. *Sir Casimir Stanislaus Gzowski.* Toronto: Burns and MacEachern, 1959.

Lamb, W. Kaye. *History of the Canadian Pacific Railway.* New York: Macmillan Publishing Co., 1977.

Laslett, John H.M. *Labor and the Left: A Study of Socialist and Radical Influences in the American Labor Movement, 1881-1924.* New York: Basic Books, 1970.

Lupul, Manoly R. *The Roman Catholic Church and the North-West School Question: A Study in Church-State Relations in Western Canada, 1875-1905.* Toronto: University of Toronto Press, 1974.

Macbeth, R. C. *Sir Augustus Nanton: A Biography.* Toronto: Macmillan Company of Canada, 1931.

McCormack, Ross. *Reformers, Rebels and Revolutionaries.* Toronto: University of Toronto Press, 1977.

Macdonald, Norman. *Canada, 1763-1841: Immigration and Settlement, The Administration of the Imperial Land Regulations.* London: Longmans, Green and Co., 1939.

Macdonald, Norman. *Canada: Immigration and Colonization, 1841-1903.* Toronto: Macmillan of Canada, 1966.

Macleod, R. C. *The North-West Mounted Police and Law Enforcement, 1873-1905.* Toronto: University of Toronto Press, 1976.

Malone, Michael P., and Roeder, Richard B., eds. *The Montana Past: An Anthology.* Missoula: University of Montana Press, 1969.

Martin, Albro. *James J. Hill and the Opening of the Northwest.* New York: Oxford University Press, 1976.

Martin, Chester. *"Dominion Lands" Policy*. Edited by Lewis H. Thomas. Carleton Library, No. 69. Toronto: McClelland and Stewart, 1973.

Morgan, Henry James. *The Canadian Men and Women of the Time: A Hand Book of Canadian Biography*. Toronto: William Briggs, 1898.

Morgan, Henry James. *The Canadian Men and Women of the Time: A Hand Book of Canadian Biography of Living Characters*. Toronto: W. Briggs, 1912.

Morton, W. L. *Manitoba: A History*. Toronto: University of Toronto Press, 1957.

Morton, W. L. *The Critical Years: The Union of British North America, 1857-1873*. Toronto: McClelland Stewart, 1965.

Nelson, J. G. *The Last Refuge*. Montreal: Harvest House, 1973.

Nelson, J. G. *Man's Impact on the Western Canadian Landscape*. Carleton Library, No. 90. Toronto: McClelland and Stewart, 1976.

Paterson, Donald G. *British Direct Investment in Canada, 1890-1914: Estimates and Determinants*. Toronto: University of Toronto Press, 1976.

Paul, Rodman Wilson. *Mining Frontiers of the Far West, 1848-1880*. New York: Holt, Rinehart and Winston, 1963.

Porter, Glen. *The Rise of Big Business, 1860-1910*. New York: Thomas Y. Crowell Company, 1973.

Regehr, T. D. *The Canadian Northern Railway: Pioneer Road of the Northern Prairies, 1895-1918*. Toronto: Macmillan, 1975.

Riessen, H. van. *The Society of the Future*. Philadelphia: The Presbyterian and Reformed Publishing Co., 1952.

Sharp, Paul F. *Whoop-Up Country: the Canadian-American West, 1865-1885*. Minneapolis: University of Minnesota Press, 1955.

Skelton, Oscar Douglas. *Life and Times of Sir Alexander Tilloch Galt*. Carleton Library, No. 26. Toronto: McClelland and Stewart, 1966.

Springett, Evelyn Cartier. *For My Children's Children*. Montreal: Unity Press, 1937.

Stafford Peat, Annie Laurie. *Nineteenth Century Lethbridge*. Occasional Paper No. 8. Lethbridge: Whoop-Up Country Chapter, Historical Society of Alberta, 1978.

Stanley, George F. G. *The Birth of Western Canada: A History of the Riel Rebellions*. Toronto: University of Toronto Press, 1961.

Stevens, G. R. *Canadian National Railways*, Vol. I: *Sixty Years of Trial and Error (1836-1896)*. Toronto: Clarke, Irwin, 1960.

Tulchinsky, Gerald J. J. *The River Barons: Montreal Businessmen and the Growth of Industry and Transportation, 1837-53*. Toronto: University of Toronto Press, 1977.

van Riessen, H. *See* Riessen, H. van.

Waite, P. B. *The Life and Times of Confederation, 1864-1867*. Toronto: University of Toronto Press, 1962.

Articles

Barnett, D. F. "The Galt Protective Tariff: Incidental or Effective Protection?" *Canadian Journal of Economics* 9 (August 1976): 389-407.

Cameron, James M. "The Canada Company and Land Settlement as Resource Development in the Guelph Block." In *Perspectives on Landscape and Settlement in Nineteenth Century Ontario.* Edited by J. David Wood. Carleton Library, No. 91. Toronto: McClelland and Stewart, 1975.

Dreisziger, N. F. "The Canadian-American Irrigation Frontier Revisited: The International Origins of Irrigation in Southern Alberta." Canadian Historical Association, *Historical Papers, 1975,* pp. 211–30.

Dubofsky, Melvin. "The Origins of Western Working Class Radicalism, 1890–1905." *Labour History* 7 (Spring, 1966): 131–54.

Dunbar, G. S. "Isotherms and Politics: Perception of the Northwest in the 1850's." In *Prairie Perspectives 2,* edited by Anthony W. Rasporich and Henry C. Klassen. Toronto: Holt, Rinehart and Winston of Canada, 1973.

Greenberg, Dolores. "A Study of Capital Alliances: The St. Paul & Pacific." *Canadian Historical Review* 57 (March 1976): 25–39.

Gutman, Herbert G. "Work, Culture, and Society in Industrializing America, 1915–1919." *American Historical Review* 78 (June 1973): 531–88.

Hagell, Edward. *"The Lethbridge News, 1885," The Story of the Press.* Battleford: Canadian North-West Historical Society Publications, 1928.

Hall, D. J. "Clifford Sifton: Immigration and Settlement Policy, 1896–1905." In *The Settlement of the West* edited by H. Palmer. Calgary: Comprint Publishing Company, 1977.

Karr, Clarence G. "The Two Sides of John Galt." In *Historical Essays on Upper Canada* edited by J. K. Johnson. Carleton Library, No. 82. Toronto: McClelland and Stewart, 1975.

Longley, Richmond W. "Climate and Weather Patterns." In *Alberta: A Natural History* edited by W. G. Hardy. Edmonton: M. G. Hurtig, 1967.

Macleod, R. C. "Canadianizing the West: The North-West Mounted Police as Agents of the National Policy, 1873–1905." In *Essays on Western History* edited by Lewis H. Thomas. Edmonton: University of Alberta Press, 1976.

Mitchell, Elaine Allan. "Edward Watkin and the Buying Out of the Hudson's Bay Company." *Canadian Historical Review* 34 (September 1953): 219–44.

Polsby, Nelson W. "Power in Middletown: Fact and Value in Community Research." *The Canadian Journal of Economics and Political Science* 26 (November 1960): 592–603.

Roe, F. G. "An Unsolved Problem in Canadian History." Canadian Historical Association, *Annual Report 1936,* 65–77.

Ross, Mike. "Mike Ross Talks About the Life Style of the Coal Miner." *United Mine Workers Journal,* 1 July 1970, pp. 12–15.

Rutherford, P. F. W. "The Western Press and Regionalism, 1870–1896." *Canadian Historical Review* 52 (September 1971): 287–305.

Van Tichem, Frank. "Father Leonard van Tichem, O.M.I." *Alberta Historical Review* 12 (Winter 1964): 17–21.

Warkentin, John. "Steppe, Desert and Empire." In *Prairie Perspectives 2* edited by Anthony W. Rasporich and Henry C. Klassen. Toronto: Holt, Rinehart and Winston of Canada, 1973.

Webb, Robert; Johnston, Alexander; and Soper, J. Dewey. "The Prairie World." In *Alberta: A Natural History* edited by W. G. Hardy. Edmonton: M. G. Hurtig, 1967.

Wilson, E. H. "Lethbridge and the A.R. & I." *The Lethbridge Herald*, December 1947:9.

Young, Brian J. "Railway Politics in Montreal, 1867–1878." Canadian Historical Association, *Historical Papers 1972*, pp. 89–108.

Unpublished Theses and Manuscripts

Baker, William M. "The Mediator and the Miners: Mackenzie King and the 1906 Lethbridge Strike," unpublished paper.

Bjarnason, Emil. "Collective Bargaining in the Coal Mining Industry of Canada, 1825–1938." M.A. thesis, Queen's University, 1965.

Bliss, John William Michael. "A Living Profit: Studies in the Social History of Canadian Business, 1883–1911." Ph.D. dissertation, University of Toronto, 1972.

Breen, David H. "The Canadian West and the Ranching Frontier, 1875–1922." Ph.D. dissertation, University of Alberta, 1973.

Cousins, William James. "A History of the Crow's Nest Pass." M.A. thesis, University of Alberta, 1952.

Foran, Maxwell Lawrence. "The Calgary Town Council, 1884–1895: A Study of Local Government in a Frontier Environment." M.A. thesis, University of Calgary, 1970.

Jacobsen, W. L. "Biographical Sketch of William Harmon Fairfield (1874–1961)." In *History of Irrigation in Western Canada. History of Agriculture.* A Glenbow Foundation Research Project, 1959–1960: 1–8.

Johnston, Alex. "Early Agriculture and the Dominion Experimental Station, Lethbridge." Paper read to the Historical Society of Alberta, 1973.

Lalonde, André N. "Settlement in the North-West Territories by Colonization Companies, 1881–1891." Ph.D. dissertation, Laval University, 1969.

McMillan, Charles J. "Trade Unionism in District 18, 1900–1925: A Case Study." M.B.A. thesis, University of Alberta, 1969.

Mitchner, E. Alyn. "William Pearce and Federal Government Activity in Western Canada, 1882–1904." Ph.D. dissertation, University of Alberta, 1970.

Porter, Sam G., and Raley, Charles. "A Brief History of the Development of Irrigation in the Lethbridge District." Lethbridge Public Library, 1925, copy in GAI.

Tagg, Melvin S. "A History of the Church of Jesus Christ of Latter-Day Saints in Canada, 1830–1963." Ph.D. dissertation, Brigham Young University, 1963.

Turner, Wesley Barry. "Colonial Self-government and the Colonial Agency: Changing Concepts of Permanent Canadian Representation in London, 1848 to 1880." Ph.D. dissertation, Duke University, 1970.

Index